MERCHANTS'
DAUGHTERS

MERCHANTS' DAUGHTERS

WOMEN, COMMERCE, AND REGIONAL CULTURE IN SOUTH CHINA

Edited by Helen F. Siu

香港大學出版社

HONG KONG UNIVERSITY PRESS

Hong Kong University Press
14/F Hing Wai Centre
7 Tin Wan Praya Road
Aberdeen
Hong Kong
www.hkupress.org

ISBN 978-988-8083-48-0

British Library Cataloguing-in-Publication Data
A catalogue record for this book is available from the British Library.

10 9 8 7 6 5 4 3 2

Printed and bound by Goodrich International Co. Ltd., Hong Kong, China

Contents

Acknowledgments

It is embarrassing to mention how long this project has taken from start to finish. The idea of a volume on women, commerce, and regional culture emerged from a conference in 1994 organized by Chi-cheung Choi at the Hong Kong University of Science and Technology, which focused on merchant cultures in South China. At the time, David Faure and I just finished editing a volume, *Down to Earth: The Territorial Bond in South China*, for Stanford University Press. We were keenly aware that gender was not given adequate attention. With a few colleagues who loosely constituted the "South China gang," we embarked on a project on the region's women, attempting to reconceptualize their lives in material, imaginary, and discursive terms. A regional framework was important to us. We hoped to highlight the women's predicaments at crucial historical junctures that had lasting significance. Some colleagues grew tired of us and moved on. A few joined with degrees of curiosity. Others who were persuaded to commit to the project probably did not know what they were getting into.

Despite the project's long gestation, its collective authors and participants have shared exciting intellectual discoveries that cross boundaries in academic disciplines, regional studies, theory and methods in historical and ethnographic research. A few years back, David Faure happily declared his exit from South China. With this volume completed, I can head towards Mumbai and Dubai in good conscience.

We collectively thank funding organizations and academic institutions that have supported our authors' research at various stages. I am most grateful to numerous colleagues and students who have added inspiration and companionship to the project over the decade. In particular, I would like to thank Muriel Bell, Susan Brownell, Chen Chunsheng, Deborah Davis, Kathryn Dudley, Patrick Hase, Gail Hershatter, William Kelly, Dorothy Ko, Angela Leung, Tik-sang Liu, Susan Mann, Ngai Pun, Elizabeth Sinn, Maria Tam, James and Rubie Watson. Wing-hoi Chan, Elizabeth Sinn, and Angela Leung have given special attention to the overall themes that shape the volume and introduction. The late Carl Smith was with us all along, inspiring us with his faith in uncovering the voices of the unheard.

The reviewers have been constructively critical and have offered valuable suggestions for revisions. Colin Day, Michael Duckworth, and Clara Ho of Hong Kong University Press have, as always, given the project patient and thoughtful attention. I thank the Hong Kong Young Women's Christian Association for kindly providing two images for the cover. Yan Lijun, Zhang Jun, and Yang Meijian have tried their best to make Endnotes work for classical Chinese bibliographical entries. I am most grateful to Kwok-leung Yu, Emily Ip, Venus Lee, and Natalie Wong who have provided meticulous editorial and technical support in preparing the manuscript for publication. I thank the Council on East Asian Studies at Yale University, and the Hong Kong Institute for the Humanities and Social Sciences at the University of Hong Kong for their generous financial and institutional support over the years.

Our gratitude ultimately goes to the women and men in the region whose life experiences form the core of the historical and ethnographic texts that have enriched our intellectual pursuits and humanist sensibilities.

Helen F. Siu

Contributors

Wing-hoi Chan is an assistant professor in the Department of Social Sciences at the Hong Kong Institute of Education. An anthropologist, Chan focuses on kinship, marriage and their performance aspects in South China, the political contexts of local and transnational ethnic identities, and the politics of representations of the countryside. Recent publications include "Migration and Ethnic Identities in a Mountainous Region: The Case of 'She Bandits'," in *Empire at the Margins: Culture, Ethnicity, and Frontier in Early Modern China*, ed. Pamela Kyle Crossley, Helen F. Siu and Donald S. Sutton (Berkeley: University of California Press, 2006); "A Sense of Place in Hong Kong: The Case of Tai O," in *Hong Kong Mobile: Making a Global Population*, ed. Helen F. Siu and Agnes Ku (Hong Kong: Hong Kong University Press, 2008).

Pheng Cheah is a professor in the Department of Rhetoric, University of California at Berkeley. He is the author of *Spectral Nationality: Passages of Freedom from Kant to Postcolonial Literatures of Liberation* (New York: Columbia University Press, 2003) and *Inhuman Conditions: On Cosmopolitanism and Human Rights* (Cambridge: Harvard University Press, 2006). He is also the co-editor of *Cosmopolitics: Thinking and Feeling Beyond the Nation* (Minneapolis: University of Minnesota Press, 1998); *Grounds of Comparison: Around the Work of Benedict Anderson* (New York; London: Routledge, 2003); and *Derrida and the Time of the Political* (Durham: Duke University Press, 2009). He is currently working on a book on world literature in an era of global financialization.

May-bo Ching is a professor of history and a research fellow of the Centre for Historical Anthropology at Sun Yat-sen University. Her major research interest is the social and cultural history of modern China. Her recent publications include *Regional Culture and National Identity: The Shaping of "Guangdong Culture" Since the Late Qing* (in Chinese; Beijing: Joint Publishing House, 2006), which discusses changes in the articulation of regional identity against the rise of nationalism. Her current projects include a preliminary study of the introduction of natural history drawings and knowledge into China since the late eighteenth century and a social history of Cantonese opera from the 1860s to 1950s.

Chi-cheung Choi is a professor in the History Department at the Chinese University of Hong Kong. His major publications include *Jiao: Festival and Local Communities in Hong Kong* (Hong Kong: Joint Publishing Co., 2000); and "Competition among Brothers: The Kin Tye Lung Company and Its Associate Companies," in Rajeswary Brown, ed., *Chinese Business Enterprise in Asia* (New York; London: Routledge, 1995).

Po-king Choi is an associate professor of education administration and policy at the Chinese University of Hong Kong. Her areas of interest are education policy and gender studies, Hong Kong culture and identity, and life histories. Her recent publications include: "The Best Students Will Learn English: Ultra-utilitarianism and Linguistic Imperialism in Education in Post-1997 Hong Kong," in *Journal of Education Policy* 18, no. 6 (2003): 673–94; "The Politics of Identity: The Women's Movement in Hong Kong," in Benjamin Leung, *Hong Kong: Legacies and Prospects of Development* (Aldershot, Hants: Ashgate, 2003); and *Threads and Needles: Oral Histories of Hong Kong Garment Workers*, editor (Hong Kong: Stepforward Multimedia Ltd., 2008).

David Faure is a professor of history at the Chinese University of Hong Kong. He specializes in social and economic history from the Ming dynasty to the Second World War, and the history of Hong Kong. His publications include *Colonialism and the Hong Kong Mentality* (Hong Kong: Centre of Asian Studies, the University of Hong Kong, 2003); *A Documentary History of Hong Kong, Vol. 3 Economy* (co-editor Pui-tak Lee, Hong Kong: Hong Kong University Press, 2004); *China and Capitalism: A History of Business Enterprise in Modern China* (Hong Kong: Hong Kong University Press, 2006); *Emperor and Ancestor: State and Lineage in South China* (Stanford: Stanford University Press, 2007).

Liu Zhiwei is a professor of history and the director of the Centre for Historical Anthropology at Sun Yat-sen University. His areas of research are Chinese economic and social history of the Ming and Qing periods and studies of popular religion and rural society. His publications include "Lineage on the Sands: The Case of Shawan," in David Faure and Helen F. Siu, eds., *Down to Earth: The Territorial Bond in South China* (Stanford: Stanford University Press, 1995), and *Between State and Society: Studies of the Household Registration and Taxation Systems in Guangdong in the Ming-Qing periods* (in Chinese; Guangzhou: Sun Yat-sen University Press, 1997).

Helen F. Siu is a professor of anthropology at Yale University. She has conducted long-term field research in South China and Hong Kong. Her publications include *Mao's Harvest: Voices of China's New Generation* (co-editor Zelda Stern, Oxford, 1983); *Agents and Victims in South China: Accomplices in Rural Revolution* (New Haven: Yale University Press, 1989); *Furrows: Peasants, Intellectuals, and the State* (Stanford: Stanford University Press, 1990); *Down to Earth: The Territorial Bond in South China* (co-editor David Faure, Stanford University Press, 1995); *Empire at the Margins: Culture, Ethnicity, and Frontier in Early Modern China* (co-editors Pamela Kyle Crossley and Donald S. Sutton, Berkeley: University of California Press, 2006); *SARS: Reception and Interpretation in Three Chinese Cities* (co-editor Deborah Davis, New York; London: Routledge, 2007); and *Hong Kong Mobile: Making a Global Population* (co-editor Agnes Ku, Hong Kong: Hong Kong University Press, 2008).

The late **Carl T. Smith**, honorary vice-president, the Royal Asiatic Society Hong Kong Branch, came to Hong Kong in 1961 to teach theology, first at the Church of Christ in China's Theological Institute. Between 1962 and 1983, he taught at the Chung Chi Seminary and its successor, the Chinese University of Hong Kong. Faced with a lack of information on Chinese converts and on what Christianity meant to them, he devoted decades to meticulous research into the lives and social organization of the Chinese populations in Hong Kong and Macau. His publications include *Chinese Christians: Elites, Middlemen, and the Church in Hong Kong* (Hong Kong: Hong Kong University Press, 2005) and *A Sense of History: Studies in the Social and Urban History of Hong Kong* (Hong Kong: Hong Kong Educational Publishing Co., 1995). Mr Smith passed away in 2008.

Josephine Lai-kuen Wong is currently working at the Hong Kong Museum of History. She joined the museum in 1998 and completed the postgraduate program in museum studies at the University of Sydney in 2001. Her research interests include Hong Kong history, women's history, and cultural studies.

Yan Lijun received her MA degree in anthropology from Sun Yat-sen University, and worked as a journalist with the Nanfang Media Group, Guangzhou. In 2007, she joined the Hong Kong Institute for the Humanities and Social Sciences, the University of Hong Kong, as its China program coordinator.

Yang Meijian received her MA degree from Sun Yat-sen University and is a doctoral student in the Department of Anthropology, Yale University. She has conducted extensive fieldwork in Guangzhou and Yunnan.

Taotao Zhang majored in history at Yale University. Her senior thesis was on early twentieth-century Fujian. Since graduation, she has been working for a global consulting firm in Hong Kong.

Introduction

Helen F. Siu and Wing-hoi Chan

Gender, Regional Culture, and Women's Positioning

The study of Chinese women has contributed significantly to gender theories. The construction of gender differences and women's negotiation of cultural space in restrictive power contexts have been given ample attention.[1] This volume continues the analytical direction by using materials from South China to illuminate the junctures of history, gender subjectivities, and power play. The authors, an interdisciplinary team, have done extensive archival and fieldwork in South China. Like many before them, they challenge static and dichotomous frameworks that stress patriarchy, women's subjugation, and resistance. Moreover, the choice of South China signifies an additional analytical agenda. The authors hope to highlight the contingencies, ambiguities, significations, and implications of women's positioning that arose from the intense commercialization that was characteristic of the region from the late imperial to the post-reform periods. They use historical, ethnographic, and literary research to underscore the mutually constitutive processes of a dynamic regional culture, gender constructions, and women's lived experiences.

The volume organizes case materials in ways that engage with historians Dorothy Ko and Susan Mann who, in their studies of the Yangzi River Delta, focus on women's agency that intertwined with regional histories.[2] While Ko and Mann may have taken commercialized Jiangnan as a given background for their analyses of women's agency, the authors of this volume hope to foreground South China as a historical process and cultural construct. They turn their analytical attention to crucial moments of state-making and commercialization that have significantly framed the cultural mapping of particular localities. Residents of the Pearl River Delta and Hong Kong, two important localities in South China, were culturally, economically, and politically undifferentiated in the late imperial period. They went separate ways along colonial and revolutionary paths in the twentieth century, but boundaries between them are rapidly blurred in China's post-reform era. The changing relationship became entwined with the negotiations of gender meanings and relationships.

Using the South China region to explore the nuances of women's positioning has particular relevance for Chinese anthropology because the seminal works of Maurice Freedman on territorial lineage formation have long associated the region with patrilineal descent, corporate property ownership by male agnates, and patriarchy.[3] On the other hand, unusual forms of marriage and social bonding are not lost to later scholars. The delayed transfer marriages, and the sworn spinsterhoods are well-known examples.[4] The task here is to appreciate how dominant cultural notions and divergent pursuit have been mutually constitutive in the evolution of a region, a Weberian task we began in an earlier volume.[5] Instead of accepting the South China region as a geographical or administrative unit that has been a repository for Confucian patriarchy, the authors of this volume ask what a regional culture means to those actively involved in its making. A rereading of South China's cultural history may question the assumption of the lineage complex. Differing from the "marriage resistance" literature, Siu's analysis of the delayed transfer marriage in the Pearl River Delta shows that apparent gender anomalies to a Confucian mindset might turn out to be the regional norm.[6] The question is how these "anomalies" acquired the aura of cultural mainstream. The process probably reflects how the practitioners of a particular region forged their identities through instrumental and symbolic means to engage with an expanding empire. This conceptual agenda permits the questioning of the lineage paradigm, adds nuance to notions of resistance, challenges the woman-as-victim script, and recenters certain priorities of mercantile society and their modern transformations. They strive for historization of gender consciousness and subtler appreciation of the varieties of women's roles. These identities intertwined with the regional culture of South China where the domination of the lineage paradigm has too often been assumed.[7]

To appreciate the fluidity of women's positioning, actively pursued in this cultural/spatial frame of reference, the volume focuses its attention on three significant historical junctures in the region's transformation broadly conceived. First, it highlights local self-fashioning in the Ming and Qing dynasties. Women's and men's practices intertwined based on local indigenous cultural backgrounds and specific moments of late imperial state-making. The rise of particular lineage formations in the region complicated gender and kinship hierarchies, when "women" assumed kinship positions that cannot be reduced to their gender.[8]

A second juncture of regional history the volume underscores was trade, empire, emigration, and reform in colonial Hong Kong and Republican South China. In Hong Kong, the colonial encounters between Chinese and other mercantile elites were fraught with Confucian pretensions and racial politics but also enriched by enlightened missionary efforts, formally recognized legal rights, and a wider range of properties. They unexpectedly opened up spaces as well as dangers for both elite and working women. The same applied to emigrant communities along the South China coast.

In the mainland from the late Qing to the Republican period, gender politics was by no means static. Kang Youwei, a leading Cantonese scholar/reformist in the last decades of the Qing Empire, and nationalist women's suffragists in the first two Republican decades pushed gender consciousness to new heights.[9] The latter development in Guangdong and the movement to abolish the bond maidservant system in Hong Kong during the 1920s owed much to shared social and cultural impact of foreign missionaries. Political border did not prevent mutual influences in gender-related reforms.[10]

The volume focuses on the postwar decades as the third significant juncture of regional development and gender dynamics. Progress was made on the mainland in gender equality, but the cultural and political environment remained unfavorable to the rise of women as a force in civil society. In contrast, colonial rule using a conservative male merchant elite to "represent" the Chinese community had been a major obstacle to legal and political reforms to address gender issues until the 1970s, making Hong Kong "the most laggard of modern Chinese society in eradicating the concubinage institution."[11] That said, the economic and cultural transformations in Hong Kong amid political changes in more recent decades prepared women for leading public roles and collective action. In contemporary Hong Kong, one finds a meeting of women's work experiences and civic movements where women's groups participate in larger causes while maintaining their own agendas. The political developments in anticipation of 1997 heightened such gendered consciousness and civic activism.

Looking ahead as neoliberal market forces have turned the region into a global factory and haven of consumption, opportunities and vulnerabilities will continue to be created for women and men. Politicians on both sides of the border focus on infrastructural linkages for a mobile work force in the region. On the software of development, how does the new range of cross-border interactions shape gender dynamics and subjectivities? Where can "tender sprouts of a Chinese feminist public sphere" be found?[12]

Images beyond the Confucian Imagination

It was April 28, 1899. J. Stewart Lockhart, Colonial Secretary of Hong Kong, wrote a report to the Governor while returning from the newly established border posts in the New Territories.

> We left Wo Hang yesterday morning and proceeded to Starling Inlet, to the point where the British boundary begins [Sha Tau Kok] . . . From Starling Inlet we crossed in boats to Luk King . . . From Luk King we proceeded to Plover Cove and walked through the villages in that district. . . . We reached Tai Po at 6 p.m. after having marched about 25 miles. . . . I may mention that out of 111 persons employed yesterday at Wo Hang to carry our baggage, 70 were women, who came with us all the way from Wo Hang to the Camp here.[13]

Nearly a century after Lockhart's march, Siu was with a boatload of villagers who returned in 1992 to a remote corner of the New Territories near the Chinese border. She was attending a major religious ceremony of the community, the *jiao*. Some came from as far as various parts of Britain where they or their fathers had emigrated. The men eagerly described to her the wide range of work that they remembered women in the village had performed. When Siu asked the men what was left for them (the men) to do, they gave her a rather nonchalant answer, "We hung around, fished a little, and played with the children."

Anyone familiar with South China will acknowledge that women visibly worked outside the home in a variety of trades. That was the norm. Those wearing wide-brimmed hats made of black cloth were seen working in the Hakka villages of Eastern Guangdong and the New Territories of Hong Kong. In the fishing communities known as Dan, women carried children on their backs, fished, mended nets, marketed their catch, and maneuvered boats with sturdy finesse. In the plains where farmers engaged in intensive production of cash crops — vegetables and fruits, mulberry and silk, pigs and wine — women were vital to the family economy. They were skillful farmhands, enterprising peddlers in the market, and dependable keepers of family finances.[14]

Some of those from families with comfortable means in the heart of the Pearl River Delta were given the opportunity to be educated alongside their brothers. It was not uncommon to give women landed property as dowry or to allocate provisions of grain to them in documents of family division.[15] In prosperous counties in the delta, brides were known to be bold. Local folklore pointed out that brides readily claimed to have brought their own grain and needed only water from their husbands' households (*dai mi shi shui*). Furthermore, women's voices shared with those of men to sustain an oral tradition of funeral and bridal songs. Intimate sentiments of sisterhood and religious devotion were expressed in popular rituals and not considered problematic in a male-oriented world. They were documented in genealogies, deeds, ritual, and business records.[16] In a word, local practices were far more nuanced and complicated than a Confucian language was able to contain.

In the late imperial period, South China, in particular the Pearl River Delta, was known for its high degree of commercial activities. They were reflected in the large-scale reclamation of the sands financed by lineage and merchant estates, in a vibrant land market and layered tenancy, and in the growing and long-distance marketing of cash crops. Moreover, commerce in coastal South China was tied to foreign trade. As early as the Tang and Song periods, Arab traders came via the Indian Ocean and Southeast Asia. Portuguese, Dutch, and, later, British traders arrived in the Ming and Qing. They too left their mark. Over the centuries, despite ebbs and flows in dynastic policies, traders were major players in the making of society in the region.[17] Coastal cities in the southeast (such as Guangzhou and Quanzhou) came to assume culturally mixed characteristics. Mosques, cemeteries, and European-style architecture were interspersed with Buddhist temples, Daoist shrines, and family graveyards. One can argue that these were enclaves of different faiths and communities, but their existence at the level of everyday lives and popular culture showed a relatively diffuse influence.[18]

From the perspective of the political center, coastal South China was a volatile region at the margins of empire — affluent but unfamiliar, not entirely out of reach but hard to control. The local populations were resourceful and productive. In their cultural strategies, they tapped the empire's civilizing language. However, their identities were ambiguous and their loyalties unpredictable. Officials at times labeled them *yiyu jiangun* (operators in unfamiliar territory). In peaceful times, some of them were identified as merchants and boat masters. During dynastic turmoil, they were branded pirates and rebels.[19]

Moreover, religion and Confucian values were interwoven with mercantile interests and popular culture. As early as the seventeenth century, the colorful career of Monk Dashan (1633–1705) captured the ethos of a cultural renaissance and an unorthodox business ethic.[20] Dashan had a network of monasteries under his care in Guangdong, Jiangxi, and Macao in the turbulent Ming-Qing transition. He bought silk from Suzhou for the Vietnam kings and brokered tribute trade when he went overseas to lecture. His monasteries were sites for gatherings of scholars, with wine, song, poetry, dance, and theatrical performances. The likes of Dashan were master cultural brokers with broad horizons. They turned places at the margins into energizing nodes and centers of intense production, exchange, and consumption. Institutional identities and national boundaries were crossed.

Could the combination of Confucian morality, scholarly tastes, mercantile resourcefulness, and religious refuge have provided an unusual space for the region's women? In the twentieth century, Lady Clara Hotung's founding of Tung Lin Kok Yuen may have been a shining example. Fast forward to contemporary Hong Kong, the enterprising energies of the nuns in the newly established Zhilian Jingyuan have also attracted wealthy patrons and public personalities from a global Chinese network. At the extreme other end of the glamour scale, woman shaman in the region have also built careers by founding temples and creating a following even in the most god-forsaken corners.[21]

One also needs to explore the cultural orientation of merchant families. In Guangzhou, merchants who engaged in foreign trade rose to prominence in the eighteenth century when the region produced a wide range of everyday consumer products for foreign buyers. They were worldly and at times unorthodox in their business practices, but they bought the necessary bureaucratic connections and scholarly etiquette with their astonishing wealth and conspicuous consumption.[22] Their daughters were to be brought up genteel if only for marriage strategy. The China Trade genre of paintings depicting the era of commerce and diplomacy along the China coast in the eighteenth and nineteenth centuries contained fascinating details of social life that were at once local, imperial, and multicultural.[23] The Peabody Museum in Salem, Massachusetts, shows a rich variety of the household goods produced — wallpaper, European style furniture, Chinaware, silverware, clocks, and decorative items, made to order by Chinese craftsmen in Guangzhou and transported across the Indian Ocean and the Atlantic. These technically sophisticated products reflect the interpenetration of European tastes and Chinese cultural imaginations. If educated women in the region managed household budgets and were the major creators of taste in the household's production and consumption, how would their resourcefulness become intertwined with the unorthodox world of their men?[24]

Fieldwork in the Pearl River Delta reveals that successful merchants in the Republican era often maintained separate households in their native communities and places of sojourn. Wives and concubines managed these households, which were nodes in the entrepreneurs' business networks.[25] Moreover, sons educated away from home or entering family businesses would circulate among these nodes, at times cared for by and apprenticing with their fathers' women.[26] Profits were invested in land and occasionally in the form of lineage estates. As a cultural strategy for social mobility, contributions were made to temples and community charities to cast a diverse network.[27] How these investments reinforced or eroded male-centered priorities would not be straightforward. As women in emigrant communities had to be resourceful for everyday survival due to long-term absence of male household members, one would at least expect the public and private lives of women in these communities to be loaded with conflicting notions.

Moreover, the Pearl River Delta was linked to city culture through a dynamic network of market towns where powerful lineages and merchants were based. Cities at the turn of the twentieth century constituted a vibrant landscape of conspicuous consumption by metropolitan merchants that involved women as both subject and object. In the images created by popular literature and media, women occupied visible public space as accomplished courtesans and hostesses, opera singers, and, in the later decades, as actresses with distinctive talents in film.[28]

Extending beyond Guangzhou's cosmopolitan environment at the time, the interracial and multicultural setting of Hong Kong presented women with further unusual opportunities. Women were by no means cloistered in Confucian submissiveness. Through the promotion of Western style, co-educational schools, property laws, missionary and other charitable organizations, women in the region had access to multiple channels of mobility.[29] Dan women provisioned merchant fleets from Europe and America when the ships moored in the Victoria Harbor or Macao. Some cohabited with the traders and officers and were left with properties and resources. Some wisely speculated in real estate, whereas others operated businesses, including houses of prostitution. Their experiences can be fruitfully contrasted with forms of prostitution in other regions of China around the same time (as described by Gail Hershatter), where social hierarchies were maintained by rituals of kinship and marriage infused with traditional cultural norms.[30] In Hong Kong, the fortunate ones whose children obtained European education rose from the margins of both societies to become matriarchs of well-connected Eurasian families. But, opportunities also came with dangers and misfortune. The Po Leung Kuk archives have shown that many women fugitives whom the charity protected had escaped from abusive masters, abductors, and fraudulent marriage arrangements.[31]

As historians have pointed out, in China the late Qing and early Republican years provided opportunities that activists in the women's suffrage movement were quick to grasp. Many of female members of Sun Yat-sen's Revolutionary Alliance invoked their contribution to the nationalist cause to demand recognition of women's election rights as well as constitutional clauses for broader issues of gender equality.[32]

Thanks to such efforts progresses were made in Guangdong at the provincial level in 1912. In 1919, in the wake of the May Fourth protest and anticipation of the drafting of a constitution, Wu Zhimei, a Guomindang politician who graduated from the Hackett Medical College for Women in Canton founded by medical missionaries, organized a Guangdong Federation of Women's Circles. These efforts won success in 1922.[33] As a revolutionary center for the Guomindang in alliance with the Chinese Communist Party, and with support from the Comintern, Guangdong was the site of women's mobilization in the mid-1920s but the effects seemed limited and short-lived.[34] But the women's suffrage activists' eventual "gains include the Tutelate Constitution, the Double Fifth Draft and the 1947 National Constitution."[35] As already mentioned, colonial rule, with its cooptation of conservative Chinese compradors, was an obstacle to similar legal reforms in Hong Kong, but Chinese Christians and Chinese nationalism were important factors to a movement to abolish female slavery known as *mui-tsai* in the 1920s and Guangdong developments were an important impetus of the activism.

Half a century of socialist ideology and state-building further separated Hong Kong from South China in the mid-twentieth century. Millions of women on the mainland rose through the revolutionary ranks, aided by laws and political organizations in the new regime. They were institutionally visible as a work force and as cadres in government-sponsored women's organizations. Skeptics might view images of women occupying "half the sky" as socialist rhetoric in the party-controlled media, but for a great many women growing up in the cities, education, health, social mobility, and self-confidence were real.[36]

Hong Kong, on the other hand, developed postwar institutions by reorienting its economy towards Europe and North America. From the 1970s to the 1990s, it made a transition from an immigrant city to an industrial and international financial center. The educated, locally born women and men enjoyed unprecedented social mobility to become Hong Kong's professional middle class. Social movements, expanded social services, and more recently political reforms contributed greatly to improvements in gender equality. For example, the equal pay campaign begun by government-employed expatriate women teachers in 1960 made considerable progress by 1965 but equal pay policy was not extended to female nurses until 1971.[37] The emergence of a local feminist movement accompanying rapid upward mobility, decolonization, and expanded political participation since the 1980s greatly raised gender consciousness and contributed to public awareness of related issues and legal reforms, and civic activism.[38]

In the media today, three categories of working women have come to dominate public attention in ways quite separate from their counterparts on the mainland. One sees women as wielders of power and consumers of commodities. Class and ethnic issues complicate women's opportunities for empowerment. At the privileged end are accomplished professionals in international finance, jet-setting heads of family corporations, high-ranking civil servants and legislators, and patrons of the arts and charity organizations.[39] Many appear able to maintain vigorous professions and manage their families because other women's labor in the form of domestic help is cheap and available. The presence of over 250,000 female migrant workers from Southeast Asia has meant that middle-income families can afford full-time help at home.[40]

At the sorrowful end of a gendered social hierarchy are Chinese immigrants from rural Guangdong and Fujian who have joined their husbands in Hong Kong in the last two decades. They are part of an increasingly gendered social landscape that straddles the border between Hong Kong and the mainland. Images of their plight are vividly contrasted with the professional women in the local media. Living at the rural fringes of Fujian and Guangdong, they married older working men and immigrants.[41] In Hong Kong, they are easily singled out because of their rural accents and styles and labeled "new immigrants" by a hostile public. Although many have, in fact, found work and successfully adjusted to life in urban Hong Kong, the mass media continues to present them as desperately poor, welfare recipients isolated from extended kin. Many are also victims of abusive husbands and are seen by a large segment of the host community as social burdens.[42] Hong Kong men who have ventured north for work since 1997 have found spouses from among the tens of millions of *dagongmei* (working sisters) who are resourceful and have adjusted to urban industrial life in Guangdong.[43] Although discriminated against, these women are seeking help from existing women's groups and joining community activism.

On the consumption front, new wealth in the region complicates the cross-border gender landscape. Differences in the prices of commodities, services, and entertainment on the mainland also attract consumers across the border. Extramarital affairs are common, triggering family unhappiness and resulting in tragic human dramas.[44] The intruding presence of mistresses in Hong Kong families has much to do with the Special Economic Zone in Shenzhen and in the boomtowns of the Pearl River Delta.[45] A culture of conspicuous consumption has spread among the newly rich who are reeling from decades of deprivation. Lavish banquets, song, dance, and women are visible symbols of the good life on a fast track. Entire neighborhoods, named "mistress villages" (*ernai cun*), have sprung up along the border where men who commute between Hong Kong and South China seek the services of women for a fraction of the price they pay in Hong Kong. Tens of thousands of migrant women have come to the area from poorer provinces seeking fortune. In a morally uncertain post-reform era not unlike nineteenth century Hong Kong as described by historians Carl Smith and Elizabeth Sinn, many seem to consider the sex industry an opportunity. Hong Kong's reintegration with China highlights once again the exploitation, the dominant cultural assumptions, and the desperate maneuvers of young women who try to claim liberating spaces for themselves. These features, sensationalized by popular media, fuel public debates about gender and lived experiences.[46] On the mainland side, the widening of the gender gap in income and occupation and the apparent return of "traditional" biases in the course of economic liberalization are noted by the provincial Women's Federations and feminist scholars in Guangdong, some of whom are active in newly formed NGOs.[47] Their interventions to issues such as the exclusion of married "daughters" from sharing dividends from newly urbanized villages are hindered by a legal system under which individual's rights are difficult to assert against local government.[48]

This volume examines how gender notions and women's positioning have been woven into the evolution of this region over the last two centuries. The substantive chapters are organized into three clusters, each based on a significant historical moment of the region's transformation.

Cultural Spaces between State-Making and Kinship in the Late Imperial Period

The volume begins with Liu Zhiwei's meticulous reading of an important ritual practiced by a prominent lineage in Guangdong in the late Qing — the annual visit to a tomb of two female ancestors, the *gusaofen*. Panyu, a county in a prosperous part of the Pearl River Delta, was populated by territorially based groups that traced common descent from male focal ancestors. Their solidarities were reinforced by corporate estates, ornate ancestral halls adorned with literati honors, and public rituals that often excluded female participation. The He lineage in Shawan was a magnate lineage on the edge of the river marshes in Panyu. It claimed tremendous territorial dominance and flaunted its wealth and literati pedigree. Its social, ritual, and political presence centered around the focal ancestral hall, the Liugeng Tang, and the Beidi Temple where the deity, in rare military garb, was seen as symbolic of Ming imperial power.[49] In this context, the elaborate annual pilgrimage to Guangzhou, dedicated to the wife and sister of the legendary focal ancestor, might have seemed out of place.

Reading between the lines of local gazetteers and lineage genealogies and substantiating his interpretations with ethnographic materials, Liu delineates a complex process of cultural mixing and matching whereby an indigenous population in South China used material and symbolic means to acquire an authoritative place in the evolving empire. The process he describes challenges conventional wisdom about "sinicization," which assumes that South China was settled by Han Chinese migrants from the Central Plains (Zhongyuan) who brought with them Confucian cultural values and institutions. Instead, Liu argues that state-making in the area during the Ming and Qing dynasties might have involved local populations weaving what they had imagined to be authoritative cultural norms from "the center" into their own practices. The cultural products on the ground highlighted the complicated agency of indigenous inhabitants who claimed to be Han Chinese on their own terms. Their divergent strategies, while aggressively adopting the Confucian literati language, gave women a great deal more nominative space and made patriarchy more contingent than Freedman's lineage paradigm might have acknowledged.[50]

Liu Zhiwei's chapter on public rituals is followed by David Faure's equally meticulous reading of biographies and private family letters during the Ming and Qing. Faure focuses primarily on the writings by a few prominent local scholars about their mothers. Much emotion went into the essays. These were private sentiments interlaced with Confucian narrative styles. The motherly images progressed from those of intimate caretakers in the earlier period to competent household managers and educated tutors. The mundane details of social life and family networks, however, have to be gleaned from writings framed by formulaic ideals of gentility and literati pretensions by the early nineteenth century. Faure's reading shows that "mothering" took on different meanings and substance for the sons over a long historical period, which allows us to appreciate different degrees of social space beyond prescribed Confucian expectations. Subjectivities changed with the percolation of highly moralized images as Guangdong went through convulsions of late imperial state-making, a process layered with commercial prosperity and literati refinement.[51] But the sons' actual experiences of their mothers survived between the lines. If Confucian ideals are not taken as the cultural/historical baseline for this region, it is interesting to question why, when, and by what means these ideals became moral authority. To what extent were local practices agentive improvisations?

The chapter by May-bo Ching explores the expressive cultures of bridal laments in relation to *muyushu* (songbooks of various popular narratives in the Cantonese vernacular). Comparing the highly innovative performances in the Hakka and Dan communities with those of the more settled Punti farmers, she examines the finer meanings of the positioning of women and marriage practices in the region in the late imperial and early Republican periods. Her subject matter engages with three issues. First, gendered notions embedded in the laments seemed to have been deviations from Confucian ideals but were treated as the norm by locals. Could this have been another long process of cultural mixing and matching by indigenous populations, a theme highlighted by Liu Zhiwei's earlier treatment of lineage rituals? Second, on the intimate emotions involved, do the bridal laments represent experiences with no cultural basis outside liminal time, as Fred Blake has described? Or, do the laments reveal feelings of women in a bind — daughters who have fully internalized Confucian values of filial piety and duties in marriage, and are torn in moments of forsaking one and embracing the other, as Rubie Watson would argue? Agonized voices or not, there are issues of authenticity and interpretation. Authorship and audience complicate the gender issue, because men can be centrally involved in the production and performance of these ritual laments. In fact, Ching points to the more restrictive features of the songbooks vis-à-vis the oral performances and relates the difference to an urban-based print market that was dominated by literate men in the early twentieth century.[52]

Focusing on women's work and women's food in the New Territories of Hong Kong in the twentieth century, Wing-hoi Chan's chapter further decenters the lineage paradigm by offering social details and changing subjectivities related to the evolution of a commercialized regional economy. The details serve the point of how dichotomous approaches to women's activities may reinforce exaggerated models of patriliny. He combines British colonial records with women's oral accounts of local economic life and argues against a scholarly preoccupation with the rice paddy and the lineage. Chan highlights women's work in the production of hogs for the market and their consumption of sweet potatoes, a crop of little market value. Chan also suggests that the relationship of women to commercialization in the area was one of intensified exploitation. A mediating factor came with natal and matrilateral ties that were economically important to peasant families. Nevertheless, Chan contrasts the carefree spaces given to unmarried daughters with the hardship of young married women who were subjected to strict control in both production and consumption.

Agency in Emigrant, Colonial, and Mercantile Societies

In this section, Chi-cheung Choi focuses on women in Chaozhou (eastern Guangdong) during the late imperial and early Republican periods. In the rural areas of Chaozhou, a long history of emigration resulted in women taking over many managerial roles at home and in business transactions, as buyers and sellers of land and property, and as guarantors and witnesses to legal contracts. However, Choi explores why women in this area, as contrasted with those in the Pearl River Delta, continued to be confined by male-dominated social ethos. Women were only able to step outside of home in the treaty port of Chaozhou when foreign legal and business institutions gave a generation of women entrepreneurs new protection and recognition.

In the two chapters on Hong Kong, one finds equally mobile populations where laws and moralities associated with trading empires and multi-ethnic colonial encounters created unusual dangers and opportunities for enterprising women. The chapter by the late Carl Smith explores court documents in colonial Hong Kong to find numerous Dan women from the Portuguese colony of Macao who had inherited property under the protection of British law. It traces the case of Ng Akew in mid-nineteenth century, a Dan woman in Macao who lived with and bore children by James Bridges Endicott, an American ship captain who engaged in the opium trade. Starting from the social and economic fringes of both British and Chinese society, she thrived in an interracial relationship and fully exploited her power among British colonial officials, American traders, Muslim shopkeepers, and Chinese pirates. Her social mobility illustrates the opportunities open to some women who were able to enrich their lives by claiming protection from British colonial institutions and a relatively open mercantile society. Smith's significant observations are not limited to the intimate interracial relationships between European and Muslim men and their Chinese women. For these women, relationships with their "protectors" were often short-lived. However, some were left with properties. Their Eurasian children, if fortunate, were provided with schooling. An important fact behind this was that despite racial and political overtones in most colonial encounters, the legal system had recognized property and a range of other rights for these women even after their men had left the scene. Historian Elizabeth Sinn's 2007 study of prostitution houses operated by these women has noted their shrewd business maneuvers.[53]

Merchants cultivated power through charity.[54] Its connection to colonial administration and missionary morality in Hong Kong provided some unusual refuges for women. From the archives of the Tung Wah Hospital and the Po Leung Kuk, Sinn has written extensively on public health, prostitution, and the protection of fugitive women from the mid-nineteenth century to the early decades of the twentieth. These were charitable organizations established within the British legal framework and run by Chinese merchant elites. The women who came under the protection of the Po Leung Kuk were originally bought by their masters at a young age (*zhuhua*) and raised for the purpose of future work.[55] Some were sold into domestic servitude. Known as *muitsai*, domestic bondservants were often physically and sexually abused. Many who fled their masters fell into the hands of human traffickers who supplied houses of prostitution. The fortunate ones took shelter in the Po Leung Kuk. Sinn's study shows that past prostitutes and protected women who had been left with resources by their foreign male patrons often succeeded in the trade. In an environment full of dangers and opportunities, their gain could be other women's misfortune.[56]

In describing the world of expatriate women in Hong Kong, Susanna Hoe and others reveal the political impact that these women brought to the lives of the most exploited through charity, Victorian morality, Christian sensibilities, and legislation. The issue of women's servitude was an emotional and controversial one not only for politicians, colonial officers, missionaries, and expatriates, but also for Chinese merchant households and elite women. Scholars have explored private letters, diaries, official documents, and missionary records to reconstruct the concerted efforts of those who opposed female servitude, campaigned for the licensing of prostitutes for public health purposes, and sheltered fugitive women.[57] The efforts took many decades to become a force in society. Based on moral outrage, political ambition, and religious commitment, the unlikely alliance of reformers and politicians in Whitehall and Hong Kong eventually forced its way into the Chinese merchant community.

The commercial environment provided opportunities for the children of interracial unions. Those fortunate enough to receive a Chinese-English education became successful professionals and brokers for trading empires that needed cross-cultural skills. They intermarried, and their mothers, wives, and daughters became matriarchs of prominent businesses and property-owning families in Hong Kong. They settled and put down roots in Hong Kong, confirmed by their burial ground — the Chiu Yuen Cemetery.[58] It is true that the early colonial society was sharply demarcated along racial lines. Prejudice prevailed with both Confucian and Victorian moralities. But the Eurasian background of these families did not bar them from positions of influence. They became master cultural brokers.

Another group directly involved in the cultural encounter in the colony were Chinese Christians, whose influences were limited by the colonial government's cooptation of the more traditional compradors. Wai-ching Wong argues that despite conservative doctrinal elements, Christian women evangelists provided female students in missionary schools role models beyond those of wife and mother.[59] By 1921, inspired by their faith and nationalism, Chinese Christians in Hong Kong organized the Anti-Mui Tsai Society to push for abolition of the *mui tsai* system. On the organization's executive committee in 1921 was Chinese Christian woman Ma Fok Hing-tong, who drew support for the cause from the Chinese YWCA she cofounded not long before. According to Wong's interpretation of the records, Ma and other Chinese Christian women "seized the opportunity to campaign not only for the abolition of girl servants but also for the equality of men and women."[60]

On the other side of the debate was conservative compradors including Eurasians like Sir Robert Hotung.[61] He was known for his business success and philanthropy. He was first knighted in 1915 and received numerous honors from the Pope and the governments of China, Portugal, France, Germany, and Annam. A wife of Sir Robert, Lady Clara Hotung (also known as Ho Cheung Lin-kok) came also from a Eurasian family. As illustrated by Josephine Lai-kuen Wong's chapter, Lady Clara was a remarkable figure who advocated for Buddhist charity causes and led a vigorous and well-respected public life until her death in 1938. She saw her children married into equally prominent families among the Hong Kong elites. As the most significant lay patron of the Tung Lin Kok Yuen, a Buddhist institution that she established in 1935, she helped redefine Buddhist faith and practice by integrating a place of worship into an urban setting and founding free Buddhist schools for women.[62] Gentry sponsorship of Buddhism was well known in Chinese history.[63] Lady Hotung's patronage was uniquely placed at a period of "New Culture" in the mainland after the May Fourth Movement when religion and cultural norms were challenged. Her Eurasian background made her efforts all the more unique. Her support for Buddhism thus introduced elements of Christian charity, education, and public service. While her polygynous marriage might have precluded her participation in the anti-Mui Tsai movement in which Chinese Christian Ma Fok Hing-tong was very active, Lady Clara used her resources to benefit other women by innovations likely to be inspired by the missionary practices. For her generation of women to whom formal institutional channels were not culturally or politically permissible, religion and charity could have been their best expressions of activism.

Work and Activism in a Gendered Age

Although a colony, Hong Kong was never a bounded physical entity. It was established as a node in the crossroads of empires, trading, and diasporic communities. The border between Hong Kong, mainland China, and the world was porous for almost a hundred years until after the Communist Revolution in China. Culturally, the South China region encompassed a highly commercialized Pearl River Delta and two regions with long histories of emigration, Siyi (Sze Yap) and Chaozhou. Hong Kong was linked to these regions as a vibrant space of flow. Before the 1950s, administrative barriers for the movement of people and goods had been light and often not enforceable. Making use of institutions unavailable on the mainland and elsewhere, a diverse range of people entered and exited Hong Kong in various phases of their lives and careers. According to historian Elizabeth Sinn, from the late nineteenth century to 1939, over 6.3 million emigrants had embarked at Hong Kong for a foreign destination, and over 7.7 million returned to China through the colony. They brought with them goods, capital, diverse cultural styles, worldly information, and new horizons.[64]

However, the political changeover of China in 1949 brought drastic changes to the region as movements across the border became restrictive. Until the 1970s, Hong Kong society was colonial in administrative structure and cultural orientation. Although politically and culturally cut off from the mainland, it remained a node for world industrial assembly lines, and, in recent decades, global finance, consumption, and media. While China turned inward in the Maoist phases of its socialist revolution, Hong Kong was therefore projected to the world, almost by default. Although the colony received waves of legal and illegal migrants from China, a homegrown population came of age in the 1970s with urban, middle class, Western-oriented education and professional careers. In their cultural identity, institutional practices, and political orientations, they drew a hard line between Hong Kong and China.[65]

The chapters in this section use particular historical moments, when the border between the mainland and Hong Kong hardened and softened, to frame their analyses of women's positioning in the South China region. A range of institutional channels enabled women to be publicly active. In colonial Hong Kong, civil service jobs opened up for women because competitive male candidates had stayed away from what they considered dead-end careers. As highlighted by Helen Siu's chapter, women might have started their civil service careers as strategic response to inequality, but they rose through the colonial system by taking jobs their male colleagues had shunned. Over time, they created their own identity and social recognition. When Anson Chan was appointed chief secretary of the Hong Kong government in the autumn of 1993, there were few raised eyebrows that the first Chinese chief civil servant would be a woman. The absence of fanfare then and now for the presence of senior women in the administrative and business hierarchies contrasts sharply with China, where forty years of ideological promotion to uphold "half the sky" seem to have reaped only token appointments.[66] The situation in Hong Kong can also be distinguished from that of Japan where societal affluence does not seem to fundamentally alter gender relationships, and high-ranking women within corporate or government structures are rare.[67] Granted, the term "women of influence" (*nü qiangren*) discloses a degree of gender bias because there is no equivalent prefix for distinguished men, it no longer arouses the sense of awe in Hong Kong that it did when it first appeared in the 1970s. One may argue that for the term to have lost its poignancy in the public mind is a good indicator of the progressive acceptance of women's achievements in the last thirty years.

In an introduction to a collection of works on women in Hong Kong, Veronica Pearson and Benjamin Leung argue that social and legal improvements for women are substantial. However, they have not altered some deep-seated hierarchies. The persistence of gender inequality has to do with Hong Kong's unique history — a combination of Chinese patriarchy, colonial laissez-faire, and the peculiar demands of a postwar industrial economy.[68] Their arguments are most relevant for understanding the "working daughters" in Janet Salaff's classic work on postwar Hong Kong. Inequality is found not only among working class families. Until recently, women were represented less in managerial and administrative positions than professional/technical ones. Nevertheless, a fast-moving industrial and service economy has allowed a large number of women to acquire education and to reach white-collar jobs.

Gendered opportunities are not confined to civil servants and professionals. A dense public culture in popular print, radio, and film from the 1960s helped project new images of women. In film, *The Seven Sisters*, with leading actresses, such as Siu Fong Fong and Chan Po Chu, became popular in the 1960s in their portrayal of college girls and young factory women. "Jane Bond" movies showed martial women kicking men while acknowledging "family values."[69] Working daughters of that period flocked to their fan clubs and identified with the actresses in movies that centered on family conflicts, dilemmas in marriage and romance, and hopes for personal fulfillment. The consumption practices associated with fandom were used to assert autonomy and independence.[70] Thus popular media instead of the state responded to the emergence of a large female audience and contributed to a new gender consciousness that matured in later decades amid political changes.

Po-king Choi uses oral histories to describe a generation of "daughters" who started factory work at a tender age in postwar Hong Kong. Today they look back on their lives as daughters, wives, mothers, and assembly line workers at the height of Hong Kong's industrial development in the 1970s. These women were distinguished by an intense desire for self-improvement. Opportunities in Hong Kong allowed them to attend night schools, to climb their way up to white-collar employment, and to attain personal fulfillment in social activism outside the home.[71] They fashioned their own moral universe against many odds. Choi also highlights how they have built on their past resourcefulness to face difficult circumstances today. In her previous works and a postscript in her chapter, Po-king Choi focuses on union activism among skilled and semi-skilled workers who have been displaced by the movement of Hong Kong factories across the physical border. Many of Hong Kong's middle-age working women experienced "withering of the Hong Kong dream" because, as Ching-kwan Lee (1999) has argued, that sexual discrimination at Hong Kong factories decades earlier prepared men for the economic integration with South China (in terms of management and technical jobs) and not for the women. While fighting for improving their life chances in uncertain times, some have extended their activism to other disadvantaged groups, such as sex workers and abused women. Choi sees the rise of their conscious, critical activism as a crucial component of post-1970s Hong Kong, where civic organizations, combined with the beginning of political negotiations on Hong Kong's future, created an unprecedented public forum.

Across the border on the mainland, public images of women in the socialist decades were in sharp contrast to those in Hong Kong. The liberated women were selfless workers who sacrificed personal lives for revolutionary causes. Tens of millions of young women rose through the cadre ranks of the Chinese communist party. Unlike the civil servants or working daughters in Hong Kong, the cadres garnered very different political resources, which were based on their assigned class positions and ideological affinity to the party-state. Sustained government efforts to improve women's material and social positions did bring visible results. Several generations in the cities enjoyed relatively good health care and education. The oral histories collected by Yan Lijun and Yang Meijian of former student activists turned senior administrators in Guangzhou clearly demonstrate the energies, ambivalences, and the structural constraints the socialist revolution had imposed. Women have had special ideological roles and institutional spaces in post-1949 China. Revolutionary rhetoric and political practice promoted the ideal for women to become "steel maidens" equal to men in their labor contributions. The process of achieving the ideal could be both liberating and alienating. Mobility strategies were relatively one-dimensional when the historically porous border between South China and the world outside became hardened by a language of the state and revolution to the exclusion of other social possibilities. Still, proximity to Hong Kong allowed the adventurous and desperate in Guangdong to cross boundaries in physical, cultural, and political terms.

Post-Mao liberalizations from the early 1980s on triggered drastic changes. The border between Hong Kong and the mainland softened with unprecedented speed and intensity. As shown in Ching-kwan Lee's work, by the mid-1980s, middle-aged women workers in Hong Kong found themselves displaced because factories had moved across the border. On the other hand, these factory jobs in Guangdong have given tens of millions of young women in the surrounding provinces the ultimate opportunity. Ngai Pun's work focuses on the conflicting worlds of the largely female migrant workers in Dongguan, an area with a concentration of foreign direct investment from Hong Kong, Taiwan, and Japan. Everyday, the workers juggle the harsh conditions of low-skilled assembly-line work and abusive factory management. Cramped in temporary dormitories, they create complicated bonding networks based on native place and invented particularistic ties. Their initial goals are to make enough money during a temporary sojourn to return home with a handsome dowry and support their families in the villages if necessary. Increasingly, the more resourceful ones are drawn to enterprising sideline work in the service industries. Pun captures the women's agency in defining their identity and social horizons.[72]

In the post-reform era, sudden exposure to the affluence of Hong Kong and foreign cultures has been disorienting for the construction of gender subjectivities. Among the newly rich, women are often reduced to a commodity — as cheap, compliant labor in factories and the sex industry. In the thriving consumption industries, hostesses in their *qipao* fill the reception halls of restaurants, karaoke bars, massage parlors, and nightclubs. They solicit eager customers in entertainment quarters and train stations. Many become "contract mistresses" kept by truck drivers and commuting businessmen in the boomtowns along the Hong Kong-Guangdong border.

The final chapter in this volume returns to images. Pheng Cheah meticulously analyzes cross-border prostitution as hauntingly portrayed in Fruit Chan's film, *Durian Durian*. The protagonist is one of the tens of millions of enterprising women who are "on the move" to southern China, looking for opportunities. These migrant women fight against the "controlling gaze" of the state media and popular consumption that expect filial daughters and docile sex objects. The agency of these women migrants is complicated and at times contradictory. One often asks if one should view their performances as empowerment and resistance or as acts of desperation by victims who see few alternatives.[73] Their sojourn can be summed up by sad images of the migrant returnee in Fruit Chan's film. The main character travels to Hong Kong to become a prostitute, subjecting herself to inhumane conditions. She returns to her hometown where family and friends shower her with attention for her "accomplishments" as a businesswoman and make demands on her savings. She watches her life fall apart under the pressure of collective pretense. Her only solace is a durian fruit sent to her from Hong Kong by a young illegal immigrant girl who is as much a fugitive as she is in every sense of the word. The historical baggage she carries is heavy. Although the chapter focuses on issues of representation, the film's realistic images force the audience to ask sharp questions about real life situations. Do women like her feel compelled to move on in a fast forward mode?[74]

This volume reflects interdisciplinary work over a decade. The authors have shared interests in the historical evolution of South China. They are intrigued by the peculiar intertwining of the mercantile, the literati, and the modern in the construction of gendered space. A regional focus does not necessarily divert attention from broader theoretical issues about gender. Instead, by unveiling the complex historical processes juxtaposed with the essentialized images of tradition and patriarchy, the authors hope to sharpen the analytical tools for examining cultural fluidity that enables and is transformed by human agency. By using three historical junctures to organize the empirical materials, the authors also explore how the fluidity consolidated and made lasting significance.

The subject area of Chinese women and the theoretical issues of agency and resistance are widely taught and researched. South China with its historical links with trade and the Chinese diaspora has been a focus for historians. Moreover, contemporary cross-border fluidities between the Pearl River Delta and Hong Kong have gained much analytical attention due to China's market turn, the influx of global capital, emerging labor regimes, and consumption fever. The implications of state-making processes to gender equality and women's agency on either side of the Hong Kong-mainland border have attracted scholarly attention.

The volume aims to integrate these interests with interdisciplinary focus, historical depth, and ethnographic details. For historians and anthropologists who are interested in the works of the "South China gang" since the publication of *Down to Earth: The Territorial Bond in South China* (Stanford 1995), this volume provides further theoretical application of a "regional construct" that appreciates process and transcends definitive powers of administrative borders. Moreover, by focusing on women's agency shaped by historical moments, the volume brings out gender dimensions that were not adequately treated in the previous volume. It also stresses that to understand gender in historical or contemporary South China, the cultural dynamics in Hong Kong provides valuable materials for comparison and connection.

Likewise, for scholars interested in modern Hong Kong society, the volume intends to refocus their attention to cultural dynamics in the larger South China region of which Hong Kong has been an integral part. Traditional concerns of family, lineage, and women's place characteristic of South China continue to shape women's public image and self-identity in modern Hong Kong. Ironically, the Maoist Revolution across the border has decimated traditional cultural resources. It is interesting to examine how cultural fragments are being reconstituted by intense cross-border activities today.

For an audience generally interested in gender issues in China or elsewhere, the organization of case studies in this volume illuminate the important historical processes in which layers of social, political, and economic activities intersected to constitute gendered notions and strategies in an evolving regional space. This engages with critical perspectives that refuse to treat women and gender as static, essentialized cultural categories. Each section in the volume highlights particular junctures in the development of South China that have significant impact on the predicaments of women and their identities and mobility strategies. Substantial gaps in knowledge remain. The authors nonetheless hope that a regional historical perspective on gender subjectivities is a worthwhile direction to explore.

I
Cultural Spaces between State-Making and Kinship

The Lingnan region has long seen a curious juxtaposition of powerful lineages, male-dominated ancestral estates and rituals, and remarkable anomalies from the Confucian ideals in marriage practices. The four chapters in this section deal with the historical evolution of this region and argue that compelling gender notions and divergent energies have been mutually constitutive over centuries of state-making and cultural transformation when an indigenous population claimed its respective place in the expanding Chinese empire. The chapters use four different topics to engage with the argument. Liu Zhiwei applies a careful "reading" of a ritual by a powerful lineage in the Qing that focused on the worship of two female ancestors. By unveiling how indigenous customs and a Confucian literati language intertwined at agentive moments of becoming Han Chinese in the Ming and Qing, the chapter recovers gender space that has been locked within a lineage paradigm and its associated assumptions of patriarchy.

David Faure continues the exercise in critical reading by examining images of mother in the writings of prominent Ming and Qing scholar-officials. From the changing images gleaned from the texts, Faure highlights the dissonance between the rich emotional bonding between mother and son and the discursive ordering frame of Confucian literati writing that stressed propriety and distance from a male point of view.

To explore unusual gender space, May-bo Ching turns to an oral tradition of ballads sung by local women in the region. Were the ambivalent emotions expressed in these ballads resistance to a Confucian patriarchy or fragments of indigenous cultures woven between the lines? The irony is, as she points out, that by the early twentieth century, the production and circulation of these ballads in print form were shaped by a commercial market and writing styles in the world of literate men. As indicated in the chapters by Liu and Faure, to what extent were these women's voices intertwined with those of their male counterparts?

The theme of an increasingly commercialized region and its effect on the circumstances of village women is the focus of Wing-hoi Chan's chapter. His meticulous examination of the microeconomics of farming in the poor Hakka villages of the New Territories in colonial Hong Kong shows complicated division of labor and well-being not only in gendered terms, but also in marital circumstances among young women. The network of natal and matrilateral kin, crucial to the economic circumstances of peasant families, might have given village women more room to maneuver than a dichotomous framework that exaggerates the force of patriliny.

1

Women's Images Reconstructed: The Sisters-in-Law Tomb and Its Legend*

Liu Zhiwei

Women in Ming-Qing literature were portrayed in extremes. Most were, if not virtuous virgins or chaste widows, then dissolute women or lascivious girls. These images of women were literati constructions based on the morality of Neo-Confucian thought in the Song-Ming periods.[1] Reinforcing notions of male superiority, the images were prevalent in the central plain (*zhongyuan*) region but were more nuanced in the Lingnan region.[2] When Lingnan gradually became part of the imperial order in political and cultural terms, the reconstitution of women's images was an important means adopted by the literati to spread "civilization" to their own localities. Layers of meaning were embedded into such reconstitution. I would like to use the "Sisters-in-Law Tomb" near Guangzhou and the evolution of its legend to illuminate such historical processes.

---

* This historical survey is part of a research project about the society and culture of the Pearl River Delta, guided by David Faure, Helen F. Siu, and Ye Xian'en, and funded by the Institute of Chinese Studies, the Chinese University of Hong Kong, and the Wenner-Gren Foundation for Anthropological Research. Fieldwork was conducted by Helen F. Siu, Dai He, Chen Chunsheng, and me. I would like to thank them for their valuable input and permission to use their materials.

The "Sisters-in-Law Tomb" and the Early History of the He Lineage in Shawan

Today, the "Sisters-in-Law Tomb" is situated at the foot of the Baiyun Mountain north of Guangzhou. Old residents of the city are well aware that this is an ancestral tomb under the He lineage, a renowned lineage in the town of Shawan, at the heart of the Pearl River Delta. Those buried in the tomb were the wife and sister of He Renjian, a fourth-generation ancestor who first settled in Shawan. Legends about the Sisters-in-Law Tomb circulated around Guangzhou, and two versions were recorded in *Folk Stories of Canton*, edited by Liu Wanzhang in 1929. They are as follows:

> The younger sister and wife of He Renjian got along very well together. In fact, they were so fond of each other that they vowed to die on the same day, even though they could not have been born on the same day. One day, He's wife was struck with a serious illness. Sensing that her sister-in-law was near death, He's sister hurried to prepare the funeral clothing. Unfortunately, He's sister was too anxious and, while walking, she fell down from the upper floor of the house and died. Saddened by the terrible news, He's wife also died. To respect the wishes of his wife and sister, He Renjian looked for a suitable site to bury them. Guided by a kind Earth Goddess, who appeared as an ordinary old woman, He Renjian successfully found a site to bury the two women together. The site was said to be so auspicious that it brought good fortune to the He lineage for generations thereafter.

The second version of the Sisters-in-Law Tomb legend, collected by Liu Wanzhang, alleged that the "sisters-in-law" actually referred to the mother and aunt, rather than sister and wife, of He Renjian.[3]

However, what attracts our attention is not the legend itself, but that this particular tomb for the sisters-in-law was, and still is, being worshipped as an ancestral tomb by one of the most distinguished lineages in the Pearl River Delta region. One may wonder if this ritual was an unusual local custom that evolved out of a complex historical-cultural process. To understand the issue, we must look into the early history of the He lineage in Shawan.

According to the genealogy of the He lineage,[4] four other tombs with ancestors of the He lineage should be present near the Sisters-in-Law Tomb. These included the tomb of He Chen, the third-generation ancestor; the tomb of He Renduo, who was referred to as the brother of He Renjian, or a cousin who did not share the same He ancestor in Shawan; the tomb of He Zhiteng, the ninth-generation ancestor of the Yi branch (*fang*); and an "auspicious tomb" (*jimu*) situated among the three abovementioned tombs.[5]

In 1994, the hill on which the Sisters-in-Law Tomb was situated was flattened to make way for urban expansion in Guangzhou. Although the Sisters-in-Law Tomb was declared a cultural heritage site just in time to stop its destruction, it still had to move 30 kilometers north of its original position. After this incident, archeologists investigated the tomb and the two other tombs nearby. They could not find either the tomb of He Chen or that of "granduncle Zhiteng." The three surviving tombs were the Sisters-in-Law Tomb, the tomb of He Renduo, both of which were second burials, and a tomb at the presumed site of granduncle Zhiteng's tomb, with a tablet that bears the words: "Madam Li, the wife of the eleventh-generation ancestor." All three were brick-chambered types constructed in the Ming dynasty.[6] It is important to note that as one of the most important places for ancestral worship for the He lineage in Shawan, this site is dominated by tombs for women. Another major site for the ancestral tombs of the He lineage is located on Wo Mountain in a suburb northeast of Guangzhou, where He Renjian, their fourth-generation ancestor, his second wife, and the wives of the fifth-generation ancestors were buried.

Before 1949, all members of the Shawan He lineage went annually to Guangzhou to visit these tombs and conduct elaborate rituals of worship that lasted for two days. They worshipped the Sisters-in-Law Tomb on the first day and then the tomb of He Renjian on Wo Mountain on the second.[7] While conducting fieldwork in Shawan, we discovered that the local people always talked about the Sisters-in-Law Tomb but rarely mentioned the tomb of He Renjian. The Sisters-in-Law Tomb appeared much more important to the local people. What was even more interesting was the claim of the Hes in Shawan that the tomb of He Chen should have been situated next to the Sisters-in-Law Tomb, and that before 1949, "[they] burned incense and lighted candles at the site of He Chen's tomb first, worshipping and sweeping [it] in the same way."[8] However, narratives provided by members of the He lineage often mentioned rituals only for the Sisters-in-Law Tomb. Although He Chen's tomb had fallen into ruins, there were no attempts to restore it. It therefore appeared that the primary focus of the Hes' annual worship had been the Sisters-in-Law Tomb and not others.

Why did the He family assign top priority in ancestral worship to the tomb of two female ancestors, but not to their first ancestor, or their third-generation male ancestor? Such practice seemed to have deviated from the conventional expectations of a lineage that was grounded in Confucian propriety. We must turn to the early history of the He lineage for clues.

The Hes in Shawan have claimed that their ancestors migrated to Guangzhou as early as in the Song dynasty. According to their accounts, their fourth-generation ancestor, He Renjian, settled in Shawan, Panyu county, in 1233 and has since been considered the founding ancestor of the lineage. The eighth-generation ancestor, He Zihai, obtained a metropolitan graduate degree in the early years of the Hongwu period (1368–1398) when civil service examinations were first carried out by the Ming government. The *Guangdong Provincial Gazetteer* (*Guangdong Tongzhi*) also recorded an epitaph written by the minister of personnel in the Zhengtong period of the Ming dynasty (1436–1449) in commemoration of He Zihai.[9] These accounts demonstrated that since their settlement in Shawan, the history of the Hes was recorded with some clarity and it is reasonable for us to regard the history behind the Sisters-in-Law Tomb as credible. Because one of the stories stated that the sisters-in-law were buried next to the tombs of their "ancestors," we may assume that these "ancestors," that is, the ancestors of the He lineage prior to He Renjian, are the key to understanding the Sisters-in-Law Tomb. In a previous paper,[10] I have examined in detail the history of the He lineage before their settlement in Shawan and shall discuss it only briefly in the following paragraphs.

According to the genealogies of the He lineage, the names of the ancestors in the three generations prior to He Renjian were He Yuanchong, He Mi, and He Chen, respectively. However, these names were "acquired" from the genealogies of the Hes after the mid-Ming from places other than Shawan. Moreover, their tablets often bore peculiar official titles, such as "Liu Xueshi" (Sixth scholar), "Sanjiu Chengshilang" (Three-nine official in charge) and "Niansan Chengshilang" (Twenty-third official in charge). Their descendants at that time interpreted the term "Xueshi" to mean "Hanlin Academician" and took up absurd titles, such as "Sanjiu Chengshilang," as the official titles of their ancestors. All of these interpretations were fallacious. Hanlin Academician was a highly respected official position in the Song dynasty. Although the ranking of the Gentleman for Managing Affairs was as low as the eighth rank, upper class, it was still reserved for officials serving in the capital and was "the starting official title bestowed on the sons of the principal graduate or those of the Grand Councilor."[11] If the earliest ancestors of the He lineage in Shawan were indeed Hanlin Academicians, how could it be possible that their names and genealogical accounts were so unclear for such a long time? One may question why the Hes in Shawan did not make their earliest ancestors, who were supposed to be Hanlin Academicians, the center of their worship, but instead worshiped He Renjian as their founding ancestor, whose official title ranked the lowest among those in the earliest four generations of the He lineage? The official title of He Renjian was apparently "Gentleman for Rendering Service," which was of the eighth rank, lower class. Even that rank was questionable.

He Zihai began compiling genealogies of the Hes in Shawan in the *Genealogical Chart* (*Putu*) in the early years of the Ming dynasty. But he disdained the practice of forging ancestors' genealogical accounts and fabricating relationships with renowned and virtuous people, a common practice for compiling genealogies at the time. In fact, he criticized these customs as "reckless." Although he did mention vaguely in another document that two of his ancestors had been metropolitan graduates from Panyu in the Tang dynasty, when he traced his family history in the preface of the *Genealogical Chart*, he simply wrote, "Our family has accumulated merits of more than a hundred years since [the time] of Fupan *gong* [i.e., He Renjian]." He mentioned nothing about the generations before He Renjian.

The 1561 edition of the *Guangdong Provincial Gazetteer* mentioned the Hes of Shawan by listing the names of their ancestors from the Tang to the Yuan dynasties, namely, He Ding (Tang), He Ze (Song), and He Ruji (Yuan).[12] Such an account was probably composed by official scholars with positions as prestigious as that of He Zihai. However, this account did not mention the ancestral characters that were highlighted by the Hes in Shawan. Examples of such characters were the so-called founding ancestor in Nanxiong; an Attendant Censor of the Posterior Jin dynasty, He Chang; the three metropolitan graduates of the Northern Song dynasty who were known as the "three phoenixes of the He family," namely, He Ji, He Li, and He Qu; and the first-generation ancestor, He Yuanchong, who was portrayed as a Hanlin Academician. *Guangdong Provincial Gazetteer* was by no means the sole credible source. The compilation of the Hes' presettlement history in it was supplemented with numerous amendments and additions after the mid-Ming period. The additions bridged the gap between He Ze and He Renjian, hence connecting the history of the He lineage in Shawan with the legend of Nanxiong Zhuji *xiang*.[13] Because information about the generations prior to He Renjian was only "acquired" from others after the mid-Ming period, details about these figures, such as their names, genealogies, and the time and route of migration were unclear and subject to dispute. Even the Hes today, who have paid much attention to the examination of their own lineage history, can only sigh and remark, "Whether the accounts are true, only the ancestors themselves would know. We can only suspect what has already been suspected, and trust what has already been trusted."[14]

If the Hes prior to He Renjian were unidentifiable, the statement that the sisters-in-law were buried next to the tomb of an "ancestor" should thus be questioned. Both the Qing gazetteer's account[15] and explanations given by the Hes stated that the "ancestor" referred to He Chen, the third-generation ancestor, who was supposed to be the father of the *gu* (the sister or aunt of He Renjian, depending on the version of the legend) and the father-in-law of the *sao* (the wife or mother). If this had been true, He Chen's tomb should have been more significant than both the Sisters-in-Law Tomb and that of He Renduo. However, the genealogical account of the He lineage stated:

> The tomb of Ancestor Xi'an [that is, He Chen] had long been demolished. Many of its bricks and stones were seized by others for use on tombs nearby. It was not until 1407–08 that [He] Zhizhong and [He] Zhiyi were selected to be responsible for restoration, and all the [new bricks] were marked with the characters "the tomb bricks of the Hes in Shawan." In 1408–1409, Huang Shouxing, a man from Guangzhou, trespassed upon the tomb site [of He Chen]. Subsequently, [the He lineage members] selected [He] Zhilin, [He] Zhizhong, [He] Zhiyong, and [He] Zhiyi to present their charges [against Huang] to the prefecture and county courts. The case remained unsettled after three years, so [the Hes] reported the case to the Provincial Surveillance Commission, which then took it up to the Provincial Administrative Commissioner. [The Provincial Administrative Commissioner then] appointed an official to handle and investigate the case. [After] examination, [Huang] was found guilty.

and

> During the Tianshun period (1457–1464), the tomb [of He Chen] was again trespassed upon by He Cize from Guangzhou. [The Hes] thus authorized three descendants of the tenth generation, namely, [He] Shaoda, [He] Shaopu, and [He] Shaogui, to act as plaintiffs [against He Chize]. Chize was then found guilty.

We have not been able to verify either court case. However, considering the status and prestige enjoyed by the He lineage of Shawan in the region, it seemed unlikely that there were such recurring trespassers. I suspect that the existence of He Chen's tomb was actually confirmed after the Hes won these court cases. However, even if He Chen's tomb had already been identified in Ming, it could not replace the Sisters-in-Law Tomb in terms of its importance in the He traditions of worship. In sharp contrast is the well-preserved tomb of He Renduo, who was only an ancestor of a collateral branch of the Hes in Shawan and whose descendents cannot be identified today. Archeological investigations show that the Hes in Shawan restored tombs near the Sisters-in-Law Tomb during the Jiajing period of the Ming (1522–1566) and the Qiaolong period of the Qing (1736–1796). If He Chen's tomb had been the most important one among the Hes' many ancestral tombs, it could not have been left unattended.

It is not my intention to recompile a genealogy for the He lineage or to assess the disputes over the tombs. I want to illustrate that among the sites for ancestral worship by the He lineage of Shawan, the Sisters-in-Law Tomb is far more important than those of their male ancestors. Moreover, in the following sections I will show that the significance of He Chen's tomb could only be illustrated with a literati interpretation of the legend of the Sisters-in-Law Tomb.

The Indigenous Images of Women in the Pearl River Delta

The storyline in the legend behind the Sisters-in-Law Tomb is simple, and its content not remarkable. Without sufficient firsthand evidence, it is difficult to formulate an explanation of why the Hes worshipped the Sisters-in-Law Tomb in such an elaborate manner. Nevertheless, to demystify this ritual practice, it is valuable to examine the socio-cultural context on which the legend of the Sisters-in-Law Tomb was established and in particular, women's status in the local cultural tradition.

Women in the Lingnan region — including the "*zishunu*" of the Pearl River Delta region in the late Qing and early republican periods, and the working women in Hong Kong today — have contributed a great deal to the modern transformation of family and society. Many appreciate this as women's empowerment and liberation. However, I would argue that the status of women in the Lingnan region had a very different "cultural starting point" from that of women from the "central plain" region. Makino Tatsumi has studied this in detail.[16] Using the case of the Sisters-in-Law Tomb, I hope to show a possible correlation between a local cultural tradition and the ritual respect given to women ancestors.

Many historical literatures identify the Lingnan region as a part of China from the Qin-Han period. However, historical records show that before the Ming dynasty, the cultural customs of Guangdong was substantially different from the "Han-Chinese culture." In his *An Account of Moving the Guangzhou Prefectural School* (*Guangzhoufu yixue ji*), Zhang Zi, the Prefect of Guangzhou in the Song dynasty, stated:

> Guangdong and Guangxi are situated south of the Five Mountains. Together [the two places] comprise more than forty prefectures, with Panyu being one of the largest towns. However, the number of renowned scholars there

is particularly small, and the number of people studying at schools and obtaining degrees is also much lower than other regions. . . . Moreover, people there indulge in leisure and pleasure and are not ashamed of bickering. Wives go to courts to make accusations on behalf of their husbands. These women act in courts as if they were at home, fabricating excuses and arguments, bawling and boasting without restrain. Everyday women are whipped to chase them out of court. It is never considered improper [even when] fathers and sons of large lineages live separately. Blood brothers do not help each other in emergencies. Juniors offend seniors, and the elders take advantage of the young. Occasionally there are those who marry without matchmakers, and their parents do not prohibit [them from doing so]. Funeral rituals are excessively lavish and out of control. [Even though the expenses] reduce the rich in the morning to paupers by night, people are perfectly willing [to continue such practices].[17]

The descriptions above present a vivid picture of the indigenous society in the Song dynasty through the lens of Confucian officials. If the geographical names had been omitted, one would probably not identify it as a region under the direct administration of the "Chinese Empire." Prefect Zhang intelligently attributed the differences to the fact that the "imperial civilization had not yet spread [to Lingnan]." Within such a cultural context, it is no longer surprising that women's images and social roles were different from the archetype described by the Confucian scholar-officials. Another Song document stated:

Guangzhou women are strong, but men are feeble. Eight or nine out of ten women dress their hair up and wrap it with black gauze, wear black clothes with half of their arms exposed, and are known to "wander the streets carrying children on their backs."[18]

The social manners described above stood out in the historical Lingnan region.[19] Similar characteristics were observed in Guangxi during the Qing dynasty. In the chapter entitled "Barbarous customs" in *A Collection of Accounts on Guangxi* by Wang Sen, one finds the following entry:

The people of Wuzhou cultivate, but do not engage in crafts. Sorcery is commonly practiced, and women in markets are numerous. With their hair dressed and feet bare, they buy grains and sell firewood. In marriage ceremonies, betel nuts are always used, and men and women do not perform pledge rituals. Brothers are addressed as sisters. Uncles and nephews are largely addressed as grandfathers and grandchildren. It is men who usually "marry" into the wives' family (*jia*) and inherit the properties of their wives' fathers. It is the women who take in their husbands in marriage (*cu*), giving properties to their husbands. There are cases of men changing their surnames to adopt those of their wives or adding to their surnames those of their wives, never returning to their lineage of origin. People feel no shame if a woman marries another man after she has been betrothed.[20]

Wuzhou lies in the same cultural-linguistic zone as the Xi River and Pearl River Delta regions of Guangdong. The regions are known to have retained variations of many aboriginal cultural practices until recently.[21] Confucian scholars such as Huang Zuo asserted that since the Song dynasty, Guangdong had become a place where "the emperor's commands and teachings penetrated everyday lives," that "customs gradually followed those of the ancient times"; "the robes and caps people wear, and the rituals and music people practice are no different from those of the central region." However, in reality, only "women from reputable families" would abide by the etiquette and standards exemplified in Confucian sayings such as "women should never step outside of their homes, and fathers-in-law and brothers-in-law should never see their daughters-in-law and sisters-in-law respectively except during festive occasions." Commoners in the Pearl River Delta region continued practicing indigenous customs, retaining a strong sense of local culture until the Ming-Qing and Republican periods. This rings especially true with regard to the customs related to women. For example:

> When a family of commoners marries out their daughter, women gather to sing and say goodbye [to the bride.] [The place where they sing] is called the singing hall (*getang*). Although this tradition has gradually been abandoned, it can still be found in some villages. In the past, singers held hands and tapped their feet to keep rhythm. They often brought objects forward as metaphors, similes, or as subtle means of communication. [Their songs] are comparable to the verses of *Ziye* and *Zhuzhi*. The last phrase always end with "*niang laili*", "*ma laili*," "*shui dang di*" (water agitating a little brother), and "*niang shiji*" (how old are you, the girl in her teens?). All these songs are duets sung as questions and answers between men and women with intention to tease. Village girls who ignore the rules call one another "*wanji*" (binding one's hair together). Whenever they are working in the fields, they sing songs to tease one another.[22]

These social norms differed entirely from the Confucian standards for women's conduct. The statement that such practices were gradually abandoned may partially reflect the cultural transformations that took place in the Pearl River Delta region after the Ming dynasty. It more likely reflected the ideals held by the literati, such as Huang Zuo, who strived to promote Confucian teachings in indigenous societies.

Women's social status in the Pearl River Delta region can also be understood from the position of daughters. When we conducted fieldwork in Shawan in 1989, an eighty-six-year-old man (now deceased) strongly asserted that the daughters of Shawan were very "fierce." He said that family finances were usually kept by the daughters, especially by those *zishunu* who were quite wealthy and whom he called "fierce aunts" (*egupuo*). The old man's complaints against these social norms might have resulted from difficult personal experiences. However, his opinion is generally shared by inhabitants in the Pearl River Delta region. One phenomenon in the region that has attracted scholarly attention was the extravagance of the dowry presented by the bride's family. It often outshone the betrothal gifts offered by the groom's family.[23] This practice has had a long history. The 1561 edition of the *Guangdong Provincial Gazetteer* noted that in Guangzhou, when marrying out their daughters, families often competed in the amount of trousseaux, candies, and cakes presented, leading some to bankruptcy. The 1548 edition of the *Xiangshan County Gazetteer* (*Xiangshan xianzhi*) described the lavishness of marriage practice, stating that in response to some families on the groom's side who offered more than a hundred teals of gold as betrothal, some families on the bride's side had presented ornaments as dowries worth several times the price of the bride, with land occasionally added to the trousseaux list. Such extravagant dowries may allow one to argue that the status and rights maintained at home by women in Lingnan were not as marginal as described in scholarly literatures.

Along with the privileges enjoyed by daughters were the duties to which they were subjected at home. In historical literature, one frequently finds accounts of certain "great-aunts," who pledged to not marry (to take up her family's burden) and were thus worshipped by her natal family's descendents after death. For example, in the chapter on virtuous women, in the 1774 edition of the *Panyu County Gazetteer* (*Panyu xianzhi*), an entry recorded how a certain Aunt Chen Guijie, in view of the death of her elder brother and parents, vowed not to marry to take care of her orphaned nephew and her widowed sisters-in-law.[24]

This story closely resembled one of the versions of the Sisters-in-Law Tomb legend. Moreover, similar stories could be found in counties other than Panyu. One such example was the story of Madam Nie from Xinhui County. Madam Nie's husband died within a year after their marriage. After her own parents passed away, Madam Nie returned to her natal home and vowed never to remarry in order to take care of her orphaned nephew. Moved by the virtue of Madam Nie, her younger sister also pledged not to marry. Together, they raised their nephew. After their deaths, the two women were worshipped by the Nies, and their tablets were placed on the porch to the left of the Nie's ancestral hall.[25]

These daughters of the Pearl River Delta region who bore particular responsibilities and duties in their families appear somewhat related to the local customs of *zishunu* (girls who ritually pinned up their hair, formed sisterhoods, and took elaborate vows not to marry) and *buluojia* (wives who did not live with their husbands and instead resided in their natal homes). Some scholars associate the *zishunu* practice with the silk industry that boomed in the nineteenth century, which gave women workers economic independence. However, such an argument stems from a misunderstanding of the cultural traditions in the Pearl River Delta region, where women did not assume humble positions and subordinate roles. In fact, both *zishunu* and *buluojia* were ancient customs that originated from indigenous groups in southwestern China.[26] Evidence of such practices can be found in local literatures published after the Qianlong period (1736–1795), long before the rise of the silk industry in the nineteenth century:

> Virgins in villages very often established spinsterhood with other village girls. They relied on and maintained close relationships with each other and were unwilling to marry. Even if they were forced to marry, they would return to their parents' home and remain there for a long time, unwilling to go back to their husbands' homes.[27]

Traces of the *zishunu* and *buluojia* customs can be found in the legend of the Sisters-in-Law Tomb in Shawan. One, the husband's sister vowed not to marry. (In fact, locals use the term "pinning-up one's hair" [*shuqi*] to describe the resistance of the husband's sister to marriage, where *shuqi* usually signifies the status of a *zishunu*.) Two, although the brother's wife in the Sisters-in-Law Tomb legend did not practice the *buluojia* custom, she did not live with her husband, He Renjian. Rather, she and her sister-in-law "depended on each other for their livelihoods." Furthermore, she did not give birth to any children. All the sons of He Renjian were born to his concubine, who was buried with him. Despite being He Renjian's proper wife, the *sao* was buried with the *gu* in a separate tomb. Whether this practice is associated with that of the "husband and wife living separately," as mentioned by Makino Tatsumi, is a separate question that is worth exploring. I cannot determine if the *gu* in this legend is a *zishunu*, or if the relationship between the sisters-in-law is one of "spinsterhood" between *zishunu*. However, considering that the legend has remained credible and sensible to the locals in Shawan for a long time, it is reasonable to assume that this legend is closely related to the local *zishunu* and *buluojia* practices.

It is worth noting that the abovementioned custom of "grooms marrying into the bride's family" (*ruzhui*)[28] as recorded in *A Collection of Accounts of Guangxi* is also different from the *ruzhui* practices in other parts of China. Because a *ruzhui* son-in-law could inherit the property of his wife's family, *ruzhui* was, at one time, a major way for men from distant places to enter local Lingnan society. This is evident in the chapter "Chaps from other provinces" in *An Account of What [I] Hear and Observe in Guangdong* by Zhang Qu: "Men who sojourn in Guangdong and marry locally are often detained by their wives' families. They cannot return [to their home villages]."[29] In fact, many genealogies from Guangdong recorded how the founding ancestors of a lineage settled in Guangdong by means of *ruzhui*. According to the He's genealogy, the founding ancestor of the Hes in Shawan, He Renjian, settled in Shawan by building up a relationship with Li Maoying, a Guangzhou native who became an official during the Song dynasty. Since then, the Hes and the Lis maintained close relationships for several hundred years. According to some local legends, He Renjian also took Li Maoying's maidservant as a concubine, and his son married the niece of Li Maoying. These stories indicated that the Hes settled in Shawan because some had married into the Lis family.

The relationship between the custom of *ruzhui* and the worship female ancestors in the Pearl River Delta region is difficult to establish. However, legends concerning the settlement of numerous lineages in the Pearl River Delta region are associated with female ancestors. There were stories other than the one from Shawan, which involved the tombs of female ancestors as an important part of a lineage's ancestral worship custom. A family comparable in status to the Hes is the Chens at Waihai in Xinhui county. Among the family's ancestral tombs is one of their founding grandmother who is said to be the granddaughter of Li Maoying. She had brought from her parents' family trousseau fields that became the foundation of the Chen lineage's prosperity.[30] Another example is the Wangs in Zhongshan county, who for a long time worshipped their "great grandmother" (*taipo*, a female ancestor) but not their "great grandfather" (*taigong*, a male ancestor). They did not "retrieve" their "great grandfather" until they linked their lineage with another Wangs from Shawan.[31] Similar traditions of worshiping female ancestors also exist for the Liangs at Chakeng xiang and the Chens at Tianma xiang. In the founding legends of both of these renowned lineages from

Xinhui county, the "great grandmother" (*taipo*, or *bopo*) enjoyed a very prominent status.[32] Another lineage that worships its great grandaunt is the Li family in Panyu County. In addition to worshiping the "Tomb of Virtuous Aunt Li," the Lis built her a separate hall.[33]

It should be noted that this female-centered cultural tradition was not confined to the Pearl River Delta region or to Guangdong and Guangxi. Remains of similar traditions had probably appeared in various forms in different periods within ancient Yue culture. Nonetheless, the uniqueness of Lingnan should not be overstated. The so-called "indigenous" culture could probably be found in the rural or marginal areas of central and northern China. To assess the degree of influence by Confucian scholar officials, one should also take into account differences in urban and rural environments and in social status of families. Nevertheless, it appeared that historical inhabitants in the Lingnan region were not as male-centered as they have been portrayed in much of the scholarly literature. Although a particular local orientation cannot fully explain the legend of the "Sisters-in-Law Tomb," it had a socio-cultural context. Evidence is limited, but we can at least acknowledge a relationship between this legend and the cultural traditions indigenous to the Pearl River Delta region.

Thematic Changes in the Sisters-in-Law Tomb Legend

As mentioned earlier in the chapter, there are different versions of the Sisters-in-Law Tomb legend. According to the version told to us in Shawan during fieldwork in 1989, the sisters-in-law got along very well, as if they were real sisters, to the point that the *gu* refused to marry (Here, the narrator used the term "*shuqi*.") to stay with the *sao*. Later, the *sao* fell seriously sick, and in her efforts to get funeral clothes for her sister-in-law, she accidentally fell to her death. It was also said that the *gu* died immediately from sorrow when she learned of her sister-in law's misfortune. Subsequently, the sisters-in-law were buried in the same tomb.[34]

This version of the legend basically matches the one recorded by Liu Wanzhang in 1929 and shows relative consistency as a legend that has long been passed on orally among local commoners. The structure of this legend is similar to the versions recorded in early literature, as demonstrated by one I have encountered concerning graves and tombs, in the 1774 edition of the *Panyu County Gazetteer*. It has the following passage:

The Sisters-in-Law Tomb of the Song dynasty is situated in Pujian. The *gu* is the daughter of He Chen in Shawan. Her brother, Renjian, marries a daughter of the Shis. The *gu* and the *sao* are very close. [Later,] the *sao* passes away. The *gu* does not marry and dies at home. So, they are buried together.[35]

However, this account was immediately challenged by a contemporary literatus. In 1756, while serving as the Principal Examiner of Guangdong, Liang Guozhi found the Sisters-in-Law Tomb offensive to Confucian propriety.[36] Twenty years later, Liang was promoted to Grand Secretary, and was invited by a member of the gentry of the He lineage to compose the *Tablet Inscriptions of the Sisters-in-Law Tomb*. In it, Liang stated:

In the year of Bingzi (1756), I undertook the appointment of supervisor for the civil service examinations in Guangdong. Traveling past the Yu Mountain, I read geographical accounts from Guangdong about the mountains and the celebrated sites I passed through, [and found that] none of these places was as cultivated as the provincial capital. To the north of the City of the Rams (Guangzhou), mountain ranges ran in all directions, with temples, pavilions, and caves of immortals and hidden land. I particularly went to take a look at the Santai Mountain situated west of Xianyan, which was the recorded location of the Sisters-in-Law Tomb. Never had there been a tradition of burying a husband's sister and a brother's wife since the ancient times, so why [was there such a tomb] burying [a pair of sisters-in-law in Guangdong] and why had it become so distinguished? Was it because the tomb site was propitious? Or was it because the people buried there were illustrious? At the beginning, I was not able to obtain any details about [the tomb].

After the examination results had been announced, He Quanxing, a student from Panyu County, was selected by his native fellow townsmen to undertake the rituals of paying respects to teachers. So, I posed my questions about the Sisters-in-Law Tomb to him. He stood up and said: [The brother's wife and the husband's sister] were the wife and sister of my fourth-generation ancestor. Our third-generation ancestor, Xi'an *gong*, had resigned from office and suffered from illnesses from time to time. [But] the situation of the state was so chaotic at that time that our fourth-generation ancestor, Fupan *gong*, had to run the state affairs and so was often away from home. [Fupan *gong*'s] sister and wife took care of [Xi'an *gong*] in the mornings and at nights, [which kept them so busy that they did not even have the time] to loosen the girdle of their dresses. [Wanting] to show her gratitude to her own father, and considering the virtue and diligence of her brother's wife, the *gu* broke her bracelet and vow not to marry. The *gu* and the *sao* depended on each other for their livelihoods, which pleased Xi'an *gong* so much that he forgot about his old age. Xi'an *gong* died a few years later, and the *sao* bore such sorrow that she died from illnesses soon afterwards. The *gu* was fine at first, but later, she was so moved [by her sister-in-law] that she fell into a coma and passed away on the same day. Recognizing their virtue, Fupan *gong* showed his sympathy by allowing them to be buried together next to the tombs of our ancestors, fulfilling their wishes. The county record only noted the close relationship between the sisters-in-law, but it certainly was not complete.

I said, ". . . Nothing can sustain a woman's reputation through the generations besides her chastity and filial piety. They circumscribe normal courses of action, but they are [actually] tied to obligations and the teachings of sages. For this particular pair [of women], the daughter-in-law treated [her father-in-law] well, and the daughter [assumed] the righteous responsibility [of taking care of her own father]. Their characters can be regarded as everlasting." On this account, I briefly recorded the story, and ordered the postman to send my writing back [to Panyu], for it to be inscribed onto a stone tablet and for people to observe local morals as well as to examine the traces [of the legend].[37]

Another written record of the legend can be found in an essay entitled "Writing after the genealogy of the Chens of Waihai," composed by Long Tinghuai, a renowned member of the gentry from Shunde county, around the Jiaqing (1796–1820) and Daoguang (1821–1850) periods. It stated:

The number of lineage members for the Chens of Waihai in Xinhui and the Hes of Shawan in Panyu rank first within the locality. Their ancestral tombs are situated side by side outside the northern gate of the provincial capital's city wall . . . The founding ancestor of the Hes died early and left a child. Fearing that her brother's wife could not pledge to raise the orphan, nor place her heart into nurturing the He descendents, the sister [of the founding ancestor] vowed along with [her brother's wife] not to marry. [Together, they] took care of the orphan until he grew up. [Later], when the *gu* died, she was buried in the same tomb, though in a different cave, as the *sao*. Even today, people still call it the Sisters-in-Law Tomb. Even the shepherds and woodcutters who pass by the tomb can recount the chastity and righteousness of the sisters-in-law.[38]

A comparison among the different versions of the same legend of the Sisters-in-Law Tomb proves very intriguing. The entry in *Panyu County Gazetteer was* too brief, but the content and structure of this early account were consistent with the oral version. The only difference was the cause and sequence of deaths of the sisters-in-law. I believe that the following was the original version of the legend. The two female characters of the story were a "brother's wife" who seemed not to have lived with her husband and a "husband's sister" who vowed not to marry. The "brother's wife" was not buried with her husband, but instead with her husband's sister, and the tomb had become the center of the lineage's ancestral worship. This version emphasizes the close relationship between the sisters-in-law, and its theme was centered on women. However, this theme and its moral implications fundamentally contradicted conventional Confucian ethics.

The *Tablet Inscription of the Sisters-in-Law Tomb* clearly stated that, to the literati, the Sisters-in-Law Tomb and its legend were incompatible with orthodox conventions. The story recorded in the inscription was made up by a man who had already become a member of the gentry. He solved a puzzle raised by an official who felt that the Sisters-in-Law Tomb had deviated from conventional values. This explanation was subsequently accepted by a high official because the story had been modified according to literati criteria. To the Hes of Shawan, a renowned lineage of the Ming-Qing Pearl River Delta region, one that had always been proud of its allegiance to orthodox propriety, it seemed necessary to reconcile the conflicts between its indigenous custom of worshipping the Sisters-in-Law Tomb and the orthodox tradition identified by members of Confucian scholar officials within the lineage. The Hes were able to accomplish this by manipulating various cultural symbols to express their appreciation of literati culture. For example, by forging and altering the names and genealogical accounts of their ancestors, members of a lineage could "prove" that they were descendants from nobles and officials of the Ji surname in the Zhou dynasty. Nevertheless, they could not easily change the tradition of worship at the Sisters-in-Law Tomb. Although it was incompatible with the literati's cultural standards, it had taken place every year for generations. The easiest solution, therefore, was to reinterpret the legend. In short, the *Tablet Inscription of the Sisters-in-Law Tomb* was a literati version of the Sisters-in-Law Tomb legend constructed out of pragmatic necessity.

One of the major differences between Liang's and Long's account is the character for whom the sisters-in-law cared. In Liang's account, it was the father/father-in-law. In Long's account, it was the orphaned nephew/son. The part of the story that described the sisters-in-law bringing up the orphan, as recorded by Long, is incompatible with descriptions on the third- to fifth-generation ancestors (as told by the Hes of Shawan). Long's version is probably a modification of an earlier version that was composed by people not in the He family. It nonetheless offers the most reasonable explanation for the Hes' belief in the Sisters-in-Law Tomb.

The three written accounts, namely, the one in the *Panyu County Gazetteer,* the one written by Liang Guozhi, and the one by Long Tinghuai, told different versions of the legend. We consider the oral version provided by our interviewees and the one in *Panyu County Gazetteer* as one, because the content and structure of both are basically the same. They all contain the common storyline in which the *gu* vows not to marry and lives with her brother's wife for life. This fundamental structure in the Sisters-in-Law Tomb legend clearly focuses on the relationship between the husband's sister and the brother's wife — a point further supported by the criticism in the *Tablet Inscription of the Sisters-in-Law Tomb.*[39] Whether the sisters-in-law "took care of the father" or "raised the orphan," the acts rendered the legend more compatible with the ethical standards of the literati. They were probably added at a later date.

This reinterpretation transformed the legend from an ordinary folk account to an event that promoted Confucian moral teachings. A story that originally described only the affection between a pair of sisters-in-law was introduced with new elements in the *Tablet Inscription of the Sisters-in-Law Tomb*: in Liang Guozhi's version, the sisters-in-law paid respect to the father (or father-in-law) and the brother (or husband); in Long Tinghuai's version, the sisters-in-law took care of an orphan. Through these additions, the love between the two women became a sacrifice for their male-centered family. In Liang's version, the women played the roles of "wife," "daughter-in-law," and "daughter"; in Long's version, they are "mother" and "aunt." These roles are defined from a male point of view and fit into a cultural hierarchy established by the scholar-officials.

Because the version in the *Tablet Inscription of the Sisters-in-Law Tomb* best conforms to literati ethics, the addition into the story of two male ancestors becomes particularly crucial to the change of themes in the legend. Subsequently, the tomb of He Chen, as discussed in the first section of this study, becomes a very significant symbol. The existence of his tomb indicates that the story's core lies in the respect the sisters-in-law paid to the father-in-law (or father) and the husband (or brother). He Chen's tomb was inserted into the story to place the affectionate relationship between the women within a Confucian ethical paradigm. The Hes' lineage records document that members of the family seized the land of He Chen's tomb because of their social status and the support of local, high-ranking officials early during the Yongle (1403–1424) and the Tianshun (1457–1464) periods of the Ming dynasty, hence verifying the tomb's existence. The importance of He Chen's tomb in demonstrating the male-centered theme is again corroborated in a document recently written by the members of the He lineage. In January

1994, during the relocation and restoration of the Sisters-in-Law Tomb, members of the Hes in Shawan acted as the "Group for Managing the Restoration of the Sisters-in-Law Tomb, Shawan Town, Panyu County," and presented a letter to the Committee for Managing Cultural Relics of Guangzhou. They asked for "a restoration of He Chen's tomb during the repair period of the Sisters-in-Law Tomb." The reason for the request was provided in the letter:

> At this moment, as the Sisters-in-Law Tomb undergoes restoration, we are seriously reflecting on the land around the "Sisters-in-Law Tomb" at Santai *ling*, Baiyun Mountain, where the ancestral tombs of He Liugeng *tang* are located. The first person to be buried there was ancestor He Chen, (see *Guangzhou Prefectural Gazetteer, juan* 87.9, and the Li's edition of *Panyu County Gazetteer, juan* 24.6) who was the father of the husband's sister and the father-in-law of the brother's wife. The tomb of He Chen was situated at the upper right-hand corner of the Sisters-in-Law Tomb. It was taken over twice by other people for burying [their family members] during the Yongle and the Tianshun periods, and thus has gradually dilapidated. However, during every Qingming festival and worshipping occasion, [we] continue to burn incense and light candles, worship and sweep [the tomb of He Chen] at its original location.
>
> Recently, the "Sisters-in-Law Tomb" was fortunate enough to have been included as a site for preservation on the fourth list of Guangzhou's ancient remains. As it is going to be restored soon, we propose that the tomb of our third-generation ancestor, He Chen, should also be restored. Although only the "Sisters-in-Law Tomb" was recognized as an important cultural relic, in our opinion, the admirable hard work and female decorum of the brother's wife, who attended to her father-in-law mornings and evenings without taking time to change her clothes at night, would not have been demonstrated had ancestor He Chen not fallen sick and died. This is our first point. The praiseworthy chastity and filial piety of the husband's sister towards her father, as well as her profound affection towards her brother's wife, would not have been realized either. This is our second point. Furthermore, the love between the sisters-in-law moved our ancestor Qianpan *gong*, Renjian (that is, our founding ancestor who first settled in Shawan). To recognize their honor and show his sympathy to them, he allowed the [bodies of the sisters-in-law] to be buried to the left of the family ancestor's tomb (that is, the third-generation ancestor), fulfilling their wish. This is our third point. These three points are inseparable from [the history] of our third ancestor, He Chen *gong*. Therefore, if his tomb is not restored, [the site and the history of the Sisters-in-Law Tomb] will become a laughing stock for visitors and the scholarly community.[40]

This passage is fascinating because it clearly illustrates the paramount role played by He Chen's tomb in constructing the literati version of the Sisters-in-Law Tomb legend. However, the question now becomes whether He Chen was indeed the first person to be buried in this site. Did the Sisters-in-Law Tomb come into existence before the tomb of He Chen, or was it the other way around? My conjecture is that the Sisters-in-Law Tomb is older than He Chen's tomb. This is, of course a speculation. However, that the tomb of He Chen has long fallen into ruin while the other three tombs are still intact demonstrates that the literati interpretation of the Sisters-in-Law Tomb legend has not been fully accepted by the commoners in local society. Because this interpretation only expresses recognition of Confucian scholarly culture and values, it may not be of particular significance to most members of the He lineage. Their annual worship of the Sisters-in-Law Tomb is a local tradition continued from previous generations. Attention is given to He Chen's tomb out of a need to reinterpret their traditions from a literati point of view, but his tomb never replaced the Sisters-in-Law Tomb in terms of its importance in the local traditions of ancestral worship. The account written by Long Tinghuai clearly demonstrates that, to commoners, the He family's ancestral tombs are defined by the Sisters-in-Law Tomb. Although He Chen's tomb has not been forgotten entirely, it is not worth mentioning.

Moreover, according to the oral account of the legend, He Renjian picked the site for the Sisters-in-Law Tomb in accordance to the directions given by an "Earth Goddess."[41] This oral account may not be more credible, but it demonstrates that the scholar-official version of the legend, in which the sisters-in-law were buried next to He Chen's tomb, has not been accepted in the oral tradition. The two members of the He lineage who narrated the legend to us have read the *Tablet Inscriptions of the Sisters-in-Law Tomb*, yet, they only related to us the version as transmitted orally among the commoners. This indicates that there are two separate traditions guiding the He lineage's worship of the Sisters-in-Law Tomb that were intertwined over centuries of representation. Through uncovering fragments of historical story telling, we can detect the tension and conflicts underlying them. The reconstitution of the image of women appears to have been instrumental in allowing a local society to be integrated into an orthodox cultural hierarchy.

It is interesting to note that members of the He family in the 1990s continued to use a mixture of Confucian and indigenous values as expressed in the legend to support their request to preserve the Sisters-in-Law Tomb. In an official letter sent on 15 August 1993 to the Office for Constructing and Managing the Baiyun Mountain of Guangzhou, the Shawan Township Government explained its case:

"The Sisters-in-Law Tomb" is a famous ancient tomb, rare in history. On the one hand, it [signifies the virtue of] "honoring the kin and respecting the aged," serving as a model [for righteousness]; on the other, it demonstrates that the relationship between sisters-in-law is as close and affectionate as mixing water with milk.

In another letter sent to the Office for Constructing and Managing the Baiyun Mountain of Guangzhou, the Hong Kong Panyu Shawan Native Place Association stated:

For a women's tomb to be held at such a high esteem during the feudal era is extremely rare in our country. A great number of the seniors in Guangzhou are fond of talking about [the tomb]. Even people from the towns and villages outside Guangzhou, in appreciation of the fame [of the tomb], come especially to worship and show reverence, so as to educate their juniors about filial piety and harmony among siblings.

Whether from an "antique" perspective of furthering moral obligations and teachings from the sages, or from a contemporary perspective of "resurrecting a spiritual civilization," the ideal of "filial piety and harmony among siblings" remains the thematic motivation for local elites and the government to acknowledge the Sisters-in-Law Tomb. By changing the theme in the Sisters-in-Law Tomb legend, the scholar-officials, who strived to promote moral teachings in their localities, successfully reconstituted the image of women in accordance with their moral universe. This drawn-out process of cultural invention implies, on the one hand, recognition of and integration with state orthodoxy, and on the other, a manipulation of cultural strategies by resourceful local populations during centuries of state-making. Reconstitution has been mutual. As the scholar-officials made efforts to transform an indigenous culture, literati priorities were also refashioned with diverse local ingenuity. The ultimate question is: have women been given their deserved agency in our analyses?

2 Images of Mother: The Place of Women in South China

David Faure

Research on the history of the family in south China is both important and difficult. It is important because the family obviously occupies a crucial position in the Chinese psyche, but difficult because available records tend to bear on the lineage rather than the family as such. That is to say, the record tends to dwell on men and their connections rather than women and theirs.

A viable source on the history of the family would be biographies of women, many of which are included in genealogies and essay collections. One might, for instance, focus on biographies written in memory of the writers' own mothers, in the hope that an emotional element might bear on descriptions that would be strongly tinted by the stereotypes. Nevertheless, not even the trauma of death and separation, which were usually the occasions for such essays, provided a means for breaking the stereotypical deadlock. Biographies of mothers recorded in genealogies were written by men, chiefly of literati inclination or pretension, and they expected their mothers to have nursed them, prodded them to hard work, held the family together in times of hardship, managed the servants without having herself avoided hard work, and abided by the standards of filial piety to the husband's parents. Accounts written by writers on their own mothers were not always very different from the formalistic descriptions of virtuous wives and loving mothers written on behalf of little-known acquaintances. The structural view of the family, as expressed in the formalistic records, is only a construct of what the family should have been, not an account which might have touched the emotions as one should expect from ingrained memories. Without the emotions, the image of mother has to be unreal.[1]

However, it is not easy to catch the literati unaware for an eyewitness element to motherhood. The following examples have to remain anecdotal and suggestive, rather than thorough. This is a first attempt to probe the records for feelings expressed by men for their mothers, an effort in the hope that they might, if only by a little, subvert the stereotypes.

What Does Mother Do But Suckle?

A well-known account about a mother is the famous memorial to the emperor by the philosopher Chen Baisha (1428–1500) excusing himself from service at the capital. Chen noted that he was not weaned until he was nine *sui*, and he cited this fact to emphasize the debt he owed his mother.[2]

Chen's father died at twenty-seven *sui* before Baisha was born, his mother was then twenty-four *sui*. Baisha made his reputation in Guangdong long before he accepted high office at the capital in 1483, and he gave it up in less than a year. In his petition for permission to retire, he pleaded illness and the need to take care of his mother. Baisha was, by then, fifty-six *sui* and his mother seventy-nine, but his memorial carried a strong tinge that because he was weak in health, his mother had continued to take a nursing interest in him. This was filial piety, no doubt, and might be corroborated by numerous statements scattered in Baisha's writings detailing his concern for his mother's health and safety, but the closeness of mother and son as expressed in this debt of sucking mother's milk up to nine *sui* is probably atypical even of most essays in memory of mother. Throughout his life he was quite close to his brother, five years his senior: one poem recalls movingly how he feared for elder brother when the latter was out collecting rent during a rain storm. There might also have been some deference to his elder brother as would have been advocated by the *Zhuji jiali*, Zhu Xi's family regulations, that Chen supported and propagated. At Chen Baisha's house at Jiangmen, on the principal altar are placed tablets of five generations, ending with Baisha's elder brother, Baisha's own tablet being set up on a side altar. In accordance with the *Zhuji jiali*, the tablets indicate single-line descent down the senior male line. This was a rare practice in the ancestral halls of the Pearl River Delta. Chen Baisha had two wives and children of his own, whom he seldom wrote about. If the tablets are indicative of domestic sacrifice set up during Baisha's life time, and this I think very likely, whatever Baisha's emotional relationships with his wives and children, his domestic circle incorporated his mother and his elder brother in some prominence.

What part mother played in this circle has to remain an open question: Chen Baisha tells us little of it. Perhaps he was a very private person who would resent our prying into his emotional life, but in view of his frequent reference to his own filial piety, more likely, filial piety did not require assigning mother a role in the extended family. Perhaps this is being unfair to Chen, for after all, what we have from him is a petition to serve his own end rather than an essay in memory of mother. But mother who suckled and left no impact on son's intellectual or social development must stand as one extreme of how intellectual men might consider to be the place of women.

Family Values

Chen Baisha was an influential thinker in the Pearl River Delta, not so much because of his philosophy, as because of his support for the establishment of orthodoxy in Guangzhou and its surroundings in the late fifteenth and the early sixteenth century. The breast-feeding mother was an image that was propagated with this orthodoxy. Huang Zuo's *Taiquan xiangli* (Mr Taiquan's family rituals) makes this very clear:

> Remember, your body is born of your parents. You are carried in the womb for ten months, and suckled for three years. If you are killed, you would have wasted your parent's deep kindness . . . Every morning, take your children to bow to your parents, and present a fresh pot of tea. At breakfast, lunch and dinner, ask your parents to sit at the head of the table, and stand on one side with your wife to take care of their food and drink. When they go to bed at night, go up to the bed to take a look. When you go out of doors, tell your parents and bow. When you return, make another bow. If parents have passed away, when you rise in the morning, go to their spirit seats and bow in front of it. When you drink tea or have rice, feed them as if they were living.[3]

The *Taiquan xiangli* was written a generation after Chen Baisha's death. It rose from the tradition that Chen actively perpetuated. Village regulations were being reformed under official guidance as military action was restoring order among the Yao in the Pearl River Delta in the late fifteenth century. As this chapter of the *xiangli* specifies in an earlier paragraph, the objective of these regulations on filial piety was to civilize these barbarians. There was, therefore, a hidden message in this image of the breast-feeding mother. Mother provided the physical sustenance of life, just as ancestors provided the line of descent. Offerings on the ancestral altar made up retribution for birth and sustenance. Mother was not only shunned as a social being, she really only provided a service to the descent line.

The Place of Affines

Li Suiqiu (d. 1644), the poet, went through a very different experience from Chen Baisha. We know next to nothing about his mother, except that she begged Guanyin deity for a child before Suiqiu was born because her husband's hair was turning gray and she had yet not produced a son. Suiqiu's father was a teacher, who spent much of his time away from home. Suiqiu grew up in Guangzhou, living next door to his mother's brother and her stepmother. It was his step-grandmother who brought him up. When he was ill, it was step-grandmother who stayed up to take care of him. This is possibly the reason we find in his writings more about his relatives on his mother's side than we do about those on his father's side. When he was small, his family was close to the family of his mother's aunt (*gumu*):

> The two families went to each other with their walking sticks during the festivals. They are not required to stand on ceremony. Whenever there is an invitation to dinner, something is given to the other family. They order their servant girls about, and in matters of salt and rice are not shy of asking from each other.[4]

The development of very close relationships among affines is further brought out by his description of one Peng Yuzhuan, whom he described as an "outside nephew of his aunt's family" (*yu yijia waisheng*). As nearly as I can interpret the term, Peng's grandmother could have been Li Suiqiu's mother's sister, and for that reason, Peng looked upon Li as an uncle (*jiu*). Nor was that all, Li's aunt's brother-in-law became Li's good friend from the time they were boys, while nephew Peng was later to become Li's elder sister's son-in-law. The impression one can form from all this is that of a vibrant community linked to the mother's family.[5]

Mother's family had not been fortunate. Her own mother had died while she was small. She and her two younger brothers were brought up by step-grandmother. Step-grandmother survived the two stepsons, and lived with mother's third younger brother, who was probably adopted because Li Suiqiu noted that step-grandmother did not give birth. The two deceased stepsons left only one surviving son, who was blind, and when the third son and his wife died, step-grandmother lived alone with the blind grandson and some great grandchildren. She also had a daughter who married out and died early. Interestingly, mother did not appear in any prominence in Li Suiqiu's description of step-grandmother. Instead, mother lived, not with Suiqiu, but with his two younger brothers from his father's concubine. No sense of filial piety is indicated between Suiqiu's mother and his step-grandmother. When he spoke about his mother, it was when he pleaded with Chen Zizhuang, who was to become the rallying point of late Ming loyalism for which cause Li Suiqiu finally gave his life, that he might be spared from office. Devotion to step-grandmother was derived from a sense of retribution for the nursing care he had been given; devotion to mother was a convenient excuse.[6]

Mother as nurse and mother as focus of a social childhood network — the uterine family[7] — form complementary images, even though they do not necessarily converge on a single person. How far the subsuming of Chen Baisha's domestic relationships under the shadow of his brother, and the intimacy of Li Suiqiu with his affines was the consequence of a rural-urban distinction is an open question. We know, almost instinctively, that relatives on mother's side must count for a great deal in the building of social networks, and the more marriages took place among neighboring communities, the more relatives and neighbors would be indistinguishable. None of this gives ground for expecting any discernible progression in the evolution of the family. We should not be surprised that affines mattered unless we have fallen for the extreme view of mother's social irrelevance.

The Incorporation of Gentility from the Ming to the Qing

With the little that is known about the family, and the enormous variations that must have existed across social classes, geographic regions, ethnic or religious affiliations, it is difficult to the extreme to generalize about historical patterns relating to the subject of the mother's relationship to her sons within the dynastic period. Perhaps the one pattern that emerges from reminiscences of mother is the adoption of genteel manners along with upward mobility, as exhibited in essays included in the genealogy of the Huo surname of Foshan from the Ming to the Qing.[8]

Huo was a common surname in Ming and Qing Foshan. It was prominently represented among the leaders of 1450 in the Huang Xiaoyang uprising, and until then, did not appear as a unified lineage. Clusters of Huo surname people lived as neighbors, and probably did not make their lineage connections until well after Huo Tao had built his ancestral hall in

1525. The Foshan Huo surname did not compile a common genealogy until 1686, and even then, it was not clear there was a common ancestral hall for all persons of the surname, even though by then individual lines of descent would have built them for themselves. Active in lineage building was a line that traced its descent to one Junxue (1628–1703) of the seventeenth generation, which left quite a few biographical essays on members of the lineage, including three reminiscences of mothers by their sons. These biographies spanned four generations, the first being written possibly after 1660 and the last in 1704. Quite aside from encompassing the Ming-Qing transition, these several accounts, therefore, also came within the period when the lineage as a structure built around ancestral halls and genealogies came to have been established among the Foshan Huo. The question arises if adopting the lineage outlook made any impact on family life.

As might be expected, we do not know very much about the family before written biographies were prepared and kept. The first biography details the life of Madam Chen (1556–1632), wife of fourteenth generation ancestor Weicheng (1543–1605), the first man of this line to have achieved official status. Madam Chen came from a notable family and had married Weicheng upon the death of his first wife. She is portrayed as someone who was capable of withstanding hardship. While her husband served as an official in Sichuan province, she nursed her father-in-law in his illness, and sold her ornaments to pay for his funeral upon his death. The family was poor even upon Weicheng's return at the news of the death, but Madam Chen made sure that there was enough rice in the household of several tens of people. She also nursed her mother-in-law through a tumor, and prayed to the deities when doctors declared that she could not be cured. When her two stepsons were ill from what might appear as a recognized infectious disease, and members of the family withdrew to avoid them, Madam Chen was there with their wives and maidservants to nurse them. Upon Weicheng's death in 1605, the two elder stepbrothers of the author of the biography sold the family's land properties, houses, and even the ancestral trust properties. The author remembers living in his teens in temporary quarters, without savings and having to face the demands of creditors. The point he made, however, was that it was in these circumstances that mother encouraged him to study. He passed the official examination in 1632, and his mother knew of his success shortly before her death.

We have the biographies of some of the men in the fifteenth generation, but not of the women. The next biography of a mother describes the life of another Madam Chen (1613–1675), wife of sixteenth generation ancestor

Yu (1599–1665), Weicheng's grandson on the senior line of descent. However, the men's biographies of the fifteenth generation are important for the background with which we may interpret the rather short biography we have of this later Madam Chen. Despite what the previous biographer had said about his elder brothers losing the family estate, Tingdong of the fifteenth generation (dates not recorded), whose biography was written by the same man who had written the biography of the senior Madam Chen, was portrayed as a devoted scholar. Like many others in Guangzhou and Foshan in the late sixteenth and seventeenth centuries, this up-and-rising scholarly family had fallen under the influence of the new learning associated with the name of Wang Yangming, and in the Pearl River Delta, with Chen Baisha. This was not a teaching that made any impact on the treatment of women in the home; the teaching stressed self-cultivation and quiet sitting, and combined this with an interest in political commentary. More relevant to the family probably was the fact that Tingdong, saddled with illness, was by middle age very much confined to the village. It was the biographer, Dezhi, who achieved high office, who brought Yu's son with him to Nanjing just as the Ming dynasty was collapsing. Yu's son, Junxue, would only have been in his teens at the time, and so while Dezhi stayed at Nanjing, he was sent home. Junxue's biography, written by his son, notes the harsh conditions that the family faced in the aftermath of the political turmoil. They lived in a tiny house amidst broken furniture and farmed with their own hands until 1650, when Junxue achieved *boshi dizi* student status. The scholarly tradition continued, and he was appointed Instructor at Yangchun county by 1690.

Madam Chen, Yu's wife, has a somewhat nondescript biography. She came from a reputable family, married at twenty *sui*, and aside from other feminine virtues, was noted as being kind to her servants. She was not in favor of whipping them, and when her sons reprimanded the servants, she told them that while nobility and servility might differ, people were fundamentally all one (*guijian xushu, renze yi ye*). She dressed simply, even though her relatives were now adorned in finery. She personally spun and wove. There were many mouths to feed, and the family managed without difficulties only because she was a capable manageress.

The implication of the passage, on its own, is not obvious. However, if it is taken in conjunction with the family history, we can detect in it a pattern of development. The subject of the third biography is Madam Liang, Junxue's wife. Again, she came from a reputable family, married at twenty-two *sui*, and took care of her parents-in-law. The biography indicates that the family had fallen upon hard times, and so when she spun day and night, she did it then to find an income even though later in life she maintained the practice as self-discipline. The biography does not go as far as to comment on her literary accomplishments, but much is made of her insistence that a scholarly tradition be maintained within the family. She had grown up in a scholarly family, and she knew of scholarship as the family enterprise (*dushu wei chuanjia shiye*). She encouraged her husband to sit the official examination, and she put great store on the education of her children, both her sons and her daughters. She seems to have had definite ideas about the value of early childhood education, and believed in training her daughters for their duties as wives and mothers. She believed in keeping the women apart from the world outside the home: no woman of the demeaned classes (*liupo*) were to set foot in her house, and even in her old age, refused to have her portrait painted because she was not to be gazed by a man who was not a member of the family. Hidden in all this was the maxim that the biography quoted her as saying:

> Wealth and nobility are maintained by providence (*ming*) and cannot be forced. However, the fragrance of the book must not be severed. If the fragrance of the book is severed, the family's reputation becomes lowly and servile. When the family reputation is lowly and servile, the people it produces will be mean and corrupt. When people are mean and corrupt, they cannot make friends with gentlemen on high, and do not have the wisdom to make a livelihood below. If they can be satisfied as farmers and wood-cutters, there can still be goodness. However, in their stupidity they may remain ambitious, their disregard for propriety will compare with the lowly and servile, and they will carry out stubborn and dangerous acts. I cannot bear to speak of life that reaches this stage.[9]

There seems to be an ideology in all this, which follows in a progressive sequence in the lives of the three women. Madam Chen of the fourteenth generation was the rustic woman who was not disturbed by the dirty and messy. Madam Chen of the sixteenth generation had moved easily into a family that boasted of a scholarly lifestyle that befitted the fashion of the time. Madam Liang of the seventeenth generation was clinging on to a scholarly tradition that she feared might be slipping from her family. The imitation and maintenance of the scholarly life style imposed a specific position on the woman. She was always the virtuous wife and good mother, but in this family, at least, it was probably in the early Qing that the ideal required her to remain within the four walls of the household.

Until Dorothy Ko documented the role of domestic woman teachers in eighteenth-century China, the image of the literati mother in the Ming and the Qing was almost a contradiction in terms.[10] Following Ko's documentation for the prevalence of woman teachers, the literate mother must have been quite common in scholarly families even if the number of women who were literate remained smaller than the number of literate men. Women who learned to read, like men who learned to read, would have been taught that the social spectrum was headed by the fully literate, who was not the reader, but the writer of reading material. Gazetteer biographies give us an impression of the progression of this ideology: there certainly were highly literate women in the Ming, but by the early Qing, gazetteers recorded women whose literate skills were considered accomplished. It is possible to demonstrate that from the 1500s, various practices associated with the veneration of ancestors in ancestral halls built to a particular style started to become more widespread, and that the spread of these practices had much to do with the spread of a culture in which scholarship and the achievement of official status were regarded as the epitome of career success. Along with this development would have come the popularization of scholarship in the family. Women might be educated, educated women might set themselves apart from menial tasks associated with the sick and the dead, indoor work such as spinning and weaving was to be encouraged, but eulogies of mothers did not speak of their engaging in outdoor labor even though women did commonly work in the fields. Moreover, mothers retained their positions as managers of the family. It was not at all uncommon for the family to suffer financial hardship when father was posted away from home, and, so, it was mother who strived to make ends meet to hold the family together. There was emerging out of all this an image of the mother of the genteel family, where father remained the family head, but mother was cast in an indispensable supportive role.

Supportive Mother and Filial Daughter-in-Law

Not knowing anything about Chen Baisha's mother, we are hardly in a position to question if she was literate. Fifteenth-century Xinhui county, however, was located on the outer reaches of the Pearl River Delta, and Chen Baisha's achievement had come largely through his own merit rather than his family's connections. Even though it is possible to detect the character of the genteel family taking hold of upper class Guangzhou in the fifteenth century, it was unlikely, therefore, that Chen Baisha's mother would have had much to do with that. A contrast to that would be the account of his mother by Luo Tianchi (1686–1766), writer and local historian, and a member of the powerful Luo lineage at the Shunde county city of Daliang.

For three generations, Luo Tianchi's family were uncommon scholars. Nevertheless, it seems to be their family tradition that they should not attempt high office. Luo Tianchi's grandfather was a *jinshi* of 1658, but his appointment to office coincided with the feudatories' rebellion and thereafter he did not accept further appointment. He associated with late Ming supporters, turned his attention to lineage welfare, and came to be known for refusing to associate with people in high office. Tianchi's father continued this arrogance towards high status, but he also developed an appreciation for the predicament of maidservants. His biography notes that he wrote an essay while he visited Huizhou (Anhui province) to advise owners of maidservants to allow them to marry. It mattered not if they were married to manservants, farmers or merchants, or if they were sent home or even kept as concubines, for it was the natural order that people should seek fulfillment as parents, husbands and wives. Charitable perhaps, the essay reemphasized the centrality of the family rather than the individual.[11]

However, Luo Tianchi had this story to tell in his collection of miscellanies, the *Wushan jilin* (A forest of anecdotes from the Five Hills):

> A certain woman was a native of Shunde. Her husband was too poor to marry. His mother sold herself for four pieces of silver so that he might marry. When the woman came into the family and knew about it, she cried, saying, "Has my husband for the sake of his wife made his mother sell herself so that he might marry her? This is losing a mother to obtain a wife. Has the wife for the sake of the husband made the mother-in-law sell herself so that she might be wedded to him? This is obtaining a husband and losing a mother-in-law. These are unfilial acts. However, where can the silver be found to redeem mother-in-law?" She begged her father and borrowed four pieces of silver and asked someone to redeem the mother-in-law.[12]

Luo Tianchi cited variations of this story to give the impression that it was quite commonly told in Shunde. In one variation, it was the man who sold himself, but the moral was similar. It was not servitude but separation from mother that was the cause of sorrow.

The *Wushan jilin* contains numerous other stories that would support the view that family values were subtly being transformed. The stories are familiar: virtuous women loyal to the betrothal bond insisted on entering the families of their betrothed even when the men had died before the wedding. Some women committed suicide when their parents opposed these decisions, and while Luo Tianchi found such suicide pointless, he also demanded consistency in social practice. Luo drew a political lesson from all that. On balance, it was loyalty that mattered more than life.[13] The linking of the life-blood of the individual to the descent line was one thing, as indicated in the discussion on Chen Baishan and Huang Zuo above, the acquisition of gentility as a strategy or consequence of upward mobility was another. Nevertheless, the reinstating of orthodoxy as political feelings for the Ming was yet another strand in the make-up of the popular family ideology. In a real sense, in the *Wushan jilin* family was supported in the reconstitution of the social order. The late Ming loyalist tradition would have agreed with the upwardly mobile status-seekers of the early Qing in tightening social mores.

The account that Luo Tianchi wrote of his mother, therefore, does not differ significantly from the image that may be constructed from the Huo family biographies. Father was sufficiently well known to have had his biography included in the county gazetteer, but mother's life would not have circulated beyond the family group if a biography of her had not been written. Mother had come from a magistrate's family. She married at nineteen *sui*. She had been a filial daughter before marriage, and despite her well-off natal family, she was capable of maintaining a frugal household. She served her mother-in-law well, but maintained strict discipline on her son. The writer recalled his being spoilt by grandmother but taken in hand by mother. Mother was a good home manager, and saw to it that the family did not suffer from want when father was away in the capital. She survived three daughters-in-law and brought up three grandchildren. Much emotion went into the essay, but the product remained stereotypical. It was a stereotype that probably agreed well with the writer's belief.[14]

Mother as Manager

The reminiscences of mother recall her managerial abilities, but none actually spells out what they might consist of. Household management would have been made up of many chores, and perhaps a considerable amount also of the close interpersonal relationships such as the stuff of which soap operas are made. The biography would have been too formal to portray mundane affairs of daily life. A better source would have been correspondence.

A set of letters between a son and his mother originating from a Hong Kong secondhand bookstore gives some clues. Like so much that comes from secondhand bookstores, all that we know must be derived from the documents themselves. The writer was living in Guangzhou, apparently working for a business but attempting also to continue his education. The letters are dated, but no year is given. They were likely to have been written some time in the Republican period, but well before 1930.

As one might expect with family letters, they do not deal systematically with any subject, but wander among a host of issues. Common themes that occur deal with the sending of money or medicine from Guangzhou back to mother, and people coming from the home village bearing news. By the third letter to mother from the correspondent, it is clear that the writer had married and his wife was not staying with his mother but back at her own home village. It might also be that she had been a cousin on the mother's side, for he said:

> Yesterday, Uncle (mother's younger brother) Liu came and said that father was seriously ill and almost died. From his description, it seems that the situation is serious. I wonder if someone has gone to see him. [Your] daughter-in-law has to serve her father. It is the responsibility of a child [to his or her parents]. Please do not make her come home quickly. It is important that she acts responsibly to people close to her.

The very next sentence in the letter goes into another subject:

> Conditions are difficult this year. If our family can manage at the new year, [a line beginning with 'do not' deleted] . . . If Uncle Jin is really very poor, do not push him for the rent from his first crop. It will be no use asking him. Just let things take their natural course. If he brings it, then take it. However, if our family cannot manage and is worse off than he is, then it is impossible not to push him. I have little left over this year, but if conditions in the family are not very good for the new year, I shall strive to send home ten taels. Mother, there is no need to worry.[15]

It transpires in a later letter that the writer had only recently married and he might also have become somewhat worried about his wife coming home.

> Please send someone to Anjiao to ask Liu [his wife] to return early in the month.[16]

His wife came back. In no fewer than four letters, he pleaded with mother to integrate her into the family.

> Now that your daughter-in-law, Liu, has returned, please teach her what is happening at home, however big or small. Also, please let her know what had happened in the past, what is said to be right, what wrong, so

that daughter-in-law might appreciate the reason behind them. Let her know how things should be done, so that in future, when things happen, she would have some opinions. Please stop her listening to other people's affairs, or gossip about other people . . .

If someone is needed at night to keep you company as you sleep, ask her to do that. She may usefully get up to make tea [for you]. She should not be shy at home. What she sees and talks about relates to people in the house. To show her the proper women's manners, don't make her sit for a long time in her room. Even when there are visitors, this should apply; she should not be shy. Tell her how the family is managing. Teach her to manage the home frugally, not to gossip . . . [17]

These were Shunde women, among whom returning to the natal home after wedding was common.[18] Mother, in fact, worried that the writer's sister, recently married, might refuse to return to her husband's household after she came home.

Financial management also comes into the picture. Elder sister living back in the village had lent money on the guarantee of a third party. Our writer advised that his correspondent must give her a note to record the debt. Talking about his wife yet again, he advised that pork should be eaten every six days and five chickens should be raised at any time. One of these was to be eaten every month.

Of course, mother was involved in the management of the family. Of course, the integration of the newly married daughter-in-law would have been a matter that had to be handled with tact. Of course, there would have been the management of loans and credit. Biographies allude to these aspects of social relationships, but only in personal letters do we see how in the mundane affairs of life they were carried out.

Conclusion

Models of mother as the provider of sustenance, as a model of gentility and as manager of home if not always estate, are probably quite universal. The form that each of these models might take in any society has as much to do with broad changes in food and subsistence, social styles and mobility, and management as a whole as with the status of women vis-à-vis men which itself has to be related to political ideology. In Guangdong, a case can probably be made that these changes were related to the emergence of a particular way of regulating lineage relationships that had to do with social and ritual changes in the mid-Ming, that is to say, in the fifteenth and sixteenth centuries.

We know next to nothing about social relationships in rural communities prior to the fifteenth century and would be hard-pressed to discuss how family relationships were transformed by these changes. The few references we have of women donating substantial estates to monasteries before the Ming, and of substantial amounts of land given as dowry in the early Ming, suggest that women might have held land with greater ease at an earlier time than in the Ming and Qing. However, there is no reason to suppose that descent had not been traced unilineally along the male line or that the uxorilocal marriages referred to in the records as exceptions were not indeed exceptions. The place of woman was probably secondary to begin with before the fifteenth century.

Into this background came the spread of literacy, the enforcement of household and land registration, and then degree-holding statuses in the Ming. The focus on mother as source of life would have related to the stress on lineage that resulted from these developments, and gentility would have come with the upward mobility. However, the impact of affines and the management role of mother would have been continuation from previous practices, even though the manner in which these aspects of family life might continue would have been affected by the many other historical changes that characterize the Pearl River Delta in the Ming and the Qing, namely urbanization, commercial growth, prosperity, and the continuing flow of information with the lower Yangzi, the heartland of prosperity in China and in all likelihood the source of many fashions.

Following this line of thinking, one might argue that it was not the shortage of managerial skills that would have kept women secondary. Nevertheless, any position that required association with the state would have been taken by a man, even though we know that women went of their accord to the magistracy in the event of litigation. Political patronage was for the most part provided by men. Insofar as the state recognized the household rather than the family, the head of the household would by definition have been a man. In these circumstances, a woman might hold a domestic position of responsibility, but she could not have been the head of the household. In the environment of status-conscious lineage politics, neither would have been many men.

3

"What Alternative Do You Have, Sixth Aunt?" — Women and Marriage in Cantonese Ballads*

May-bo Ching

Does Sixth Aunt Have an Alternative?

Sixth Aunt is about to marry a man she has never met. Unappealing and fond of gambling, this man is by no means an ideal husband. Does Sixth Aunt have an alternative? She is supposed to have. Growing up in the Pearl River Delta region, she could have chosen to become a "*zishunu.*" Women had formed sisterhoods with other female companions and taken vows not to marry. She could also have chosen to practice *buluojia* by not cohabiting with her husband after marriage.[1] Nonetheless, Sixth Aunt is not free to decide her fate because she is merely a fictitious character portrayed in a Cantonese ballad *muyushu*. She is bound by the narrative and textual structure to submit to the arranged marriage. She is obliged to speak and sing in the prescribed text compiled by others.

Sixth Aunt (Liugu) is the major female character of a Cantonese *muyushu* (literally, wooden-fish book). It is one among many booklets for chanting, written in a verse style of seven-character lines in colloquial Cantonese and entitled *Liugu huimen* (Sixth Aunt returning to her natal home). In the story, Sixth Aunt is the cherished sixth daughter of a certain

* An earlier version of this chapter was originally presented at the *Conference on Merchants and Local Cultures*, organized by the Division of Humanities, Hong Kong University of Science and Technology in August 1994, entitled "Does Sixth Aunt have an alternative? – Women and marriage in the late Qing and early Republican Cantonese ballads." It has had subsequent revisions.

Hu family. She is engaged to an undesirable man, Li Guanwang. Her mother has been misled by a matchmaker who claims that Li is from a well-to-do family. The unfortunate match is portrayed as "the Goddess of Mercy soon to be paired with a lowly spirit!"[2] On the eve of her wedding, like many Cantonese brides in real life, Sixth Aunt sorrowfully sings her bridal laments. The *muyushu* text, on this occasion, is interwoven with a series of bridal laments. The musical and textual characters of a different genre of *muyushu* would have been easily identified by local readers.

The story continues with a rather established plot. Immediately after their marriage, Guanwang pawns all of Sixth Aunt's fine clothing and jewelry for money to satisfy his gambling habit. As expected, he loses all the money. Without a single set of decent clothes to wear, Sixth Aunt is too ashamed to perform the *huimen* rituals of returning to her natal home on the third day of her wedding celebration. She is able to pay a visit only two months later, after she has borrowed a fine, yet unfit dress from another woman.

Appreciating Sixth Aunt's sorrow, her mother and her best female friend dissuade Sixth Aunt from returning to her husband's home. Noticing that Sixth Aunt has already stayed at her natal home for a while, Guanwang is encouraged by his stepmother to pay his in-laws a visit. He puts on the clothes left by his ancestors, but his apparent poverty invites only scorn and ridicule. Guanwang is so angry that he considers taking a concubine and ignoring his wife. However, he is cautioned by his stepmother who encourages him to improve his circumstances to win back Sixth Aunt.

Despite the grim prospects, Sixth Aunt feels that she has to return to her husband's house because she is "his woman in life and his ghost in death."[3] At that juncture, the story line twists dramatically. When Sixth Aunt arrives at her husband's house, she has a pleasant surprise and a change of fate. Guanwang has unexpectedly acquired some wealth in a rather short time through gambling, ridiculous as it seems. The *Liugu huimen* thus guarantees a happy ending. Sixth Aunt and her family change their attitude towards Guanwang. She gives birth to several children, and they live happily ever after.

A *muyushu* bearing a similar title — *Sangu huimen* (Third Aunt returning to her natal home), presents a simpler and happier story than *Liugu huimen*. With the introduction of a matchmaker, the Qiu family delivers their beloved third daughter, Third Aunt, to a marriage with the son of the Wang family. The matchmaker has assured them that the Wang family is wealthy, and the fiancé of Third Aunt, a diligent student, is also keen to start his own business. The text says:

It was heard yesterday that he is going to open a shop to sell silk;
He has already drawn up the [shop] regulations, and he is determined
. . .
Never does he visit prostitutes or gambling houses.
He is the kind of man who can hold onto what he has achieved, no doubt.[4]

In other words, Wang is an ideal husband for Third Aunt, and, more important, an ideal son-in-law for his wife's family. With such a promising start, readers are told that Third Aunt has nothing to worry about after her marriage. Hence, unlike Sixth Aunt who laments on the eve of her wedding, Third Aunt sings the bridal songs while practicing the pinning rite. She "only pretends to be mournful."[5] Similar to the way *Liugu huimen* is sung, bridal laments are inserted into the text of *Sangu huimen* as an easily identifiable separate genre.

The promising beginning of *Sangu huimen* also ends happily. When Third Aunt goes back to her natal home to visit her parents three days after her marriage, she decorates herself with fine clothing and precious jewelry, showing off the fortunes of her husband's family. She tells her mother and female relatives and friends that the words of the matchmaker are true. As expected, Third Aunt bears a number of sons and daughters and lives a happy life.

The stories of *Liugu huimen* and *Sangu huimen* are so typical among popular fiction that most readers would find the two narratives unremarkable. Rather than focusing on the story, I will show how the literary format of *muyushu* might have painted certain images of women in the Pearl River Delta region. Despite the constraints in real life, what alternative choices would women imagine that they have that are different from those of fictional characters? Furthermore, how might various forms of communication within the same genre of song (in this case bridal laments) — oral, manuscript, or print media — have given the singers and their audience different cultural messages and opportunities for improvisation? Finally, because these ballads are sung in Cantonese and written in a Chinese script mixed with invented Cantonese words, it will be interesting to explore the local flavor of this genre of literature.

Muyushu and the Late Qing Local Literature

Muyushu is used as a collective term for the songbooks of various popular narratives in Cantonese, particularly the *nanyin* (southern tone) and *longzhou* (dragon boat) types.[6] Although scholars try to assign them clear definitions, the three terms often appear interchangeably in texts.[7] Whereas the term *longzhou* refers to texts that are three to four pages long, the terms *muyu* and *nanyin* are used interchangeably for exceedingly long pieces. Written in a verse style of basically seven-character lines, the language used is not full colloquial Cantonese. Instead, classical language is mixed with Cantonese usages, which, in some cases, can only be written in made-up characters. In performance, the three terms refer to three different forms of singing. Thus, the same text can be sung in the style of *muyu* (oratorio without the accompaniment of a musical instrument), in the style of *longzhou* (singing with a regular interlude played with a "dragon-boat drum," often performed by beggar-like jugglers in villages), or in the style of *nanyin* (singing accompanied by more elaborate and standard prelude and interlude, often performed with a Chinese vertical bamboo flute or *yehu* made from coconut shell). This generalization masks variations that have evolved over a few centuries.

What is clear is that the term *muyu* appears in texts as early as the late Ming period. Two late Ming/early Qing men, Kuang Lu (1604–1650) and Wang Shizhen (1634–1711), mentioned in their poems the practice of singing *muyu* in Guangdong.[8] Qu Dajun's (1630–1696) *Guangdong xinyu* (New accounts of Guangdong, first published in 1700) also provides some references for the use of these texts. Qu mentions that women invited blind musicians to sing the *moyuge* (touching-fish songs) in their gatherings.[9] The earliest extant *muyushu* song texts, *Huajian ji* (The story of the flowered letters), date back to 1713 and is now archived at the Bibliothèque nationale de France.[10] Literati considered many of these popular texts vulgar and worthless, and few of the early editions survived. Most of the extant *muyu* texts available in public collections are Republican publications.

Muyushu, nanyin and *longzhou* have varied contents — historical narratives, mythological tales, stories of famous men, love stories, and descriptions of local rituals and customs.[11] Historical narratives tell the stories of the "ancients" (*guren*). The themes of "talented students and beautiful ladies" (*caizi jiaren*) are most popular. In spite of their abundance of titles and subjects, many *muyushu* share an underlying narrative structure and ideology. They begin with a brief mentioning of the geographic setting, and continue with a narrative of the family background of the major characters, a portrait of the major characters, several tangled plots of the story, a happy ending, and, finally, the moral of the story, told by the author in the first person. Among the 158 sets of *muyushu* collected at the University of Hong Kong, over one hundred have a happy ending. Of these, the final section of sixty-eight is entitled "so-and-so *tuanyuan*" (literally, "uniting as a perfect circle"), regardless of how miserable the previous part of the story might have been. As in modern television soap operas, happy endings are appealing to the majority of the audience, especially among the poor and marginalized. Wing-hoi Chan's study on the use of *muyushu* among the Hakka population in the New Territories shows that the *Gao Wenju zhenzhu ji* was one of the most favorite texts among female readers because the story mirrored their hard lives. Many of their husbands had migrated overseas, and these Hakka women endured the burden of raising their families and hoped only that their lives could end happily one day.[12]

Liugu huimen and *Sangu huimen* are two of the published *muyushu* with a happy ending. The publication dates of both texts are unknown.[13] However, if we judge from the printing style and the background knowledge about the publisher, Wuguitang, it is reasonable to speculate that the existing copies of *Liugu huimen* and *Sangu huimen* that I have read were late Qing and early Republican publications. That *Sangu huimen* was published in Guangzhou suggests that it may be a late Qing or early Republican publication, because Wuguitang had its headquarters in Guangzhou from the mid-Guangxu (1875–1908) period on. That *Liugu huimen* was published by the Hong Kong branch of Wuguitang and had a color-printed cover indicates a more definite publication date. Because Wuguitang did not use color-printed covers for its *muyushu* texts until the 1950s,[14] the existing copy of *Liugu huimen* was most likely published in or after the 1950s. However, if *Sangu huimen* was a late Qing or early Republican publication, given the similarities in title and subject matter, it is reasonable to assume that an earlier edition of *Liugu huimen* existed.

My speculation is also based on the assumption that the mid- and late Qing periods witnessed the increasing adaptation of local happenings in literature and, in particular, in vernacular writings. A traceable example is the case of Liang Tianlai, a Panyu native whose family members were murdered by burglars in 1727. Legend has it that the murders were plotted by a certain Ling Guiqing, who wanted to seize Liang's house for geomancy reasons. Because Ling bribed the officials involved, the lawsuit never received a fair trail until the Emperor heard of the case and appointed a commissioner to intervene in 1731. Based on the legend, a story entitled "Yunkai xuehen" (Wiping out a grievance while clouds apart) was written sixty years later by Ou Su and collected in his *Ailou yizhi* (A record of indolence at the cloudy tower), miscellaneous notes on local hearsay, prefaced in 1794.[15] In 1809, a *muyushu* entitled *Liang Tianlai jingfu qishu* (A spectacular book about Liang Tianlai, [written to] warn the riches) was published, which was followed by another novel, *Jingfu qishu*, published in the same year.[16] Another *muyushu* called *Liang Tianlai gao yuzhuang* (Liang Tianlai suing at the imperial court) was published at a later date, probably in the late Qing period.[17] The *Jingfu qishu* was then adapted by Wu Jianren, a Panyu writer, and rewritten under the title of *Jiuming qiyuan* (A remarkably unfair case involving nine lives) in 1907. Cantonese operas based on the same story were then composed during the Republican period.[18] The various adaptations from the late eighteenth to the early twentieth century of the story of Liang Tianlai indicate the growth of a local audience that was large enough to support a sizable local literature market that depicted local events that had taken place in local settings. *Sangu huimen* and *Liugu huimen* might have been two examples reflecting the "localization" of subject matter in the late Qing popular literature in Guangdong.[19]

Detailing the Role of Women in Vernacular Literature and Local Culture

Both *Sangu huimen* and *Liugu huimen* can be considered "local" in the sense that they describe in detail many peculiar local marriage practices, and, like the majority of the *muyushu*, are composed mainly in Cantonese and are supposed to be chanted in Cantonese. By further analyzing how local marriage practices are narrated in *Sangu huimen*, *Liugu huimen* and a number of other titles and by reviewing the Cantonese singing traditions in the New Territories,[20] I will evaluate the role of women in the construction of a vernacular literature and the "local" cultural meanings embedded in it.

The laments

Bridal laments in Cantonese occupy a considerable part of the text of both *Liugu huimen* and *Sangu huimen*. The practice of singing laments in marriage and funeral rituals was, and still is, common in various parts of China. This practice has been studied by both Chinese and Western scholars.[21] A very striking image in bridal laments concerns death, especially in reference to the groom and his family. In addition, Wing-hoi Chan and other scholars have observed that bridal laments sung among the Punti, the Dan,[22] and the Hakka share similar themes. First, they count the bride's debts and credits in relation to her parents. They highlight the bride's ties to her natal lineage and they curse the matchmaker. They blame the bride's parents for marrying her off, and stress sisterhood feelings for her female companions. Finally, they make derogatory references to the women married to men of her natal lineage. Improvisations are common and mostly in the form of claims, accusations, and self-defense.[23]

Chan's study further reveals that the bridal laments sung among the Dan fishermen are much more individualized and contextualized.[24] For example, in one lament composed by a Woman To from Kat O, who emigrated to the Netherlands, she tells her younger sister, the bride, how hard it is to run a restaurant in the Netherlands.[25] Accusations against the father of a certain Woman Shek are sung by her female relatives at Ap Chau when she is sent off to Ko Lau Wan. He is portrayed as mean because he would not lend money to his younger brother when the latter needed resources to buy an apartment. He is also not ready to hold a feast for his daughter's wedding.[26]

In contrast, the bridal laments sung among the Punti women are tailored more to the situation than the person. The bridal laments of Woman Law of Siu Lik Yuen are sung at certain stages during marriage rituals, such as when "packing clothes into the suitcase" (*diegui*) and upon "the arrival of the sedan chair" (*jiaolai*). The laments sung by Woman Tsang of Tung Tau Tsuen are so specific that, not only are they addressed to her siblings, but some songs also address female relatives with particular backgrounds, such as those who are young widows, widows with several sons, or widows who have daughters but no sons.

In areas such as Yuen Long-Sheung Shui-Fanling, there have been "girl houses" (*mawu*). Those who congregate there work hard to memorize the difficult lament texts. A local elder once explained that the sophisticated form of previously composed repertoire made it difficult to invent new texts.[27] Moreover, some women composers are fond of and proud of adopting certain literary forms into their bridal laments. Woman Cheung of Tai O has adapted a number of stories by "ancients" (*guren*). The "ancients," such as Di Qing, Mu Guiying, Liang Shanbo, and Zhu Yingtai are historical or fictional figures to whom Woman Cheung has only slight exposure through local operas.[28] Woman Tsang of Tung Tau Tsuen also emphasizes that her efforts to compose the laments parallel those of a student who diligently follows established rules.

One may argue that women who lack the command of literacy enjoy a degree of creativity and individuality when they compose the bridal laments precisely because they do not feel bound by the rules and cultural assumptions of a written tradition. Chan acknowledges that bridal songs "have a certain degree of autonomy from the immediate context of their individual performance," but argues that rather than representing the voice of an individual woman, bridal laments are collective voices expressed through the brides to highlight the line drawn between the brides' natal kin and the grooms'. They also illustrate the power relationship between the two.[29]

If we compare the language and contents of the laments that are actually sung with those printed on *muyushu*, we learn that whereas the bridal laments in an oral tradition are very often claims, accusations, and self-defense expressed orally by women, those in printed form are expressed in a more literary manner and were probably penned by men. To an extent, the bridal laments in both the *Sangu huimen* and *Liugu huimen* appear closer to those composed and sung among the Punti population. They remain restrained in tone and stick closer to the moralistic ideals of a written tradition. When compared to laments sung by the Hakka and the Dan fishermen, *Sangu huimen* and *Liugu huimen* pale in the degree of self-expression.

In the *Sangu huimen*, it is said that because "numerous women want to listen to the laments," and "neighbors flock to [Third Aunt's] home to wait for the performance," Third Aunt ends up not being able to sing with her own full voice. In the exceedingly long bridal laments that appear in the following section of the text subtitled "*dakai tancheng*" (literally, "opening up the charcoal jar" — *tancheng*, the homophone in Cantonese of *tanqing*, which means "unleashing of feelings"), Third Aunt's mournful feelings are false and her singing is reluctant. Third Aunt's mood in the performance is largely determined by her happy relationships with her natal family and a marriage full of future promise. As arranged by the author of the texts, she has no reason to grieve.[30]

In only one aspect are the bridal laments sung by Third Aunt and her "sisters" similar to those sung in the New Territories, namely, the adoption of death imagery. However, Third Aunt makes no accusations or comments about her own family members, which occasionally are found in oral performances. She only sends greetings to her seniors and warnings to her juniors. She does not even accuse the groom's family and the matchmaker, as would have been expected in performances. Therefore, the death and hell imageries in the text of *Sangu huimen* remain superficial imitations of those employed in the laments that are actually sung. The difference between insiders (the bride's natal-kin group) and outsiders (the groom's family) is not asserted.

In the *Liugu huimen*, the deceit in the match making is seen as the root of Sixth Aunt's sorrow, as presented in the bridal laments in the later passages of the text. In fact, a distinguishing feature of the *Liugu huimen*'s laments is her severe and direct accusations against the matchmaker. She says:

Harming others, [her] intention is not simple.
This person will never be tolerated by the Heavenly code.
Whoever harms others will eventually harm herself; this has always been true from of old.
Retribution and compensation are sure to follow.

[I] pray for you that the older you are, the worse-off you become, and the harder your life will be.
For a whole day, no water and rice will touch your lips.
Three times a day your body will stick to the [sleeping] mat.
For a whole year, you cannot avoid any disease.[31]

Cursing the matchmaker is a common theme found in the bridal laments sung among the Punti and Hakka populations.[32] In a real-life situation, a bride's accusation against a matchmaker may not be a genuine accusation but merely an expression of uncertainty and anxiety about her own future. However, the accusation presented in the *Liugu huimen* appears much more valid and justifiable because of the background narratives given in advance.

In addition to being a "story," both the *Sangu huimen* and *Liugu huimen* were meant to be up-to-date and handy song texts. The *Sangu huimen* is subtitled "an up-to-date song text for sending off a daughter from her chamber, a newly selected, comprehensive edition." The *Liugu huimen* is subtitled "an up-to-date lament text for marrying off a daughter, a revised, newly selected, and comprehensive edition." Such handbook-like song texts are not uncommon in Cantonese vernacular literature. Two early Republican publications, the *Shikuan hanshu* (Up-to-date book of laments) and the *Furu xige buqiuren* (Women and children learning songs without asking the others), are examples of printed bridal laments. Putting aside the storylines of *Sangu huimen* and *Liugu huimen*, we may consider the two *muyushu* as samples of these singing handbooks. Understandably, these mass-produced, standardized song texts can incorporate no individual and contextual messages. They contain primarily an abundance of such literary devices as metaphors or the breaking of a character into several parts to become parts of a poem. It is doubtful that these songbooks would have been used on the occasion of an actual wedding. Where singing bridal laments was a necessary practice, women would have learned from their female seniors to sing or compose their own bridal laments. These seniors, in most cases, lacked the command of literacy to consult any handbook. Brought up in an oral culture, they had their own ways of transmitting the singing practice from one generation to the next.

We should further distinguish the bridal laments that exist in a manuscript tradition from those in a print tradition — although both belong to the category of written culture. A manuscript entitled *Hunyin sangji hanshu* (A book of laments used in marriages and funerals), collected at the Guangdong Provincial Library in Guangzhou, might shed light on this issue. The manuscript illustrates contemporary social circumstances and the personal situations of the people involved. For example, in a paragraph sung at a funeral during the rite of "buying water," the following appears: "The Republic has invented a new order of fashion. . . . The old court pearls should no longer be worn, so as not to be mocked by others as being foolish!" In the same text, foreign fashions and commodities, such as Western-style suits (*xizhuang*), British pounds sterling, and American dollars are listed.[33] Such timely improvisations do not easily find their way into the printed form of the *muyushu*.

The marriage

Both *Sangu huimen* and *Liugu huimen* attempt to incorporate the details of local marriage rituals into the stories. These rites, as indicated by the subtitles of the text, include "matching the birthdays of bride and groom" (*he niangeng*), "seeing the bride off" (*songjia*), "pinning the hair and making up the face" (*shangtou kaimian*), "eating rice at the warm chamber" (*shi nuanfangfan*), "making fun of the bride and the groom at their newly-decorated bedroom" (*nao xinfang*), and, finally, "[the bride] going back to the natal home" (*huimen*, usually practiced by the bride three days after her marriage). A detailed illustration of these marriage rituals is simultaneously a demonstration of norms. Yet in the real-life situation of the Pearl River Delta region, the "norms" of marriage could have been multiple. As indicated at the beginning of this study, *zishunu* (forming sisterhoods with other female companions and taking vows not to marry) and *buluojia* (not cohabiting with one's husband after marriage) used to be common practices. In *Liugu huimen*, Sixth Aunt is at one point open to one of these two possibilities. When she returns to her natal home to express her miseries, her mother is so distressed by her daughter's situation that she suggests:

He is so poor, he cannot stay long.
[If he dies,] I shall find you another husband and tie up another good knot.[34]

A second possibility offered to Sixth Aunt is proposed by one of her closest female *xiangzhi* (literally, friends knowing each other very well). She says:

> Yesterday there were ten pieces of dates of birth [submitted by the matchmaker],
> I said that I would not marry from then on and was willing to stay with my father and mother.
> I would like to stay at home with you.
> Don't endure the bitterness and sorrow [caused by] the disloyal bloke.
> [Because] you can make shoes and I can have threads unknotted,
> Together we can work diligently and save some money.
> If our parents do not allow us to do so,
> We can live in the nunnery.
> Eating vegetarian meals, I would like to be a nun.[35]

Nevertheless, the author of the text has already determined how the story should end, and remarrying or resisting marriage are not options. The matchmaker's fabrications and Guanwang's addiction to gambling are, from the author's point of view, of little consequence. It is the obligation of Sixth Aunt to be patient and hope for the best. Sixth Aunt is left with no choice. Her moral character (in accordance with Confucian principles) is appreciated once again towards the end of the text:

> You can see how Sixth Aunt is content with the lot she has.
> Being able to wait until the cloud parts, she [finally] sees the brightness of the moon.[36]

Here, the idea of "marriage resistance" proposed by the *xiangzhi* is particularly worth exploring. It is not a coincidence that intimate relationships among females are mentioned in both *Sangu huimen* and *Liugu huimen*. In *Sangu huimen*, among all the bridal laments illustrated, the most dramatic scenes come from those sung between Third Aunt and her "sisters" — her female relatives and friends in a general sense. They probably have no blood relationship with Third Aunt but are described as "sharing the same heart" (*tongxin*) with her. By using various names of flowers, insects, birds, vegetables, and herbal medicines as metaphors, the laments express the sorrow of Third Aunt and her "sisters" and expose the conflicts between their intimacy (*qing*) and a conjugal relationship between Third Aunt and her would-be husband. This illustration paves the way for the main subject of the story — Third Aunt must return to her natal home not only because she has to visit her parents, but also because she has promised to report to her "sisters" about her married life. It is also with these *tongxin* that Third Aunt can share with her most intimate feelings. She tells them how caring her husband is — something she is too shy to tell her own mother.

I would like to suggest that this *tongxin* and *xiangzhi* relationship and particularly the proposal of marriage resistance that appear in the texts are a superficial imitation, or even a distortion of the *zishunu* and *buluojia* customs that were prevalent in some areas in the Pearl River Delta.[37] In fact, both *zishunu* and *buluojia* are the two most common local subject matters adapted in *muyushu,* although the terms seldom appear in the texts. Examples of these *muyushu* include the *Shisiqi* (For ten times [I] think about), *Jinxiu shizhai* (Jinxiu eating vegetarian feast), *Shi'er shichen* (Twelve [Chinese] hours), *Dalan laopo gui* (Breaking the wife's cupboard), *Chai waimu wu* (Tearing down the mother-in-law's house) and *Jie xielan* (Untying the carrying basket), which also incorporates the *Yuchan fujian jinlan* (Yuchan sending a letter to her "golden-orchid" sister), *Yuchan tan wugeng* (Yuchan unleashing her sadness throughout ten hours), and *Yuchan wenxi* (Yuhan inquiring the sorcerer).[38]

Opinions of the practices of *zishunu* and *buluojia* that are reflected in various *muyushu* are surprisingly consistent — they are at least ambivalent if not totally negative. In some cases, the authors simply designed the story as a statement about the love-sickness of a girl who has committed to a sisterhood.[39] In others, the authors designed the story as a tragedy and did not forget to give readers a lesson that such relationships are undesirable. In the *Chuixiao yiyou* (Playing the flute [she] misses [her] friend), a girl finds fault with her "golden-orchid friend" for not keeping in touch since they have lived apart. She concludes with bitterness that committing to "a golden-orchid [relationship] is like [obtaining] a ticket to see the Emperor of Hell. It damages the remaining years of my life."[40] In the *Menglan yiyou* (Menglan missing her friend), the major female character, Menglan, has a similar painful experience. She thus "advises the 'red-powder girls'; that, never should they take up the sadness of mine [hers]."[41] In the *Riye shichen* (*Hours through days and nights*), one finds a similar message: "[I] advise the girls that they ought not to seek [such] joy. That they should never engage in a 'knowing-each-other-well' relationship" is clearly conveyed towards the end of the text.[42]

An exceedingly elaborate example of such stories is the *Jie xielan*. The major female character of the story, Yuan Qingchan, believes the rumors that her "golden-orchid" sister, Jin Yuchan, has fallen in love with another girl, and she intends to end their former relationship. Qingchan is so depressed that she finally commits suicide. Yuchan and her mother later communicate with the ghost of Qingchan through a sorcerer and explain to her that the rumors were untrue. The clarification is, of course, too late. Yuchan can only live the rest of her life with great regret.[43]

In *Shi'er shichen*, Bilan cannot sleep well because she is remembering her intimate relationship with her "golden-orchid" sister, Qingyu, who has recently married and broken their former relationship. At the beginning of the text, Bilan remembers how "scrumptious" (*yewei*) such a "golden-orchid" relationship is. Yet she regrettably says at the end that:

> At the beginning I supposed you were of true affinity and fidelity.
> I did not expect you would hurt me as such.
> This is a good lesson for all others —
> One should never become involved in a "same-heart" relationship again![44]

In some cases, the authors reject the ideas of *buluojia* and *zishunu* and offer a compromising solution. In the *Chai waimu wu*, the *buluojia* practice is not treated favorably: the husband is angry with his wife because she prefers to stay with her "golden-orchid" sister and does not return to join him for three years. He throws stones at his mother-in-law's house and wishes to negotiate with his wife. His mother-in-law finally makes a compromise by allowing him to stay with her daughter at her home.[45] In the *Jinxiu shizhai*, the *zishunu* custom is recognized only when it is practiced in another form — Jinxiu's refusal to marry is accepted because she chooses to become a nun. Her determination is appreciated in the text only because her actions fit the ideal of chastity (*zhenjie*).[46] Another *muyushu*, *Mei Li zheng hua*, is regionally set in Fujian. It shares the same idea that it is not desirable for women to reject married life. When the major male character of the story, Mr Mei, suggests marriage to the two young women who have saved his life, both decline his proposal because they have a *tongxin* (same heart) relationship. However, in the author's hand, a few lines of persuasion are enough to change their mind — the young women are ultimately willing to "entrust" their "humble bodies to the man"[47]

In other cases, authors proposed a total abandonment of *zishunu* and *buluojia* practices. In *Husinu zitan* (A woman silk worker lamenting on her own), a woman spinster is initially very proud of her ability to earn her livelihood by working in a silk factory. Thus, she pins up her own hair (*shuqi*) and pledges in front of her relatives that she will never marry and will take care of her parents from then on. However, her parents die unexpectedly when the woman is in her thirties. She spends all her savings on their funerals and is unable to retrieve the funds she has entrusted to others to invest. By that time, she is too old to work as efficiently as she did in her younger days and is thus rejected by her employer. She regrets her former decision to remain unmarried and decides to find a husband for herself. According to the story, she realizes that this is the only guarantee of happiness for the rest of her life.[48]

In *Yejian Jinlan* (Warning Jinlan at night), Jinlan does not go to her husband's house and stays with her "golden-orchid sisters." One night, the Goddess of Mercy appears in her dream and says to her that:

> The practice of not returning to husband's house is objectionable.
> If the husband's family is poor and does not have a descendent,
> The ghost of his ancestor will cry sorrowfully.
> They will go to the Emperor of Hell to seek a resolution,
> And [the Emperor of Hell] will put you, such an unscrupulous girl, in the
> "tower of looking back to your native village" (i.e., put her to death).[49]

Taking the advice of the Goddess, Jinlan gives up her *buluojia* practice and even manages to persuade her "golden-orchid" sisters to abandon their *buluojia* practice entirely.

The ambivalent attitudes held by the *muyushu* authors towards the ideas of *buluojia* and *zishunu* appear to be consistent with the orthodox viewpoints commonly held by the literati. However, these attitudes are equally ambivalent when compared to those held by local literati in Guangdong. Helen Siu has clearly shown that the practices of *buluojia* and *zishunu* were, in fact, accepted as the norm by some elite families in the Shunde and Xiangshan regions, at least until 1949. It is very possible that the *muyushu* authors did not come from regions such as Shunde and Xiangshan. Having only heard about the *buluojia* and *zishunu* practices, the *muyushu* authors might have approached the matter with an orthodox mindset. Given that most of the *muyushu* reviewed in this article are Republican productions, it is also reasonable to speculate that these *muyushu* authors might well be trying to identify with the modern Chinese intellectuals, who often found the indigenous customs exotic and incomprehensible.[50]

It is interesting to contrast the marriage prospects of men and women characters portrayed in various *muyushu*. Unlike the tragic mood presented in the previous stories, polygamy is often narrated with a joyful ending in *muyushu*. When I first examined the table of contents of all the *muyushu* collected at the University of Hong Kong, I was struck by the frequency of similar subtitles, "*Er / San mei tuanyuan / tonghuan* or so and so" (literally, "uniting as a perfect circle with / being happy together with two / three beautiful ladies"). I selected those stories marked with similar subtitles for further examination. As expected, all the selected texts conveyed a similar message, namely, that the major male character is able to marry two or three young women of equal status at the same time without any one of them becoming a concubine. Moreover, starting with the famous *Huajian ji* of the 1700s, these stories provided similar justifications for polygamy — the man is separated by default from the first woman to whom he has become engaged. During his adventures, in which he is from time to time in danger, he is rescued by other women. He finally marries the other women in addition to his *yuanpei* (literally, the first wife). This is understandable because he is only showing gratitude to his benefactor(s). His decision is happily supported or even encouraged by his *yuanpei*. Although women are, in most cases, left with no choices in the *muyushu*, men seem to be more able to pursue their own agendas.[51]

Although women might have more space to maneuver in an oral tradition, their reflections in a written tradition are, in most cases, drawn up by men. To claim that the *muyushu* are written by women probably focuses too much on the audience's side of the commercial commodity and does not consider enough about its authorship and production in print. The authorship of *muyushu* is, in most cases, unknown. As in the cases of *Sangu Huimen* and *Liugu huimen*, only a pseudonym, "Xianqing jushi" (a retired scholar at leisure), is noted. Because men were for a long time in a more advantageous position in a written culture, they were more likely to be the authors of the *muyushu*. The insights for composing vernacular literature may come from women in an oral, real-life context, but it is more likely that men put the ideas into written words and had them simplified, purified, and repackaged for a market of printed matter that entertains both male and female readers.[52]

The language

It is undeniable that Cantonese vernacular terminologies constitute the major "local" characteristics for *muyushu*. As Wu Ruiqing points out, despite the fact that she includes two of the *muyushu* titles in her study, namely, *Liu Quan jingua* and *Shijiu wenlu*, they do not have a Guangdong background because they originate from *Xiyouji* and *Liang Shanbo yu Zhu Yingtai* respectively. But in both texts, cuisine, fruits, and animals are articulated in Cantonese terms.[53] However, one should question how "local" the Cantonese is or which type of Cantonese is being used in a *muyushu*. Not being a linguist, I am unable to examine in detail the regional differences of

Cantonese. However, some obvious examples are useful to illustrate the complex issues. For example, in *Sangu huimen,* ways of addressing people are the "standard" ones that we learn in a written context — *taigong, taipo* for great grandparents; *fuqin* and *muqin* for parents, *gumu* and *yima* for paternal and maternal aunts respectively. Yet, the kinship terminology used in real life can be much more complicated. Leaving aside the Hakka and the Dan fishermen, the Cantonese ways of addressing father varies, at least, from *A Ye, A Bo, A Shu, A Die* to *A Ba* , and for mother, it can vary from *A Nai, A Jie, A Niang, A Mu, A Dai* (in Cantonese) to *A Ei* (in Cantonese).[54] The Cantonese used in the *muyushu* is probably the most common Cantonese that could be understood by the majority of the literate or semi-literate Cantonese.

It is not impossible to consider the specialities of Cantonese spoken in various regions when the vernacular is put into written form. This is demonstrated in a Christian pamphlet entitled *You yinghua qianxue qimeng shu yi* (Translated from an English primer of enlightenment), which was published in the Cantonese spoken in the four counties, namely, Xinhui, Enping, Kaiping and Taishan.[55] Obviously, unlike the Christian missionary, the publishers of *muyushu* and other Cantonese vernacular literatures can only bypass any factors that would inhibit the production and circulation of their mass-produced product. Hence, by saying that the *muyushu* is "local," one overlooks the commercial nature of the publishing business of *muyushu*. *Muyushu* and much other popular literature and handbooks, such as almanacs, are supported by a low-quality printing industry operated at low cost in major cities and towns, such as Guangzhou, Foshan, Dongguan, Hong Kong, and various Chinatowns in North America.[56] In most cases, one edition of stories was used without revision, and thus one printing block was reused over the centuries without regard for the changing time-space contexts. After all, being "trans-local" would guarantee wider market appeal.

Conclusion

An abundant use of Cantonese vernacular and the adaptation of local happenings are the two most distinguishable features that give *muyushu* a significantly "local" outlook. However, the discussion above also shows that the language used in the printed documents is mixed with a considerable amount of classical Chinese and northern vernacular. The finer details of "local" Cantonese are often excluded. The subject matter of the *muyushu* that I have selected for this study expresses a strong local touch. However, it is clear that the authors do not appreciate the local practices that they note because they appear "unorthodox" and unfamiliar. The intertwining of a seemingly scholar-gentry, state-wide orthodoxy and local customs described in *muyushu* is illustrative of a larger cultural process in an evolving regional political economy. One may wish to read between the lines to appreciate how "local practices" are portrayed and, more significant, how they are marginalized and excluded for local consumption.

If these texts become the established guidebooks for local performance, does this suggest that the possible alternatives for women in a local context are limited? Women in any real life context are never free to act according to their own will. Many studies of the area have demonstrated that women have been agents, victims, and simultaneously empowered when they went through various stages of marriage. There are intense negotiations among the brides and their female friends, their natal kin and their husbands' families, and there are ways to seek refuge, recourse, and social recognition. The point of this study is that, whereas in an oral tradition, women are involved more in the creative process and thus have more opportunities to express themselves, in a written tradition, women generally become a mere audience or even an object of mocking because they lack the command of literacy. The ambiguous wording of *muyushu* suggests that women might not have much of a voice in a written tradition that is dominated by literate men — even if the written literature is composed in a vernacular language, their "*mother*-tongue."

4 Women's Work and Women's Food in Lineage Land[*]

Wing-hoi Chan

Introduction

Patrilineal descent has dominated the study of Chinese society in late imperial and early modern periods. The lineage model has been under considerable critical scrutiny.[1] But the influences of the paradigm on the study of women and gender in South China have not received comparable attention.

In fact, influential studies on Chinese women seem to reinforce the lineage model rather than challenge it. For example, Margery Wolf's[2] theory of women and the family in Taiwan is based on a single "Chinese concept of family" equated to patrilineal descent, outside of which women are supposed to have constructed "uterine families," which are used to explain phenomena such as the difficult relationship between mother-in-law and daughter-in-law. A more recent, influential formulation equating women's active roles in relationships across family and descent group boundaries to "women's community" implies that peasant men lived entirely within their lineage.[3] D. K. Feil has observed a very similar tendency in the study of Highland New Guinea society:

* Initial research on which this chapter is based was supported by Yale University's Center for International and Area Studies, its Council on East Asian Studies, and Graduate School. Additional research, especially on land records, was carried out when the author was a postdoctoral fellow at Centre of Asian Studies, The University of Hong Kong.

> [T]ies of kinship and descent, and affinity as well, are frequently separated
> or disproportionally analyzed in Highlands social structural studies and
> are usually, if subtly, attached to the domain of one sex or another.[4]

Feil's study of a Highlands society highlights structures mediated by
women. Comparison of South China to Highland New Guinea may seem
far-fetched, not least because familiar image of Chinese lineages based on
rice farming.[5] However, building on a project re-examining the relationship
between representations of descent and gender in South China,[6] this chapter
will argue that, in the study of early modern South China, the lineage model
has obscured sweet potatoes and swine, and women's roles in their
consumption and production, and in economic aspects of peasant families'
ties beyond the descent group. The chapter further demonstrates that an
extreme version of the lineage model and a dichotomous approach to the
study of women reinforce each other.

Since its beginning, scholarship on Chinese lineages has emphasized
the rice land endowment of such groups. Most of the extensive studies
attempted to understand the historical Chinese lineage through Hong Kong's
rural communities, although for the latter the earliest detailed data are
colonial records from the 1900s and ethnographic fieldwork from around
1960. The picture of dominant patrilineages as a community closed in on
itself for its male peasant members has become influential and received
little critical scrutiny. As a result, gender aspects of the rural economy have
been obscured, despite increased attention to class and gender inequalities
within powerful lineages.

The new study of oral accounts and land records presented here will
show that since long before the arrival of the first anthropologist in rural
Hong Kong in the 1950s, rice farming was unable to meet the needs of
such communities. Women's work to produce other food and income and
their consumption of a larger proportion of an alternative staple were major
elements in the rural economy. These features of the economic system were
important factors to some aspects of gender and family relations often
attributed to the kinship system.

Double-cropping irrigated rice land in southeastern China, with a high
potential for rent extraction, is considered a major factor to the rise and
maintenance of large localized descent groups. It was the most important
kind of asset set aside to produce income for the worship of ancestors and,
where the income is large enough, other benefits for their descendants.
Some advantages of rice land for lineage development are clear enough.
The opportunity to develop such land might promote the establishment of

extended social organization; the high profitability of the asset provided support for ritual and other activities that help maintain a descent group and its subdivisions.

However, various authors have gone further in emphasizing the power of the lineages found in Hong Kong and the nearby region to argue that lineage members generally derived material benefits from corporate landholdings, and those benefits, among other factors, kept them inside their own descent group. In contrast, this chapter argues that preoccupation with corporate ownership of rice land has obscured the rural economy's reliance on an alternative staple crop, on animal husbandry, on gender patterns in the production and consumption of both kinds of farm products, and on economic relationships between peasant families and their affines mediated by married women.

Freedman is among the first to argue that poor tenant families derived tenancy advantages from their membership in a lineage. He writes:

> When the landlord was often the agnatic group of which the tenant was a member, and when being a member . . . meant having a prior right to tenancy, the poorer people had every reason to stay in the community rather than go to try their luck elsewhere.[7]

Later authors seem more sensitive to the factor of what is called "segmentation" in the literature on Chinese lineages: when there is a trust set up for an ancestor other than ancestors common to the entire lineage, the group consisting of beneficiaries of such a trust is known as a "segment."[8] As scholars since Freedman have recognized, many members of Chinese lineages did not belong to any well-endowed segments, and many others had only very small shares in segment with relatively small assets.

One of these scholars, Jack Potter, while taking Freedman's argument further, also acknowledged such complications.[9] However, he concludes:

> . . . in spite of these exceptions, it does seem that ancestral property did give economic advantages (if only in terms of secure tenure) to some poorer members of a lineage.[10]

Subsequent scholarship does not seriously question "secure tenure" as an important benefit enjoyed by lineage members before postwar transformations, but some does reveal the importance of other crops and incomes as well as women's very important role in the economy. Elizabeth L. Johnson's biography[11] of Great-Aunt Yeung, a Hakka woman in Tsuen Wan, shows the importance of women's roles in wage labor and production of swine and sweet potato. The importance of sweet potato was not unique to the Hakka. Rubie Watson's report reveals that situations in Punti dominant lineages were probably not very different. Sweet potato provided important supplement to rice in Ha Tsuen:

> Older women reported that in the past they had eaten two meals a day. . . . Sweet potatoes were usually mixed with rice to make a kind of gruel, and when there was no rice, sweet potatoes were eaten alone.[12]

Watson mentions a woman who found herself in the latter situation when she married into a landless family in the village in 1918. It is worth noting that by Watson's estimate, about 55% of a representative hamlet's households were landless. She also observes, "contemporary villagers . . . often refer to the past as 'the time when we ate sweet potatoes.'"[13] She moreover mentions livestock such as pigs and refers to women's role in growing sweet potato.

However, the importance of sweet potatoes and farm animals is obscured by the same author's overall argument, which seems to have gone further than previous authors to assert the benefits of membership in dominant lineages. Referring to Ha Tsuen, Watson states, "Most farmers were able to rent land sufficient for their household's [sic] needs."[14]

The claim of sufficiency which received reinforcement from Watson's overall argument that peasant men in dominant lineages were encapsulated by the descent group.[15] Myron Cohen[16] corroborates such a reading when he explores the relationship between family and lineage, especially in Freedman's "Type Z" lineage, i.e. one that was "powerful, well endowed, had a long history and a relatively large and compact membership," which approximates Rubie Watson's "dominant lineage." Referring to Rubie Watson's finding, Cohen argues that ". . . while it might be commonly the case that the majority in a type Z lineage were members of poor tenant families . . ., such families had as their only assets whatever their shares in the main lineage estate might have been."[17] To Cohen, in type Z lineages the dependency on the descent group weakened peasant families as social units and accounted for much reduced importance of affinal ties. The argument, however, suggests not only a peasant family's necessity to depend on the lineage but also the sufficiency of lineage resources, without which it would have to pursue outside opportunities and other kin ties.

Rubie Watson seems to give a different picture a few pages later in the source cited above: "For many households, fishing or wage labor might well have meant the difference between having enough to eat and going hungry."[18] Poor lineage members might be heavily dependent on the lineage but they seldom had access to sufficient rice land through the lineage as suggested by the claim of encapsulation. Nor was Ha Tsuen unique in this respect. James Watson finds in nearby San Tin a serious land shortage, as well as the readiness of poorer members of the lineage to search for outside opportunities during the first half of the twentieth century. Watson finds one third of the thirty-eight households he surveyed in the village to have a male who worked as a seaman within the first four decades of the twentieth century. Of the sailors Watson met, only one took the job "for reasons other than immediate necessity."[19] Even Ha Tsuen men pursued opportunities outside of the lineage, especially as seaman on ships. In a paragraph on the importance of the sea for the livelihood of Ha Tsuen villagers Rubie Watson states:

> In the 1930s there were at least three households in the hamlets of Sik King Wai whose sole source of income was remittances from sailors. Other families were partially dependent on absentee sailors.[20]

It is very likely, therefore, that the proportion of families entirely or partially dependent sailors amounted to around 10% of the seventy-one households Rubie Watson estimated for 1905. But there seems to be much variation in the extent of involvement in seafaring among lineages, and that variation might be attributed to the scarcity of such jobs rather than lineage type. It seems that not only is seafaring often male employment outside of the lineage, but they were often obtained through kinship ties beyond descent too. J. Watson[21] reports that peasant men in San Tin sometimes used ties through married women to obtain such jobs during the prewar period. He refers to a man whose father could not rent enough land for three sons. The young man "spoke with a maternal cousin who was a sailor from a nearby village, and soon afterward was on his way to Singapore."

Overshadowed by the big lineage model are several important features of the rural economy. These include a system of gender inequality under which women worked beyond paddy farming and household duties and consumed a variety of food considered inferior to rice. Another important feature, women's maintenance of natal and affinal ties was obscured when this important activity of women is treated as "women's community" serving peasant women's needs in lineages that took good care of its land-poor male members. Such activities could be considered as "work," in the sense of "the work of kinship" coined by Micaela di Leonardo[22] to overcome dichotomous approaches to women's active involvement in contact across households either as "women's culture" or "another way in which men, the economy, and the state extract labor from women without a fair return."

The Case of Sheung Shui

Sheung Shui is one of Hong Kong's rural communities through which anthropologists tried to understand the historical Chinese lineage. The rise of the Liao (Liu in Cantonese) of the village took place around the transition between the Ming and Qing dynasties in the first half of the seventeenth century.[23] The village's individual members and trusts established for ancestral worship probably expanded their holdings in Sheung Shui plain, one of the two most fertile areas of the New Territories. Their ownership of land in other parts of the district probably benefited from reclamation by Hakka immigrants who came in the seventeenth and eighteenth centuries.[24]

The rise of Sheung Shui was probably enabled by claimed and actual connections to government officials. The elite of Sheung Shui gained considerable political influence in the area since early in the eighteenth century by obtaining imperial degrees.[25] In or shortly before 1751, the lineage built an ancestral hall named Wanshi *tang*, which is alluding to a claim that a distant collateral agnate and his sons were high officials.[26] The worship of ancestors at the hall was heavily gentrified and the ceremonies honored senior male and excluded women as participants.[27]

Although British rule started in 1898 and brought many changes, agriculture had been the most important source of livelihood until the 1950s.[28] Official records suggest that land have been abundant within the lineage. But the elderly women of Sheung Shui told very different stories.

One of my informants married into Sheung Shui in the late 1940s. For years her family had no access to rice land. It was very difficult to find any to lease. One time her husband and his brother together successfully bid a one-year lease from an ancestral trust, but it was because they tendered very competitive rent. Not until the 1950s could the family find a long-term lease for about 0.5 acre of paddy land.[29] But these improvements were possible precisely because by then growth in non-agricultural employment opportunities reduced the demand for rice fields. Another woman married into an owner-farmer family in the same decade. Her father-in-law, though not among the very wealthy (*caizhu*), had "quite a landholding." The land was farmed with the help of several annual farm laborers and "teaming" partners, but the land was insufficient for his many sons when they grew up.

The scarcity of paddy fields and the importance of sweet potato are already evident in the life stories of women who married into Sheung Shui families in the first and second half of 1930s. Two of the families were well-off one or two generations before but their fortunes had since dwindled. The young wives had to farm for their families' livelihood, but there was no rice land. Another informant's family probably had more access to paddy fields. They owned about 0.33 acres and could produced "just enough rice for their own consumption" — when supplemented by other crops and incomes (see below). She was born around 1918 and married a Sheung Shui man in about 1938. She recalled that her family by marriage occasionally had the use of additional land by bidding one-year leases. The family sometimes kept a cow and sometimes formed a "teaming" relationship and used the cow of the wealthier partner. The arrangement was for poorer partners worked the fields of a wealthier partner in exchange for meals on workdays plus plowing service for their own plots.

Rice land shortage existed long before the 1930s and 1940s. Analysis of data on landownership and productivity shows that there was not enough paddy land for the poorer members of the community since the 1900s, the earliest period for which land records are available.

To assess land sufficiency in Sheung Shui, it is useful to introduce Baker's distinction between land within and outside what he calls Liu "territory," i.e. a core area adjoining the village formed by contiguous plots owned by Liu individuals or trusts. The area accounted for two thirds of the Liu holdings, and was mostly within a half-mile radius from the center of the village. It could be used to approximate the portion of Liu holdings available for use by lineage members.[30] Most Liu-owned plots of land outside the cluster were leased to outsiders.[31]

Under British rule, land records grade agricultural land into first-class, second-class and third-class. All first-class land was paddy fields that produced two crops a year. Fields among third-class land was suitable for dry cultivation only. In the Sheung Shui area, second-class is probably an in-between category for plots with lower productivity or only portions suitable for paddy cultivation.

Landownership was very skewed. Based on unique Liu individual or joint house-owners named in the House Block Crown Lease from the 1900s, the number of households can be estimated at 358 — the number of uniquely named home-owners. Analysis of Block Crown Lease data shows that 20% of these Liu households owned 145 acres of the 174 acres of first-class core-area land. Among them were some landlords. Members of this class in the Sheung Shui area, like those in Ha Tsuen of northwestern New

Territories studied by Rubie Watson, were distinguished from most owners of smaller holdings. They and their family members played no role in agricultural production.[32] In Sheung Shui, there were quite a number of owners of more modest holdings who personally farmed assisted by *changgong* laborers hired on annual basis and "teaming" partners.

Most other members of the lineage had to rent most of the land they used to grow rice. Information introduced above implies that 80% of Sheung Shui families together owned only twenty-nine acres of first-class and fifteen acres of second-class land in Liu "territory." They could have access to land by renting from some of those among the top 20%. But among the latter, only those with holdings of four acres or more of land in the first-class or second-class grade were likely to rent out.[33] We find that about ten owners met the criteria, and they together held sixty and fifteen acres of first-class and second-class land respectively.

Peasants could also rent from ancestral and communal trusts, which Baker has found to hold as much land as individual members of the community did in the 1900s. But he also makes it clear that members of the lineage were not equal beneficiaries of the trusts. Paddy land owned by Wanshi tang, the trust whose beneficiary was the entire lineage, amounted to only about nine acres.[34] There are other trusts, each shared by the descendants of one or a few ancestors, corresponding to a lineage "segment."[35] The distribution of wealth among the trusts was very uneven. The wealthiest trust, in honor of an ancestor of the sixteenth generation and holding 51.83 acres in 1906, included among its surviving beneficiaries grandsons of the ancestor during Baker's fieldwork.[36] However, Baker finds the average holding of trusts to be only 3.02 acres,[37] and a member of one poorer segment "belongs to no [trust] closer than seven generations from him."[38] That often means that a large number of beneficiaries share the incomes from a small endowment.

A man in the lineage might have access to rice land held by segments of which he was not a member. With few exceptions, land in trust ownership was rented out for income. Some trust land was set aside for temporary leases by auction. Some informants suggested that that bidding was very competitive and the resulting rent was sometimes much higher than that of long-term leases. Moreover, there is documentary data suggesting about 40% of "territory" trust land might have been rented to those among the top 20% land owning Liu families. For an optimistic estimate, here it is assumed that all territory trust land was rented to the bottom 80% of Liu households.[39]

Based on the considerations presented above, landownership in 1906 within the "core area" is summarized below.[40]

Table 4.1   Estimated agricultural landholdings in core area by grade and ownership

	First-class acres	Second-class acres	Third-class acres	Total acres
All private	174	41	118	333
Less: top 20% owned	<u>145</u>	<u>26</u>	<u>68</u>	
Bottom 80% owned	29	15	50	
Rented from top 20% owners (est.)	60	15		
Available from trusts	155	41	103	<u>299</u>
Total				632

For an estimate of land sufficiency, specific data on consumption needs and productivity are essential. Four hundred catties is used here as a level of income that may be able to meet subsistence needs plus some minimal expenses.[41] A 65% conversion from paddy to rice approximates local report at "sixty something."[42] The average productivity of paddy fields in the Sheung Shui area was reported to be between 250 catties to 300 catties per *douzhong*, which is equivalent to about 1,650 catties per acre.[43] Based on two cycles per year, the average annual productivity of first-class land would be 3,300 catties per acre. The corresponding second-class figures are estimated here at 70% of their first-class counterparts. Rent in Sheung Shui, charged by trusts and private owners, amounted to around 50% of yield.[44] A deduction of 10% should be made to allow for village watch levy (about 5%), seed (about 3%), and irrigation charges (unknown).[45]

According to the figures introduced above, each first-class acre owned by the farmer will produce 2,970 catties of unhusked rice net of deductions, and the grain would feed 4.8 persons. If the land was rented, the tenant's net income would amount to only 1,320 catties, which would feed 2.15 people.

Given the data and optimistic assumptions presented above, 739 people or 64% of the bottom 80% of the Sheung Shui population reported in the 1911 census could be supported by paddy farming.[46] Sheung Shui was not unique. A very similar estimate of 63% can be made for a hamlet of Ha Tsuen under some optimistic assumptions using data published by Rubie Watson and others.[47]

It is therefore clear that dominant lineages did not have sufficient land for its members. How did peasant families cope with land shortage?

Table 4.2   Rice land (in)sufficiency for the bottom 80% land owners

	First-class acres	Second-class acres	First-class feeds	Second-class feeds	Total feeds
Owned in Core Area	29	15	141	51	192
Rented from landlords (est.)	60	15	130	23	153
Rented from trusts	155	41	332	62	_394
Total					_739
Compare 80 % of population (1,441) in 1911				80%	1,153
Sufficiency					64%

Women's Food and Women's Work

In the study of the Chinese lineage, commercialization has been considered an important factor. For example, Freedman[48] describes the economic aspect of the lineage as "a complex of agricultural and commercial institution," acknowledging the prominence of crops other than rice in some communities, and links that to foreign trade. Potter has put even more emphasis on commerce as a factor in the geographical distribution of lineages, observing that powerful lineages are likely to be concentrated "in the central and southern regions of the empire, and especially in the more commercially developed areas."[49] However, neither author pays much attention to the production of farm products other than rice for the market, not to mention the gendered nature of such production, non-commercialized crops grown on other land, or gender patterns in the consumption of such crops. To the elderly women of Sheung Shui, these were important aspects of the local economic situation before Japanese occupation.

Their families, like many others in Sheung Shui and other dominant lineages, could survive because they did not live solely on farming rice land owned by trusts and landlords in the lineage. Shortage in paddy land was alleviated to a small extent by some outside labor opportunities but more generally by substituting rice with sweet potato and raising hogs for sale. Most families grew sweet potato, in many cases on their own land, which was not good enough for rice. They also cooked its vines to feed the animals.[50] Both tasks were mainly assigned to young married women.[51] More than other family members, married women substituted sweet potato for rice and thus reduced a family's rice consumption needs. These factors, along with some outside employment for the men and "teaming" arrangements for the women, made it possible for many families to cope although they did not have sufficient access to rice fields.

Pig raising had been important since before the New Territories was brought under British rule. During the relevant period, pork was not part of the average villager's everyday diet. Instead, hog meat was a delicacy reserved for banquets and major holidays. Pigs were raised mainly for sale. The colonial official who investigated the area in 1898 reports that pig raising was carried on "in almost every village" for export.[52]

Pig raising was a very important source of income because the prices were good and each family produced a few annually.

Pigs fetched rather high prices relative to paddy. The women I interviewed in Sheung Shui do not remember historical prices. But a male informant in Ho Sheung Heung recalled that before Japanese occupation a pig was sold for at least $20 whereas paddy went for $3.6 a picul (hundred catties), implying 5.5 piculs of paddy for an average pig. The average pig being sold in the New Territories during the prewar years probably weighted no less than 120 catties if they were comparable to those in nearby parts of South China,[53] although official sources from Hong Kong implied that imported hogs had an average weight of about a picul.[54] Based on the latter figure, documentary data can be used to estimate the price in piculs of paddy averaged five around 1935.[55] The ratio should have been considerably higher before the impact of economic depression in the 1930s.[56]

Production in 1941 could be estimated at close to 0.47 per capita.[57] The average villager could raise pigs in a small scale because there was no need to purchase feed grain.[58] For the same reason, large specialized farms, if they existed at all at the time, could account for only a very small fraction of the number. Poorer families in rural areas with lower transportation costs and fewer other opportunities probably produced more. In Sheung Shui, one woman recalled that in some years she sold three grown pigs and many more piglets, another informant said that she sold four in some years. Their numbers were probably not extraordinarily high: each had no pigsty or spare house and had to keep the animals in her home's front section, which also served as the kitchen.

Even at the lowest price ratio mentioned above, proceeds from the sale of three pigs would be equivalent to about 1,500 catties of unhusked rice, slightly more than the needs of 2.43 persons according to the estimate used in the previous section.[59] Many families might have raised fewer, but, as one woman explained, it was because in later periods engagement in casual wage labor made it hard for them to keep more swine.

Although Baker[60] mentions that formerly pigs foraged within the village, and that many still did during his fieldwork in the 1960s, pigs had to be fed. By the 1960s some of my informants used leftovers from nearby restaurants. Before then, families in these communities reared swine using feed prepared mostly from the vines of sweet potato and some of its smaller tubers. Married women were the ones to prepare pig feed. Many remembered the hardship of cooking the fodder in the evening, filling a small house with heat, humidity, and an unpleasant smell.[61]

Sweet potato was used not only as material for pig feed. The importance of sweet potato in China is recognized by many historians. The crop was introduced into various coastal localities of China in the mid-sixteenth century and became an important food for the poor.[62] Some of the discussion is directly relevant to the New Territories. Chen Shuping has referred to a legend recorded in a gazetteer of Dongguan County, the administrative district that at the time included the New Territories area, claiming that a native brought the crop back from Southeast Asia. Chen's other sources indicate that sweet potato was important in Guangdong Province within a century of the alleged event.[63]

Among Sheung Shui women whose families had insufficient access to rice land, sweet potato was always important as food. One informant's father-in-law gave her and her husband two parcels of agricultural land to farm. The larger of those was about 0.5 acres in size,[64] and both were suitable for growing sweet potato and groundnuts only. Two other informants similarly explained that their families had only the kind of land fit for sweet potato and could not find paddy land to rent. Although in these two cases the lack of access to rice land might be related to earlier wealth and the husbands' non-agricultural occupations, they reflect the general situation where shortage in rice land and the nature of the varieties of land and crops are concerned.

Reports indicate that each *douzhong* (about 0.16 acres) of land produced 1,000 catties of sweet potato per cycle and there was very little difference between good and poor land in this respect. Sweet potato can be grown on most paddy fields between rice cycles. The high productivity may mean it was possible to produce enough sweet potatoes as a catch crop on rice land. But it might be difficult to store sweet potato produced in one season for the rest of the year. Moreover, as many families had no access to rice fields at all, they grew sweet potato on land that was not fertile enough for rice. Two to three cycles of sweet potato could be grown on such land annually. Each *douzhong* can produce close to 3,000 catties annually, which might be enough to replace rice for close to three people.[65]

Sweet potato was considered inferior food, although the perception was not elaborated upon in Chinese medical terms or otherwise. It was grown mainly for the farming family's own consumption. According to an informant's anecdote about her father who was a merchant in Canton, shop employees in the city or the rural households of landlords did not eat the tuber. From Ha Tsuen, Rubie Watson[66] provides corroboration when she reports, "[S]weet potatoes were one of the few crops that were not marketed." A source on the Guangdong Province indicates that some quantity of the crop was actually traded even in the early decades of the twentieth century. But it also suggests that it was not profitable to sell.[67]

If sweet potato was considered inferior food, it was women, especially married women, who ate more of the crop than rice. The necessity to eat a lot of sweet potato when they preferred rice added to their unhappiness. In most families in Sheung Shui and the villages from which their brides had come, both men and women ate sweet potato, but my informants made it clear that men and to a lesser extent unmarried women were allowed to indulge in eating less sweet potato and more rice. Married women ate the largest share of the inferior food. In Ho Sheung Heung, a grandmother recalled that she ate more sweet potatoes in order that her sons could have more rice to eat. But many informants at Sheung Shui told me a daughter-in-law did not have much choice than to eat more of the tuber and less rice. Moreover, my impression from informant accounts is that they were solely responsible for all the work in sweet potato fields except plowing. Rubie Watson[68] had very similar findings from Ha Tsuen.

In British government land records, dry fields, on which sweet potato could be grown, are classified as third-class land. The latter also covers threshing floor, garden, orchard, and wasteland, but those together represent a small percentage.[69] Also grown on dry fields were some cash crops, especially groundnuts and sugarcane. A government source from 1940 cited above reports that groundnuts accounted for 4.4% of agricultural land in Hong Kong and sugarcane took up another 4.2%.[70] Sweet potato accounted for 17.4%, about twice of what was used to grow the two cash crops taken together. There was probably not much demand for groundnuts in Sheung Shui despite the fact that there was a factory in the nearby market that used it to make edible oil.[71] Most rural families seem to have produced groundnuts mainly for their own consumption, e.g. as an ingredient for pastries and other snacks. Sugarcane was probably more important during an earlier time. But Sheung Shui itself was not involved in growing sugarcane. The crop was concentrated in some other areas of the New Territories.[72]

The lower importance of cash crops like sugarcane and groundnuts implies less demand for third-class land and more of such land left in peasant families, including those who had lost their rice fields to landlord-merchants. In fact, the difference between irrigated rice land and dry fields correlated with the difference between descent group ownership and individual family ownership. Land held by trusts established to generate income included a much higher percentage of paddy fields because the latter produced the grain widely traded at much higher prices. Baker's[73] analysis of land holding in his sample survey areas in the vicinity of Sheung Shui suggests more than the low commercial value of dry fields and the crops produced in them. He also finds 40% of individual holdings to be "third-class land." In comparison, only 28% of trust holdings are of the same grade. Similarly, J. Watson's account of San Tin gives an even stronger impression that irrigated rice land was tied to the lineage and dry land fit for growing sweet potato was associated with individual families.

The low value of sweet potato and the land on which it was grown reinforced the crop's unique position as feed material and subsistence crop in a highly commercialized economy. It seems scholarly preoccupation with lineage and rice land has led to neglect of these aspects of local economy that were less dependent on the lineage.[74]

In Sheung Shui, third-class landownership reflected in the Block Crown Lease was lower than what might be expected from oral accounts. Among house owners in the bottom 80% in terms of first-class land ownership, only slightly more than half owned 0.17 acres or more of third-class land. There is documentary evidence that third-class land was under-reported in the Block Crown Lease to avoid liability to Crown Rent, which not all were willing to shoulder when the land could not produce crops of high commercial value.[75] Families might have been able to continue *de facto* ownership of such land until they were sold as Crown land by the government.

There were other sources of income in cash or in kind during the first half of the twentieth century. One informant was in a "teaming" relationship with a wealthier family and worked occasionally as a wage laborer for truck gardens and a nearby brick factory even before her husband found a "real" job (instead of helping at the gambling den and taking home very little money). Others had similar experiences. One of them recalled that she had to work for the principal partner in a teaming arrangement not only in rice farming but also in growing peanuts, sweet potato, and fruits and in cutting firewood. Therefore, married women not only shouldered heavy workload owing to rearing pigs in addition to growing sweet potato, and even those who farmed no rice fields were often in arrangements under which they labored for a wealthier family involved in paddy farming.

There were occasional wage labor opportunities for women in pre-war British New Territories. Those intensified somewhat during the few years between World War II as the government responded to the influx of refugees from nearby parts of China. Some informants recall friendships and experiences in labor in the nearby areas. But the economic opportunities were not regular enough to foster women's independence from their families.

Work, Consumption, and Power

The importance of women's contributions in the rural economy of South China is a familiar point. In the literature this has been most visibly associated with silk production and its apparent link to varieties of "marriage resistance," a form of spinsterhood sanctioned by ritual, and "delayed transfer marriage," in which the bride lived apart from her husband during much of the marriage. There has been a tendency to link such apparent manifestations of "women power" to work. But Helen Siu's study[76] compellingly argued against such explanations, showing instead how delayed transfer marriage was linked to regional culture and tight networks of kinship involving both men and women. "Women power" in the later form of spinsterhood might be partly attributed to economic independence associated with work in the silk district. To what extent was women's family-based labor in the lineages of New Territories empowering?[77]

All the hard work and sacrifices did not give young married women in New Territories lineages more power. Quite the contrary, parents-in-law often pressured them to work harder and harder.[78]

The experience of a Sheung Shui daughter born in the later 1910s was not atypical. She recalled the situation after she married at the age of eighteen. She had to get up at five each morning. After combing her hair, she swept the floor, boiled water to prepare tea, and made offerings to the gods and ancestors. Then she fetched about a dozen buckets of water to her in-laws' house and her own house. When these chores were done she went to work in the fields. Upon her return she husked rice and prepared the meal. The family raised pigs for sale. In the evening she had to collect "pig vegetables" such as sweet potato vines and use them to make pig feed. It was often well after midnight when she finished the day's work. Her husband, like a few other men of his generation, left home to work as a seaman, in this case, soon after marriage. This meant even heavier workload, among other disadvantages for the woman. Both her mother-in-law and father-in-law treated her harshly, most probably in order to push her for more labor. She recalled that although there were many chores to finish before she could leave for the fields, she was scolded for not going out earlier. When she returned from working outside, she was scolded for coming home early. Actually she did not return to rest. A lot of work awaited her. When on a different day she returned at a later hour, she was scolded again, this time for delaying preparation of the meal. My informants in Sheung Shui had very similar experiences. They were luckier than some others in their community who were beaten by their in-laws.[79] Many a mother-in-law was said to have acted harsh in the beginning of the relationship in order to have more control on a new daughter-in-law. Harsh treatment actually continued for a long time partly for the same reason.

Patterns of married women's work and consumption are reinforced by gender socialization. Village women were trained to be frugal and hardworking since their early years and among many the habits continue to this day.

One of my regular informants drew my attention to a communal building in her hamlet, pointing out that men played mahjong in air-conditioned rooms inside while women played their card games outside even on hot and humid days. She mentioned this as an instance of sexual inequality. The contrast between male and female users of the communal building does reflect a sharp gender difference slightly clouded by generational difference. Nowadays, men and younger women often play mahjong games outside of homes. Many village shops were established and survived on the money people spent on mahjong tables. Tea ("Western tea" with milk and sugar), coffee, and sandwiches could be ordered there. The stakes are relatively high and deductions from money won by players pays for the electricity consumed by air conditioners. The women's card game, in contrast, is played with very small stakes, typically up to a few Hong Kong dollars, i.e. fractions of US $1, per player. Also, it usually takes place at the home of one of the players. Part of the deductions may be used to pay for a new set of cards. It is certainly not enough to cover electricity for air-conditioning. Sometimes the players have snacks during the game, but those are homemade rather than bought from the market.

It was not because they have less disposable income that older women do not play mahjong or card games at the shops. Many of them receive rent from houses owned by their sons who have emigrated (typically to Europe). These women made it clear that the rent receipts, often amounting to between US$500 and US$1,000, are intended for their own use. But they practice a level of frugality their circumstances do not call for. Some of them do eat outside in the morning but they always go to the cheapest places, and order the lowest-priced items. It is common that sons and daughter who come back from abroad to visit urge them to eat more and better food, but such prompting seems to have very little effect.[80]

The long-standing gender patterning of consumption behavior is clearly evident in informant accounts of the use of tobacco. I was told that in the old days tobacco was bought in big packs each costing "twenty cents," which, a male informant assured me, was inexpensive by the standard of those days. He was probably referring to the period before World War II, when the cost would be close to the daily wage of an agricultural laborer hired on annual basis. The relatively low cost made it possible for many males to start smoking at the age of twelve when they went to school. It was common for both men and women to smoke. However, women did not start until they were quite old. Although many of them apparently smoked for no particular reason, women's use of tobacco had to be justified as a remedy for "wetness" (one of the most common medical conditions defined in Chinese medicine) and the latter was considered a problem that came with old age. Informants said that if a woman started smoking before she was "old enough," she would be told that she had not reached the age yet.

The foregoing does not mean that the expectations on women's work and consumption were not at least sometimes resented and challenged. It was probably not uncommon for young married women to voice their discontent. The Sheung Shui daughter mentioned above recalled that she protested aloud in her parents-in-law's presence a few years after her marriage. One occasion was when her in-laws asked her to learn to plow, which was usually men's work. She refused and retorted that the more work she learned to do the more she would be given to do. On another occasion she protested that in every five cents the family made, she contributed three cents' worth of work, but despite her years of hard work, her in-laws did not buy her anything. I asked whether her protest brought any changes. She replied that all the neighbors were aware of the situation even before she spoke out. So it seems that the protests had no clear impact partly because such treatment of young married women was commonplace and considered internal matter of the family.

In addition to gender expectations, kinship ideas also reinforced the pattern of work and consumption. The difference between expectations for daughters and daughters-in-law are evident in my informants' nostalgic accounts of their days as daughters. They think that they had a lot of freedom until they married. As they put it, they could "go sideways or go forward" (*hengxing dianzou*, *dian* being the opposite of *heng* "sideways," "horizontal" or "across" in Cantonese). They were allowed to be at least occasionally picky about food and choose to eat rice alone without mixing with sweet potato. Moreover, girls had lighter workloads than their married sisters. Peasant girls participated in household chores and farm work. But they had fewer responsibilities than women who married into their village. That was why they could sometimes helped a "sister-in-law" husk rice and do other chores so that she would have the time to teach them bridal songs, many of which describe married life as miserable.

Many informants remembered the time they spent at a "girls' house," which was usually the home of a widow who also supervised the girls who stayed the nights with her, for several years before marriage. Life at a girls' house was remembered as happy and carefree. Although the practice of "sworn sisterhood" was uncommon in this area, girls who shared a house were close to one another and those who shared a bed tended to be good friends. The young women of the house played card games, prepared snacks like peanut candy, and made their own clothes. They went to the house not only in the evening but also in other times when they were free. For example, it was remembered that they commonly gathered in the "girls' house" on rainy days to have fun.

When I asked my informants (in their seventies and eighties during my visits in the mid-1990s) why a mother-in-law, having had experience of being bullied as young daughter-in-law herself, would not treat their daughters-in-law nicer. A typical answer is that being a mother-in-law and being a daughter-in-law are like two stages in transmigration, so the mother-in-law would think that in time the younger woman will be in her position. Implicitly there seems to be a similar view that daughter years and daughter-in-law years were two separate stages each with a different set of expectations.

But daughter and daughter-in-law were not just two stages in a lifecycle because being a daughter was not just a memory of the years before marriage. A married woman remained a daughter to her natal family and the relationship was important to her.[81] Like the Sheung Shui daughter whose story is retold above, a woman in the community remembered that her husband was told by his mother not to give her any spending money. Another woman in Sheung Shui also told me she did all the work and did not receive from her mother-in-law any spending money. She added that she got that from her natal family, probably when she returned to visit from time to time, and she considers her case typical.

Although informants like to contrast support from the natal family against the harsh treatment by the in-laws, the two seem to have reinforced one another. Elsewhere I have described[82] cultural conceptions among women of the Sheung Shui area linking procreation and body to feelings, and argued the importance of bond of kinship for married women. Certainly such cultural conceptions might help justify harsh treatment of young married women as daughter-in-laws as well as a caring relationship based on biological bonds. While conflicts between mother-in-law and daughter-in-law in the area appear similar to Wolf's account of women and family in Taiwan, the tensions seem attributable not to patrilineal descent versus "uterine family" but to a more nuanced kinship system and weaknesses in the "lineage" economy.

Women's "Kin Work" and Economic Links outside the Lineage

If lineage land was not enough for its peasant members, did they pursue opportunities outside the descent group? If so, did women's natal ties, extending beyond the confines of their husbands' lineages, contribute to cooperation between families or individuals who were related through them?

Rubie Watson observes that women in peasant families in Ha Tsuen took an active role in affinal relationships and their male counterparts did not. It is commonly reported in the New Territories that boys stopped going with their mothers to visit relatives by the time they became adolescents and some adult men tend to shy away from banquets hosted by such relatives, in some cases even those by their married sisters. However, in these activities women were actively participating partly on behalf of their husbands (e.g. interacting with husband's married sister) or as parents and brothers' as grandparents and maternal uncles of their children. The phenomenon appears to be similar to those Micaela di Leonardo found in contemporary United States, as well as Mexico, Japan, and Australia. She observes, "the very existence of kin contact and holiday celebration depended on the presence of an adult woman in the household." di Leonardo argues that there is a need to transcend dichotomous explanations that attribute such gender roles as either yet another way in which women were exploited or manifestation of women's altruism and mutual support. Using the term "kin work" to analyze women's role in maintaining and creating cross-household kin ties, she proposes that such a role is "women's labor from which men and children benefit," and at the same time "undertaken in order to create obligations in men and children and to gain power over one another." In this chapter, "kin work" helps also to highlight the economic importance of such ties where lineages did not provide its male members with secure resources as alleged by scholars reviewed above.

Watson's analysis of her Ha Tsuen material may be seen as a dichotomous approach similar to those di Leonardo tries to overcome. Watson argues that before cultural changes in the post-War decades, peasant men in dominant lineages were not involved in affinal relationships, and women took an active role in those relationships for a "women's community" rather than kinship involving both men and women. She states that only men in the merchant and landlord class used affinal relationships for economic and political purposes.[83] To what extent does the difference between the models offered by di Leonardo and Watson reflect differences in reality? Did a peasant man in the New Territories and more generally in South China benefit from his womenfolk's kin work and became in their debt for it? Did women take initiative in such interactions and if so why?

Obviously, peasant families had fewer economic, social, and political resources to share with relatives than their landlord-merchant counterparts did. But did they share other resources? In a study based on interviews with refugees from Guangdong province Martin Whyte[84] finds that in the past affinal ties provided a crucial framework for sharing labor during busy seasons:

> Households [in villages] formed on the basis of patrilocal residence often grew similar crops on much the same schedule, and they had to reach outside of the village to get extra labor during peak agricultural seasons. Affinal kin, living in different villages often a good distance away, and therefore growing their crops on a slightly different schedule, formed a primary source of such peak-season labor.[85]

I have come across similar cases in villages near Sheung Shui. Two male informants recalled helping their married sisters during the busy agricultural seasons and explained to me that it was common practice. A Ho Sheung Heung man remembered very well the locations of the pieces of land belonging to his married sister's husband and sons at Fan Ling because he helped work the fields at various times. He also recalled helping another married sister at San Tin a few times in the 1930s. A Tsung Pak Long villager remembered helping his married sister, also at San Tin, sometime before he married around 1946. Ho Sheung Heung and especially Tsung Pak Long may not count as "dominant lineages." But these cases involved Fan Ling and San Tin, both of which were strong lineages.

The fact that I did not come across such cases in Sheung Shui itself may be attributed to the facts that many marriages there were with families across the border, and that the Sino-Japanese War and the Chinese Civil War made the sharing of labor more difficult. For the same reasons, other uses of affinal ties and women's natal ties was very visible in Sheung Shui. The second Sino-Japanese War began in 1937 and did not directly involve Hong Kong until a few years later, when the conflict became merged with the Second World War. Before then, when the Japanese occupied parts of South China, including villages in the mainland side of the border, many villagers on the Chinese side crossed the border to live temporarily in Hong Kong villages where they had relatives. These immigrants included many married Liu daughters who returned with their husbands, children, and in-laws. When Japanese troops eventually entered Hong Kong and occupied the territory, such immigrants from mainland China left for their homes across the border. But many came again around 1949 after the communist took over mainland China. That was why Baker[86] observes that residents of Sheung Shui since the early postwar period include, "not unnaturally," some Liu daughters' families by marriage. Sometimes more distant kinship ties through women were involved. One informant's husband moved to Sheung Shui where a Liu wife was an "elder sister" from his neighborhood in a village across the border. Some villagers addressed his wife using the term for "father's mother's brother," after his relatives in the village.

Affines also helped each other out in other circumstances than harvest season and war. At Ho Sheung Heung, a woman who married in the early 1930s remembered that her husband's family could afford to entertain local villagers for days (it was an obligation to do so) because his sister, married to a wealthy Sheung Shui man, brought plenty of food. In Sheung Shui itself, a promising young man could pursue his education thanks to financial help from a sister's husband. In both cases, the beneficiaries were among the poorest in their communities.

When a peasant family had more than their labor to share with relatives as a result of economic change, there was no sign of hesitation to honor and use ties outside of the lineage. For example, they had shared employment opportunities since those became more available.

Trucking and seafaring represented new opportunities of outside employment during the first few decades of the twentieth century for Sheung Shui and Ho Sheung Heung men. Emigration overseas was important in many communities in South China since the late nineteenth century.[87] There is no direct indication of what percentage of Sheung Shui men were involved in seafaring jobs and emigration, but these kinds of employment must have been of considerable importance.

Relationships through men and women allowed such new employment opportunities to be shared. One man interviewed by the Oral History Project was hired as a sailor through the agency.[88] However, in the same period, some other Sheung Shui men obtained the same kind of job through a Ho Sheung Heung villager who was a senior seaman, probably the head of the Chinese crew on one ship. In the latter village, there were a few seamen,[89] and the wife of one of them recalled the senior seaman's wife was from Sheung Shui, and that was why he introduced a number of Sheung Shui men who were relatives through his wife to seafaring jobs before he helped some Ho Sheung Heung villagers described as "his own people" in a similar way.

Trucking provided employment opportunities for a small number of Sheung Shui men before the war. Palmer[90] mentions that several Lius "became specialists in the road-hauling business," and that two lineage members operated the largest trucking business of the area in the 1920s. There were at least two other trucking businesses run by members of the community. One owner of such firms could be identified to be from a wealthy family.[91] But there are indications that the drivers were from poorer families. According to the widow of a driver who was in the trade in the 1930s, he had to find work when he was fourteen to fifteen years old because the family was poor, probably starting as an apprentice who helped with loading and unloading. A younger driver who began as such an apprentice in the late 1940s for a firm owned by another member of the lineage. He noted that the employer did not give jobs to the Lius only. Among the employees were his "relatives," including a sister's son.

Mass immigration and inflow of capital and manufacturing know-how into the colony during the late 1940s and late 1950s brought major changes to the colony with influence on Sheung Shui amplified because of its proximity to the town that grew out of the nearby market formerly controlled by the lineage. Employment opportunities in the market town and further afield were augmented by the government enhancement of public services in response to a huge population growth.[92] More important was the rise of the Chinese restaurant trade in Western Europe, which offered additional employment opportunities that were often shared by affines. In the late 1950s, a Liu from a family that owned no rice fields emigrated to Europe to work in a Chinese restaurant through arrangements made by a sister's husband, a villager of Chau Tau. In Ho Sheung Heung I knew of a few similar cases and it is said that during those times it was more common to get help from relatives than someone in one's own village. In the cases I know of, none of the families involved were landlord-merchants.[93] In many cases, a woman asked her husband or son (who tended to be based overseas at the time) to help one of her brothers or their sons.

Emigrated men often left more agricultural work to the wives until farming was abandoned in the 1960s. In the case of one informant, the departure of her husband in the late 1950s almost coincided with the arrival of her brother and sister from their natal village in mainland China. She could cope with the agricultural work (which had increased in part because the family could rent more paddy land as some men who had left for outside employment gave up their leases) because her siblings helped. Although the particulars of the circumstances were unique to that period, my informants assured me sharing between two families initiated by married women was not a new development among ordinary villagers.

It is clear that the women at least sometimes took the initiative to ask their husbands or brothers to help their families by marriage. Their crucial roles in these economically important affinal and matrilateral interactions are sometimes obscured in informant accounts by a tendency to credit the male relative who had more direct access to the resource.

Conclusion

Although theorists of the Chinese lineages have emphasized the importance of rice agriculture, and one influential case suggests that members of dominant descent groups enjoyed sufficient access to paddy fields, women's oral accounts of economic life in rural Hong Kong suggests heavy reliance on growing sweet potato and raising pigs.[94] In South China rice coexisted with sweet potatoes, and the two crops had very different degrees of commercialization and gender associations. Analysis of landownership, tenure, and productivity numbers suggests that the locality in question is not exempted from the serious rice land insufficiency problem historians find elsewhere in China during the same period. Therefore, the claim of lineages' ability to provide economic security and perpetuate social encapsulation for its peasant men is clearly problematic. Recognizing this helps to bring into focus women's work in producing hogs for the market, their consumption of a crop of very little market value, and their maintenance and proactive use of non-patrilineal kinship ties as important factors in the local economy.

Peasant women's relationship to commercialization was one of intensified exploitation reinforced by socialization, which discouraged them from spending money and consuming market products. The pattern of women's work and women's food was probably also reinforced by conceptions that daughters and daughters-in-law were very different kinds of kin. Instead of viewing the antagonism between daughter-in-law and mother-in-law as a consequence of women's strategy in a kinship system that can be equated to descent,[95] one may see the tension as part of an economic system in which young married woman were subject to intensive control in both production and consumption.

The highly commercialized economy in the New Territories of Hong Kong and in South China in general contrasts with the exchange of hogs based on ties through married women among the Tombema of Papua New Guinea studied by Feil.[96] But the latter's criticism of dichotomous approaches to kinship cited above applies here. In the New Territories and South China ties outside of the husbands' lineages were important not just to women themselves. It provided a framework for pooling labor, providing temporary shelter during war and other disturbances, and sharing employment opportunities. Therefore, in the sense of economic importance of such kinship ties and women's participation partly on behalf of others and partly for themselves, women's roles in kinship could be considered "work" as di Leonardo has argued.

The analysis of rural economics and its gender dimensions presented here call into question an exaggeration of the influences of the lineage which has shaped the analysis of Chinese society and culture in general and women's predicament and voices in particular. While the Chinese lineage is no longer a major focus of research as it used to be, new foci such as gender might perpetuate and even amplify problems in the lineage paradigm by interpreting phenomena such as those presented above simply as evidences of change or resistance.[97]

II

Agency in Emigrant, Colonial, and Mercantile Societies

In the previous section, the chapters outline an emergent Confucian moral order during agentive historical moments of state-making in the late imperial period, the upward mobility of local populations, and an increasingly commercialized regional economy. In the process, women experienced ambiguous positioning. For merchant families, gentility signified upward mobility along a rather orthodox path shaped by literati pretensions. As in Jiangnan, education made daughters marriageable. They became respectable wives and mothers in the inner chambers and were competent household managers. Although culturally binding in the construction of gender expectations and in the cultivation of social capital, mercantile South China was also a fluid environment due to its connection with multiethnic trading empires and their mixed religious traditions and political-legal sensibilities.

Chi-cheung Choi focuses on women's roles in Chaozhou, a region in eastern Guangdong known for its long history of overseas emigration. In the absence of male members of households, women took over many managerial tasks, working to make ends meet for the family, functioning as buyers and sellers of property, acting as guarantors and witnesses in business transactions. However, Choi argues that culturally, they continued to be subordinated to Confucian morality and largely confined at home. Stepping out was realized only after Chaozhou city became a treaty port, with foreign business and legal institutions providing protection and recognition for a new generation of women entrepreneurs.

Colonial encounters in Hong Kong and Macao added another layer of complexity. The following two chapters highlight the cultural dynamics generated for and by women in the Hong Kong-Macao region where colonialism, trading empires, and multiethnic unions intersected. The interstitial spaces provided for women's mobility were unusual. Carl Smith traces the "careers" of some Dan fisherwomen who cohabited with foreign traders and officers and were left with property in Macao and Hong Kong. Although situated at the margins of traditional Chinese and colonial societies marked by sharp racial and social lines, these "protected women" were able to maneuver between racial politics and overlapping legal and administrative institutions. They established themselves as shrewd entrepreneurs in real estate, the opium trade, piracy, and other adventures.

The characters in Carl Smith's chapter remained at the margins of society, but history tells us that many offspring of interracial unions became successful professionals for the trading empires where cross-cultural finesse was an asset. As unusual cultural brokers crossing racial, social, and gendered boundaries set by Confucian and Victorian moralities, members of Eurasian families, women and men were able to negotiate a visible presence in mainstream Hong Kong society in the nineteenth and early twentieth centuries. The life and work of Lady Clara Hotung, wife of Sir Robert Hotung, as narrated by Josephine Lai-kuen Wong, is a case in point.

5 Stepping out? Women in the Chaoshan Emigrant Communities, 1850–1950[*]

Chi-cheung Choi

Introduction

Although Chinese women have been viewed throughout history as exploited and oppressed with little ability to control their fates, for the Chinese women themselves, this was not always true. Studies have revealed, especially during the late imperial period that women were powerful, independent, and content with their status within society.[1] In different parts of China, they are described as domestic financial managers as well as supporters of the family budget.[2] Myron Cohen, for example, has distinguished the differences between the family head and manager. The former is usually a male member of the most senior generation while the latter, an able female.[3] Chinese fiction and nonfiction, such as *Hong Lao Meng* (Dream of the Red Chamber) or the autobiography of Zeng Zifan, conformed to this observation.[4] Genealogical records in the Pearl River Delta (usually compiled by male members of the lineage), for example the He of Xi Chao, noted that the daughter, who was married out yet still took care of the family budget while the father and brothers conducted business in Macau.[5] In the lower strata of the Chinese society, it was not uncommon to find women wage earners

[*] An earlier version of this chapter was presented at the conference on "Entering the Chinese City" organized by the Institute of History and Philosophy, Academia Sinica, December 13–15, 2007. Research of this paper was supported by the Hong Kong Research Grant Council (project number HKUST512/94H) and the CUHK Direct Allocation Grant (project code 2010334).

and supporters of the family. The Hakka women with their unbound feet, were observed by many Western travelers and missionaries, for their major role as manual workers in the field, construction sites, and in the mountains collecting wood.[6] In the cities and towns, since the late nineteenth century, women, especially those from Hunan, were recruited as factory workers in Shanghai and many in the Pearl River Delta as well as the Yangzi Delta, were involved in the silk industry.[7]

However, until 1949, the Chinese society was, and still is largely men's domain. In the state level, women were forbidden to participate in imperial examinations, hence, were deprived of their chance to enter the bureaucratic hierarchy.[8] In the local society, women were denied of holding a lineage position as well as position in business institutions such as the Chamber of Commerce. In the business arena, merchants' status and influence were institutionalized in 1904 when the State founded a Bureau of Commerce to balance the existing six bureaus of Personnel, Household, Diplomatic, Military, Legal, and Public Work. Commercial Law was drawn to encourage the establishment of various Chambers of Commerce to promote business in various cities. Chinese women, however, found no position in these new institutional arrangements. The business world, like lineage, remained largely, until very recently, a man's world.

It took a long time for women to step out from the family and enter the public area of business. For instance, in 1988, about 130 years after its establishment and thirteen years after its registration in the Hong Kong Government's Company registrar as a limited liability company, the Kin Tye *Lung* company, the oldest existing Chinese *Nanbei hang* ("import-export company") in Hong Kong, amended its company articles to allow shares of the company to be transferred by a member not only to male subjects (such as son, grandson, father, brother of such person), but also to any female subject including daughter, granddaughter, mother, or sister.[9] In 1992, the first time in the company's 140 years' history, female members were registered officially as shareholding members of the company.[10] Female members of Kin Tye *Lung* began to play more dominant roles in the running of the company.[11]

This chapter will use Chaozhou as an example to argue firstly, that economic determination cannot explain why women in mainland China, though given chance and capital, could not enter the public sphere of the business world, and secondly, that in order to enter the business world, it was dependent on the degree of institutional protection a woman, just as men, received, rather than gender per se. Given the special social conditions in the rural as well as city areas of Chaozhou since the mid-nineteenth century, this paper intends to analyze the opportunities that might have allowed women to step out from the family and discuss how such opportunities were subordinate to the male social ethics. It was not until non-Chinese institutional support was received, were the women able to step out.

Emigrant Community and Women in the Village: The Chaoshan District

Chen Ta defined emigrant community as a community where "the majority of the inhabitants depend for their living in part on remittances that come from members of the family who are abroad."[12] Chaoshan district has a long history of emigration; many male members emigrated to Southeast Asia. In 1949, of the 5.6 million immigrant Chinese in Southeast Asia (who originated from Guangdong province) about 40% came from Chaoshan district (see Table 5.1). In the 1930s, remittance received from Chaozhou emigrants made up 20% or more of the total national revenue (see Table 5.2). These figures indicate that in the rural Chaoshan communities where there were more women than men there was an abundance of money.

Table 5.1 Number of Chinese in Southeast Asia in 1949

	Chaozhou	Hakka	Cantonese	Hainanese
Siam	1,167,000	333,000	146,000	250,000
Malaysia	230,000	43,000	490,000	111,000
Singapore	184,000	47,000	172,000	60,000
Indonesia	168,000	315,000	315,000	63,000
Vietnam	374,000	85,000	378,500	40,000
Others	24,500	122,000	129,005	20,600
Total*	2,148,500	945,000	1,631,000	544,500

* number on this row adjusted.

Sources: Data from Pan Xingnong, *Malaiya Chaoqiao tongjian* (Gazetteer of the Chaozhou Chinese in Malaya) (Singapore: Nandao Chuban She, 1950), 20; Xia Chenghua, *Jindai Guangdong sheng qiaohui yanjiu (1862–1949)* (Study of Remittance of Guangdong Province in the modern period [1862–1949]): Using Guangzhou, Chaozhou, Meizhou and Qiongzhou districts as examples) (Singapore: Xinjiapo Nanyang Xuehui, 1992), 27.

Table 5.2   1933 Remittance (million dollar)

	Siam	Singapore	Vietnam	Others	Total	% of national share
1930	40	30	10	20	100	
1931	35	28	10	17	90	22
1932	32	25	6	12	75	21.9
1933	27	25	6	12	70	20.5
1934	20	18	4	8	50	20.2

Source: Data from Wu Chengxi, "Shantou di huaqiao huikuan" (Overseas Chinese Remittance in Shantou), *Huaqio Banyuekan*, vol. 99–100 (Nanjing 1937): 13–14.

Xiao Guanying, head of the municipal department of the Shantou city in the 1920s, noted in his 1925 book that "(because many men left home) all major or minor household matters, including cultivation, household chores, other manual work and social activities, all relied on women. "[13] Chen Ta, based on his survey in the early 1930s asserted that in such families, ". . . usually it is the wife of the (family) head who looks after the affairs at home while he is away (not an aged father or mother); only occasionally, when the wife is not sufficiently experienced, may another older woman act as head of the household and take charge of all the matters that affect the immediate family circle. This may at times include important decisions having to do with business, education, marriage, religious observances, and other matters that require considerable judgment."[14] During the absence of male members, women stepped into the role vacated by their male members as decision makers, even in important transactions like the sale and purchase of lands.

Land and Land Deeds

Land is the foundation of a patrilineal society. Sale of land to any non-lineage buyer has the potential to harm the foundation of a lineage community. It is therefore interesting to investigate a woman's role in land transactions in a community where large numbers of the male population were absent. The following is an analysis of 230 land deeds owned by the Chens of Kin Tye *Lung*, a merchant family who came from Qianmei village of Raoping county, Chaozhou prefecture. All the transactions date from mid-nineteenth century to mid-twentieth century with around 78% executed after the fall of the imperial government in 1911.[15]

Besides names of the buyers and sellers, the 230 land deeds also recorded (i) the guarantors or mediators, (ii) the contract writers, and (iii) the witnesses. In general, a married-in wife can be recognized from term of address such as *mao mao shi* (madam XX) or *mao men mao shi* (madam X of family Y). Female figures can also be identified if she is addressed by female kinship terms, such as *zumu* (grandmother), *mu* (mother), *ci* (mother), *da po* (senior wife), *ma* (grandmother or mother), *qi* (wife), *xi* (daughter-in-law), or *nu* (daughter). Throughout the 230 land deeds, eighty-four (or 37%) recorded a total of 106 female members. Of the total 477 guarantors, only one was female. Similarly, of the 114 land deed writers, only one was female, the seller's daughter. Out of 106 females recorded in the land deeds, 104 were recorded as witnesses or sellers.

Witness

Thirty-five land deeds recorded a total of forty "witnesses." Most of these witnesses were female (twenty-nine female in twenty-seven deeds, or 73% female in 77% land deeds). As shown in Table 5.3, most of them were members more senior than the sellers (for example: grandmother, mother, or senior wife). This was likely due to the absence of senior male members in the family. In the absence of senior male members, women, be they the grandmother, mother, or wife, played an important role in land transactions. A mother held the right of intervention in dealing with her children's "inherited" property.[16] Land deed 10-2-2 shows that the extension of intervention is closely related to the nature of landownership: a certain Wu Zhenliang had two wives, a Liu and a Chen. Zhenliang went to Thailand and died there without leaving any fortune. Wife Chen, in order to repay the debts owed by Zhenliang, decided to sell the field her husband inherited from his father. Probably because Zhenliang's parents were both deceased, when Zhenliang's minor wife decided to sell the land, she had to consult the senior wife as well as her sister-in-law, both of whom had the right to intervene a transaction.[17]

Sellers

Seventy-two females appeared as sellers in sixty land deeds (26% of the total transactions). From Table 5.4, we see that one third (twenty) of these land deeds were signed under the name of *mao mao shi* ("madam X") or "wife of a certain male." About half (twenty-nine) of these land deeds were signed together with the son, husband, or grandson. Of the remaining eleven deeds, female sellers appeared as members of an extended family or lineage branch.

Table 5.3 Relation of female "witness" and the land seller

Witness's kinship term	No. of land deeds	Land seller						
		$mu+zi$	zi	qi	sun	Male	Female	$erxi$
Zumu	2	0	0	0	2	0	0	0
Mu	19	4	14	0	0	0	0	1
mu + mu	1	0	1	0	0	0	0	0
guzhang + dapo	1	0	0	1	0	0	0	0
ci + mu	1	0	1	0	0	0	0	0
Male (same surname)	6	3	0	1	0	2	0	0
Female (same surname)	1	0	0	0	0	1	0	0
Female (different surname)	1	0	0	0	0	1	0	0
nan	2	0	0	0	0	2	0	0
ma	1	0	0	0	0	0	1	0
Total	35	7	16	2	2	6	1	1

zumu=grandmother; mu=mother, guzhang=father sister husband, dapo=husband's major wife, ci=father major wife, nan=son, ma=grandmother, zi=son, qi=wife, sun=grandson, erxi=daughter-in-law

Source: Data from Choi Chi-cheung, *Business Documents and Land Deeds Collected by Dr. James Hayes: Kin Tye Lung Document, vol. 1, Land Deeds of the Chaoshan region* (Tokyo: The Institute of Oriental Culture, Tokyo University, 1995), 271, Table 10.

The land deeds recorded the nature of land ownership. These included "*chengzu*" ("inherited from ancestor"), *chengzu yingfeng huo zhifeng ji feng* ("own shared inherited from ancestor"), *cheng fu* ("inherited from father"), or *cheng fu* ("inherited from husband"). One hundred and twenty-two of the 230 land deeds mentioned that the lands were inherited from ancestors. Of the land deeds that involved a female as the seller, 60% (thirty-five) clearly stated that the land was either acquired through the effort of the ego and/or her husband (nineteen) or obtained from family division (sixteen). When a piece of land was sold using solely the name of a female (wife or *mao mao shi*), 75% of which stated clearly that the land was owned by the ego or her husband. On the contrary, when a female appeared as one of the members of the extended family or a lineage branch, less than half (46%) indicated vaguely that the land was inherited (*chengzu*).

Table 5.4 Nature of land ownership and kin relationship of the buyer and seller in land deeds which recorded female(s)

Kinship term	Kin relation				Nature of land ownership						
	L	S-N	S-DV	DS-DV	Zu	Zu-S	F	H	H-S	Own	Total
Grandmother and grandson	0	0	0	1	1	0	0	0	0	0	1
Mother and son	2	5	5	10	11	3	2	4	0	2	22
Mother and daughter-in-law	0	0	0	2	2	0	0	0	0	0	2
Mother, son and daughter-in-law	0	0	0	1	0	0	0	1	0	0	1
Mother, son and grandson	0	1	0	1	0	0	0	2	0	0	2
Husband and wife	0	0	0	1	1	0	0	0	0	0	1
Wife	2	0	0	3	2	3	0	0	0	0	5
Wife of a branch	0	0	3	0	0	3	0	0	0	0	3
Madam X	6	1	1	7	3	6	0	1	5	0	15
Madam	0	1	1	6	5	1	0	0	0	2	8
Total	10	8	10	32	25	16	2	8	5	4	60

L=same lineage, same village; S-N=same surname, neighboring village; S-DV=same surname, different village; DS-DV=different surname, different village.

Zu=inherited from an ancestor; Zu-S= land acquired as a share inherited from an ancestor; F=inherited from father; H=inherited from husband; H-S=land acquired as a share inherited from husband; Own=self landownership.

Source: Data from Choi Chi-cheung, *Business Documents and Land Deeds Collected by Dr. James Hayes: Kin Tye Lung Document, vol. 1, Land Deeds of the Chaoshan Region* (Tokyo: The Institute of Oriental Culture, Tokyo University, 1995), 271, Table 11.

When the nature of land ownership is clear, any unnecessary disputes with relatives outside the family can be avoided. In the rural community, landownership tied neatly with the right of settlement, which is the foundation of a male-oriented lineage. Therefore, control of landownership is a crucial factor for the maintenance of a patrilineal society.

The Chaozhou district, especially Raoping and Chenghai counties, witnessed a high rate of male emigration. According to a 1987 statistic, more than 70% of the population and 50% of registered households of Longdu district, Chenghai County, had members living overseas.[18] Ancestors of most of these households ventured to Southeast Asia after the second half of the nineteenth century. Chen Ta claimed that it was not only the beginning of the "dual head family" system, but also sparked the inevitable rise of female power.[19] In fact, in the three cases illustrated by Chen Ta, wives of absentee male members were described as family heads, regardless of the social status of the family or whether there were senior male members in the family. Statistics of land transactions further confirmed the pivotal role of women in emigrant communities. However, as shown in the land deeds, women's dominant role in the emigrant community was restricted to the sphere of the "family" (nuclear or extended). Her involvement in land transactions was very much decided by the nature of land ownership. When transaction was related to the lineage, the woman's role inevitably became secondary.[20] Only one out of 477 guarantors recorded in the land deeds was a woman. This indicated that when warranty was needed, women did not have the credential to guaranty a transaction that traditionally belonged to men.

Women as Wage Earners

In the rural Chaoshan region, since the mid-nineteenth century, many men were forced to leave home in search of employment in Southeast Asia. Some families, however, remained in poverty and had to rely on their female members to sustain the family. According to Chen Ta, girls and married women worked at home to make clothes, engaged in cross-stitching, and helped to make pottery and joss paper.[21] Products of these light industries were exported overseas via Shantou, the treaty port which opened in 1860. For example, cross-stitching, which was introduced by members of the American Baptist Mission at Shantou by the end of the Qing dynasty, had an annual return of more than one million yuan in the early 1920s. It was one of the four major profitable businesses in the Chaoshan district. Products were made and embroidered by more than 30,000 women in Chaozhou, Jieyang, Chaoyang, and Chenghai counties before export to overseas through the Shantou port.[22]

Joss paper making was another major handicraft through which many girls and married women in rural Chaoshan region earned subsidiary incomes. For example, in the Nanyang district of Chenghai county, 80% of the total 100,000 population engaged in the making of joss paper. Joss paper was exported to Shaodong, Hebei, Dongsan sheng, Henan, Shanxi, and Shaanxi, and through the southern route to Siam, Singapore, and Vietnam.[23]

In other words, besides working in the field, many women in the rural areas earned subsidiary incomes from light industries. The opening of Shantou as a treaty port in 1860, the profit from exporting textile products, the need for joss paper and other local products from fellow emigrant villagers provided job opportunities for women in the rural Chaoshan district. Yet, unlike their counterparts in the silk industry area in the Pearl River Delta, these women failed to establish themselves in the public domain. Chen Ta pointed out that his 1920s observation was similar to the statement quoted in the 1893 *Gazetteer of Chaozhou* that "Girls and women are chiefly engaged in embroidery, spinning and weaving. They are seldom seen on the streets or employed in outdoor labor on the farms. When they live near the mountains, women become foresters; when near the sea, they catch marine products to help earn a living"[24] Dyer Ball, a contemporary Western writer, also observed the difference between the Pearl River Delta and the Chaoshan region: ". . . to one accustomed in Canton and neighbourhood to the constant presence of women in the fields and streets and on the river and sea, busy with various kinds of manual labor, it is strange to note their entire absence, with but trifling exceptions, in the country around Swatow."[25]

Male overseas migration and the opening of Shantou as treaty port created an environment that helped promote women's social status and image in the public. However, these new social environments also encouraged local suspicion. The story of "Boar blocking the path" (*zhugong lanlu*) in Zhanglin, a major port for emigration before the establishment of Shantou, highlighted the male dominated rural community's anxiety against the rise of women. The story was about a widow whose son had to seek a living in Southeast Asia. The woman, after staying at home in poverty for some years, decided it was time to marry again. Three times, when she was on her way to meet the matchmaker, a big black boar blocked her path. Failing to pass the boar three times, the widow felt that it was fate that she should maintain her chastity. When the son returned home from Southeast Asia with his fortune, he realized that without the mysterious boar, he would have had to bear a life-long shame of having an unfaithful mother. In order to thank the boar, he donated money to make a statue of a boar in the local Tianhou temple. Instead of guarding the temple's entrance, the statue of the boar was erected symbolically facing, diagonally towards the holy goddess. Local people believe, in a community of absentee men, the Lord Boar (*Hai ye*) was responsible to guard the chastity of local women.[26] The eye-catching presentation of the boar facing the goddess is a social reminder for women to remain faithful. Women's public fate, hence, was based on the interpretation of men, disregarding her influence as family head and wage earner. Their public image was subjected to cultural sanction.

Women of Merchant Families: The Chens of the Kin Tye *Lung*-Wanglee Company

The Chaoshan region also produced many wealthy families that made their fortune from overseas. According to Suehiro Akira, the largest rice millers and six of the eight wealthiest Chinese merchant families in Bangkok, Siam, in the beginning of the twentieth century, came from this region.[27] Wanglee, an associate company of Kin Tye *Lung* in Hong Kong, and Koh Man Wah, associate company of Yuanfa hang in Hong Kong, were two of them. Founders of these two companies came from Qianmei village of Longdu district, Raoping county (under the jurisdiction of Chenghai since 1945), and the capital of Chenghai county respectively. Both of them founded their import-export business in Hong Kong in the early 1850s and expanded to Bangkok, Singapore, Cholon, and Shantou in the 1880s. Utilizing their network of associate companies, they extended their business from 1880s to 1930s, to rice milling, shipping, remittance, warehouse and real estate, insurance, and also invested in various stock companies such as HSBC.[28]

A result of drastic multidirectional business expansion is growth of the family internationally. Many offspring were born outside China, by wives whom they married while overseas. At the same time, in their hometown they purchased land, built enormous houses, reconstructed ancestral halls, and even built a "new village" for family members of their employees who belonged to the same lineage. In the case of the Chens of Kin Tye *Lung*-Wanglee family, their hometown provided them with their first wife and was final place of retirement for the first and second generation.[29] Since the beginning of the Republican period, sons born by overseas wives did not reside in the village. The houses served as domestic residences for their Chinese wives and concubines sent home from overseas,[30] and a temporary resting place for their coffins.[31] Until 1930s, male members born overseas were sent home to be educated until they were ready to help in the family business. In general, the enormous houses, one of which has ninety-nine rooms, were occupied mostly by women (wives, concubines, and daughters), young sons, adopted sons, and servants. The houses and land (853 acres of which were bought from 1900 to 1949) were managed by the Chinese wives, their adopted sons, and housekeepers who were remote relatives.[32] Women of the family were highly educated and included a poet and a herbalist. Though the herbalist provided free medical advice, it was said that she rarely ventured out of the confines of her own home. It was said that in the 1920s and 1930s, during the procession of deities in the beginning of the year, villagers had to carry the deities into the houses for the Kin Tye *Lung-*

Wanglee women to worship. Music and opera troupes were invited to perform inside the house compounds. In brief, the wealth provided by their husbands and sons overseas inevitably created a wall which separated the women from their fellow villagers. These women were kept at "home," guarded and respected. The "dual-head" family structure described by Chen Ta underwent transformation in the 1920s; before the 1920s, the home in China was the "major home" whereas after the 1920s, second-generation business-oriented male members began to regard their overseas home as the "major home." Where they used to go back to China upon retirement, or were buried in China in death, this was no longer the case. The male dominated hometown in China served to produce loyal employees and safeguard the chastity and loyalty of their young concubines after their deaths.

In brief, from the mid-nineteenth century to the 1930s emigration of their menfolk and increased business opportunities provided a social environment that allowed women to step out from their traditional domestic domains. In the rural Chaoshan region, on the lower social strata, women were major wage earners, if not also the sole breadwinner who worked hard to support their families and their absentee husbands. On the upper end women were able to enjoy extravagant lifestyles with the remittance received. In the absence of male members, women, be they poor or wealthy, controlled not only family finances but also took over as head of family in key decision-making. However, even though the particular social context provided females an opportunity to step beyond the family, they were culturally sanctioned by the male dominated lineage community, which emphasized female chastity and loyalty.

Women in the City

Shantou was an alluvial sandbank located at the southern exit of the Han River in the eastern part of the Guangdong Province. Until the late seventeenth century, it was recorded as a desolate place visited only occasionally by pirates and nearby fishermen.[33] In 1715, "Sha Shantou" was established as one of the coastal batteries guarding the region. While officially recognized maritime trade was conducted at the western exits of the Han River, illegal business trade increased gradually at the southern entrance of the Han river. In other words, since the early eighteenth century, more boats began to anchor at Shantou. Seeing opportunities, ". . . local people started to build mat-shed shops and tile-roofed houses to facilitate trade. A market was subsequently created."[34] Business transactions conducted at Shantou were not taxed and therefore, were regarded as illegal. In the beginning of the nineteenth century, a market was established. Tax was levied on shops. In addition, a sub-station of the Chaozhou Station, Guangdong Maritime Customs was established at Shantou to collect a transaction tax.[35] The government then recognized Shantou as a maritime port attached to the capital of Chaozhou prefecture. In 1858, under the Tientsin Treaty, the capital of Chaozhou prefecture was opened as a treaty port. However, when the British started to establish their consulate at Chaozhou City, they received strong resistance from the local people. Therefore, the port open to foreign countries was changed from Chaozhou City to Shantou. In 1860, the Chaozhou Maritime Customs was established at the Mayu Island near Shantou. This was then moved to the city area of Shantou in 1863. Shantou, a treaty port under the jurisdiction of the Tuopu si of Chenghai County, was limited to a very small area. Attempts to extend the city area by foreign traders in 1865 were unsuccessful.[36] In 1867, along with the escalating volume of trade, a sub-office of the Hui-Chao-Jia *prefecture* was set up at Shantou to handle foreign affairs.[37] Expansion of the territorial boundary of Shantou City probably started from this period. In 1921, Shantou became a Shi (city), and became independent of Chenghai County. After the city became independent, the land area of the city increased rapidly, ". . . from a few Chinese miles to 365 Chinese miles, and the maritime area increased to 327 Chinese miles.[38]

As a city surrounded by three conventional administrative districts, Chao'an, Chaoyang, and Jieyang, but being newly developed it was independent of influence from the three districts. Hence, Shantou was the best neutral place to develop a government to administer the region. It was also a city without a traditional indigenous power; therefore, various immigrant groups could compete with each other. Factions were founded among sub-dialect (different Chaozhou tones) and dialect (Chaozhou and Hakka) groups.[39]

Since the beginning of the twentieth century, the port replaced Chaozhou city as the region's political and administrative headquarters. Together with political importance, its administrative territory expanded dramatically in the 1920s and 1930s. However, until the 1920s, Western businessmen described Shantou as a port not favorable for modern commercial transactions; the city did not have modern financial or industrial institutions.[40] Its economy relied heavily on overseas and hinterland connections that facilitated the growth of small-scale business activities. Large-scale businesses had to rely on financial organizations in Hong Kong, Guangzhou, or Shanghai. Businessmen in extensive business activities usually had their headquarters in Hong Kong. In brief, while Shantou became important politically, it did not develop into a modern financial center.

Shantou was a commercial city. Its prosperity relied heavily on shipping, remittance, and monetary exchange, and import-export.[41] Embroidery works like Chaozhou Chousha (a kind of drawn work on silk products) was the only significant industry in the region. These businesses linked Shantou's fate with its hinterland and with Hong Kong and Southeast Asia. It was also these businesses that provided opportunities for women to step out from their families.

As an immigrant city, Shantou's female population was comparatively low. Compared with men, female education became popular only after 1928. Shantou had a gynecology training school exclusively for females, which trained many professional female gynecological doctors and nurses in the society.[42] However, in general, females received lower regular education (see Tables 5.5 and 5.6), which as a consequence, affected the type of work they engaged in.

Shipping, Import and Export, and Female Petty "Entrepreneurs"

Shipping can be understood in two categories, that is, the transportation of human beings and the transportation of goods. The number of ferries and junks that entered or left the Shantou port increased from 161 in the 1860s (or 59,236 tons) to 2,496 in the 1920s (or more than two million tons), and 4,010 in the 1930s (or 5,735,828 tons). Table 5.7 shows the sharp increase in volume of both goods and people carried.

With the arrival of the steamship, large numbers of Chaozhou natives could travel overseas and back. In the 1850s, Shantou replaced Xiamen as the major port for the transfer of coolies. Coolie trade agents ran hostels and coolie kennels. Coolies from Shantou's hinterland were recruited by brokers and transported to Shantou via steamships. There, they were kept in hostels until the day of departure. From 1852 to 1853, more than 3,450 coolies were sent abroad. In 1855, this number increased to 6,300. After Shantou became a treaty port, more Chinese from inland districts went overseas via this port. The Chaozhou merchants provided an efficient infrastructure assisting these new immigrants: from transporting them to assisting them in settling down in the host country. According to a 1935 statistic, about two million Chaozhou Chinese lived in Southeast Asia at that time (Table 5.1). This figure is 40% of the five million population of the Chaoshan region.[43]

Table 5.5   Local schools in Shantou city (1923)

	Secondary school			Business	Vocational	Total
	Private	Municipal	Edu. Bureau	Provincial	Private	
Number of schools	3	1	4	1	2	11
Boy			3		1	4
Girl		1	1		1	3
Co-ed	3			1		4
Teachers						212
Male	59	4	84	21	20	188
Female	3	6	12	0	3	24
Students						2094
Boy	445	0	970	180	108	1703
Girl	52	78	136	0	125	391

Note: This table does not include five missionary schools, two British, two American and one French.

Source: Data from Xiao Guanying, *Liu shi nian lai zhi Lingdong jilue* (A Memoir of Southeastern China of the Past Sixty Years) (Guangdong: Guangdong Renmin Chuban She, 1996 [reprint of 1925]), 132 (inserted).

Table 5.6   Number of male and female students in Shantou

	High	Junior	Primary High	Primary Junior	Kindergarten	Supplementary	Vocational
1928	Total population: 129,588						
Boy	184	940	1,228	3,424	196	1,072	324
Girl	34	282	383	1,543	166	140	124
B:G	0.19	0.3	0.31	0.45	0.85	0.13	0.38
1936	Total population: about 200,000						
Boy	506	1,612	2,071	6,860	714	929	1,496
Girl	176	551	818	3,128	482	228	1,899*
B:G	0.35	0.34	0.40	0.46	0.68	0.25	1.27

* Female Gynecology and Nurse Training Schools

Source: Data from Xie Xueying (comp.) *Chao Mei Xianxiang* (Conditions in the Chaozhou-Mei Xian Area) (Shantou: Shantou Shi Tongxun She, 1935), 135.

Table 5.7   Cargo volume number of passengers 1860–1930

Year	No. of ships	Tonnage	Customs (Total customs tael)	No. of immigrants	No. of emigrants	Total overseas settler
1860	161	59,236	6,176,293	–	–	
1870	414	204,968	9,455,850	–	22,282	
1880	866	627,886	21,275,667	28,013	38,005	9,992
1890	1,649	1,573,542	25,070,981	50,062	65,475	15,413
1900	2,127	2,185,554	40,030,734	71,850	93,640	21,790
1910	2,592	2,960,744	54,014,382	108,833	132,928	24,095
1920	2,496	2,921,531	65,497,958	68,525	109,251	40,726
1930	4,010	5,735,828	108,879,407	94,726	123,724	28,998

Sources: Data from Maritime Customs Decennial reports, 1860–1930.

The large number of Chaozhou natives living overseas naturally gave rise to an increase in demand for Chaozhou goods, as well as the need for remittance services.

Until the 1920s, emigration of females and children was not encouraged. To prevent involuntary or forced migration, the Shantou municipal government required all women and children who intended to travel to Southeast Asia to be interviewed before tickets could be issued.[44] According to Lee, female labor migration to Malaya was insignificant before 1920. However, "[t]he 1930s witnessed a large influx of Chinese women (in Malaya), but this was offset by high U-turn migration, presumably of Chinese men"[45] (see Tables 5.8 and 5.9).

Before Shantou was established as a treaty port, smuggling was the way of life for the people who lived in the region. Opium, which occupied about 75% of the revenue drawn from import until 1910, was replaced by the importation of cotton yarn, sugar, and canned food. In 1926, rice, sugar, cotton, and charcoal were main imports. Major exports included paper and peanut oil. Major imports from other parts of China included bean cake, cotton yarn, beans, and peanuts, while exports to other parts of China included paper, sugar, and clothes. As we can see from Table 5.10, the Shantou-Hong Kong-Southeast Asia trade occupied about 70% of the total trade return.

Besides producing export items like embroidery works and joss papers, the trading environment provided women in this region with at least two types of occupations. According to a Shantou correspondent, when the 1928

Table 5.8   Percentage of female immigrations in Malaya

	Chinese migration to Malaya (total arrivals)	Percentage female	Total departure
1860s		NA	
1870s		NA	
1880s	1,145,682	3	
1890s	1,520,995	5–6	
1900s	1,894,262	7	
1910s	1,689,582	7–8	
1920s	2,301,869	13	1,236,175
1930s	1,265,074	25	1,236,175

Sources: Data from Sharon M. Lee, "Female Immigrants and Labor in Colonial Malaya: 1860–1947," *International Migration Review*, vol. 23, no. 2 (Summer, 1989), Tables 2 and 3.[46]

Table 5.9   Migrants from the Chaoshan region

	Emigration				Immigration			
Year	Male	Female	Children	Total	Male	Female	Children	Total
1930	78,598	22,335	22,771	123,704	62,525	14,583	17,615	94,723
1931	50,978	14,656	14,568	80,202	52,726	17,516	11,720	81,962
1932	23,261	7,711	5,852	36,824	38,905	20,128	11,831	70,864
1933	26,903	9,014	8,941	44,858	31,999	10,368	17,355	59,722
1934	32,603	12,170	11,531	56,304	23,641	6,187	10,672	40,500

Source: Data from Xie Xueying (comp.), *Chao Mei Xianxiang* (Conditions in the Chaozhou-Mei Xian Area) (Shantou: Shantou Shi Tongxun She, 1935), 40.

Table 5.10   1926 trade return of Shantou port (Haiguan tael)

	Import	Export	Total	Percentage
Hong Kong	4,436,535	733,911	5,170,446	16.90
Siam	3,776,891	2,929,592	6,706,483	21.90
Straits Settlement	307,728	4,819,929	5,127,657	16.70
Vietnam	2,097,286	2,223,188	4,320,474	14.10
Sub-total	10,618,440	10,706,620	21,325,060	69.6
Other Countries	8,628,153	681,359	9,309,512	30.4
Total	19,246,593	11,387,979	30,634,572	100

Source: Data from "*Xin Shantou*" (New Swatow) (Shantou: Shantou Shi Shizhengting Bianji Gu, 1928), 10.

world economic crisis finally destabilized the light industries in Shantou, many women were forced to become porters. As observed by a contemporary reporter, ". . . whenever one goes to the Shantou maritime customs, one will always see thirty to fifty female porters waiting for their services . . . one can also find these female porters at the Swire pier carrying bean cakes into the warehouses . . . [each time] they could earn three to five cents or up to one yuan . . . there are increasingly more and more healthy women coming for this kind of job . . . every 3 or 5 days, they will go back to their village."[47] Exporting of local goods to Southeast Asia also attracted many women who transported dried seafood from other coastal areas to Shantou.[48] Some women even engaged in cross-border trading. According to the same reporter, at least 1,000 women smugglers (*shuike*) traded between Hong Kong and Shantou:

> . . . they travel to Hong Kong four times a month, using a capital of 30 to 50 yuan to buy goods like matches, sugar, dried mushroom, abalone, sharks fins, or jinseng. They will travel back to Shantou on Sunday because on this day more than 4 ships will arrive at the same port. They usually use their female charm or persuasive power to obtain sympathy from the customs officer. If caught, . . . they are usually more successful than male smugglers . . . [49]

In brief, the Shantou maritime trading environment facilitated the emergence of a group of female petty entrepreneurs who traded between Shantou and its hinterlands. These female itinerants, as noted by the 1935 reporter, either went home once every few days or three or four times a month. In the absence of male members, when jobs could not be found at home because of economic recession, the city provided new job opportunities for women of lower social status.[50]

Women, Maternal Kin, and Business: The Case of Yuanfa Hang

As mentioned above, since the beginning of the twentieth century, remittance was a major source of income for many households in the Chaoshan region. For families who are better off, like the Chens of Kin Tye *Lung* and the Gaos of Yuanfa *hang* remittance received by women was used not only to buy land and build magnificent houses, but also used to invest in business in the city. Some women held private accounts in companies owned by their husbands or paternal kin;[51] others invested in small firms through their brothers or fathers.[52]

Shantou did not have any large-scale companies before the Second World War. There was only one modern bank, the Bank of Taiwan, which handled foreign exchange. The Hong Kong and Shanghai Bank had only a small agent there.[53] Transactions in the Shantou City were usually small and are handled by local native banks (*quan zhuan*). According to Rao Zongyi, there were 3,441 firms with a total capital of 57,684,000 silver yuan or an average capital of 10,769 in Shantou in 1933. During this period, the largest firms in Shantou were exchange (*hui dui*), remittance (*qiao pi*), and import-export trading firms (*nanbei gang hang*). The average capital of these firms did not exceed 150,000 yuan (see Table 5.11).[54] Therefore, firms in Shantou were comparatively small. Their source of capital is a point of interest and the case of Yuanfa *hang* may offer some leads to their role in business in Shantou.

Table 5.11   Size of firms in 1933 Shantou

Type of firm	No. of firm	Total capital (yuan)	Average capital per firm
Exchange (banking)	58	14,500,000	250,000
Remittance	55	1,100,000	20,000
Import-export	70	7,000,000	100,000
Sub-total	183	22,600,000	123,497
Other firms	3,258	35,084,000	10,769
Total firms	3,441	57,684,000	16,763

Source: Data from Rao Zongyi, *Chaozhou Zhi Huibian* (Collection of Chaozhou Gazetteers) (Hong Kong: Longmen Shu Dian, 1965), 868–70.

Yuanfa *hang* began in the early 1850s as a trading company in Hong Kong founded by Gao Chuxiang (or Koh Mah Wah as he is known in Bangkok) of Chenghai county. From the 1850s until 1930s, the company expanded its businesses activities and established ". . . marketing networks and financial channels in the intra-Asian trade, mainly through the three major entrepots of Swatou [Shantou], Hong Kong and Singapore."[55] Yuanfa *hang*, one of the most prominent Chinese import and export trading companies in Hong Kong, imported rice and other products like spice and sugar from Southeast Asia and re-exported them to Chinese coastal cities like Shantou and Guangzhou (Canton). In return, it exported Chinese, especially Chaozhou, local products to Southeast Asia. Besides trading, the company's second major business activity was as shipping agent for the

Scottish Oriental Steamship Company and the Dutch Norddeutscher Lloyd Steamship Company, and, after 1919, the Butterfield and Swire Steamship Company. Its cargo and passenger ships traveled frequently between Hong Kong and Bangkok. After the 1870s, similar to the Chens of Kin Tye *Lung*, the Gaos of Yuanfa *hang* further expanded their business activities: firstly, they established associate companies in Japan, Thailand, Singapore, and Malaysia. Secondly, they expanded from trading and shipping to rice milling, real estate, and finance.[56]

Gao Chuxiang had nine sons, the eldest adopted while the rest by his four wives. In 1883, when Chuxiang died, Yuanfa *hang* became a "common or public company" of the nine sons and their descendants. The precise distribution of power among the nine brothers is not clear although we know that the eldest adopted son remained in Chenghai to take charge of land properties. Shunqin, the second son by Chuxiang's Thai wife was the head of the enterprise and, Huishi, the seventh son, took care of the business in Thailand.[57] The sons, each holding a private account in the company, also conducted their own businesses. Shunqin used Shunji as the account name in the company; under that name Shunqin engaged in various businesses like real estate, insurance, trading, and finance. Shares and directors of many of these companies overlapped.[58] According to an account given by one of Shunqin's sons, the "common company" [*gongjia*] also held shares in these private companies [*siren*].[59] Moreover, two directors of the "common company," a maternal uncle Chen Chunquan and later, his son Chen Dianchen, were also shareholders and directors of some of these companies.[60]

Shunqin died in 1909. Before his death, he appointed his eldest son Shengzhi to head the "common company," though business in Thailand was said to be managed by Shunqin's Thai wife and her sons. Shengzhi was known as a revolutionist and a patriotic entrepreneur. He founded an electric company, a water company, and a textile factory in Shantou. Most of the managers of these companies were brothers and nephews of Shunqin's Chinese wife (see Figure 5.1). Shengzhi died in 1913 and the business was passed on to his eldest son Bo'ang. Their maternal uncle Chen Chunchuan continued to be managing director of Yuan Fat *hang* until 1922 when his son succeeded him. After 1914, the Gaos ventured further into the financial field, including investment in four Chinese native banks.[61]

According to Gao Zhenbai, descendants of Chuxiang actively developed their own respective businesses from the beginning of the twentieth century. They took the profits from the "common company." However, whenever a crisis arose, only the descendants of Chuxiang's first, second, and fourth

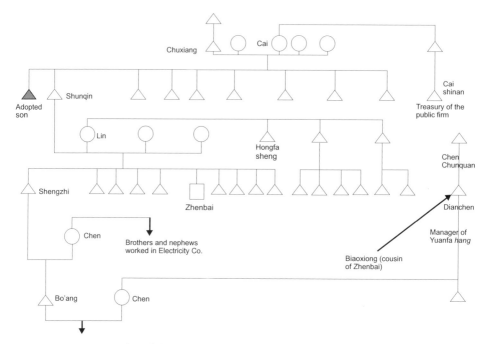

Figure 5.1   Kinship of the *Gao*s of *Yuan Fat Hong* (maternal kin who held key positions in *Yuan Fat Hong* and its associate companies)

Sources: Lin Xi, "Yijiu Sansan Nian Shantou Jinrong Fengchao" (The 1933 Financial Crisis in Shantou), *Da Cheng* (1967), no. 22: 1–4; Lin Xi, "Cong Xianggang di Yuanfa Hang Tanqi" (Talking from Yuanfa Hang in Hong Kong), *Da Cheng* (1983), no. 117–21; Lin Xi, *Tingyu Lou Suibi* (Essays Written in the Rain Hearing Chamber) (Hong Kong, 1991). Lin Xi is the pseudonym of Gao Zhenbai.

sons were willing to assist. Between 1926 and 1927, Yuanfa *hang* was heavily in debt and many shareholding branches hastily abandoned their shares instead of contributing liquidity to strengthen the parent company. In 1928, the company was forced to restructure with the help of Chen Dianchen, Bo'ang's father-in-law. The company was, from 1928 to 1932, jointly owned by the Gao family, headed by Gao Bo'ang, and Chen Dianchen. It was during this period that Yuanfa *hang*'s associate companies in Bangkok were declared bankrupt and this was followed by the winding up of businesses owned by other branches. In 1932, the relationship between Chen Dianchen and Gao Bo'ang deteriorated. Chen was forced to give up his shares in the company. A year later, following the fall of the four closely related Chinese native banks in Shantou, Yuanfa *hang* and other "private" companies affiliated with it also collapsed.

The development of Yuanfa *hang* and its associate companies reveals a process of expansion of their business activities as well as the conflict between "common" and "private" companies. Like Kin Tye *Lung*, the control of Yuanfa *hang* gradually concentrated into one pedigree, from Shunqin, to Shengzhi and Bo'ang. But unlike Kin Tye *Lung*, Yuanfa *hang* relied heavily on its maternal relatives in management and financing. According to Gao Zhenbai's description, the Gaos' maternal kin were employed not only as managers in business sections, but also as managing directors and treasurers. Most of these maternal relatives were related to the dominant pedigree of the Gao family (see Figure 5.1). They were relatives of Chuxiang's wife, Shunqin's wife, Shengzhi's wife, and Bo'ang's wife. It is worth noting the relationship between the Gaos of Yuanfa *hang* and Chen Chunchuan and Chen Dianchen. Chen Chunchuan came from Chenghai county and was Shunqin's maternal cousin. Chunchuan started working for Yuanfa *hang* in the 1860s. He soon became manager of Yuanfa *hang* in the early 1880s. Chunchuan retired in 1922 when his son Dianchen succeeded him as managing director of the company. Both Chunchuan and Dianchen were highly respected by the Chinese community in Hong Kong, especially those in Nanbei *hang* and the Chaozhou circles. In 1921, Chen Chunchuan was invited to inaugurate the Chaozhou Chamber of Commerce.[62] His son, Dianchen was a *Juren* imperial degree holder and a JP (Justice of Peace); he was Director of the Donghua Hospital and chairperson of the Chaozhou Chamber of Commerce.[63] Chunchuan was not only manager of Yuanfa *hang*. He also ran his own import-export business. Together with Shunqin, he opened a Yude Sheng in Hong Kong and a Chengfa *hang* in Canton. As general managers of the company, Chunchuan and Dianchen not only managed the operational side of business, but also of the company finances.[64] They could access the company's safe in which important title deeds and paintings were kept.[65] Moreover, as a maternal uncle, Chunchuan played a crucial role in the family affairs such as the division of family (*fenjia*) after the death of Chuxiang. Thus, Gao Zhenbai asserted that the one who actually controlled the company and the real decision maker was Chen Chunchuan, the maternal uncle.[66] It was perhaps because of this that, when Bo'ang wanted to resume control over the company in 1933, he had to replace Chen Dianchen with his own natal brother, Chenglie.[67]

There were several factors that contributed to the Gaos' reliance on maternal kin. It was partly because their businesses had expanded so rapidly to such an extent that the Gaos did not have enough close agnates to fill up key positions, particularly those that control the finances of the company. On the other hand, it was also because of the lack of support from their own localized lineage, which resulted in the employment of maternal kin as managing directors and treasurers. This lack of lineage support is also reflected in the expulsion of Rixi, Chuxiang's father, from his village. It is clear that without a strong lineage foundation, the Gaos of Yuanfa *hang* had to rely on kin related by marriage to support their expansion. The cost of relying on maternal kin was high: from 1928 to 1933, conflicts among brothers, cousins and affines led to the breakup of the corporate group. Since the beginning of the twentieth century, "privatization process of the "common company" accelerated Bo'ang's uncles' distrust and anxiety. When the "common company" faced difficulties in the 1920s and 1930s, the kin, be they maternal or paternal, were reluctant to inject financial resources. Therefore, following the financial crisis in 1933, eighteen firms related to the Yuanfa *hang* were closed. They included nine Chinese native banks, three shipping companies, a company in Canton, one each in Singapore, Shanghai, and Bangkok, and two companies in Hong Kong.[68]

In brief, in the case of Yuanfa *hang*, women were a crucial hub connecting her husband's family with her own paternal kin. Maternal kin provided services for the company and financial assistance, like the case of Chen Chunquan and his son Dianchen, when the paternal kin failed to assist during a crisis.

Shantou as a city provided job opportunities for women, facilitated the emergence of female petty entrepreneurs, absorbed excess capital in the village, and allowed women of the affluent class to serve as the networking hub in the business arena. However, in the business sector, women did not have any significant managerial and decisive roles in any registered company.

Conclusion

In 1988, about 140 years since its establishment and twelve years after its registration as limited liability company, Kin Tye *Lung* revised its company regulation to accept females as shareholders. In 1992, fifteen female members inherited 62,132 shares (or 11% of the total shares) of the company.[69] This revision marks the end of a male-dominated, patriarchal institution and the beginning of one that disregarded gender differences. Southeast Asian women, however, were accepted into the business world earlier than their counterparts in China. William Skinner, in his 1957 book, noted that ". . . Thai women — not their menfolk — were the traders in the indigenous population; they had a certain amount of business know-how and could appreciate the advantages of an industrious Chinese husband . . ."[70] For him, the advantages of a Chinese having a Thai wife were that: (1) they could easily deal with Thai customers, (2) more readily obtain loans, (3) a wedding in Thailand was less expensive than a wedding in China. Therefore, in the nineteenth century, marriage with Thai women was the rule for Chinese immigrants when occupation and financial status permitted.[71] Wives and daughters of Chinese business tycoons played crucial roles in the family business. For instance, Thongpoon Wanglee, wife of Chen Shouming who was head of the Wanglee company, was the decision maker in the family business after Shouming was assassinated in 1945.[72] In Suehiro and Nanbara's study of Chinese capitalists in Thailand, almost all major Chinese business families had at least one female member who held an important managerial role in the family business, or even founded their own companies.[73] From court cases in the early twentieth century Singapore, we also found women entrepreneurs. Some of these court cases could be found in *Text book of Documentary Chinese: Selected and Designed for the Special Use of Members of the Civil Services of the Straits Settlements and the Protected Native States*, edited by G. T. Hare. For instance, case 71 recorded a woman who operated a Gambier shop and case 110 recorded a woman who operated a transport company that owns more than twenty rickshaws.[74]

Studies on women in China often focused on their subordinate status relative to men. In fact, as we saw in the cases of women in Kin Tye *Lung*, Yuanfa *hang*, and the less wealthy, they played a far greater role in their own destinies than commonly assumed. As pointed out by various scholars, given the particular environment in the inner court, the silk industry in rural Pearl River Delta or in time of social uncertainty, women could rise up as teachers, religious leaders, and many were actually economically independent.[75] This chapter, however, attempts to use the Chanshan region as an example to illustrate that in the traditionally male dominated lineage and business arenas, particular social environments such as the absence of menfolk, the emergence of a city, and the influx of capital not only did not create a gateway for women to step out of their domestic confines. They at times sanctioned such movement.

To step out, Chinese women need fundamental change of the social structure.

6 Abandoned into Prosperity: Women on the Fringe of Expatriate Society

Carl T. Smith

Extract from letter of "Eurasian," 1895:

> The wonder is, truly, that we are as well off and as educated as many of us find ourselves today. It certainly reflects the utmost credit on our unfortunate mothers. . . . In some cases our mothers have only themselves to blame for what they are wont to speak of as "cruel desertion". . . our fathers are well we know not where. I freely admit some of our fathers act like men and have . . . settled a dowry on our mothers and have left us the means of keeping our family respectable.[1]

Statement of Dr E. J. Eitel, 1879 to an inquiry into female servitude:

> Women kept by foreigners in Hong Kong are, as a rule, rather raised in their own esteem by the connection, of the immorality of which they have no idea. They usually are provided for by foreigners when the connection is severed. These women are usually thrifty and able to save money, which they invest in Bank deposits, also in house property, but principally in buying female infants whom they rear for sale to or concubinage with foreigners, for which they generally gain a competency in about ten years.[2]

Intercultural and Interracial Relations in China

Chinese and Eurasian women lived on the edge of expatriate society in the China coast cities where the cultures and peoples of trading empires met. The passage of time has altered the nature of these relationships. As the world moves in fits and starts towards globalization, there is increasingly greater interrelation of peoples, a breakdown of racial exclusiveness, and a blurring of cultural distinctions.

The initiation of this interracial and intercultural movement began when the first foreigners arrived on the edges of the Middle Kingdom. European vessels touched the China coast in the sixteenth century, with Portugal leading the way. The Portuguese established a permanent settlement at Macau in 1557.[3] The official Chinese policy was to control contact between the foreigners and the Chinese and limit it to trade and the provisioning of the settlement. Chinese were not to stay overnight within the "Christian" city. In practice, there was a steady absorption of Chinese into the Macanese population through conversion, adoption of foundlings, and purchase of children. In such cases the Chinese who lost their ethnic identity were given Portuguese names, spoke the language, wore Western-style clothing, and followed foreign customs. These practices continued until the nineteenth century.[4]

A different relationship between Chinese and foreigners was established in the late eighteenth century when other foreigners began trading at Guangzhou. With the British in possession of Hong Kong and the opening of the treaty ports to foreign residents, a policy of social and, if possible, geographic separation was followed. No Chinese, except servants, were allowed to live on the Peak in Hong Kong or on the foreign concession of Shameen Island at Guangzhou.

Social separation based on race did not preclude some men in the expatriate community having casual, temporary, or permanent sexual relationships with Chinese women. The casual relationship brought a financial reward to the prostitute. The temporary relationship could last a number of years before the connection ended with the return of the expatriate to his home country. Permanent relationships usually were based on marriage. In each type of relationship, there was a financial aspect: the casual was normally based on prostitute-client terms; the temporary meant maintenance as long as the relationship lasted and often ended with provisions for the future needs of the woman; marriage ensured the right of inheritance.

Boat Women: A Distinctive Lifestyle[5]

According to the nineteenth-century Hong Kong historian, E. J. Eitel, most of the women who had children by foreigners were *Tanka* (*danjia*) boatwomen.[6] These women were on the fringes of both Chinese and expatriate society.

Marriage between *Tanka* and those who lived on land was prohibited. The men could not sit for the imperial examinations. They were a distinct group with their own lifestyle and occupations. Their marginalization was geographic and economic. The *Tanka* lived on small boats moored in harbors and inlets in the river deltas and along the coast. They were not a part of the basic farmer-merchant economy of China. Their livelihood depended on fishing and water transport. After the arrival of foreigners, men served as pilots, and women supplied foreign vessels with provisions and services. The women washed cloths, repaired clothing, and transported passengers and goods from ship to shore in their sampans. These contacts allowed them to become familiar with the strange appearance and customs of the *fan kwai* — foreign devil. The foreigner, for his part, responded to the friendly, open attitude of these people, which contrasted with the frequently encountered xenophobia and cultural arrogance of the land populations.

European views and attitudes towards the boat women are reflected in the sketches and pictures of them by the China Coast artist, George Chinnery, and in contemporary accounts by foreigners. A traveler, Charles Toogood Downing, observed in 1837, "They were good-natured, pretty-looking young women, and smiled frequently, exhibiting beautiful teeth. One of them seemed to have taken a good deal of pains in adorning herself, and had arranged some artificial flowers in her hair."[7] Another European, William Maxwell Wood, described them as "picturesque, white teethed, laughing-mouthed, bandana kerchief-headed nymphs."[8]

To their Western clients, the woman appeared to be free agents. It was only they who rowed the small boats. It was women who came in their boats to greet foreign ships when they arrived. About their menfolk, William Maxwell Wood remarked, "Where the men live, and how, I do not know."[9] It was as if their own men had abandoned them. Doubtless they had not, but they remained out of sight to the casual Western observer.

This male absence created an area of freedom for the women. Within this freedom there were opportunities for making money. For her services, of whatever nature, a woman received pay. She probably would have handed it over to the men, but if she had the will, she could surreptitiously reserve a portion for herself. The man would not have been present when she bargained for the price or when she rendered the service, because many services were performed on board foreign ships.

The area of freedom she enjoyed would have given her opportunities to manage her own sexuality. As Downing was being conveyed in one of the boats, he was attracted to one of the two women who were rowing and he touched her arms. She withdrew, telling him in pidgin that the Chinese authorities might be watching, but then in a low voice she said, "Nightie time come, no man see."[10]

Most of the woman who were "abandoned into prosperity" by foreigners in the nineteenth century came from this group of marginal Chinese. Their marginality, however, proved to be a door of opportunity in the settlement of Chinese in urban Hong Kong after the British claimed it in the name of Her Majesty in 1841. Policy at the time was to grant lots in the Chinese Bazaar to those Chinese who had assisted the British during their war with China.

Macau Boatwomen: Early Landowners in Hong Kong

There is evidence, though it is scanty, that in early Hong Kong there was a group of Macau boatwomen who owned lots in the Upper Bazaar in Hong Kong. This Bazaar was three rows of lots on the hillside above Queen's Road. They are the present Lower and Upper Lascar Rows and that portion of Hollywood Road that is above them.[11]

There was an interval between the first allotment of the lots and confirmation of ownership in 1845 when Crown Leases were granted. In the meantime, properties changed hands, but transactions were not recorded because the Land Registry was not opened until 1844. Certain terms used for grantors and grantees indicate ownership of lots by Macau boatwomen, such as *O-Mun yan* (Macau person), *Chue-ka* (householder — this term appears to apply to females), and *Shuen-nui* (boatwoman), along with status terms, such as single, spinsters, unmarried, widow, wife, married woman, and concubine.

Following are the records of women who owned property in the Upper Bazaar. They provide an insight into female landowners in early Hong Kong and how some formed alliances with Muslim men as the area became a center for the recruiting, lodging, provisioning, and entertainment of lascar seamen.[12]

In December 1850, Chang Aye,[13] otherwise Chan A-yee, of Macau/ *O Mun yan*, bought for $120, Inland Lot 246 with buildings from the original Crown Leasee, Aheen, otherwise Tam A-hoy, of Heangshan, that is Hsiang-shan District, adjoining Macau.[14] She sold the lot in October the following year for $190, realizing a profit of $70 or one-third over a period of ten months. The purchaser was Le Amung, otherwise Li A-man, Macau. The Chinese character designation of both grantor and grantee was *O-Mun-Yan Chue-Ka*.[15] A-man, boat woman, Hong Kong, sold the lot in August 1853 to Mahomet Arab, *serang*[16] for $550. Over two years she realized a profit of $360, almost double the price she had paid for it.[17]

Sin chow eep, of Macau, otherwise Sin Chau-ip (*O Mun yan, chue ka*) purchased Inland Lot 247D in October 1850 from the original Crown Leasee Hee Aqui, native of Pun U, otherwise He A-kwei. No consideration price is mentioned. In May 1852, she sold the lot for $210 to Mahomet Arab.[18]

Low lim kim, a Chinese female, otherwise Lau Lin-kam (*O Mun yan, nui yan*) purchased Inland Lot 248C for $200 from Peroa, *ghaut serang*. A witness to the transaction was Sea Tso, mariner, otherwise Shi Tsoh, *O Mun yan, hang shuen*. His occupation of mariner suggests a connection of the purchaser with the boat population of Macau. She sold the lot for $180 in January 1851 to Mahomet Arab.[19] In this instance the woman suffered a $20 loss.

Mahomet Arab, who had purchased the above lots, had been present when the British flag was raised at Possession Point in February 1841[20] and was one of the early Muslim settlers in the Upper Bazaar where he operated a lascar boarding house. He was a licensed *ghaut serang*. Over the years he acquired a number of the Upper Bazaar lots. He lived with three women, one of whom was Chinese. His principal wife was a Muslim from his homeland; secondary wives were a Malay and a Chinese mistress, A-hoy, probably a *Tanka* boatwoman. In his will he made provisions for her and her son Hajee Mahomed.[21]

Heu Atai, boatwoman, otherwise Hui A-tsai, *O Mun Yan, chue ka* purchased Inland Lot 248 in February 1851 from the original Crown Leasee, Cheang Afoo, shopkeeper at Kowloon. No consideration price is mentioned.[22] She was still in possession of the lot in 1872.

Sheak Afuh (otherwise Shek A-fuk), *Heung Shan yan, chue ka* in 1849 bought Inland Lot 258C at an execution for unpaid debts of Chun Foo. She paid only $20 for the lot. Sheak afut, of Pwanyu, shopkeeper, sold the lot in 1851 for $30.[23] I can offer no explanation for the discrepancy between the designation in the memorials of 1849 and 1851.

Other female landowners in the Upper Bazaar were associated with Muslim men.

Chan Tai-sing was the wife of Akbar, a Muslim from India. He died at sea in May 1845. He was the owner of Inland Lot 294B. One-third share went to his widow and two-thirds to his only child, a daughter named Hack Moy. In 1853 Hack Moy assigned her share in the property to her mother by deed of gift.[24] In April 1855, Chan Tai-sing, the widow, sold a part of the lot to Me Achut, otherwise Mei A-chut, shopkeeper, for $350. In 1859 the widow inquired of the registrar if she could transfer the remaining part of the property to her daughter. He informed her she could do so, if she paid the expenses of the transaction and an outstanding debt of $35.12 her husband's estate owed the government. He had purchased the house and lot in March 1845, a few months before his death, for $150 from Izam Mahomed, a Bengalese resident of Victoria [Hong Kong]. The original document was in Gujarati.[25]

Leong A-peen, the wife of Shaik Madar, died in 1863; she was survived by her husband and an unmarried adult daughter, Ahsay. At the time of her death, A-peen was the owner of Inland Lots 256 and 166. Lot 256 was on Hollywood Road and had been purchased by the deceased in 1860.[26] Lot 166 was on Lower Lascar Row and had been conveyed to her in 1849 for $120 by Leang Ashap, shopkeeper. In 1864 Shaik Madar, A-peen's widower, transferred Lot 166 for a consideration of $5 to the daughter Aysah, then married to Abdul Kurreem, clothier. She and her husband sold the lot in 1871.[27]

The Arab, Madar, and Kurreem/Curreem families were prominent members of what became known as "local Muslims." Descendants of these families are still living in Hong Kong.[28]

A micro study of the land records for the Upper Bazaar reveals that at its earliest development, it had an unexpected number of Macau boatwomen as landowners and residents. It attracted a small Muslim population that provided the lascar crews of vessels in the harbor such services as recruiting offices, lodging houses, lemonade, and coffee shops, clothing, and provision stores. Some of the Muslims established relationships with the boatwomen.

The Lam Sisters: Matriarchs and Property Owners

A Chinese woman surnamed Lam had four daughters by a foreigner named Bartou. Three of these daughters had children who became the progenitors of an emergent wealthy and influential Eurasian network in the closing decades of the nineteenth century.[29]

The four sisters became property owners in Hong Kong. The first of the sisters, Lam Fong-kew, died intestate in Hong Kong in 1871. She had purchased subsection 1 of Section A of Inland Lot 110 on Graham Street, south of Hollywood Road in 1867 from the Hong Kong and Shanghai Bank for $3,650.[30] Lam Fong-kew was survived by three unmarried sisters, "who were her sole next of kin," namely, Lam Kew-fong, to whom letters of administration on her estate were granted in 1875, Lam A-shui, and Lam Tsat-tai. They were entitled to her property as tenants in common. The sister A-shui subsequently died intestate without having married.[31] Her death left two unmarried sisters, Lam Tsat-tai and Lam Kew-fong, as her surviving next of kin. In 1891, they assigned the property on Graham Street "for divers good causes" to Chan Kai-ming and Chan Kai-cheung.[32]

Either Lam Fong-kew or her sister Lam Kew-fong was the protected woman of George Tyson,[33] a partner of the American firm of Russell and Co. He retired from the firm in 1867. George Tyson purchased No. 47 Graham Street, being Section A of Inland Lot 450, in 1869. Tyson must have left Hong Kong about this time. He died in Philadelphia, Pennsylvania, in 1881. His executor in 1889 conveyed the property to Chan Kai-ming, the son of Lam Kew-fong.[34] According to the Hong Kong Rate and Assessment Books, Lam Fong-kew resided on the premises from 1868 until her death in 1871. It then was occupied by her sister Lam Tsat-tai and her family. In 1885 it is listed as a brothel.

Lam Kew-fong, the administrator of her sister Lam Fong-kew, was protected by the American merchant Albert Farley Heard. He was in China from 1854 to 1873. After his departure, he married Mary Livingston. Before his departure in May 1873 he conveyed a Section B of Inland Lot 94 at the corner of Aberdeen and Staunton Streets to Lam Kew-fong for $1,000.[35] In July of the same year he conveyed a property in Macau to her.[36] She lived at the Aberdeen Street house with her family until she sold it in 1881 to Fung Sui-ho, a single woman, for $3,600.

Lam Kew-fong in 1873 bought from the Parsee merchant, Dadabhoy Cowasjee Tata, the remaining part of Inland Lot 110, No. 52 Hollywood Road, for $4,400. Six years later she sold it for $8,000 to Wong Shu-tong, a compradore.[37]

Lam Kew-fong bought Inland Lots 183 and 184, on Gage Street in July 1878 for $17,000. A new house was built on the premise in 1879 and 1880 and was occupied by Lam Kew-fong after she sold her Aberdeen Street property. In October 1878, she sold the remaining part of Lot 183 to Leung A-woon, a protected woman, for $2,842, and Section A of Lot 184 to Lee Hok-mui, also a protected woman, for $2,784. In 1891, Lam Kew-fong transferred Section A and the remaining part of Lot 184 to her son, Chan Kai-ming, for $10,000.[38]

Lam Tsat-tai was first protected by Gustav Overbeck, later Baron von Overbeck, a partner in Dent and Co., and then by an American, Edward Constant Ray.

Gustav Overbeck married an American woman in 1870. In the previous year, he had conveyed two lots at Sai Ying Poon to Lam Tsat-tai, unmarried woman, "to provide for her and her children." She sold these lots in 1875 to a Chinese trader, for $6,500.[39]

In 1873, Lam Tsat-tai bought section D of Inland Lot 110, a large three-story house on Hollywood Road (now No. 54) for $4,000; she sold it in 1896.[40] In 1876, she bought an adjoining property on Graham Street, sub section 2 of section A of Inland Lot 110, from John Murray Forbes, Junior, of the firm Russell and Co., who was acting as trustee for the children of the deceased Kwok A-cheong. She had been a protected woman of one of the men connected with Russell and Co. Lam Tsat-tai sold it in 1899.[41] These two properties were leased in 1886 for five years to Belle Emerson, a popular brothel keeper. No. 52 Hollywood Road, owned by Lam Kew-fong was also occupied by a succession of European prostitutes. Owners were able to get good rent for the properties used by prostitutes.[42]

This detailed recital of property transactions of the Lam sisters is the foundation for understanding one of the methods used by women who had been abandoned by their protectors to build up substantial estates from rent and the purchase and sale of properties. Such women were the fortunate ones who had generous protectors who ensured their financial security and who used their business acumen to add to their initial seed money.

Ng Akew: An Enterprising Business Woman

Ng Akew[43] was a boatwoman acquired by the American ship captain, James Bridges Endicott, upon his arrival in China in 1842.[44] She was then about twenty-two years old. As the principal in the "Cumsingmun Affair" in 1849, she was described as a "shrewd, intelligent woman." The facts of the case support this description and attest to her enterprise in business matters.

Soon after her connection with Endicott, she began trading on her own account. In a typhoon in 1848 the British ship *Isabella Robertson* was wrecked. Captains Endicott and Lungley bought the ship's damaged opium. Akew bought eight chests from them on credit, but Endicott paid Lungley on behalf of Akew. She sent these eight chests on one of her vessels to be sold on Hainan Island. However, before it could be sold, it was seized by pirates.

As a boatwoman Akew was well acquainted with the practices and haunts of pirates. She resolved to haunt their leader Shap-ng-tsai at Tin-pak and bully him into handing the opium back or paying compensation to her. She threatened him with vengeance from her foreign protector and his friends. Shap-ng-tsai agreed to give her a quantity of betel-nuts. She took them to Cumsingmun and sold them, but the return did not cover the value of the opium she had lost. She was determined to return to the pirates and press for further compensation. Captain Endicott advised her to be satisfied with what she had already received and let the matter drop. She had a mind of her own, however, and a confidence in her ability to negotiate a better deal. During Endicott's absence in Canton, Akew took two boats and returned to the pirates.

Some days later, she returned to Cumsingmun with her two boats laden with cotton, cotton cloth, sugar, pepper, rice, oil cakes, oil fish, dye stuffs, etc. Her boats were accompanied by six other vessels.

Charles Jamieson, captain of an opium receiving ship at Cumsingmun, was suspicious of the flotilla, suspecting that they were not honest traders. He took upon himself to make a closer inspection. There were eight junks, six of them heavily armed. On one of the unarmed junks he found Akew. He began to question her, but she clammed up. All she would say was, "Captain Jam-mi-son, my no care for you." When Jamieson threatened to send for a longboat with reinforcements, she jumped into a sampan, which immediately scuttled away. Jamieson then ordered the hatches of the junk to be opened and found a cargo of sugar and cotton.

After consulting with Captains Wilson and Roper, also in command of receiving ships at the Cumsingmun anchorage, it was decided to send an express boat to Hong Kong to request Daniel R. Caldwell to investigate the matter. Caldwell was a police superintendent and had extensive knowledge about Chinese criminals and their activities. Instead of sending Caldwell, the Hong Kong government informed the Navy about the affair. However, they had no British vessels immediately available, and because of Akew's connection with an American citizen, word was sent to the American commodore at Macau. He dispatched a ship to Cumsingmun with instructions that, if there was any suspicion that the junks there were connected with pirates, they were to be captured or destroyed. However, they had left a day after Akew's encounter with Capt. Jamieson. The next morning a schooner belonging to Captains Endicott and Lungley took part of Akew's cargo to Macau for disposal.

On the arrival of the American at Cumsingmun, a search was made of the Chinese junks there. On two of them bales of cotton with marks of British owners were found. These junks were seized with their crews and taken to Macau. These two junks belonged to Akew. Since the American commissioner at Macau believed that the cargo had been pirated from British ships and was therefore the property of British subjects, he delivered the junks, cargo, and crews to the Hong Kong authorities. In the investigation that followed, Akew denied that the goods had been purchased from pirates but testified that they had been given to her in lieu of opium the pirates had seized from her ship. The charge of piracy could not be proven, and the seized cargo was returned to Akew. She claimed, however, that much of it was now missing.

In this affair, Akew capitalized on her past as a boatwoman and her present situation on the fringes of the foreign community. Many of the pirate community were from the boat population. They and their ways were not strange to Akew. Her association with foreigners made her a formidable opponent and a person to be reckoned with. She played her double role to the hilt. She was a woman of intelligence and independence, trading on her own, making her own decisions, and achieving results in a man's world.

Akew's circumstances changed radically in 1852. Her protector arranged for his marriage to an English woman. Two days before his new partner arrived in Hong Kong, he made arrangements for the financial security of his old partner. James B. Endicott, "master of the *Ruperall* opium receiving ship now lying in the harbor of Cumsingmoon" conveyed a portion of Inland Lot 104 on Gutzlaff Street, Hong Kong, to Douglas Lapraik and William Scott as trustees for "Ong Akew, spinster, a Chinese female residing at Macao, and mother and guardian of Achow, a Chinese infant of ten years or thereabouts."[45] On the same day, Bridges conveyed to Akew, a life interest in Inland Lot 71, a tavern property on Queen's Road in Sheung Wan. On her death, the property was to revert to the estate of Bridges.[46] At the same time, there was a division of the children of J. B. Endicott and Akew. Akew received the eldest son, the above Achow, and a daughter. Bridges retained two sons, James, Jr., Henry, and a daughter Sarah.[47]

Akew, displaying her usual initiative and independence, set about reconstructing her life under these new circumstances. She moved from Macau to Hong Kong and lived at her property on Gutzlaff Street. In 1856, she entered into a relationship with Fung Aching. He is described as her husband and as "the well known Peruvian Coolie Provider, and a man of extensive means."[48] He and Akew bought, developed, and sold lots and houses. It was a period of expansion, and profits were to be made.

Akew's reputation grew as a woman of property and capital. She extended her activities into money loan associations. Something went wrong in 1878, and a number of suits were filed against her by creditors. These ended in bankruptcy proceedings. Mr Gibbons, the Registrar General in 1880, said, "I declined to have anything to do with that bankruptcy because I believe it has to do with the keeping of brothels."[49]

Ng Akew left Hong Kong for a time, but she was assured of continued financial support because the two properties Endicott had placed in trust for her in 1852 could not be sold to meet her debts. She may have continued to live until 1914 when these lots reverted to the estate of her one-time protector and were sold by his surviving executor.[50]

"Mrs" Francis Petersen: Protected Woman of a Tavern Keeper

Death is an involuntary abandonment of those left behind. However, it can thrust a widow into an independent business career. Such was the experience of a Chinese woman, who, as wife of a Hong Kong tavern keeper, was on the fringe of expatriate society.

Lum Asing, also known as Sui San, was born about 1852 in Macau. As a girl she was a student of Miss Harriet Baxter, who had dedicated her life in Hong Kong to a ministry to the poor and the education of Chinese, Eurasians, and orphans.[51] Lum was either an orphan or a child who had been abandoned by her family to have come under the tutelage of Miss Baxter. This was her first step onto the edge of the expatriate world in Hong Kong. She may have been baptized a s a student, although I have no record of it. She was given the Christian name, Jane Francis or Frances? In her school days she acquired knowledge of English.

In 1869, at the age of seventeen, she became the protected woman of Peter Petersen, a Swede, who began his career in Hong Kong as a tavern barman and later a proprietor. In 1872, he was at the "Land We Live In"[52] and two years later at "City of Hamburg."[53] He died in 1876 at his tavern "The Royal Oak" at 208 Queen's Road at the age of 32 years after a long illness.[54] In his will, made shortly before his death in 1876, he described himself as a tavern keeper. He left $500 to his mother in Sweden and the residue of his estate to "Lum Asing, of Victoria, unmarried woman, at present living under my protection." He appointed her and his friend Johann/John Olsen,[55] also a tavern keeper, as his executors.[56] He left her with three young children, three thousand dollars, and the tavern/hotel business.

She continued the business, although women were not permitted to hold a tavern license. In 1880, in a special session of the licensing board to consider the application of Mariano Fernandes, a twenty-three old youth "of Chinese extraction" for the license of the London Inn, it was stated "the virtual management [was] in hands of a Chinese woman, by name Jane Petersen."[57] She had probably recruited Fernandes, who may already have been an employee, to act as a "front-man" for her. His application was turned down, and not long after the "widow" Petersen married by license J. J. McBreen. He was not a happy choice and the marriage did not last.

She paid for his discharge from the police and also paid off $600 of his debts. They lived at the London Inn, where J. J. McBreen is mentioned in March 1881 as the proprietor of the Hong Kong Coffee Saloon.[58] After nine months, he got a position in the military Commissariat Department. She then took a house near the American Consulate on Wyndham Street. A year after their marriage, their relationship became so strained that they separated. As a woman with capital, she did not need to depend on her husband.

After the separation, she went to Singapore where she opened a boarding house of sixteen rooms. While there she gave birth to McBreen's child.[59] Her husband was to have paid her $20 a month, but, during the nine months she was in Singapore, he paid nothing.

After her return to Hong Kong from Singapore, she and her estranged husband signed a formal agreement of separation in July 1884 with the Anglican missionary Rev. J. B. Ost acting as trustee on behalf of her and her children. In spite of her past history, she was still a concern of the church. Her children may have been placed in the school and orphanage conducted by Mrs Ost, when their mother left for Singapore.

She again went to Singapore where she operated an unlicensed boarding house on North Bridges Street. Next door, a widow, Mrs Jessie Ramsay Ormiston, also had a boarding house for policemen and sailors. In May 1889, Mrs Ormiston, then living in Hong Kong on Graham Street, gave testimony in a suit brought by Mrs McBreen against her estranged husband. Mrs Ormiston told the court, "I am a woman of easy virtue." While the same description does not necessarily apply to Mrs McBreen, she did live in the milieu of the *demi monde*.[60] As a Chinese woman, she lived on the edges of the expatriate community. She was fortunate to have acquired financial independence through this connection. McBreen could not pay the support stipulated in the separation agreement, and he was sent to the debtor's prison. He was released in September and the couple was reconciled.

Two weeks after the reconciliation Mrs McBreen was back in court, charged with selling liquor without a license. Two months earlier, she had opened a shop in Wan Chai in partnership with a Chinese man. The shop sold lemonade, ginger beer, and other nonalcoholic drinks. She had applied for a license to sell liquor, but it had been refused. The shop was closed by the police. The McBreens intended to leave Hong Kong, but their departure was not immediate because in February 1890, Mr McBreen was mentioned as a clerk in the solicitor's office of Mr Webber.[61]

The marriage of the "widow" Petersen to Mr McBreen proved to be a drain on her capital, but, even so, she was able to use what remained in various business ventures.

Discussion

When she entered into an alliance with a non-Chinese male, a Chinese woman transferred her dependent role in the traditional Chinese patriarchal family for another form of dependence. The new relationship, however, was less confining and restrictive.

Within the usual Chinese family, the activities of the women were under close supervision by the males in an extended family to preserve the purity of the bloodline and safeguard the honor of the family. In her new relationship she was accountable to only one man. During most of the day her protector would be attending to his business. He had his own bachelor establishment and would also spend time there. At times he might be absent on business or on visits to his home country. These absences left the woman on her own to manage her own affairs. Such a separation was a training experience for a possible permanent severance of the relationship when the woman would be thrown on her own resources and freed from dependence on any male. These separations also provided an opportunity for her to strengthen bonds with women in her own position and possibly the males of her natal family. An examination of wills of single women shows that such ties were maintained.

A Chinese woman who was married to a foreigner normally could expect support from her spouse until his death. If he died intestate, she would be entitled to one-third of his estate, and two-thirds would go to their children. Whatever her financial position, she would have not been accepted in expatriate society in Hong Kong in the nineteenth century.[62]

Many Hong Kong fortunes have been built on the foundations of real estate. Women in Hong Kong, who have had their own capital, have found it a good investment. As shown in this study, Chinese women on the fringes of expatriate society reaped the profits of such investments. They were in a special position, because few women in a traditional family would have had the same opportunity.

There were other opportunities for making money, such as sponsoring loan associations, lending money, financial interest in brothels, and training purchased or adopted children for prostitution, concubinage, or protection by a foreigner.

Evidence of the prosperity of some of the "abandoned" women was the purchase of common property as a "club house." Two groups of such women banded together for this purpose. One of the sisterhood houses was on Graham Street. The other was on Peel Street. Excluded from expatriate society, they formed their own network on the basis of their peculiar position. Prosperity and financial independence enabled them to have their own social centers.

Chinese women who were separated from their expatriate partners by death, departure from Hong Kong, or unilateral or mutual action could find themselves in a new situation of independence with varying degrees of financial resources, which became an economic base for various types of entrepreneurial and investment opportunities. This was an unexpected development of intercultural relations on the China coast. It presaged the modern movement of women to control their own lives and engage in business and finance.

7

The Eurasian Way of Being a Chinese Woman: Lady Clara Ho Tung and Buddhism in Prewar Hong Kong[*]

Josephine Lai-kuen Wong

This study uses a biographical account of Lady Clara Ho Tung and her contribution to Buddhist institutions in Hong Kong and China to illuminate the social, cultural "space" enjoyed by elite Eurasian women in an unusual colonial environment in the early decades of twentieth century. Lady Clara Ho Tung's marriage to Robert Ho Tung, compradore for Jardine Matheson & Co., transformed a young woman from a modest professional family into the matriarch of a distinguished Eurasian lineage. Clara dutifully bore and raised children and took care of the Ho Tung household. While enduring the sicknesses and deaths of her loved ones, she found refuge in religion. Her devotion to the Buddhist faith and her respect for Confucian values supported her claims to a Chinese cultural identity. At the same time, her global travels and social exposure in an ethnically fluid environment gave her the resources to develop visions far beyond local society. She made the best use of the political and social capital of the Ho Tung family to fulfill cultural and humanistic aspirations.

Lady Clara was an active agent who "made things happen" in prewar Hong Kong society. The seminary, Tung Lin Kok Yuen, which she founded in 1935, was a landmark in the development of Hong Kong's Buddhist

* This chapter is a revised version of my MPhil thesis, entitled *"Tung Lin Kok Yuen: Buddhist Reform in Pre-war Hong Kong"* (University of Hong Kong, 1999). I am deeply grateful to my supervisor, Dr Elizabeth Y. Y. Sinn, for her unfailing support and guidance in various ways over the years. I wish to thank Dr Irene Cheng for sharing with me meticulous details about her mother during interviews in 1996 and 1997. My gratitude goes also to my husband, Toby Ho, for his encouragement and understanding.

community. Buddhism was practiced by the local population as folk religion, with a heavy emphasis on rituals. Buddhist clergy had generally led cloistered lives in remote monasteries and hermitages, and an educated few treated the religion as an intellectual subject. The seminary, with its distinctly secular orientation in education and social services, redefined what Buddhism, Buddhists, and Buddhist institutions should be in urban colonial Hong Kong. Clara believed that the Buddhist religion should transcend its traditional ritual and spiritual realm. Using the strategies of Christian missionaries in Hong Kong, she devised ways to proselytize the faith. The intellectual aspect of Buddhism was promoted through education and public lectures. The Yuen provided a gathering place for practitioners from different sects, male and female, clergy and laity. It became a modern, urban institution that performed vital religious, educational, cultural, intellectual, and social functions for the region. As a permanent headquarters for and leadership of the local Buddhist community while China was in turmoil, it gave the faithful a refreshing sense of belonging and identity.

What Lady Clara anchored in Hong Kong can be compared to the ups and downs of a movement on the mainland. From the mid-nineteenth century to 1949, Buddhism in China underwent major changes — the ravages of the Taiping Rebellion, the early revival attempts by the lay Buddhists, the state-led education reforms, and anti-religious movement during the Republican period, the reform movements by the Buddhist clergy, and, finally, tight religious control under the Communist regime after 1949. These changes indeed went hand in hand with the political developments in China — the Self-Strengthening Movement in the 1860s, the Hundred Days Reform in 1898, the abolition of Civil Service Examination in 1905, and the May Fourth Movement in the 1920s. During the process of "remaking the nation" in China, Buddhism was simultaneously attacked and "modernized." The Republican era provided opportunities for Buddhism to respond to the times beyond the imperial protocol. Buddhist organizations were founded to have dialogues with the new regimes. The idea of forming societies, associations, and organizations was a novel expression, highlighting a new sense of being "public" and "civic." On the other hand, anti-tradition, modern nationalist sentiments of both the Nationalists and Communists made it difficult for the Buddhist religion to comfortably fit into their agenda. The Buddhist revival and reforms in China ended abruptly after the Communist revolution in 1949, yet its legacy lived on in Hong Kong. Lady Clara's efforts during these turbulent decades had played a significant historical role.

In an ethnically Chinese society, being Eurasian might not have been easy, especially because during early colonial days, mixed race unions might not have been entertained by the elite tier of society. But as Carl Smith's chapter in this volume shows, Hong Kong's multiethnic, commercial environment not only allowed chances for unexpected mobility for the class of protected women, but they were also extended to their offspring. They intermarried, and many became cultural, political brokers and professionals with powerful social networks in Hong Kong. Sir Robert Ho Tung and Sir Ho Kai Ho were among the most prominent members of these families.[1] Lady Clara's life belonged to this world but also helped shape it.

Lady Clara Ho Tung

Zhang Jingrong was born in Hong Kong on 19 December 1875. Her father Zhang Dehui and her mother, surnamed Yang, were the first generation of Eurasians in Hong Kong. "Her European blood was English and Scottish. Her grandfather was Lane, one of the founders of Lane Crawford of Hong Kong."[2] Her Chinese native place could be traced back to Baoan County in Guangdong. Clara was brought up in Shanghai and in Jiujiang Township in Guangdong where her father worked for the Chinese Customs Service. She received some education at the age of nine, but that did not last long. In 1891, her father died, and in the following year, at the age of sixteen, she brought her father's coffin back to Hong Kong for burial.[3] It is interesting to note that Clara identified Hong Kong as her family's native place. A caretaker throughout her life, she was constantly concerned about the subjects of death and the proper handling of the bodies of her deceased family members.

In Hong Kong, Clara met her cousin, Margaret Mak Sau Ying (Mai Xiuying),[4] wife of Robert Ho Tung whose story could warrant a full study.[5] Margaret married Robert in 1881 and remained childless for years. Bearing children, sons in particular, was a crucial function of marriage at that time. Sensing Robert's admiration for Clara, Margaret proposed a union between Clara and Robert, hoping that Clara could bear children for the Ho Tung family. The arrangements were formally proposed to Clara's mother and made on condition that Clara was to be a *ping qi* (an equal wife), not a concubine and was to be fetched in a red sedan chair in accordance with the traditions of a major marriage.[6] In February 1895, Clara, at the age of twenty, married Robert. In the next two decades, she gave birth to ten children — seven girls and three sons. In 1915, Robert Ho Tung received his first knighthood and the title "Sir." Margaret and Clara, being wives of Sir Robert Ho Tung, became respectively Lady Margaret (Lady Mak, Lady M or Lady Ho Tung) and Lady Clara (Lady Clara Ho Tung).[7]

Becoming a Buddhist

The process by which Clara became a devoted Buddhist and patron was related to her experience as a daughter, wife, and mother. Her grandmother and mother were both devout Buddhists. Besides Buddhism, Clara, like many Chinese people, was also brought up with Confucian values, Taoist rituals, and the general practices of Chinese folk religion. When she became a mother, she passed on the same Chinese religious practices to her children, as is related in the autobiographies written by her children Irene, Jean, and Florence.[8] Her early conception of religion was eclectic and cultural. She was both "a devout Buddhist" and "a good Confucianist." To her, Confucianism provided "the moral and ethical system" and Buddhism offered more "spiritual religion,"[9] both markers of being Chinese.

It was grief and sorrow that drew Clara even closer to religion. Throughout the 1890s, the deaths of her father, mother-in-law, and her first baby son, Henry, made her feel disillusioned and she was constantly sick. She became a vegetarian when her mother died in 1912.[10] For refuge and strength, she developed her keen interest in Buddhism. Similar experiences were shared by many lay Buddhists. In the 1910s, plagued by the health problems of her family, she continued to seek help from her Buddhist faith. She chanted and recited Buddha's name in solitude for her own peace and recovery. She took trips to China to relax, and these became a series of Buddhist pilgrimages. She chanted and prayed to trade her own remaining years for her husband's recovery.[11] As it turned out, Sir Robert Ho Tung outlived Lady Clara by eighteen years and died at the age of 94 in 1956.

Buddhist Pilgrimages

In particular, Clara's travel experiences in China were an important formative phase for her enlightenment and her sense of mission towards Buddhism. Apart from ritual knowledge, Clara turned her interests to the philosophical and intellectual aspects of Buddhism by attending lectures given by clergy during pilgrimages. It was also a transitional stage in which Clara grew from being a lay Buddhist of personal devotion to a lay patron with a public mission. By bringing back ideas and ideals of the Buddhist revival and reformation activities from China to Hong Kong, Clara acted as a bridge linking the two places.

At the beginning, Clara's Buddhist pilgrimages were family vacations and temple visits during which she prayed for deceased family members and for her own fertility.[12] Similar wishes were shared by most Chinese married women who could afford trips to temples.[13] In 1916, Clara started her first formal Buddhist pilgrimage to China. Accompanied by a few servants and her cousin Lin Lengzhen,[14] Clara visited Buddhist monasteries in some mountainous areas of the Yangzi River — Jiangsu, Jiangxi, and Zhejiang. She revisited these sites in later pilgrimages.

In 1919, Clara took her three daughters, Victoria, Eva, and Irene for a retreat, which became her second Buddhist pilgrimage in China. They went to Qingdao, Shanghai, and the Yangzi River area. In Ningbo, they visited the famous Buddhist monastery, Putuo Si to attend lectures and arrange prayers for her ancestors and her husband's families.[15] Eventually, she and her daughters took the refuge vow[16] under the abbot of the monastery. This was how Clara received her Buddhist name Lin-Kok (Lianjue), which she used thereafter as her Chinese name.[17]

Besides Buddhist monasteries, Clara also visited Taoist monasteries, Confucian temples, and the family house of Confucius's descendants in Shandong at the time when the May Fourth Movement[18] was at its zenith. Confucianism, as the icon of Chinese culture, was among those Chinese traditions being fiercely attacked by intellectuals in the May Fourth Movement. Yet, Lady Clara, in her daughter Irene Cheng's words, "had all her life regarded Confucius as the Sage," and "felt about visiting Qufu, the home village of Confucius, as a devout Christian would feel about going to Jerusalem."[19] The 1919 trip was therefore also a Confucian pilgrimage during which she reaffirmed her Chinese cultural identity.

Between 1923 and 1924, Clara made her third Buddhist pilgrimage. The initiation came from the Buddhist revival in Hong Kong. A group of monks from Nanjing and Zhenjiang came to Hong Kong in 1922 and performed Buddhist rituals to raise money for the restoration of their monasteries. Afterward they were invited back to one of Ho Tung's residences, "Idlewild" on Seymour Road, to give lectures and say prayers for Robert Ho Tung's sixtieth birthday and for his deceased mother. The monks were even invited to stay over for Chinese New Year. Then Clara left with them for China and visited their monasteries and some others in the Yangzi area for three months. The next year, she brought her son Shai Lai (Robbie) to Nanjing for military training. However, the military school was closed so she took him instead to revisit the monastery in Nanjing.

In August 1923, Clara joined her husband, Sir Robert Ho Tung, on his trips to Shanghai, Hankou, and North China to propose his idea of a "Round Table Conference" for settling disputes among warlords.[20] They were warmly received and well protected by marshals and warlords throughout the whole trip. During their spare time, they visited Buddhist monasteries in the mountains. They paid monks to arrange special rituals and say prayers for their deceased parents.[21] At Nanjing, Clara became a refugee disciple of another monk, Shi Ruo Shun of Qixia Si. The couple enjoyed the pilgrimage so much that they returned in 1929 and made a donation of $20,000 dollars to restore the Qixia Si. A plaque was later installed at the site to commemorate their generosity to the project and their long-standing patronage.[22] According to Irene, the "Round Table Conference" project drew her parents closer to mainland China in the 1920s.[23] This perhaps explains Clara's growing interest in Buddhist pilgrimage in China and her patriotic sentiment in the 1930s. This ended her Buddhist pilgrimage in China, but she continued her travels elsewhere. In 1929, she concluded her series of Buddhist pilgrimages by visiting Burma and India, which is the birthplace of Buddhism.

Clara kept detailed records of her pilgrimages in China. With the help of her Chinese tutors, she published her travelogue, *Mingshan youji (Travelogue of Famous Mountains)* in 1935.[24] The travelogue begins with five prefaces written by her clergy and lay friends. The main part comprised twenty-one articles, featuring her different pilgrimage destinations. At the back of the travelogue, she appended twenty odd pages of autobiographical notes, giving an account of her life, her family concerns, and the process by which she had become a Buddhist. Also included in the travelogue are six photographs of Clara, her family, and Buddhist institutions founded by her in Hong Kong and Macau. The travelogue remains a major source for us to understand Clara.

The travelogue was Clara's eyewitness account of changes made to Buddhism in China. For example, in Guangdong, she observed the decadence in Buddhist monasteries and among Buddhist clergy temple properties were being occupied by foreigners, such as Austrians and Japanese, some temples were being confiscated for military purposes, whereas others were left in ruins.[25] Bandits were everywhere, and some of them were clergy themselves. She laid the blame on the clergy rather than political dislocation. She wrote:

> In my opinion, the decline of Buddhism in Guangdong resulted from the decadence of Buddhist clergy themselves. Famous Buddhist sites are left

ruined and yet clergy claimed that it was all but fate, and that they could do nothing to change anything.[26]

But the travelogue also reported signs of revival and development of Chinese Buddhism. In Guangdong, some lay leaders formed their own Buddhist institutions with reform incentives. Female religious institutions also survived by gathering both Taoist and Buddhist lay worshippers:

> . . . the area fell to bandits in 1911 forcing Buddhist and Taoist clergy to flee . . . It was not until 1915, when the Republican government sent troops to arrest over hundreds of bandits, was the area finally restored. . . . Recently clergy have returned to revive their monasteries. Guanhua Si is one of the large scale Buddhist monasteries in the area. There now live several dozens of clergy who aim to renovate the monastery. They welcome other clergy to join them and seek donations wherever they could. It happens that a layman surnamed Zhao who advocates the Chan School of teaching visiting the area and hopes to reform Buddhism on Chan principle. . . .[27]

In Zhenjiang, Clara became acquainted with the monk Shi Ai Ting of Zhulin Si.[28] From him, she learned how to appreciate and embrace different sects and schools of Buddhism through education.[29] She financed him to establish a Buddhist seminary near Zhulin Si. She also made a wish that one day she would build one herself in Hong Kong.[30] Monk Ai Ting did subsequently come to Hong Kong in 1932 and lectured at Po Kok Buddhist seminary in Castle Peak and later, at Tung Lin Kok Yuen,[31] the two institutions founded by Clara. He also wrote one of the five prefaces in Clara's travelogue.[32]

Gradually, Clara developed her own views on the future of Buddhism in China. She saw the importance of Buddhist education for the next generation of clergy, and, in her view, founding Buddhist seminaries was therefore essential. Despite the reformation and modernization of Buddhism, she thought that the tradition and heritage of Chinese Buddhist architecture should also be preserved. As China was facing changes and challenges, she believed that Buddhism was the way to save the social and moral decadence of Chinese society and its people. To her, reforming Buddhism and reforming China were closely related.

In fact, Clara became such a devoted Buddhist that she took along her concern for Buddhist development wherever she went. In 1927, she took a trip to Europe and the Middle East. In London, she found some Buddhist charitable organizations but was not satisfied with their intellectual standards.[33] She also visited some charitable organizations for destitute children, which impressed her very much. She made a mental note of both the lack of proper Buddhist organizations and the proliferation of other voluntary charitable bodies in Hong Kong; and, in due course, these inspired her conception of Tung Lin Kok Yuen.[34]

Clara's series of pilgrimages, according to her daughter Jean's observation, drew her closer to the local Buddhist community in Hong Kong, because she had:

> a growing conviction that it was now necessary to have in Hong Kong an institution whereby a combination of lay and religious teaching could be (combined) and, in conjunction with this, there should be a place for worship matching, if not in tradition then at least in form, the many Buddhist temples she had seen (in China).[35]

Involvement in Local Buddhist Revival

Back in Hong Kong during the 1920s, Clara grew more and more interested in local public affairs, opening a new phase in her life as "public benefactor."[36] She took part in an anti-footbinding campaign, the Society for the Protection of Cruelty against Animals (SPCA), St. John Ambulance Brigade, and the annual Agricultural Show in the New Territories.[37] The 1920s also witnessed a revival of interest in Buddhism in Hong Kong, and Clara was one of the local patrons in the campaign:

> There was a revival of interest in Buddhism among many of the better-known Chinese families in Hong Kong. . . . After years of devoting herself to the needs of her husband and children, when [Lady Clara] felt neither any longer required her full attention, she gave her time freely to her religion, her relatives and friends, and to educational and charitable projects. Through these activities, literally thousands of people in Hong Kong got to know her or at least to know of her.[38]

Given the prominent social status of the Ho Tung family, Clara's involvement in Buddhist affairs to a certain extent did elevate the social standing of Buddhism in the local Chinese community.

At the beginning, Clara invited only clergy from China to the Ho Tung residence for lectures and rituals. In 1922, monk Shi Miao Shan, widely known as the "Living Buddha," from Jiaoshan Si, Zhejiang, came to Hong Kong and gave lectures on Lantau Island. Clara wished to attend lectures on the Island, but was advised by her husband not to, because of "the bandits and pirates activities around Hong Kong." Sir Robert instead suggested that his wife invite the monk to lecture at their home. Miao Shan accepted the invitation and visited Ho Tung's residence on 12 September, 1922. On arrival, he also managed to pray for Victoria, Clara's eldest daughter, who was delivering her first baby.[39]

Soon, inviting Buddhist clergy home became a common practice in the Ho Tung household. Three months later, in December 1922, a group of monks from Nanjing and Zhenjiang headed by Shi Ruo Shun stayed at Idlewild (the Ho Tung's residence) for Chinese New Year, as mentioned earlier. In 1925, Clara invited monk Shi Yuan Can and in 1928, Shi Bao Jing.[40] These monks who had been invited to the Ho Tung residences in due course moved to Hong Kong and established Buddhist institutions themselves.[41]

The lectures at the Ho Tung residences were sometimes opened to the interested public. For example, a lecture series was organized at Idlewild from July to September in 1925, and the response was encouraging, with some tens of thousands turning up during the three months.[42] The attempt further confirmed for Clara the positive prospect of Buddhism in Hong Kong. In fact, organizing large-scale Buddhist public activities in private venues was quite an innovative practice at the time. According to Irene:

> From then on [the 1920s] famous members of the Buddhist priesthood were often invited to Hong Kong, either to conduct special religious services or to lecture on the Buddhist Sutras [Buddhist scriptures]. Sometimes these activities were open to the public but held in our home, mostly at Idlewild as on Father's sixtieth birthday and once on an anniversary of the birthday of his mother, once it was held in our home on the Peak. Some lasted for many months. Mamma [Lady Clara] and the members of a few other families [such as the Lee Hysan Family] were the prime movers in these activities, which were participated in by thousands. All were glad to have the opportunity to learn more about their religion and to take part in activities hitherto unknown in Hong Kong.[43]

In addition to inviting clergy to her home, Clara was also active in other local Buddhist public activities. She was a patron and a major organizer of visits of Buddhist clergy from China and overseas to Hong Kong.[44] One of her significant contributions was to make Buddhist "public" activities "possible" in the first place.

In 1922, nun Shi Ding Fo initiated a seven-day *nianfohui* (praying gathering) with a "Water and Land" ritual service[45] in Hong Kong to raise money for the restoration project of Qixia Si in Nanking.[46] Monks Shi Miao Shan and Shi Ruo Shun were invited from China to officiate at the gathering. It was necessary to apply for a permit from the Hong Kong government for such a public gathering. But by two days before the gathering, the permit had still not been granted. Clara was so concerned that she sought assistance from her husband, Sir Robert Ho Tung, and his Chinese friends. After much persuasion, the permit was finally granted for the activity.[47] Besides securing the permit, she also financed the seven-day gathering[48] and invited the two monks back to the Ho Tung residence afterward.[49]

In 1924 when a fund-raising campaign was again launched in Hong Kong, Clara was responsible for publicizing the campaign among her philanthropic friends for support. Soon, there were other fund-raising campaigns launched in Hong Kong to finance Buddhist development in China.[50]

In 1928, she was responsible for another large-scale public Buddhist ritual service — Lee Hysan's funeral at Lee Gardens.[51] Lee Hysan and Sir Robert Ho Tung were friends, and Clara was a friend of Lee's second and fourth wives, who were also devout Buddhists.[52] Hearing of Lee's tragic death, she suggested that the Lee family invite monks from Qixia Si for a Buddhist funeral. The proposal was accepted,[53] and the Buddhist "Water and Land" ritual service started in May 1928 and lasted for forty-nine days:

> The Lee Theatre and the Lee Gardens were closed to the public [entertainment] for 49 days in mourning for the proprietor [Lee Hysan]. His body lay in the Lee Gardens where many friends called to pay their respects. According to old Chinese custom, the body had to be accompanied by the spouse, concubines and descendants for forty-nine days, during which time prayers are said by monks from different monasteries to ensure smooth transition into the next world.[54]

The forty-nine days ritual service, once again officiated by Ruo Shun and his Qixia Si monks, was also open to public participation. After the service, Lee Gardens and Lee Theatre became popular venues for Buddhist public lectures. In the 1930s, the Gardens became the headquarters of the Hong Kong Buddhist Studies Society, a Buddhist organization formed by a group of lay intellectuals.[55] The Lee Gardens were beautifully decorated in Chinese style with pagoda and statues of Buddha and *Guanyin*. The Lee family, by providing a venue for Buddhist public activities, was also a great patron of the local Buddhist Revival.[56]

Founding Tung Lin Kok Yuen

Perhaps Clara's most significant achievement in the local Buddhist revival in Hong Kong was the founding of Tung Lin Kok Yuen in 1935.[57] The name of Tung Lin Kok Yuen came jointly from the names of Sir Robert Ho *Tung* and Lady Clara, Cheung *Lin-kok* (Zhang Lianjue). It was built to commemorate their golden wedding anniversary on 2 December 1931, and was even recorded in the government administrative report as one of the three "buildings of importance" completed in that year.

In her travelogue, Clara stated that the founding of the Yuen was a personal ambition, a challenging and meaningful thing to do as she was approaching her sixtieth birthday:

> For life I have been a devout Buddhist, and I was eager to see a formal modern permanent institution yet to be established in Hong Kong to propagate Buddhism and to offer Buddhist education. As I also took pity on those young girls who did not have the opportunity to receive proper education, I therefore aimed to establish a free school to offer education for girls. The project was such a big one that it bothered me for years. With my husband's understanding and his financial support, my wish finally came true when I founded Tung Lin Kok Yuen on Shan Kwong Road.

Excerpted from Lady Clara's will, drafted in 1937, later reproduced in *Jueyin*.[58]

For Clara, Tung Lin Kok Yuen was a private temple to commemorate her ancestors. It was funded by and dedicated to Lady Clara's natal family, the Cheung family and the Ho Tung family as well. The ancestral chamber situated on the Yuen's second floor was reserved for housing the ancestral tablets of Clara's parents, her eldest son, Henry, who had died as a small child, her sister-in-law Bessie, and some other distant relatives of the Cheung family. A small suite of rooms comprising a bedroom and bathroom was built next to the chamber hall for Clara's private worship and occasional accommodation.[59]

Tung Lin Kok Yuen was also a public Buddhist institution open and catering to the general masses. Clara intended to make the Yuen a multifunctional Buddhist institution, unlike other previous ones. The Yuen, in Clara's eyes, was meant to be a place to preach Buddhism as a universal moralizing force, especially in times of uncertainty and disillusionment. In her autobiographical notes, she wrote:

. . . after the outbreak of the European War [the First World War], people throughout the world began to doubt the materialistic values that had been upheld so enthusiastically in the West. In fact, the outbreak of the war itself has manifested weaknesses of the Western civilization. Perhaps it is time for us to look back to the East for inspiration. What else but Buddhism can best represent the essence of oriental civilization?[60]

The historical context in which Clara lived was colonial Hong Kong where East meets West. The Yuen, with its Buddhist nature, had the special cultural mission to represent oriental values, in particular Chinese values.

One important feature of Tung Lin Kok Yuen was its openness to different sections of Buddhists, breaking the boundaries within the Buddhist community itself, as reflected in the education provided by the Yuen. Traditionally, Buddhist education was part of the monastic system and conducted between masters and disciples in the clergy community. Hierarchy and gender differences were also factors, affecting who could teach whom. For example, monks were more likely than nuns to receive education, and it was not common that an abbess would teach a group of monks. What the Yuen then offered was education to both secular and seminary, and accommodation for females, both nuns and laywomen. In addition, the Yuen was open to all Buddhists, male and female, clergy and laity. Renowned monks and those laymen well versed in Buddhist scriptures were invited to teach; clergy and laity were all welcomed to attend public lectures. Therefore the Yuen was far from being only a nunnery for females, or merely a monastic establishment for clergy, or a common temple to attract folk worshippers only, or an enclosed intellectual venue for educated lay members. Instead it functioned as all these at one time or another.

The location of Tung Lin Kok Yuen was also significant, with a different image and mission in the local Buddhist community. Clara did not choose a remote island or mountain to found the Yuen, as was true for the most famous Buddhist monasteries. Instead the Yuen was established in Happy Valley, an urban residential area at that time, with easy access to the urban masses. As Shi Yong Ming points out, the location of the Yuen signified the emergence of *shiqu fojiao* (urban Buddhism) in Hong Kong, which aimed at being a proactive missionary body propagating Buddhism, in contrast to *shanlin fojiao* (rural Buddhism), the passé mode of Buddhist existence.[61]

The Yuen's urban orientation served two main functions: to maintain close ties with the secular lay community and to reach out to the potential pool of masses for more lay recruits. Instead of relying on the laity's initiative to contact monasteries high uphill as in the past, the Yuen was situated where people lived. Its location thus broke the geographical, social, and cultural boundaries between the monastic and the secular worlds. The Yuen set an example for Buddhist institutions that no longer served only self-sufficient, segregated, and cloistered communities, but rather formed an integral part of the lives of common people.

Above all, Clara intended to make Tung Lin Kok Yuen a permanent Buddhist headquarters, or in her own words, *yongjiu genben jiguan* (a permanent fundamental organization)[62] in Hong Kong, in response to the well-organized Western Christian missionaries.

In view of the proliferation and achievements of Western Christian missionaries and the presence of a general sense of a Christian community in Hong Kong, Clara believed that there should also be an institution to promote unity among Buddhists in Hong Kong. The presence of such a Buddhist focal point could help promote the organization, coordination, and a sense of identity and belonging for the local Buddhist community. It could also be a contact point to integrate with other overseas Buddhist communities. Besides, according to Clara, the local Buddhist mission should not be only spiritual in function, but should also provide other secular social and cultural functions, such as education and charity, just as the Western missionaries were doing.[63]

This vision was inspired by the Buddhist movement and the wide proliferation of Buddhist educational institutions on the Chinese mainland at the time.[64] The Yuen in time served as a bridge between Buddhist communities in Hong Kong and China during wartime. When China was at war with Japan in the late 1930s, Tung Lin Kok Yuen served as a convenient refuge for fleeing clergy and their ideals from China.[65]

In 1937, Clara was elected vice-president of the Hong Kong Chinese Women's Relief Association and vice chairman of the New Life Association. The first association was the sister organization that Madame Chiang had originally created in China to look after "orphans as a result of the war"; the second was also a patriotic charitable body to raise funds for war relief purposes.[66]

Integrating her patriotic fervor with her Buddhist devotion, Clara mobilized students and staff at the Yuen to take part in the war efforts. As described by her daughter, Irene Cheng:

> Mamma [Lady Clara] was so enthusiastic about her war work that she decided to involve her class of two dozen students in the free Buddhist seminary. She had them temporarily discontinue their regular religious lessons in order to work on donated or borrowed sewing machines or to sew by hand in order to produce padded garments for the soldiers. She

felt that this service work also had its moral value in the development of her trainees. Compassion and universal love are strong moral principles among Buddhists, and Mamma used that expression as the motto for her school and seminary.[67] That year Mamma requested that the ritual be shortened by a couple of days, chiefly because she did not want the seminary students to take too much time off from the war work in which they were engaged.[68]

It is interesting to note how Clara justified the relationship between Buddhism and patriotism and mobilized the Yuen's participation in wartime efforts.

Promotion of Education

In particular, education was an essential part of Clara's efforts to revive and reform Buddhism in Hong Kong. As the mother of ten children, the subject of education was Clara's maternal duty. She took great care in the education her children received. Her daughter Irene was the first female admitted to the University of Hong Kong in 1921.[69] Even *mui-tsai*[70] at Ho Tung's household were encouraged to study, because Clara believed in "the importance of women being able to read and write." For her own children, education meant "to reap the maximum advantage from [their] dual heritage", namely the Chinese and Western traditions.[71] There was no difference in how her sons and daughters were educated, and according to Irene:

> It was quite natural that she should be as deeply concerned about the health of her daughters as that of her sons, but rather unusual that she was also concerned about the girls' education. She was much opposed to the false thought traditional values expressed in the old Chinese saying that "it is virtuous for a woman to be uneducated." Consequently, she laid great emphasis on our "Character Education", to which she attended herself whenever she had the opportunity. . . . She provided us with tutors and governess and sent us to the best schools she could find.[72]

In time, Clara also extended her passion for good education to her daughters' schools. During her lifetime, she sponsored two "Lady Ho Tung's Chinese Language Awards" to encourage Chinese language learning at the Diocesan Girls School. In 1932, she funded the "Practical Middle School" project for Lingnan University in Guangzhou where her daughter Irene was lecturing.[73]

In her autobiographical notes, Clara elaborated her views and ambitions to combine her religious commitment to revive Buddhism with her sense of social contribution to provide education for poor children in Hong Kong:

> . . . Now the world is in a mess, dangers are everywhere, another world war is about to erupt, there is no way to save the world except Buddhism. But Buddhism is in decline. To revive Buddhism, we must promote mass education to train the young Buddhists. It is my wish to run schools for Buddhism. . . . Once I thought that as humans, we are all equal and virtuous. I feel pity that children are not educated because of poverty, they just live their life without meaning and die without having their potential fully developed. It would be wonderful if I can offer education to the destitute, to teach them at least some basic knowledge of Buddhism, so that they can be good sons and daughters, good citizens and good people to display human's innate goodness and to make the world a better place.[74]

In particular, she clearly explained her patriotic and civil reasons behind her support for female education:

> . . . I also thought that females are mothers of nations, they must be well educated in order to run good families, and a good society is made up of good families. It is not correct that only males are offered education. For the sake of a good society and a good nation, we should promote mass education for females as well.[75]

Clara's aspirations found expression long before the founding of Tung Lin Kok Yuen. In the early 1930s, she was already active in running Buddhist seminaries and free schools in Hong Kong and Macau. These early ventures were later reorganized under the roof of Tung Lin Kok Yuen and were collectively named the Po Kok group of schools. Po Kok (*Baojue*) means "precious" and "awakening," and the character *Jue* comes from Clara's Buddhist name, *Lian Jue*.[76]

The records are confused as to whether Clara first started her Buddhist free school in Hong Kong or in Macau. The two schools were set up at almost the same time around 1930 and 1931, and together they were named the First and the Second Po Kok Free School (*Baojue diyi , dier yixue*).[77] They were situated in Rua Central (Longsong jie) in Macau, and Percival Street in Causeway Bay in Hong Kong[78] where, according to Clara, many ordinary Chinese people lived to whom the two schools could conveniently offer free education.[79]

The Po Kok Free School in Percival Street was the first Buddhist free school in Hong Kong.[80] Its premises were a two-story residential apartment, comprising three classrooms and a main praying hall. After paying two dollars admission deposit, students were offered a free education.[81] The two Po Kok Free Schools aimed to provide free primary education for poor girls, and each started off with nearly one hundred students.[82] Together they shared the same teaching staff of four, including monk Ai Ting and Lin Lengzhen.[83] As headmistress, Clara had to shuttle between the two schools on weekends.[84] Apart from the above fragments of information, not much is known about how the two free schools operated and the subsequent development of Po Kok Free School in Macau.

Around the same time — between 1930 and 1931 — Clara also ran her first Buddhist seminary, again in Macau, because the Ho Tung family "had many connections with the Portuguese Province of Macau."[85] The seminary was a joint venture with a layman named Zhang Xiubo[86] who provided a venue for seminary classes, called Gongde Lin,[87] then the largest Buddhist temple in Macau situating at No. 13 in Rua St. Jose.[88] Gongde Lin was initially a Buddhist nunnery headed by a monk from Shanghai of the *Linji* sect; the premises had been converted from Zhang's family residence in 1925. Zhang became monk Shi Guan Ben in 1931 and took up the abbotship of Gongde Lin two years later.[89]

The seminary classes at Gongde Lin were Clara's experimental attempt to run a Buddhist seminary. Very little has been written about its origin and nature; it was not even mentioned in the autobiographical note in her travelogue. As shown in a photo taken on the opening day of the seminary, there were about fifty female teenage students and eight female staff members, including Clara, Lin Lengzhen, and a nun. Besides offering education, the seminary also provided accommodation for nearly one hundred inmates.[90] For some reason, the seminary was closed in 1932, and the failure was a heart-breaking experience for Clara.[91]

Despite the failure of the seminary, Clara remained a patron of Gongde Lin. The institution was so famous that it was described under the category of "Chinese temples" in a Macau Travel Guide published in 1939 as follows:

> Gongde Lin is the biggest Buddhist institution in Macau, situating in Rua St. Jose No. 13. That site was initially Zhang family's vegetarian house (*zhaitang*). Since Master Zhang has become an ordained monk himself, he contributed his multi-storied family house and the backyard and converted it into the Gongde Lin. The institution adopts the Buddhist Forest System (*conglin zhi*), and clergy from all directions can stay there to pray. The institution used to be headed by monk Shi Chao Lin and funded by Lady Clara, who had close ties with Tung Lin Kok Yuen in Hong Kong. Now there are more than one hundred inmates, and the

institution is headed by a lay woman, Madam Lin Lengzhen. At the moment monk Shi Hai Yen is giving talks in Gongde Lin.[92]

After the failed attempt in Macau, Clara turned her attention back to Hong Kong. On 24 September 1932, she opened her second Buddhist seminary, Po Kok Buddhist Seminary (Baojue foxue yanjiushe)[93] in Castle Peak "to train professional missionaries."[94] Classes took place at a Buddhist institution called Haiyun lanruo. The photograph taken on the opening day shows a staff of fifteen members and more than one hundred female students, including both lay girls and nuns. In particular, monk Ai Ting was invited from China to head the seminary. According to the monk:

> In spring 1932, I quit the abbotship of Zhulin Si and came to Hong Kong. I knew that Lady Clara had been devoting herself to the promotion of Buddhism. Her seminary at Gongde Lin turned out to be a failure, and this made her very sad. She hoped that I could revive her Buddhist seminary work, but she could not find suitable premises for that, so I just returned to Jiangsu. In autumn, Lady Clara borrowed the venue for a seminary at Haiyun lanruo, Castle Peak. She wrote to request my help. I thought that since I am a Buddhist and promoting Buddhist education is both my mission and my wish, and Lady Clara was so enthusiastic, why not just come to help her for the founding years until she could find a more suitable abbot? That was why I agreed to come; it turned out that I stayed in Hong Kong for some five, six years.[95]

Despite the remoteness, bad hygiene, and bad weather in Castle Peak, the number of seminary students grew to 120 in 1934.[96] A year later, the seminary was incorporated into the newly founded Tung Lin Kok Yuen.

When Tung Lin Kok Yuen was founded in 1935, it combined the 108 students from Po Kok Free School at Percival Street with 120 students from Po Kok Buddhist Seminary at Castle Peak. The two schools were then renamed Po Ko Free School (Baojue yixuexiao) and Po Kok Buddhist Seminary (Baojue foxueshe). The seminary section was still headed by monk Ai Ting at the new permanent premises.

Students studying at Po Kok Buddhist Seminary came from both clergy and lay backgrounds. Apart from Buddhist scripture, subjects taught to seminary students included Chinese, English, mathematics, history, geography, science, and letter writing. Besides the Free School and Seminary, the Yuen also ran a night school after the normal daytime school schedule ended to offer Chinese and English language classes to adult working females who had missed education in their childhood.

Despite the grand opening of Tung Lin Kok Yuen, Clara's Buddhist connection with Macau remained. In the 1930s, monk Guan Ben renovated Buddhist chanting. He introduced the element of music with chanting and published *Wuhui nianfo xinsheng* (The New Voice of Buddhist Chanting in Five Patterns). He invited students at Po Kok School to experience the new chanting patterns and to record the results on records for sale. Today, the Yuen is still practicing Guan Ben's chanting patterns.[97]

Tung Lin Kok Yuen after Lady Clara

On 5 January 1938, less than three years after the founding of the Yuen, Lady Clara died at the age of sixty-three from complications arising from bronchial asthma. The funeral was conducted according to Chinese and Buddhist customs in a meticulous manner: the hair was neatly combed and pinned with a red silk flower; the body was bathed with pomelo leaves and dressed in a Buddhist outfit; a small pearl and a small piece of gold were placed in the mouth; and the face was covered with white silk handkerchief. The coffin was carried out of the Ho Tung's residence by sixteen bearers; the reception hall was manned by in the charge of two masters-of-ceremony and an orchestra of four musicians. The "highlight" of the funeral was the street procession, composed of family members, students, nuns, trucks, banners, lanterns, and wreaths, stretched all the way from Stubbs Road, passing Tung Lin Kok Yuen to the Chiu Yuen cemetery in Pokfulam. Details of the event were reported by the *South China Morning Post* the very next day.[98]

In 1937, Clara had prepared her will, instructing members of the Ho Tung family and her Buddhist friends to form a board of trustees for the Yuen so that the organization could move with the times and be well taken care of after her death.[99] The Yuen became a registered company on 26 May 1949, with a Board of Directors comprised of eight members,[100] including her daughter Irene, her son Sai Lai, and her famous lawyer son-in-law, Lo Man Kam. In 1951, her eldest daughter, Victoria, and Robbie's wife, Hesta Ho Hung Ki Fan (He Hong Qifen), were also invited to join the board.[101] The family members devoted themselves to the Yuen, and Victoria, in particular, spent the rest of her life filling her mother's role in running the Yuen with Lin Lengzhen and attending social occasions on behalf of it. According to Irene, Victoria:

> . . . became a very energetic and efficient fund raiser and champion of the Temple (i.e., Tung Lin Kok Yuen) and its group of Pok Kok Schools, for which she served as the supervisor for many years.[102]

Carrying two prominent family names, Ho Tung and Lo, Victoria continued Lady Clara's sense of mission to boost the publicity and social status of the Yuen in the local Chinese community.

Tung Lin Kok Yuen experienced its heyday in the late 1930s. It survived in the 1940s during the Japanese occupation, and its influence and popularity persisted after the war until the Hong Kong Buddhist Association was established in 1945 and other Buddhist institutions proliferated in the 1950s and 1960s. Over the years, the Yuen gradually became a focal point and an ideal venue for receiving overseas guests, hosting important local events, organizing Buddhist public lectures, and holding Buddhist ritual services. These activities were regularly publicized and reported in Buddhist periodicals circulating in Hong Kong, Macau, and China. In time, the Yuen's hosting role and the accompanying publicity helped build up its reputation and status in the local Buddhist community. In the absence of an official local Buddhist headquarters in the prewar period, the Yuen assumed that role.

The family network is still at work today, as shown by the Yuen's list of directors on the board, which includes members of the Ho Tung family. By the 1990s, family members sitting on the Yuen's board include Sai Lai's daughter, son, daughter-in-law, and grandson: Margaret Madam Ho Min Kwan, Bobbie H. N. Lo and his wife, Ho Lo Yee Man, and their son, Kevin Ho Yuan Kwong. Victoria's three children — Lo Tak Shing, Rita Lo, and Vera Lo — have also joined the board. Besides blood relations, a new generation of the Yuen's directors comes from members of the clergy and students who have formerly taught and studied at the Yuen.

Echoing Clara's vision and ambition, in 1995, some sixty years after the founding of Tung Lin Kok Yuen, Clara's grandson Bobbie Ho Hongyi established the Tung Lin Kok Yuen Canada Society in Vancouver to "provide an accessible venue for Buddhists and the general public to come together and share the value and meaning of Buddhism."[103]

Lady Clara: A Hong Kong Lady

This study has presented an account of the life of Lady Clara in her roles as a daughter of Eurasian background, wife of a millionaire, mother of ten children, philanthropist, Buddhist lay woman, Buddhist patron, Buddhist educator, and the founder of Tung Lin Kok Yuen. In particular, the founding of the Yuen reflects how she acted as an agent to revive Chinese Buddhism in prewar Hong Kong. Despite her early death, according to her daughter Irene:

Lady Clara is still the main inspiration for the work of the Tung Lin Kok Yuen, the Po Kok Vocational Middle School for Girls, and its subsidiary schools. In this religious and education work, her memory is most fittingly perpetuated.[104]

Throughout her life, Lady Clara had been exploring ways to meet standards of what she should do to create possibilities for herself as a woman. She found channels to fulfill her commitments both to her family and her religious faith in such a way that her domestic duties and her public roles complemented each other. The social status and the financial backing of the Ho Tung family enabled Clara to patronize Buddhist activities. Her extensive traveling enriched her insight to revive and reform Buddhism in Hong Kong. In return, Buddhism provided Clara with refuge and strength in times of family grief and sorrow. Her intellectual and spiritual pursuit of Buddhism allowed her to come to terms with her cultural identity as a Chinese woman.

At her death, Clara's contribution was widely recognized by the Buddhist communities in Hong Kong and China. She was depicted in her obituary in the *South China Morning Post* as "a staunch Buddhist" and a "prominent social worker" whom the colony had so sadly lost.[105] Her name and her Buddhist works were mentioned several times in the review article of Monk Shi Tai Xu, the famous Buddhist reformist in China at that time[106] and the chronology recording major developments of Chinese Buddhism between 1911 and 1943.[107] Monk Shi Ai Ting described her as an exceptional, benevolent laywoman who, during her lifetime, had devoted herself to the country (China), Chinese Buddhism, social welfare, and charity for the local community (Hong Kong), especially in the field of female education.[108] Monk Shi Le Guan regarded her as an outstanding female in modern Chinese Buddhism, who, despite her privileged social background, had been committed to promoting Buddhism among the masses.[109] There were also compliments praising Clara for her unfailing efforts to embrace not only Chinese Buddhism, but also Chinese culture, in contrast to the popular contemporary trend to follow the West.[110]

Back in Hong Kong the former governor, Sir Alexander Grantham, regarded Lady Clara as a "Chinese Lady of Hong Kong." Historian Susanna Hoe referred to Lady Clara as a "Buddhist philanthropist."[111] In a sociological research of modern Chinese firms, Professor Wong Siu-lun cites Lady Clara as an example of women's role as one "hidden dimension" of the "rise of business corporations in China from Ming to the present." Wong considers her the "matriarch of religiosity [of Buddhism]," "the moral capital [of

Confucianism]," and "the guardian of the spiritual well-being of the [Ho Tung] family."[112]

To continue the narrative on regional culture and women's positioning, this chapter argues that Hong Kong in the late nineteenth and early twentieth century presented a complicated historical moment. It is a history of trading empires, multiethnic and colonial encounters in which cross-cultural finesse was an asset for both men and women. A peculiarly open and encompassing environment in colonial Hong Kong gave Lady Clara a great deal of room for maneuver in her pursuit of family and religious fulfillment. It allowed her to cross racial, social, and gendered boundaries set by Confucian and Victorian moralities. In her life of devotion, she gave local society a great deal in return.

III
Work and Activism in a Gendered Age

How have the historical moments in the postwar decades, when the border between Hong Kong and mainland China hardened and softened, affected the subjectivities of women and their positioning? Has their gendered activism contributed to wider civic participation and political engagement? Helen Siu uses Anson Chan's generation of women in politics to illustrate how postwar manufacturing and the needs of a colonial meritocracy in Hong Kong have allowed educated women to excel beyond their own imaginations. They seem to have straddled the demands of locality, nation, and the world to perform in cultural styles that gained unusual charisma in the public mind. From the early 1970s to the late 1990s, a period the chapter focuses on, they reached the zenith of their respectability by preserving certain "traditions" of Chinese mercantile society while reaching far in their worldly domain. In the first decade of the twenty-first century, statistics on the education, wealth, and high placement of women in government and business only confirm the accumulated achievements of these postwar generations and the public acceptance of their positioning.

In Po-king Choi's chapter, the lives of working daughters in the 1970s were harsh, but Hong Kong's world industrial assembly line allowed space beyond the cultural environment of home where the nurturing of sons remained top priority and where daughters were expected to sacrifice for such family priorities. Night schools, nascent radio and film, and fan clubs created cultural aspirations for success and fulfillment for factory daughters. Although her chapter focuses on the active construction of moral selves by these women through multiple roles of daughter, worker, wife, and mother, Choi points to their union activism and the pursuit of other social causes that came with the dramatic shift of factories from Hong Kong to Guangdong across the border. In Hong Kong as it moved through decades of industrialization and deindustrialization, these working women's agency have added to the public arena where their voices are heard and their emotions felt.

Across the border in China, women activists, especially those who enjoyed education and government provisions in the cities, made gains through their public lives. Yan Lijun, Taotao Zhang, and Yang Meijian portray the career tracks of several women who came of age during the Maoist period when political rhetoric and revolutionary commitments dominated every aspect of people's lives and work. Through military service and education, they were able to link individual aspirations with limited political tracks to gain mobility. Some took advantage of the close proximity of Guangdong to Hong Kong by stowing away. They "escaped" the system altogether. The oral histories capture their energies in agentive moments and their sober self-reflections in the post-reform era.

The chapter by Pheng Cheah deals with the contemporary period when the South China region has been profoundly transformed by neoliberal global economy. As the border between China and Hong Kong is blurred by the volatile flows of capital, commodities, people, and images, women's subjectivities are correspondingly complicated, destabilized, and not bounded by territorial sensitivities. Ching-kwan Lee and Ngai Pun have written on gendered labor issues and particular factory regimes, focusing on the *dagongmei*. As in historical times, the region presents women workers with a mixture of dangers, trauma, and opportunities as social norms are transgressed. As a world factory and a booming region for brashly luxurious consumption, South China has attracted tens of millions of migrants from other provinces. Their pursuits and struggles have become a significant part of a gendered human landscape. They juggle with a lingering socialist bureaucratic structure and its entrenched discrimination towards migrants, with unbridled market forces triggered by global capital, and with the wasteful vanity of officials determined to catch up with lost time. Pheng Cheah's chapter uses a close reading of film to highlight representations of the lives of women when they choose mobility paths far beyond the factory floor. It captures the desperate energies, structural consequences, painful self-reflection, and deadening weight of collective pretense in the most intimate corners of these women's lives.

8 Women of Influence: Gendered Charisma

Helen F. Siu

Women of Influence (*Nü qiangren*)

Although working women in Hong Kong have been given analytical attention, studies of professional women and political figures are not numerous.[1] Serious biographies of female movers and shakers are rare compared to those written about male public figures.[2] When the images of these women circulate in the local culture industry, a curious mixture of qualities marks them. Popular impressions distinguish them from their counterparts in China and Taiwan. It is said that high-ranking officials in China are too "man-like" whereas their counterparts in Taiwan flaunt their "womanly ways." Hong Kong women, on the other hand, are powerful as well as charming and fashionable, commanding professional confidence on their own terms and keeping their glamour.[3] Whether or not one agrees with these general impressions, it is worth exploring the multiple meanings of *nü qiangren* and their associated charisma in a particular historical context — the colonial and postcolonial development in Hong Kong. Are women in Hong Kong "holding up half the sky" by quietly revolutionizing the workplace, home, and cultural expectations? If so, in what arenas and through what means are gender issues brought to public consciousness? If not, what are the contradictions and tensions? Following the historical chapters in this volume, this chapter uses the public lives of leading women professionals and civil servants in the late 1990s to explore the "meaningful spaces" Hong Kong's postwar development in South China has provided for them. There is no lack of women of influence in postwar Hong Kong. However, public perceptions of their accomplishments are gendered and based on mixed cultural assumptions. With remarkable finesse and charisma, two generations seem to have engaged with difficult circumstances to transform themselves and society.

The chapter focuses on the context that has allowed such engagement to take place in institutional, discursive, and personal terms. Although cramped in a small physical territory, residents in Hong Kong have drawn on the cultural resources, images, and institutions of two vast imperial empires. In the first century of its colonial history, Hong Kong was shaped by the global spread of a merchant culture that was dynamic, open, and unorthodox in practice, but conservative in its Confucian pretensions and pursuits. The trading partners of Chinese merchants and their associated multicultural moralities added other layers of cultural resources. Historian Elizabeth Sinn argues that for almost a hundred years Hong Kong was a significant node, a space of flow between China, the Americas, and Southeast Asia. It thus provided an effective environment for sojourners and settlers, male and female, to deposit layers of value and institutional practice.[4]

The postwar decades saw Hong Kong relatively cut off from a politically isolationist China. Its migrant capital and labor force became an integral part of the global spread in industrial production. In the 1960s, the world of Suzie Wong, physically represented by the bars and dance halls in the red light districts of Wan Chai and Kowloon, was contrasted with the lives of docile, diligent, and filial daughters working in factories and homes, producing wigs, toys, and plastic flowers for the world market. Local film studios produced popular images of "factory queens" and "college girls." The successful careers of several top female stars, such as Chan Po Chu and Siu Fong Fong, became the icons of the era.[5]

After the social unrest triggered by the Cultural Revolution in China in the late 1960s, the government invested heavily in the city's infrastructure, education, housing development, and social services, which required vast administrative support. The territory's strategic move into servicing international finance in the 1980s and 1990s also provided unprecedented social mobility for families with middle-class aspirations. An urban, modern, cosmopolitan outlook that stressed institutional fairness, clean government, and professional efficiency became the cultural mainstream for a maturing middle class. A generation of civil servants and leading women professionals came of age in such an environment. The term *nü qiangren*, which emerged in the media in the 1970s, became a household word in the subsequent decades.

A book on Japanese women is illuminating. *Women on the Verge* by Karen Kelsky, analyzes the hearts and minds of more than sixty women who represent a class of globally mobile, cosmopolitan professionals.

Although the book focuses on erotic imaginings that are intertwined with public discourses on modernity and occidental representations, the author provides a useful analytical framework to examine how individuals engage with mainstream ideological typifications. Agency is often charged with ambiguity, complicity, and defiance. The ironic twist in this case is that the marginal positions of women in Japan's political and corporate structures have given educated women unusual opportunities to explore foreign travel and global careers. Exploring space between racial and erotic politics, these women are able to challenge rigid expectations of sexuality, marriage, family, and career.[6] In a different cultural environment, Saba Mahmood finds agency among her ethnographic subjects in Cairo, Egypt, who intertwine professional aspirations with religious and moral expectations, which are highly gendered.

Have Hong Kong women in the postwar decades found themselves in similar circumstances? What gendered spaces and structural positions have been available to them?

They do not share the fate of millions of migrant working women who have joined global assembly lines and whose mobile bodies are often consumed in services and entertainment industries far from home. Instead, the world has come to professional Hong Kong women, who have attained high positions in business and administrative hierarchies. With what cultural images and typifications have these women engaged in their distinguished mobility tracks?

Recent data show their accomplishments. According to census data in 1996, 86% of the territory's women between the ages of fifteen and forty-four received postsecondary education. By 2006, the percentage had increased to 92%.[7] Business data show that women have surpassed men in their independent personal assets. Of those who held liquid assets of more than HK$1 million, 51% were women. For the professional "aristocrats" — those whose monthly earnings are HK$100,000 and above, 21% are women, up from 16% in the previous year. Moreover, 83% of corporations in the territory find women among their senior ranking executives.[8] In government and public service sectors, women also occupy leading positions and often top public opinion polls.[9] How have they managed to achieve such distinguished track records?

Women from wealthy families in Hong Kong have always enjoyed visibility. Their rise is attributed, according to popular opinion, to factors unrelated to their professional ability. Although some have received excellent educations overseas, their family ties by birth or marriage are highlighted. They assume honorable directorships in charitable organizations, such as the Tung Wah Group of Hospitals and the Po Leung Kuk. Some take on community work — neighborhood services for the elderly, women's welfare, and the like.[10]

Conflicting images are visible in publications that are focused on women. In library collections, one finds newsletters and annual reports of the Young Women's Christian Association, or the *Xianggang funü nianbao,* dating back decades. Today, at every newspaper stand, popular bookstore, and hotel, one finds the *Hong Kong Tattler, Qingxiu zazhi, Jiemei,* and the like.[11] At the lowbrow end, pornographic displays of women in daily Chinese newspapers and tabloids are marketed with little inhibition.

At the top of the class hierarchy, several generations of foreign-educated, cosmopolitan socialites patronize the performing arts and galleries. Many are "trendsetters," and their social presence is fodder for tabloid gossip. However, participation in charities and a degree of conspicuous consumption have been expected of wealthy families. Female members of these families shoulder some of the public responsibilities. Their visibility has not seriously changed gender expectations in a men's world.[12] When certain social liberties of the wealthy become known, the local tabloids are ecstatic. Public sentiments seldom side with the women involved.

Nonetheless, the term *nü qiangren,* which emerged in the media in the early 1970s, conjures a distinct image of one who is professionally in charge. Women might have started a quiet "revolution" by taking up administrative positions within the civil service, but they have remained relatively faceless in the public. Civil servants in the colonial era — both men and women — were trained to be committed executives behind the scenes. They did not pursue political careers. That was the colonial culture, as David Faure points out.[13] Instead, visible figures of women in charge came from the media industry and public service appointments. In a volume of essays entitled *Xianggang Xianggang,* Liu Su, a journalist, traces the history of the emergence of these public figures. He lists several prime examples of women of influence. One was Mrs Selina Chow, anchor and television executive in the 1970s, appointed Executive Council member in the 1980s. Lady Lydia Dunn, educated in the United States, became a director for the Swire Group and was later appointed chair of the Trade Development Council and chief nongovernment Executive Council member. She was given a baroness title in the 1990s and joined the House of Lords. Maria Tam was a lawyer by training, with business interests in China. In the two decades before 1997, the Hong Kong and Chinese governments appointed her to numerous public service committees. For the civil service, Anson Chan was appointed the first director of a government department in 1984. Man-yee Cheung was director of information in 1985 when she was in her thirties.[14] However, public attention focused on these women only when the nature of the civil service and the issues of press freedom emerged as major issues in the heated political negotiations leading to 1997.

As the negotiations for Hong Kong's fate continued from the mid 1980s to the few years beyond 1997, many more professional women were projected onto the public service and politics scene. Some prominent figures included a Secretary for Education and Manpower, Fanny Law; a chair of the Legislative Council, Rita Fan; a Secretary for Justice, Elsie Leung; a Secretary for Security, Regina Ip; an Executive Council member, Rosanna Wong; a chairperson of Equal Opportunities Commission (EOC), Anna Wu; a chairperson of University Grants Committee, Alice Lam; and, in the finance arena, Laura Cha. An American trained lawyer, Cha, became chair of Hong Kong's powerful Securities and Futures Commission in the 1990s, finished a three-year term as vice chair of China's Securities Commission (a deputy minister rank) in 2005. In 2007, she replaced Lam as chair of the University Grants Committee, which advises the government on policies and funding for Hong Kong's eight institutions of higher education. Christine Loh, a former legislative councilor turned public advocate on the environment, maintains her distance from government appointments. One also finds Margaret Ng, four time elected legislative councilor for the legal constituency and a leading member of the newly formed Civic Party, who advocates close public scrutiny of government policies and procedures.

In the local political arena, few women have commanded as much awe across the broad spectrum of public opinion as Anson Chan, both in Hong Kong and internationally. From Chan's appointment as Chief Secretary in 1995 to her resignation in 2001, she generated unprecedented charisma in the public imagination. After a few years of staying on the margins of the local political arena, she once again propelled herself into the limelight by entering a race in the by-election of a seat in the Legislative Council in 2007, competing with the former Secretary of Security, Regina Ip, who also flaunted her political ambitions after a few years of "retirement" from the civil service.[15] What does the public expect from these women of influence?

"Mrs Chan, Chief Secretary"

Three days after her appointment by Governor Chris Patten in 1993 as Chief Secretary, Anson Chan and seventeen members of her natal family returned to Anhui Province to attend ancestral rituals, which "traditionally" belonged to a male domain. The focus on her took on a new meaning. It reminded one of a scholar who had taken first place in the civil service examinations during the imperial period. With official appointments, he returned to his native place to pay respect to ancestors. In fact, a provincial official equated Anson's position with an "official appointment of the first grade" (*yipin guan*). The ancestral ceremonies were formally conducted to commemorate the rebuilding of the tomb of her grandfather, General Fang Zhenwu, who was remembered for fighting bravely against Japanese aggression in China during the war. The political consultative committee and the Anhui provincial government issued the invitations explicitly for such a purpose. However, there was little doubt that Anson was the center of attention, in the Hong Kong media if not in China.[16] In addition to pictures of her and her family at the newly erected tomb of General Fang, there was a prominent photo of her standing in front of the county temple for an imperial official, Judge Bao, the classic symbol of fearless, unyielding integrity and fairness. It was clear what the Hong Kong media expected of her.

The Chinese government also seemed anxious to fit her into a significant genealogy, even if it were a link with her natal family and not her husband's. With the change of Hong Kong's sovereignty fewer than four years away, Anson's appointment by the last governor could mean that she would be a significant political player in the post-1997 administration of the territory. The government seemed eager to sell patriotism to the Hong Kong Chinese, and it was important that her grandfather had been a famous general during the anti-Japanese war. The uncle, with whom she grew up, Dr Fang Xinrang, was an another bonus. Because he promoted the interests of the physically disabled, he had been friendly with the crippled son of China's supreme leader, Deng Xiaoping, and with Lu Ping, director of the Hong Kong and Macao Affairs Office of the State Council. Pro-China newspapers in Hong Kong already stressed her "strong and genuine nationalistic sentiments." In addition to her role as the first female Chief Secretary, she was also praised as the first Chinese to assume the position.[17]

In a merchant society with built-in Confucian pretensions, the public did not miss the detail that her mother had been an accomplished painter. Her mother's acceptance by the Chinese authorities was subtly hinted, because she had staged several exhibitions on the mainland. Moreover, one of Anson's brothers was a medical specialist and the other a translator at the United Nations. Like Anson, they were modern versions of the literati.

Her natal family background aside, the media portrayed her as a conscientious wife and filial daughter. The images were intended for those who cared about the duties of women and family, and newspapers dotingly described her weekly Sunday lunch with her mother at an up-scale restaurant in The Pacific Place, Central. In an interview, she admitted that if her husband had objected to her appointment, she might not have taken the job. Fitting the traditional expectations of merchant families, she was appreciated by her husband as being "presentable in both the sitting room and the kitchen." A Chinese newspaper in Hong Kong summed up her admirable qualities as "having been brought up in a traditional Chinese family and steeped in the Confucian values of loyalty and filial piety."[18]

In preparation for her career, she had attended the appropriate schools — she had received an elite English education in a Catholic secondary school and later matriculated at The University of Hong Kong, where most civil servants in Hong Kong were trained. She joined the colonial civil service with her cohort of university graduates, who eventually made up the core of local administrative officers in the years when Hong Kong changed from a marginal colonial society to a dynamic regional financial hub. When a competitive market demanded excellence and style, an elitist education system trained the territory's best, both women and men. Anson was a beneficiary of this system, and she made good use of such opportunities. At the time of her appointment as Chief Secretary, she had accumulated thirty-one years of service in the government.

What does the public then and now see in Anson Chan? Competence is not her monopoly; there are numerous administrators in and outside government who are equally competent. Her record is not impeccable. She is known to be uncompromising. When she was Secretary for Social Welfare, she was severely criticized in the incident of the "Kwok girl," when she ordered the child to be forcibly taken from an emotionally disturbed mother. She is not more articulate than many of the members of the legislative and executive councils. If wealth commands power, her personal circumstances, although comfortable, are by no means outstanding. How do her public images reflect social expectations? Have these expectations changed during the crucial years of political transition in the late 1990s? What lies ahead for prominent female civil servants like her, twelve years into the Special Administrative Region (SAR)?

During the ceremonies of the changeover in 1997, Anson attended the occasion with the chief executive, the top civil servants, and Chinese leaders. In the sea of black suits and military uniforms, she stood at the top of the empty aisle that divided two sets of officials and guests. The image of her dressed in red, in a space "in between" at the center of the stage, was remarkably unintentional. Was she representing the ambivalent position of a colonial civil service, an integral part of an unprecedented political experiment, or, for the gendered space of her generation of women professionals and public figures, an ominous turning point?

In the short ten years of Hong Kong's precarious transition, she projected herself to the world media as "Hong Kong's Iron Lady" and "the Conscience of Hong Kong" who would stand firm for her city's values.[19] As lawyer/ elected legislator Margaret Ng commented, "When she was chosen by Governor Chris Patten for the job of Chief Secretary she had seniority and stamina and the wide support of the civil service as typifying their values but little international exposure or star quality. She was groomed into the leading role and she rose elegantly to the occasion."[20] That was also why, on hearing her resignation in January 2001, no one would take her reasons at face value. Margaret Ng again puts it poignantly, "Well brought up senior civil servants do not normally resign for 'personal reasons' and 'to spend time with their families.' Undoubtedly, her resignation signifies a failed experiment — to transplant the values of Hong Kong's civil service to the post-1997 administration." Her tenure in the 1990s, however, symbolized the high point of a generation of women in the public service arena, whose positions belonged to a particular historical moment in Hong Kong's effort to straddle the world and nation. What can we learn from the lives and careers of these women, about the transformations that marked Hong Kong's distinctive character in the postwar years?

The Party of Handbags (*Shoudai dang*)

Anson Chan was not alone in her precipitous rise through the late colonial civil service. The number of female civil servants increased from 34,322 in 1980 to 61,566 in 2000, constituting 33% of government employees.[21] In the same period, an additional 19,000 plus men entered the civil service, but their ratio to the overall number dropped by 8%. Moreover, among the 1,272 civil servants who were at the directorate level and higher, twenty-two percent were women. Because eight out of the twenty-two highest ranked officials (bureau chiefs) were women, this group of female civil servants had earned the nickname of "the party of handbags" (*shoudai dang*). In the late 1990s, around the time of Hong Kong's return to China, these visibly fashionable and powerful women became household names to the Hong Kong public.[22] (See Tables 8.1 and 8.2.) The following newspaper reporting was not uncommon:

Table 8.1   Gender ratio of director-level appointments in the Hong Kong government, 2000

Grade	Female	Male
D7 or above	*5 (23%)	17 (77%)
D5 and D6	11 (18%)	49 (82%)
D4	40 (22%)	145 (78%)
D1 and D2	219 (22%)	786 (78%)
Total:	275 (22%)	997 (78%)

Source: *Apple Daily*, June 25, 2000, A12.

NB: Three more female officials were appointed as D7 or above by the HKSAR government in July 2000. It increased the total number from five to eight persons and changed the percentage to 36%. The higher the number in the D grades, the higher the position in the civil service hierarchy.

Table 8.2   Leading female civil servants, June 2000

Anson Chan (Chief Secretary)

Elsie Leung (Secretary of Justice)

Regina Ip Lau Suk-yee (Secretary for Security)

Denise Yue Chung-yee (Secretary for the Treasury)

Lily Yam Kwan Pui-ying (Secretary for Environment and Food)

Fanny Law (Secretary for Education and Manpower)

Carrie Yau Tsang Ka-lai (Secretary for Information Technology and Broadcasting)

Sandra Lee Suk-yee (Secretary for Economic Services)

Shelley Lee Lai-kuen (Director for Home Affairs)

Chan Fung Fu-chen (Director of Health)

Chung Lai-kwok (Deputy Secretary for Housing)

Cheung Man-yee (former Director of Broadcasting; became Trade Commissioner for Japan)

Jacqueline Willis (Hong Kong Commissioner for Economic and Trade Affairs, USA)

Elizabeth Wong Chi-lien (retired Secretary for Health and Welfare)

Katherine Fok Lo Shiu-ching (retired Secretary for Health and Welfare)

Source: *Apple Daily*, June 25, 2000, A12.

It is well known that inside the government, there is a "party of handbags." Party members are all high-ranking female officials. At the top of the list is Chief Secretary Anson Chan. Then there is Secretary of Health and Welfare Fok Law Siu-ching, Secretary of the Treasury Yue Chung-yee . . . former Director of News and Information Irene Yau, among others. . . . In the 1970s, Anson Chan and a group of female administrative officers formed the Association of Women Administrative Officers. Together they struggled for their future and for treatment equal to their male peers. Their emotional bonding began then. Today these highly placed comrades-in-arms have continued their regular gatherings. This includes their annual "Shanghai crab" dinner. We hear that the members are planning to launch a large-scale anniversary celebration of their struggle for equal contract terms. With such bonding among the female high officials, it is not surprising that some commented with a sigh, saying 'Why are the men like a heap of sand?'[23]

Who were these civil servants? What quality and authority did the public expect from them? How were they judged, addressed, confronted? Ma Zhenping, a long-time Beijing resident who worked in Hong Kong for a mainland Chinese business could only marvel at the opportunities Hong Kong women had enjoyed. Except for the impression that capable women seemed to have a hard time finding deserving husbands, he considered them the most fortunate of their gender in the world. Having experienced the "unisex" images of women on mainland China and what he termed the "hysterical assertiveness" of women red guards during the Cultural Revolution, he found Hong Kong professional women particularly gentle in their sophistication. However, he was baffled that, unlike in Taiwan, when feminists took to the streets — even on matters of unequal access to public toilets — Hong Kong women were unusually tolerant of the claims by their male counterparts. Moreover, as cosmopolitan and liberated as they were, many of the most powerful Hong Kong women continued to use their married name rather than their own.[24]

Ma Zhenping was not alone in his bewilderment. When Denise Yu became a secretary-level official, she dazzled the public with her good looks, her well-groomed manners, and her elegantly tailored Chinese dresses. That she had remained single was an issue for a concerned male caller on a radio talk show. "Why would such an attractive and feminine figure not have a husband and family?" he asked. Cheung Man-yee, former Director of Broadcasting, was another target for male commentary. Known for her fiery temper, uncompromising political stance, and nicknamed "Big Sister Cheung," she had been admired by friends and foes as "one of Hong Kong's most glamorous unmarried woman."[25]

There was also negative and equally gendered public opinion about some of these women in charge. Regina Ip, then Secretary for Immigration and Security, had been a very unpopular figure among the liberal minded citizens because of her harsh political views and tough "law- and-order" practices. However, rather than focusing on these issues, the tabloid media caricatured her in physically unflattering ways — her looks, her hairdo, her clothes.[26] Ip tried to sue the publishers on sex discrimination charges, claiming that her image had been distorted, but the Equal Opportunities Commission (headed by Anna Wu, a prominent liberal-minded lawyer) turned her case down for lack of an issue. Shortly after the controversy, a well-respected media anchorman interviewed her on his television program. She voiced her bitterness but also revealed her struggles as a widow and a loving mother. Even after she resigned in the wake of the government's controversial push in July 2003 to pass the Article 23 legislation for national security, public opinion for her remained divided.[27] In 2006, she returned to the Hong Kong political scene after an educational sojourn at Stanford University. Although the media was quick to comment on her "improved" hairstyle, attention has shifted to her political ambitions in Hong Kong.

What contributed to these conflicting images and expectations of women among the Hong Kong public? In the postwar decades, were these women given unprecedented career opportunities but not the cultural space for gendered expectations to be challenged? Why did their careers cluster in the public sector rather than in corporate businesses and academics?[28] Was this due to a colonial education, a late colonial career structure, and/ or an expanding white-collar, nonprofit sector in which women could excel without intruding on male territory? Or have literati pretensions of a mercantile society continued to frame modern family life and women's self-perceptions? The answers to these questions can be complex.

I do not intend to conduct an in depth sociological analysis of each and every one of these leading civil servants compared to their male counterparts. It is nonetheless useful to explore a few underlying issues. The educational backgrounds of this generation of women civil servants and of public figures were remarkably similar. They had years of missionary schooling and acquired superb English language skills and at times a religious commitment to public service. According to some who attended Catholic girl's schools, there were real life models — teachers and school administrators (foreign and local) who were women. Many graduates continued to bond with their secondary schools. In serving on school boards, giving public lectures, participating in speech-day activities, these career women were models for young school children. Table 8.3 shows some top missionary schools in the territory with long histories.

Table 8.3   Leading missionary schools and their distinguished graduates in 2007

St. Paul's Co-educational College	Selina Chow Liang (elected legislator) Maria Tam (former appointed legislator) Audrey Eu (elected legislator)
Sacred Heart Canossian College	Anson Chan (former Chief Secretary) Elsie Leung (former Secretary for Justice) Lily Yam (former Secretary for Environment and Food)
Maryknoll Sisters' School	Lau Kin-yee (elected legislator) Anna Wu (former appointed legislator and Chair of Equal Opportunities Commission) Emily Lau (elected legislator) Laura Cha (former chair of the Securities and Futures Commission) Shelley Lee (Permanent Secretary for Home Affairs)
Diocesan Girls' School	Wong Chien Chi-lien (former Secretary for Health and Welfare) Katherine Fok Lo Shiu-ching (former Secretary for Health and Welfare) Carrie Yau Tsang Ka-lai (Permanent Secretary for Health, Welfare and Food) Jacqueline Willis (former Trade and Development Commissioner for the SAR in the United States) Sandra Lee Suk-yee (former Secretary for Economic Development) Sarah Liao (former Secretary for the Environment, Transport and Works) Mrs Rebecca Lai Ko Wing-yee (former Permanent Secretary for the Civil Service)
St. Paul's Convent School	Lydia Dunn (former appointed senior legislator, former Chair of Trade Development Council) Margaret Ng (lawyer and elected legislator) Carrie Yau (Secretary for Information Technology and Broadcasting)
St. Mary's Canossian College	Fanny Law (former Secretary for Education and Manpower) Alice Tai (Ombudsman)
St. Stephen's Girls' College	Rita Fan (appointed, elected legislator and chair of the Legislative Council) Kwan Suk-wah (former Chief Executive of the Family Planning Commission) Regina Ip (former Secretary for Security) Rosanna Wong Yick-ming (former Chair of the Hong Kong Housing Authority)
Belilios Public School	Denise Yue (Secretary for the Civil Service) Nellie Fong Wong Kut-man (former member of the Executive Council of Hong Kong and Legislative Council of Hong Kong)

An English education in an elite missionary school was an important credential. It groomed the women to become the 2% who received university education in the 1970s and 1980s. Table 8.4 shows a large number of past and present women civil servants and those in public service who have attended the University of Hong Kong. According to three active women lawyers whom I interviewed, their fellow women students in secondary schools or universities were particularly good with the English language. Such language skills were necessary for recruitment into executive and administrative officer ranks in the government. Moreover, many women students chose humanities and social science subjects rather than fields traditionally considered the domain of men, such as science, medicine, and engineering. When it came to qualifications for administrative officer positions, which valued an all-round liberal education, the brightest students in the arts subjects were encouraged to apply.[29]

Table 8.4   Top civil servants in the late 1990s who attended the University of Hong Kong

Name	Major	Entry point	Year and highest position attained	
Anson Chan	English	1962	1993	Chief Secretary
Yam Kwan Pui-ying	Arts	1969	2000	Secretary for Environment and Food
Fanny Law	Chemistry	1975	2000	Secretary for Education and Manpower
Wong Chien Chi-lien	English Literature	1969	1990	Secretary for Health and Welfare
Jacqueline Willis	Arts	1969	1999	Hong Kong Commissioner for Economic and Trade Affairs, USA
Ip Lau Suk-yee	English Literature	1975	1998	Secretary for Security
Sarah Liao	Chemistry and Botany	1973	2002	Secretary for the Environment, Transport and Works
Denise Yue	History	1974	1998	Secretary for the Treasury
Alice Tai Yuen-ying	Law	1974	1999	Ombudsman
Carrie Yau	Social Sciences	1977	1995 1997 2000	Deputy Secretary for Security Director of Administration Secretary for Information Technology and Broadcasting
Rita Lau Ng Wai-lan	Arts	1976	1999	Director of Urban Services
Lee Suk-yee	Arts	1974	2000	Secretary for Economic Services
Shelley Lee	Arts	1971	1995	Director for Home Affairs

Language proficiency also allowed these women to choose law as their major. With a law degree and experience in private practice, many were appointed to the legislative and executive councils before and after 1997 and to public service organizations and government commissions.[30] The number of women lawyers in Hong Kong has been high. At the Faculty of Law at The University of Hong Kong, women students have outnumbered men in recent years. In the 1960s, 10% of the lawyers were women. By the early 1990s, there were 30%, and their organizational strength was visible in the Bar Association (headed many times by women), the Solicitors Association, and the Hong Kong Women Lawyer's Association.[31] During a reunion dinner to celebrate the ninetieth anniversary of The University of Hong Kong's founding in 2000, those who stepped onto the stage as "old girls" from the Lady Ho-Tung Hall were predominantly public figures and civil servants, led by the then Chief Secretary Anson Chan, and her Party of Handbags.[32]

One may argue that a larger number of male students also went through the same educational process. They attended top missionary schools for boys and went on to The University of Hong Kong. Why then were the women administrative officers pushed into public prominence? David Faure, in his work on the colonial history of Hong Kong, points to the inherent inequality of opportunities between local and expatriate civil servants and a culture that avoided political dialogue:

> . . . I do not think Hong Kong people were apolitical throughout the 1950s and 1960s, and yet I also said that within Hong Kong's political ideology, there has long been the sense that Hong Kong people cannot govern themselves. For this reason, I find the postwar generation of Hong Kong University graduates fascinating. Trained in the best of Eastern and Western traditions, groomed for Hong Kong's upper echelon, they should be the elite if ever there is an elite in Hong Kong society. And inculcated with a strong sense of social responsibility, should they not provide intellectual leadership? . . . Acting on a small stage, Hong Kong's great men had only the aspirations to match, and understandably, these turned to business, community service, and the professions. I have not mentioned the civil service, for even in 1945, no Chinese person graduating from Hong Kong University would have thought about a senior appointment in the civil service . . . It was not until the mid-1950s that the recruitment of Chinese people as Administrative Officers, as Cadet Officers came to be called, became a matter of routine. How far might Hong Kong University's graduates think advancement could lead? I dare say no Chinese person would have dreamt of rising to head of department (let along being Governor of Hong Kong), for localization was not even in the air.[33]

Many of the men who turned away from careers in government excelled in the private sector. There have been successful lawyers in private practice from that generation, including the legendary barrister Patrick Yu.[34] Men also more readily joined family businesses, which were rarely inherited by daughters. If the logic of Faure's argument is correct — that Hong Kong's bright male graduates did not compete with women for political careers because they had better mobility choices — the success of women civil servants was but a fortuitous historical moment rather than a real reversal of gender hierarchy. They settled into these administrative positions because they, their families, and the public did not expect much for women's careers.

Political Stars: Revisiting Political Charisma

The mixed signals for the party of handbags did not mean that traditional values governing gender relationships had not been challenged. At approximately the same time that Anson and her party of handbags rose to prominence in the civil service, another group of women professionals made their political debut. Although quite similar to the civil servants in background, training, and glamour, they occupied visible social and political spaces. The public also seemed to judge them with remarkably mixed gender notions.

Mrs Ellen Li was a very prominent "merchant's daughter" of a generation before the postwar baby-boomers, and her career spanned almost half a century. Born of Fujianese parents in Saigon in the early Republican era, she was given every educational opportunity — a boy's school in Saigon, an English boarding school (St. Stephen's Girls' College) in Hong Kong, and a university in Shanghai run by American Baptists. Her father had emigrated to Vietnam in his youth and worked his way up to become a successful rice merchant. He was rather indulgent with his only daughter, grooming her alongside his sons and making it known that she would one day help her elder brother in the family business. In her boarding school years, she was given generous allowances because her father believed that a woman should be economically independent to protect herself from temptations and vices.

After she graduated with a degree in business, Mrs Li worked for nearly ten years in the China and South Sea Bank in Hong Kong, attaining managerial ranks and the respect of her male colleagues. Although she eventually married into a family of medical professionals and spent most of her time raising her children, she fulfilled all the public duties of a wife from a politically influential family. She took up the cause of women's welfare in Hong Kong. From the 1950s to the 1980s, the government showered her with honors and public responsibilities. The University of Hong Kong awarded her an honorary doctorate. In 1993, she granted me a lunch interview at her favorite Hong Kong Country Club. In her mid-eighties, the elegant matriarch was happy about the structural changes that had resulted from her decades of effort and was eager to have the younger generation do much more.

In her autobiography, she highlighted the efforts she had made in the Hong Kong government's provision for women. This included a list of public service positions: founder and president of the Hong Kong Chinese Women Club (1938–90), the Hong Kong Family Planning Association (1951–90), the Hong Kong YWCA (board member since 1946), the Federation of University Women, and the Hong Kong Council of Women. In the popular press, she achieved four "firsts." She was the first woman in Hong Kong to receive the Commander of the British Empire honor from the Queen in 1974, the first Chinese women to receive an honorary LLD from the University of Hong Kong, the first woman to be appointed to the Urban Council and later to the Legislative Council (1965).[35] Anyone who treated her as a "tai tai" type would have seen her true colors.[36] She once resigned from the bank because it had assumed that, with a husband to support her, she did not need a salary raise. In an American Independence Day reception from which spouses were excluded, she insisted on attending as an independent legislator. Her biggest victory in the Hong Kong legislature, as she saw it, was the successful fight in 1973 against legal concubinage.

An essay in the *South China Morning Post* (October 26, 1985) succinctly summarized the public's appreciation of her. In "Portrait of a Crusader," Vernon Ram reported:

> Chinese women, who today enjoy a high profile in the professions and public life in Hong Kong, owe their success largely to the crusading zeal of one woman. That woman is Dr Ellen Li, 77, now a retired senior citizen. . . . Some of today's leading women legislators and business executives were either not born, or were mere toddlers, when Dr Li mounted a one-woman campaign for legislation for monogamous marriages to bring the law in line with those in force in China and Taiwan. Dr Li took it upon herself because the Hong Kong Government found itself increasingly involved in complex court cases arising from Chinese family disputes, mostly relating to inheritance. A seven-man committee was appointed to look into the situation and make a report. The report came out in 1949 — and was promptly shelved. Dr Li next organized a petition and presented it to the then Governor, Sir Alexander Grantham, who admitted he knew

nothing about Chinese law. So he sought the opinion of Sir Man-kam Lo who summarily vetoed the proposal. Then began a 20-year battle when Dr Li tirelessly campaigned for the long overdue reforms. Crucial to the law was the definition of a legal marriage in a social climate where concubinage left grey areas in respect of inheritance and legitimacy. About ten pieces of legislation depended on it. But thanks to sympathetic Legco members — particularly the then Attorney-General Denys (now Sir Denys) Roberts — Dr Li's efforts were crowned with success and the Marriage Reform Bill became law in 1973. Dr Li, a deceptively soft-spoken woman in an elegantly tailored cheongsam, employs a rapier-sharp wit and incisive logic — a refreshing contrast to the sledgehammer rhetoric of some latter date women's libbers — to score her points.

"There are three social injustices that I wanted put right," Dr Li said in 1968. "First: equal pay for equal work for women. Second: a marriage law, which would fully protect the rights of women. Third: amendments to the law of succession so that women would enjoy the same property inheritance rights as men. . . . It would have been a waste of my education just to play mahjong all day. I decided that with my financial training and business experience, I could help different organizations. . . . Even before the war I used to say Hong Kong was 50 years behind the rest of the world in culture and attitudes. Before the war, I did not care too much because I never thought I would stay. But now it was different. That started the drive in 1949 to get some of the inhibiting laws changed." The rest of course is history.[37]

She passed away in September 2005 at the age of ninety-eight. Granted that Dr Ellen Li's case is unusual, it is nevertheless interesting to note the underlying structure of opportunity for this class of elite women. The merchant's daughter's background in coastal south China gave her the resources, social networks, and a perspective. Transnational business contacts, a colonial structure shaken by war and revolution, and a new industrial society in the making, provided Li the space to make a life that was fulfilling and meaningful. What she enjoyed could have been rare opportunities in an uncertain time, but postwar Hong Kong has had a liberalized and expanded economy that has allowed rapid social mobility for an entire generation.

Outstanding political figures of this younger generation today are too numerous to name here.[38] This chapter will focus on three — Anna Wu, Christine Loh, and Margaret Ng. They have pursued distinguished public service careers as lawyers, members of government commissions and policy think tanks, and elected legislators. Their careers and the public's opinions of them have unveiled changing gender expectations in a historical juncture in Hong Kong when social and cultural identities are reconstituted in another turbulent political environment.

Anna Wu was a senior partner of a law firm when she was appointed by the then Governor of Hong Kong to the Legislative Council in 1992. Like many civil servants, she attended a top missionary school (Maryknoll Sisters' School) and graduated with a law degree from the University of Hong Kong in the early 1970s. She was fortunate, she says, that her parents could afford to provide equal educational opportunities for her and her brothers. As the eldest daughter, she was expected to shoulder family responsibilities. In our conversations over the years, she admits that she appreciates her parents' attention and trust, but deep down she knows that they wish she were a son.[39] However, she has had ample female professional models. Ella Cheong, her teacher who supervised her practical training, is a senior partner in the law firm Wilkinson and Gist and a world expert on patent and copyright law.

Although low-key in style, she remains a passionate and uncompromising defender of equal opportunity rights. When she joined the Legislative Council at the invitation of Governor Chris Patten, she had no particular political agenda but a sense of public duty. Gradually, she focused on women and equal opportunity issues. In 1995, while a member of the Equal Opportunities Commission (EOC), she used over a million dollars of her own funds to put together an expert study and then a comprehensive legislative bill on the topic. Her proposed bill covered discriminations based on age, gender, race/ethnicity, religion, political beliefs, and union activities. When the government struck down the bill by a massive persuasion campaign in and out of the Legislative Council, Anna Wu openly displayed her frustrations and criticized the government for "employing despicable tactics." The media, grateful for her integrity and courage, crowned her "mother of equal opportunity."[40]

In May 1999, Anson Chan, as Chief Secretary, invited Anna to become chair of the Equal Opportunities Commission. Anna accepted the challenge, although her appointment took many by surprise. Few expected the government to invite one of its most vigilant critics. True to her professional passion, she advocated proactive ways of educating the public on issues of discrimination. She vowed to seek better understanding of those marginalized (such as the mentally ill, AIDS patients, etc.) and would not hesitate to go to court on their behalf. She was also determined to investigate unfair practices in government departments and businesses.

These were not empty promises. In her three years as chair, she pursued several high profile legal battles. Among them were cases involving gender discrimination. A court in February 2001 ruled against an employer for subjecting a staff member to unlawful discrimination on the grounds of her pregnancy. A more daring case involved taking on the education department. Shortly after she took office as chair of the commission, she followed through with an investigative report on the Secondary School Places Allocation System (SSPA), which had been used by the government to allocate children to places in secondary schools since 1978. However, the allocation for girls and boys was given different queues, and there were fixed gender quotas in coeducational schools. The EOC received complaints from parents who felt their children had been unfairly denied access to schools of their choice. Despite the government's loud objections, the EOC sought a judicial review. In June 2001, the High Court ruled that the SSPA was unlawful. After the court ruling, Anna Wu stated:

> The High Court ruling offers clarity, and will create certainty for all parties. Good governance and accountability now require the Government and the Education Department to act quickly, to save further costs and to minimize the confusion for students, parents, and schools. It is a matter of enormous public importance for the Government and the Education Department to rectify the system as a basic educational concern. Our students are entitled to and deserve an education system that is open, fair, and non-discriminatory.[41]

Her professionalism contrasted sharply with the bureaucratic maneuvers of government departments, and won her public appreciation.[42] In the minds of many, she was "a woman of influence" who listened to the voices of the disadvantaged. Her eventual departure from the Commission was politically controversial, and she received a degree of public support. She has since taken up other social causes and put her efforts into private charity and legal education.

Christine Loh, a contemporary of Anna Wu, was appointed to the Legislative Council in October 1992. She was a founding member of the Observer, an organization formed in 1987 by a group of public-minded professionals. After her initial speech to the Legislative Council, the public knew they were observing a rising political star. A leading article in the English paper, *South China Morning Post*, announced "Christine Loh Speaks her Mind and Wins her Spurs." Known to be forthright, principled, and extremely articulate, Christine entered the political arena in the 1990s with agendas that were progressive and cosmopolitan — broad-minded interpretations of the arts, promotion of awareness of ethnic and other social discriminations, challenges to entrenched inheritance customs in the lineage-based villages of the New Territories, and, most important, public mobilization on environmental issues. Although seen by some as a protégé of the last governor, Chris Patten, Christine was one of the few legislators who looked beyond local politics in Hong Kong and cultivated non-government institutional ties overseas. Over the years since she has become politically visible, local media often address her using the endearing term "foreign little devil" (*gui mui tsai*). Conservative Chinese officials, however, have found her "Westernized" ways uncomfortable, because she does not play by their cultural rules nor toe the political line.

Her upbringing is not atypical of a postwar generation of children in Hong Kong who were born into very comfortable circumstances. Another "merchant's daughter," she grew up with a household full of professionally independent women.[43] Christine spent her childhood in a French convent primary school where she learned English and French, and where many of her classmates came from different parts of the world. At age thirteen, she attended a boarding school in England. Like many other professional women of her generation, she graduated with a law degree from an English university and nurtured an educated interest in the arts. Her exposure to China was early, when she worked her way up the corporate ladder of a leading multinational firm engaged in commodity trading with China.

The Hong Kong public has come to know her through her political activism. As early as 1985, she joined "Friends of the Earth," and since served twice as chair of the board. After an appointed term in the Legislative Council, she ran two successful direct election campaigns, in 1995 and 1998, receiving top votes among candidates for the Hong Kong Island geographical district. In 1994, she had started to publish the "Alternate Policy Address," along side of the annual policy address by Governor Chris Patten and later the Chief Executive. It openly challenged the entrenched assumptions of the government about major policy issues. In 1997, she set up the Citizens Party, with an agenda that focused on the environment and appealed to young, educated, and globally oriented middle class voters. In the Alternate Policy Address for 1997–1998, she advocated a "five-year plan," a bold model for economic and social enterprise. In 1999, she addressed the Chief Executive's idea of building Hong Kong into a world city. To claim competitive advantage, she argued, Hong Kong must enhance its characteristic freedoms, capitalize on the city's multicultural mix, invest aggressively in education, stay civil, open, and connected, and, last but not least, be environmentally sustainable.[44]

The public would identify her most with environmental issues. Looking back, she feels that their efforts have partially saved the Victoria Harbour.

It took a great deal of patience and years of research, she says, to stir up public voices against the government's plans to reclaim land along the harbor. The bill she drafted and introduced at the Legislative Council was finally passed in the late 1990s, drastically restricting the government proposals. She sees the value of reinforcing grassroot green movements with professional voices to create formidable pressure. Her focus on the educated classes has cost her votes, because political foes pick on her apparent lack of exposure to the conditions of Hong Kong's poor.

Her decision not to run for another term in the September 2000 election disappointed many, not the least the media, which lost one of its stars for eye-catching headlines. She was frustrated at the Legislative Council's lack of impact and decided to explore other channels of political communication on issues she cared about.[45] Fellow councilors attributed the frustration to her inability to engage with party politics. "She is a political loner," said James Tien, then co-chair of the pro-business Liberal Party.[46] In the wake of Christine's decision not to seek reelection, a leading media host pointed to the possibility that voters would soon forget her. Her answer was straightforward. She did not mind shying away from the political limelight, because appealing to an electoral public to build power had never been a direction she intended to take. She would devote much of her time to securing effective means to incite public policy debates. Rather than seeing her action as a retirement from activism, she insisted that it was a renewed involvement.[47] She has remained fiercely independent in political practice and spirit.

Her liberal democratic leanings have directed her to advocate for the environment and also for human rights, the plight of AIDS patients, avant garde art, consumer's rights, and citizen's informed political engagement. With the help of friends, she raised enough funds to set up a policy "think tank." The small research institute, Civic Exchange, churns out voluminous papers and commentaries on Hong Kong's major policy issues — the environmental hazards of further reclaiming the harbor, the coastal highway along the southwestern part of Hong Kong Island, the Disneyland project on Lantau Island, and the government's controversial Western Kowloon Cultural District proposal. There are also substantive reports, such as the one on how to better integrate Hong Kong and the economically vibrant Pearl River Delta.[48] She is particularly critical of the government's paper on "Hong Kong 2030: Planning Visions and Strategies" and urges the government to look beyond Hong Kong to better cultivate a hinterland in China. She also highlights the institutional "software" that a city like Hong Kong uniquely possesses — the rule of law, personal freedoms, open and fluid movement of information and capital, and competitive advantages that are not even mentioned in the government document.[49] Her means of reaching out is characteristically unconventional. Exploiting Internet technology, she maintains a "cyber community" of informed public opinion. In fact, protests through Christine's cyber network against the government's proposal to reclaim the Western District harbor forced the policy makers to drastically scale back the plans.[50] Environmental causes remain her major focus, and although critical of short-term government agendas, she is capable of working within the mainstream. In 2006, she joined forces with the business community, and the Hong Kong General Chamber of Commerce under the leadership of David Eldon to mobilize business and government cooperation to clean up Hong Kong's air pollution.[51]

One does not often associate Christine with a clear feminist orientation, although she has lobbied against gender discrimination.[52] Her liberal political leanings quite naturally led her on a collision course with entrenched lineage power in the New Territories. Early in 1994, she introduced a motion into the Legislature to revise the New Territories Land Exclusions Act. The motion proposed to grant equal rights of inheritance of landed property for female indigenous residents in the mostly single-surnamed, lineage villages. Representatives of the Heung Yee Kuk, composed of leaders among the New Territories lineages, organized more than one thousand protestors to demonstrate in front of the Legislature. Some even publicly threatened Christine with physical harm. Venturing into the villages to make her point, she insisted on establishing an image of someone who would passionately take on entrenched power and established conventions.[53]

Her serious politics aside, Christine maintains an aura of sophistication mixed with a touch of mischief. Her tastes are subtly expensive, and her style informal but cultured. Her comfortable family background is not lost to the media. She is known to have acquired a small, but of high quality, collection of modern art. When pressed, she nonchalantly admits that "savings" have enabled her to embark on public activism without a nine-to-five job. It might have been charisma or her skills in cultivating an image. Christine has been spared by the media, which can be savage to public figures. At the time she declared her retirement from legislative politics, she was the second most popular councilor in the public polls, overshadowing the internationally known advocate for democracy, lawyer Martin Lee. Among the 2000 *Business Week* awards for Asia's most influential, Christine was listed alongside finance, technology, and political figures, such as tycoon Li Ka-shing. Moreover, in a survey of university students that asked about their expectations of Legislative Councilors, Christine ranked second among those with whom students would like to connect.[54] In fact, political foes wonder why she continues to have inexhaustible political capital despite her relative inexperience in party politics.[55]

The issue can be a cultural one. The media brands her as belonging to the breed of "New Age" personalities, "exuding wisdom even in the way she drinks water."[56] She presents an image of a professional woman who charges ahead, raising eyebrows, turnings heads, and wreaking innocent havoc, quite unlike civil servants who work comfortably within an old institutional framework.[57] She captures the imaginations of the educated postwar middle class who came of age in the last two decades of Hong Kong's unprecedented development. Being young, culturally situated at the margins of mainstream Chinese society, and with a stylistic touch of mischief, Christine has been able to charm and disarm. The media often reports in curious but endearing terms how she cultivates a "mature woman" look with a particular brand of eyeglasses. She remains, in the public eye, an enviable free spirit. Like Ellen Li in the previous decades, Christine actively challenges political assumptions and constructs a new image of a woman in charge through the lifestyle she pursues and the values she advocates. In 2007, Britain honored her with a CBE (Commander of the British Empire) Order.

Margaret Ng is a former comrade-in-arms of Christine Loh in the Legislative Council. A leading journalist and practicing barrister, Margaret has been invincible in four successive legislative elections, representing the legal constituency.[58] With her intellectual sophistication, lucidity, and precise articulation in writing and speech, she can be devastating to friends and foes. Born in the New Territories, she, by her own account, missed the status of "indigenous village residents" by only a few days. Like many others in the generation of postwar baby-boomers, she had the opportunity to attend a leading missionary secondary school (St. Paul's Convent School). She read English literature and philosophy at the University of Hong Kong and was among the leaders in the late 1960s student movements, combining intellectual curiosity with passionate social activism. Her academic interests led her to a doctorate in philosophy in the United States.

Bored with administrative work in Hong Kong, she took off to Cambridge to read law in 1983. Her turn to law did not surprise her friends. She accumulated acute political sensitivities in the turbulent period when the Sino-British negotiations over the future of Hong Kong intensified. She spent her days in England divided between deeply intellectual pursuits at Cambridge and fiery parliamentary debates in London.[59] Friends knew that she would not remain an observer for long. On a visit to the late Sir Murray

MacLehose, a former governor, he gently hinted, "You are here just to take a break and have some fun, are you not?"

After returning to Hong Kong, she took up the post of chief editor and publisher of *Ming Pao Daily News*, a leading Chinese newspaper in Hong Kong. Her collections of literary and political commentaries were perceptive, cosmopolitan, and witty. She quickly gained a popular following. Even after she was called to the bar in 1988 and became an associate with the prestigious Chambers of Sir Oswald Cheung, she continued to write for *Ming Pao Daily News, South China Morning Post,* and *Hong Kong Economic Journal.* Her record of public service has been distinguished. Despite her critical views, governors Sir David Wilson and Chris Patten appointed her to important advisory committees, including the Independent Commission Against Corruption and the Central Policy Unit, a government think tank. Her impeccable English and razor-sharp mind also humbled many foreign dignities she interviewed.

Her brand of cosmopolitanism is unique. With a touch of nonchalance, she indulges in Chinese and English literary classics, modern poetry, oriental carpets, art auctions, and cultural performances in Europe and North America and is a connoisseur of French wines and Chinese culinary delights. She is no cultural broker. Instead, she engages with an amazing array of international personalities on their cultural terms.

The media seldom dares to be frivolous with Margaret Ng because the public issues she pursues are often dead serious. As an independent Legislative Councilor representing the legal profession in Hong Kong, she has long been regarded as a most uncompromising defender of the rule of law and related human rights issues. The political framework "One Country Two Systems" for post-1997 Hong Kong poses unprecedented challenges to legal practitioners because legal interpretations allow few gray areas. Margaret is particularly concerned that the Hong Kong legal framework, in principle and practice, should not be corrupted by political exigencies. To let it erode means that Hong Kong will lose a precious instrument and an established language to connect with the international community, in financial, political, and cultural terms. It would also lose credibility in the eyes of Hong Kong's rightful citizens. Social cohesion and moral clarity cannot be maintained in a society where cynicism abounds.

Acting on these basic principles, Margaret has taken some very unpopular legal stands. Even before the political changeover, Margaret voiced her opposition to the establishment of the Provisional Legislative Council to replace the one elected by popular vote in 1995. Her articulation of its illegality offended the Chinese government, which was eager to rid Hong

Kong of political voices picked by the then Governor Chris Patten. Her daring views might not have pleased an uninformed public, but they did not hurt her professional credibility, and she won another landslide election in 1998 and others that followed.

Two more issues made her equally unpopular, this time with the Hong Kong government. In March 1999, she led a group of Legislative Councilors to propose a vote of no confidence against the Secretary of Justice Elsie Leung. It was over the decision of the government legal department not to prosecute the chair of the Sing Tao Group for the chair's alleged complicity in the corruption trial of two company executives. Although the government was able to swing enough votes to reject the motion, issues concerning the fairness of the law, the alliance of government and business interests, and the competence of government appointees were articulated and hotly debated. It was embarrassing to the new regime, to say the least.[60]

The more significant case involved the first serious constitutional crisis faced by the SAR government, over the right of abode of thousands of mainland Chinese who were children of Hong Kong residents. The case was too complicated to be treated here, but Ng represented the five thousand or so children who challenged the government's decision to deny them the right of abode. The underlying constitutional issue had to do with the government seeking the interpretation of the law by the Standing Committee of the National People's Congress and overriding a previous Court of Final Appeal's decision to grant the children the right of abode. Many lawyers, including some in China, considered the government's action a serious affront to the autonomy of the judiciary and Hong Kong's legal independence that would result in severe political damage.

In 1999, Ng teamed up with prominent lawyers and judges to lead a march of more than six hundred colleagues and supporters. Dressed in black and walking in total silence, they marched through the administrative district and the courts. The silent protest on the streets was but the beginning of a series of political and human dramas surrounding "the new immigrants" that tore apart the already fragile social fabric of the territory. For her support of the mainland children, Margaret Ng has often annoyed Hong Kong residents who are worried about job security, social benefits, and cross-border crime. However, she cautions against using mainlanders as scapegoats, puts a human face on the complex social profiles of "the new immigrants," and sticks to her legal and constitutional principles.[61]

Popularly reelected to the Legislative Council by her constituency of lawyers since her 1995 debut, Margaret Ng's political trajectory has seemed unshakable. Despite years of exclusion by some factions of the Chinese government for her tough stance in defending the rule of law and democratic reforms, and despite organized challenges from pro-China lawyers, she has make an impact in shaping educated public opinion. The highest point of her series of challenges to the government involved Article 23 of the Basic Law, a national security legislation that the government was eager to promote. At the forefront of a pan-democratic alliance that protested against the lack of consultation on the proposed legislation and with several hundred thousands supporters who marched in the streets of Hong Kong on July 1, 2003, she and her colleagues (a group of lawyers who called themselves the Article 23 Concerned Group, and later the Article 45 Concerned Group) have become almost a barometer to gauge the professional, pro-democracy voice in the community, at times overshadowing the leaders of the Democratic Party.[62]

Her re-election in September 2004 was no surprise to her supporters. What surprised her friends and foes was the sudden attention the Chinese government in Beijing showered on her and her legal associates who also ran successfully for election. Days after her re-election, she and members of the Article 45 Concerned Group, including a popularly elected women legislator and former chair of the Bar Association, Audrey Eu, were invited by the Chinese Liaison Office in Hong Kong for serious talks.[63] This was followed by invitations to attend the national celebrations in Beijing on October 1 with other Hong Kong legislators. The political stardom was not what she or her colleagues had asked for, but, in the eyes of the media and general public opinion, the professionalism they had exerted finally produced some respectable impact. They charged ahead. In April 2005, over another controversial reinterpretation of Hong Kong's Basic Law by the Standing Committee of the National People's Congress, Margaret Ng and her colleagues in the Article 45 Concerned Group led another protest march of lawyers. Solemnly in black, the image of these well-dressed professionals could not have been more striking in the streets of Hong Kong. The front page of the *South China Morning Post*, a leading English-language newspaper, reported the event with the title "Lawyers Speak Volumes in Silent Protest." (*SCMP* April 20, 2005). The notion of *nü qiangren* has long disappeared. In the public eye, Margaret Ng and Audrey Eu were simply professional leaders in their own right.

In the ensuing months, public talk gravitated towards the question of whether the group would organize a political party. Margaret and Audrey Eu were frequently heard on the airwaves and on Internet radio shows. With a few male and female colleagues, many of whom were former chairs of the Hong Kong Bar Association, they created a regular forum for public dialogue. A free monthly newspaper, *A45* (with an electronic version that reaches far beyond Hong Kong) had Margaret Ng as the editor-in-chief. The first issue, not coincidentally, was an in-depth interview of the retired Chief Secretary, Anson Chan, who had some very harsh words to say about Hong Kong's constitutional affairs and the pace of democratic reforms. The Civic Party was eventually formed in 2006.[64] In the 2008 Legislative Council elections, while she canvassed for fellow members of the Civic Party, she overwhelmed her opponent yet again by winning two thirds of the votes in the legal constituency.

Dead serious in the pursuit of political principles, Margaret Ng never loses her sense of feminist humor. In the new journal and on her Web site for the legal constituency, there is always a column with gourmet recipes, how to get unusual pastries and Christmas pudding in London, and a few hints for finding the best Belgium chocolates.[65] The tongue-in-cheek assertion of her "professional place in the kitchen" has long generated its rightful presence for deserving friends at her dinner table as well as in her readers' imaginations.

A Historical and Regional Moment of Gendered Charisma

In their multidimensional qualities, Anson Chan, the Party of Handbags, Anna Wu, Christine Loh, Margaret Ng, and professional women like them have engaged with the changing expectations of Hong Kong society. In the process, they have created a new arena. The fluid process of negotiating new images reflects the kaleidoscopic nature of Hong Kong culture, regional history, and identity. The sources of their charisma capture several layers of reality — Hong Kong as local society, an essential region of South China, a node in the British colonial enterprise, an Asian financial hub, and a global city. The conjuncture of these historical moments and political realities has allowed glamorous and powerful professional women in Hong Kong to assert their agency. To push the historical issue further, one can argue that from the early 1970s to the late 1990s, the period of focus for this chapter, professional women in Hong Kong reached the pinnacle of respectability by preserving certain "traditions" of the Chinese merchant elites, and, at the same time, they reached out into a worldly domain through Western-style education. Expanded space is not confined to the professionals. As illustrated in Po-king Choi's chapter, Hong Kong's manufacturing and clerical needs had allowed women of all classes to work outside of home. Women took jobs not because they had to but because they wanted to. In the process, they also exerted their political agency. For the professionals, in particular, class mobility and education in the postwar decades of Hong Kong have made it possible for them to reach their goals with remarkable public visibility and charisma.

With Hong Kong twelve years into becoming a Special Administrative Region, has the position of professional women changed? The rapid "reintegration" with China has grave implications. For working women, job opportunities have long been reduced due to the shift of manufacturing activities across the border. The wives of new immigrants in Hong Kong cannot work because of a lack of appropriate education and the burden of children. Furthermore, professional and working women alike are facing a China where the new super rich in the boom towns of south China, Macao, and Hong Kong are constructing very different images and expectations of women. In their conception of life on the fast track, women are often reduced to commodities for consumption.[66] The images of women are overwhelmingly uniform — waitresses with their *qipao* (long dresses) fill the halls of seafood restaurants, karaoke bars, gambling clubs, and business receptions; street walkers solicit customers in front of beauty salons and train stations, not to mention the mistresses kept for short periods by truck drivers and commuting businessmen along the Hong Kong-Shenzhen border. The alarming point is that this style of consumption is often wrongly equated with Hong Kong's mainstream culture of "freedom and affluence," as symbols of modernization and development.[67]

After 1997, cross-border marriages have intensified. Increasingly, Hong Kong men look for affordable wives in South China. Triggered by the 2006 bi-census data from the government, public commentary on the marriage prospects of Hong Kong women has heated up. Are Hong Kong women losing in the marriage market because, in the eyes of ordinary men in Hong Kong, they are too educated, too independent, and too demanding of their spouses?[68] Professional women keenly feel the pressures of work and family, and many are making adjustments. An increasing number, according to the 2006 bi-census, are also taking spouses from across the border. To look ahead, it seems that sustaining the complicated respectability of professional women in Hong Kong today, as in historical times, is not confined to the issue of gender. It involves negotiations within the broader evolution of a regional culture and political economy. This chapter has tried to capture one of the many significant historical moments in gender positioning when the border between Hong Kong and mainland China hardened and softened.

9 Women Workers in Hong Kong, 1960s–1990s: Voices, Meanings, and Structural Constraints

Po-king Choi

This chapter tells the stories of women workers in Hong Kong during the period between the 1960s and the 1990s. These three decades witnessed the growth of a vibrant economy fuelled by rapid industrialization, which peaked in the 1970s and 1980s. Over the years, much has been written about this postwar "economic miracle,"[1] but up till now, there has been a dearth of discussion about the part played by women, who had furnished much of the labor power for this phase of industrialization.

Now, writing in the early 2000s, the story of these women industrial workers is trailing off with a note of sadness and anger. Instead of hardworking, competent women proudly bringing wages back to their natal or conjugal family (or both), we now have women, mostly in their early to late middle age, who experience job insecurity, unemployment, and enforced redomestication. These women suffer "serious affronts to (their) dignity and moral self-worth," even for those who manage to hold jobs, mostly low-paying ones in the service sector.[2] This depressing note aside, I believe that this is a good time for their stories to be told. The life stories of these women will serve as an important reminder of the human costs of capitalistic development and restructuring. Tak-wing Ngo has argued well for the rescuing of untold stories and the restoring of the agency of subordinate actors in Hong Kong's economic history, so as to explode the myths in dominant historiography.[3] Following the same line, I would argue that the telling of the stories of these marginalized women workers serves well to illuminate the role played by the invisible yet pervasive patriarchal gender substructure in the capitalistic development in Hong Kong, which, in turn, forms part of the growth of the global capitalist economy. At the same time, by inviting these women to tell their *own* stories, we can bring out their agency and resourcefulness in the shaping of their own lives despite structural limitations and even at times of social and economic displacement. As I shall show at the end of the chapter, some of these women were even able to make an impact, however small, in the public arena through their union participation and related activism.

Women in the Global Economy

Women have, for a long time, been the mainstay of industrial production in Hong Kong. David Levin estimated that, as early as the late 1930s, the number of female employees in the principal manufacturing industries, with the exception of shipbuilding and printing, had already exceeded that of males, though the absolute size of female employment was much smaller.[4] Between 1961 and 1981, during the time of rapid industrialization in Hong Kong, the number of women workers tripled. Then, the number of women workers declined with the massive relocation of industries in Guangdong, China, from the early 1980s onwards. Even so, they still comprised 46% of the total working population in manufacturing in 1986.[5] In fact, the participation of women in manufacturing has even been greater than what these statistics indicate, because of the significant proportion of women engaged in outwork.[6]

The predominance of female labor in industrial production is typical of export-led, dependent economies like Hong Kong and other Southeast and South Asian countries. In the postwar years, these countries' economies changed as international subcontracting of industrial production from the industrially advanced countries to developing countries intensified, capitalizing on the latter's ready supply of cheap labor. Lacking direct support from the colonial government, industries in Hong Kong nevertheless flourished, predominantly in the form of low capital small and medium-sized firms (SMF). Low capital yet high labor input allowed these SMF's to operate with the highest degree of flexibility in the international context of keen competition and great fluidity as well as vulnerability.[7] Apart from intensive labor input, these firms were also involved in multilayered subcontracting, which enabled them to minimize capital investment as well as labor costs, while maximizing flexibility. Such firms competed with each other for the shortest possible lead-time between placement of order to delivery,[8] made possible by the large pool of cheap female labor, as well as the many layers of subcontracting, down to the lowest layer of outwork, again done by women.

We can see, therefore, that women played a crucial role during this era of rapid industrialization. More importantly, we should be able to see beyond the purely economic function of the labor power of these women, and to realize that it had been shaped by their roles and identities not merely as workers, but also as daughters, wives, and mothers.

These working class daughters, wives, and mothers were, therefore, drawn *en masse* into the industrial labor market at the heyday of industrialization lasting between the 1970s and the 1980s. Then, when this mode of flexible manufacturing by SMFs ran out of steam as economic globalization rapidly intensified,[9] it was these same women who bore the brunt of unemployment. What emerged was, as Eliza Lee describes, a class polarization among women. Well-educated middle class women benefited from the expansion of financial and commercial services for international interests in the Chinese and Asia-Pacific markets, while poorly-educated working class women lost their jobs as industrial production was relocated in China and other South Asian countries.[10]

The Gender Substructure of Capitalist Production

In the 1990s, ethnographic studies of factories in Chinese societies, focusing on the workings of gender in capitalism, began to appear. These uncovered the fact that capitalistic production rests heavily on a patriarchal gender substructure.

Ping-chun Hsiung, for example, documented how married women in Taiwan were morally obligated to contribute their productive labor in family-owned factories through fulfillment of their traditional duties as wives, mothers, and caretakers. Patriarchy and capitalism were thus closely interlocking systems, and their linkage was deliberately manipulated by state policy. Such policy was encapsulated in slogans like "Living rooms as factories" and "Mother workshops," used in state campaigns promulgated by the ruling Nationalist Party.[11]

At about the same time but slightly later,[12] Ching-kwan Lee did a comparative study of women workers in two plants, owned by the same enterprise, in Hong Kong and Shenzhen respectively. She observed that the social organization of the respective local labor markets had produced two diverse "gendered regimes of production," featuring the "matron workers" (in Hong Kong) and "maiden workers" (in Shenzhen).[13]

Based on her year-long ethnographic study in an electronics factory in Shenzhen in the mid 1990s, Pun Ngai described the social construction of the *dagongmei* (working girls). She traced a genealogy of these women, drawing on insights from Foucault's "techniques of self" and "governmentality," while outlining a history of their subjectivities. She argued that sexual difference, apart from the urban-rural dichotomy and linguistic hierarchy, was one of the major regulatory projects of hierarchical, capitalistic practices on the shop floor.[14]

These ethnographic studies of women workers point to the significance of the gender substructure of power relations in the workplace, and the role of gender in the formation of workers' identity and subjectivities.[15] In brief, gender shapes the power relations in the workplace, so that labor discipline is maintained via the patriarchal structure, which exists both within and beyond the shop floor.

Up until now, there has not been any ethnographic research into the gender substructure of capitalist production in Hong Kong during its industrial phase. Now that the heyday of industrialization is gone, what we could do is to uncover such substructure through in-depth interviewing and, particularly, the reconstruction of life stories with the collaboration of former women workers. This is what I set out to do in this chapter.

Significance of Women's Voices

Feminist theorists have pointed to the importance of discovering and presenting the voices of women, which have been silenced in male-dominated agendas. By rescuing what has previously been ignored in the study of social life, feminists argue for the centrality of gender in the construction of power relationships as well as individuals' identities and consciousness.[16] Furthermore, close attention to the voices of individual women provides a useful corrective to overdeterminism in theorization, even in feminist studies itself.[17]

It is, therefore, important to get women to speak, either through ethnographic studies, or by engaging women in in-depth interviews. The issue, however, is a bit more complicated than this. Once we get women to speak, how do we listen to them and how do we make sense of what they say? Reformulating Gayatri Spivak's question (Can the subaltern speak?), Lee asked the question in this way: "Can we hear when the subaltern speaks?"[18]

Writing the Stories of Women Workers: A Methodological Discussion

Our concern here is a methodological one. We have to draw out and listen to the voices of the women we interview, while trying to put them in the wider context of structural inequality without forcing them into preset categories derived from our adopted theories. Joan Acker et al. spelled out the issue succinctly: "The question becomes how to produce an analysis which goes beyond the experience of the researched while still granting them full subjectivity. How do we explain the lives of others without violating their reality?"[19]

In this study, I used the oral history method, which has been found to be useful in "illuminating the connections between biography, history and social structure."[20] As each woman told her life story, most of the time in retrospect, she laid out a storyline, which was almost always linked up by key words. These might include words she used to designate the different stages of her life, the categories on which she built up the world she was living in, as well as her beliefs and value judgments, both about herself and about others. As she told her story, she was making sense of her own life.[21]

This is not to say that the woman's biography is written by herself alone, and that her life story will be presented just as it has been told. On the contrary, the researcher makes a "second-order" interpretation, i.e., she tries to make sense of the woman's life story on yet another level.

One important task in this "second-order" interpretation is to look out for multiple voices in the life story that has been told. This enables us to overcome the artificiality of the narrative continuity in a life story, and to detect fissures, displacement, and discordance that have occurred. At the same time, we must also look out for multiple voices among the women who were interviewed, as well as within the researcher herself.[22] In this way, we would avoid forcing our women participants and their actions into simplified, preset categories.

This does not mean, however, that we have no use for macro analysis. In fact, we have to constantly draw on categories offered by macro analysis, not as "compartments" to package the words of the women, but as leads or prompts in a dialogue between the researcher and the women being interviewed. In the process of analysis, therefore, the researcher "interrogates" the women's stories (and their interpretations) with concepts or categories derived from macro, structural analyses.

In this regard, Dorothy Smith's method of inquiry, "institutional ethnography,"[23] has a great deal to offer. Starting from the "actual activities of actual individuals,"[24] Smith tried to discover how these were articulated to social institutions (such as education, family, etc.). These institutions were, in turn, linked among themselves as well as to the capitalist state apparatus via ideologies. Such "institutional ideologies" have been "systematically developed to provide categories and concepts expressing the relation of local courses of action to the institution function."[25] By studying the everyday experiences of women in their contexts (such as family, work, etc.), Smith took account of the women's subjectivities on the one hand, and their articulation to the social relations of the larger social and economic process on the other. Along a similar line of thought, but put slightly differently, Jacka borrowed from Joan Scott and attended to the "historical processes that, through discourse, position subjects and produce their experiences."[26] Instead of Smith's Marxist notion of "institutional ideologies," Jacka used the Foucauldian notion of discourse, which does embody relations of power, but in a more fluid and less deterministic way.

A Brief Note on Life Stories and Supplementary Material

The following presentation is based on the life stories of five women, each told in a single in-depth interview that lasted one and half to two and half hours (two of the women, who were friends, were interviewed together). Four of these interviews took place in 2001, while the last one was done in 2002. At the time of interview, the oldest women, Ah Tim and Ping-kin, were sixty-five and sixty, while Yau-lan was fifty-three. The two youngest women, Ah Wah and Ling-hoi, were around forty-one.[27] The five women comprised, therefore, two different generations of workers. The older women started work in the 1950s or 1960s, and continued all the way up to 1990s. Meanwhile, the younger women started in the 1970s, with Ah Wah changing to white-collar employment since the early 1980s, and Ling-hoi joining full-time trade union work in the early 1990s. A brief summary of their biographical details is found in the Appendix.

Three of the women, Ah Tim, Yau-lan, and Ling Hoi, had worked in the garment industry, while Ah Wah was in electronics. While these four women had worked in medium to large factories, Ping-kin had more experience with small-scale, family-run factories (called *sanzai* factories in Hong Kong — literally, "hill-shack" factories). She had been working in small factories making candies, shoelaces, towels, cardboard boxes, etc., since around 1954 (when she was thirteen or so), all the way up to her marriage and beyond. Then, about two years after marriage, she worked closely with her husband in running a small enterprise for the finishing of bags and briefcases, until this wound down at her husband's sickness and subsequent death in 1995. She was the only woman among my participants who had similar experience to what Hsiung described as "living room factories" in Taiwan.[28]

Apart from the life histories of these five women, I shall also draw on supplementary qualitative data. This includes: transcriptions of two group discussions among the alumnae of an evening school (the Shaukiwan Canossian Evening School — SCES) about their experience of quitting school early in their teenage years, and their working life in factories; essays written by some of these alumnae about their early decision to quit school and their work lives,[29] and passages drawn from a book written with the collaboration of these alumnae.[30] These provide useful supplementary material concerning Hong Kong women workers of the seventies and early eighties, i.e., the younger group among our life stories participants.

Entry into the World of Work as Teens

The typical age of entry into work for both generations of women was around twelve. However, the cultural context, and hence the subjective meaning of entry, differed for the two generations.

"Natural" course mapped in poverty: The older generation of female workers

For the older women, starting work in their teenage years seemed to be part of a rather "natural" course to follow in life, having been born into poverty.

Ah Tim, for example, started working in a small family-styled factory in around 1949, ironing finished children's underwear when she was thirteen. In doing so, she was just following the footsteps of her elder sisters, who had all worked young to supplement her father's meager income as a rarely patronized herbalist. Ping-kin, whose well-educated and rather well-off father died from injuries inflicted by the Japanese during the Occupation (1941–45), started working in a candy factory when she was thirteen, in 1954. Compared to her two elder sisters, who had started working when they were seven and nine respectively, she had joined the workforce rather late already. As for Yau-lan, she left her family in Zhongshan, Guangdong, to come to Macao alone in 1958 when she was around ten years old. She was the eldest of eight children in her family, and with extreme poverty in China, her parents' decision was to send a daughter out to seek an opening.

Yau-lan worked as a maid for two families consecutively, and, when she was about thirteen, she asked to be taken as apprentice in her cousin's small garment factory in Macao, and later on she decided to come to Hong Kong to seek for better work opportunities.

Starting work means quitting school: Teenage workers of the 1970s

For the younger generation of women workers, entry into the world of work acquired a new meaning: that of quitting school. By that time, primary education had become almost universal, and its completion was marked by a competitive public examination for the allocation of subsidized secondary school places. For many working class teenage girls of the 1970s, graduation from primary school meant going straight to factory work, especially if they failed this exam.[31] There was no question that a working class child, and a girl in particular, could be supported by her family in private secondary schooling.

Even if they had passed the competitive examination and obtained subsidized secondary school places, girls might still have to give up schooling and work. Ling-hoi, for example, got allocated to three-year subsidized schooling and yet had to give it up in favor of her elder brother, who did not qualify for subsidized schooling and had to attend a private secondary school. Ling Hoi's fate was shared by two other women of her age, Terry and Alda, both alumnae of SCES.[32] It was through the interactive forces of social class and gender, therefore, that this generation of female teenage workers had come into being.

Cultural practice of the teenage (girl) worker and the precariousness of working class existence

While it was dire poverty that had driven some teenage girls into factory work, it seemed that for most other girls, it was due to a "cultural practice" which had channeled them to work upon the completion of primary school. In the case of the former, family mishaps such as the death of the father (breadwinner) or his loss of employment forced teenage children (boys or girls) to quit school, even at a younger age of ten or eleven.[33] Many other girls, however, could not recall a particular financial crisis that had propelled them into work. All they could tell today is that primary education was the most children (particularly girls) could have, and that it was common practice in the working class neighborhood for children, particularly girls, to start work upon its completion.[34]

Emily's story illustrates this "cultural practice" very well. Two of Emily's elder brothers had gone on to secondary school, one of whom got sent (somewhat against his own wish) to a private school because he had failed the allocation examination. Later, she also failed the examination. Unlike her brothers, however, she had to start work after primary six. She would have liked to go on with her studies, and her mother also wanted her to go on, but her father was rather lukewarm about this. Her observation today was that the family was not very poor, because there was always ample food, and the family enjoyed several meals a day. Her father was a construction worker, and there was no shortage of money when he was fully employed. As a teenager, however, Emily might not have been aware of the precariousness of employment of a construction worker, who was (and still is) taken on a daily basis. In fact, her father's words in reply to her request about going to a private secondary school were highly revealing of the insecure economic circumstances the family was living under: "If you go on studying, it'd be a bit of a strain (on family finances). If you quit school, we'd have an extra pair of hands to bring in money."[35]

Reading the stories of our women workers closely, one could easily see that precariousness of existence was a fact of life for working class families. Against this background, the "cultural practice" of sending a teenage daughter off to work after primary education was grounded on a concrete life-world shaped by the wider class structure. Within this structure, the livelihood of working class families was constantly threatened, not so much by sheer poverty or material lack, but by a lurking fear of loss of the means of livelihood. And, interestingly, heads of working class families (fathers and/ or mothers) looked to the gender division as an important cultural resource with which they built their strategy to fight this fear of loss. Girls, therefore, are "naturally" expected to help out after finishing their primary schooling.

Echoing Emily's experience, Ah Wah, the electronics worker whom I interviewed, described how she "gradually slipped into" (her own words) full-time factory work as a teenager after one year and a month of subsidized secondary schooling, which was concurrent with part-time and summer work in factories. Recalling how she had quit school three decades earlier, Ah Wah thought that, though family finances were a bit straitened, she still could have gone to school if she had wanted to. But the situation is better appreciated if one takes into account the wider economic context the family was in. This was how she had gradually learned about her family's financial situation as she grew up:

My father did long-term casual jobs (*chang san gong*). As I grew up, I'd learn more about this. . . . Sometimes Dad didn't have work for days, and no work means no money would come in. There're times when we couldn't even spare a few dollars for our school fees! . . . Then you wonder where Mom got her money to buy food. Mom wasn't employed then. She was a full-time housewife. My mom was illiterate. So, even back then, *I already knew that this (having no income) was a very dangerous thing!* [My emphasis.]

Girls/Women and Their Natal Families: Self in/outside the Collectivity?

In her study of the "working daughters" of the 1970s, Janet Salaff posed a dichotomy of the individual vs. the family. In this model, the working daughters were seen to make a major contribution towards the realization of family objectives (such as supporting their brothers' schooling), though they were still excluded from major decisions concerning the family.[36] But what did the working daughters themselves think about this state of affairs? Ching-kwan Lee rightly pointed out that researchers like Salaff had ignored the fact that women were themselves "subjects constitutive of and constituted through" the structural and institutional determinants of their subordination.[37] With this admonition in mind, I set out to look for the women's voices concerning their relationships with their natal families, which they supported through their waged labor.

The women's views and reactions to their contribution to family finances were varied, understandably. These ranged from compliance, anger, a sense of injustice, to pride and even a sense of fulfillment. Furthermore, these reactions were not necessarily discrete, but could be rather mixed.

Ready acceptance

Most of the girls who started work at the ages of eleven to thirteen complied with their parents' wish that they quit school and start work. Active bargaining or outright resistance was almost unheard of. In the case of the older women, this transition to work actually seemed to be a "natural" progression. One of them, Ping-kin, had, for example, asked to follow her elder sisters to work in their candy factory when she was thirteen. She had been studying for two years in a free school, which offered lessons lasting up to one and a half hour per day. Her mother had been very irritable, and had often taken it out on her, sparing her youngest brother, the only son in the family. Going out to work was a relief, and she was aware that her income would gain her a much higher status at home, which indeed it did. For some of the younger women, leaving school at twelve and earning money also brought them some childish delight, being free from the restrictions of school life, and having some newly acquired spending power.[38]

Sense of loss, anger, and injustice

Just then, I have said that these teenage daughters had complied with their parents' wish for them to quit school and start work, and active bargaining and resistance was almost unheard of. This was what things appeared to be on the surface. Probing into their thoughts some decades later, however, one finds that outward compliance doesn't necessarily mean passive obedience. Particularly for the younger cohort of women, the onset of compulsory secondary schooling (in 1978) was already in the air.[39] For them, therefore, quitting school at primary six could feel like an irretrievable loss — secondary schooling for them had become so near and yet so far. Some SCES alumnae, like Donna, Terry, and Alda said: "How I wish I had graduated [from primary school] two years later. By that time, [the government] would have compelled me to study. My family would not have had any excuse not to let me study."[40] One of them recalled a friend, a teenage factory worker, who had borrowed another friend's secondary school uniform to have a photo taken of herself with the uniform on. The school uniform signified to her what she would dearly love to have, but did not.

So what did these girls think, when they complied with their parents' wish for them to quit school and start work? For some, they accepted their fate without question: this was common practice in their neighborhood, and because of the lack of encouragement and support, they had not done very well in school anyway. There was also the common belief that boys in the family needed extra support from their families, simply because of their gender. Others, however, felt great anger and sadness. A sense of injustice would surface, at the point of quitting school or later. Grace, for example, had not questioned her family's decision for her to go to work at age eleven (she had failed her allocation examination), in order to help finance her elder brother's studies in Taiwan. Later on, she became a top student in the evening school, but then she was forced to quit on the eve of her taking the School Certificate Examination (the secondary school leaving exam). One of her elder brothers had used physical violence on her repeatedly, blaming her for disturbing the family's sleep while studying late into the night. On one of these occasions, she decided to leave the family and sought shelter in her boyfriend's home, and this drastic action was soon followed by an early marriage. She recounted these thoughts during that crisis:

> Who among you men at home [she had five elder brothers] have taken so much money home? Taken home the whole wage packet? I have! Why did you treat me like that? I felt that it was so unfair.[41]

Even for her counterparts who have not been subjected to such extreme injustice, a sense of anger and sadness could also arise. Alda, for example, was angry at her father who had slighted her for being allocated to a rather prestigious girls' secondary school ("Girls' school again?"), and who then made her quit school and start working in the factory. Terry, who like Grace also had several elder brothers, was simply told to start work, despite her being able to pass the allocation exam, and despite her love for study. All three turned out, in the end, to be top students in the evening school, and to have secured qualifications, through long years of arduous study, to enable them to leave factory work behind.[42]

Self-assertion under outward compliance

The world of subjectivities is one with many nuances that would remain out of sight if one takes account of outward behavior and concrete occurrences alone. I have said above that outward compliance does not necessarily entail passive acceptance. Not only that, but outward compliance could even be a form of self-assertion, if not outright resistance.

Ling-hoi was one of the teenage workers who had to give up subsidized secondary schooling allocated to her. Her maternal uncle had said that he would be willing to support her studies if she asked. Probably out of a kind of pride, however, she did not ask for her uncle's support back then. In her own words:

> I felt like I had to beg, to be given something by someone. Even as a young kid, I felt that if I got something from you, I wouldn't know for how long you would harp on it. I found it difficult to accept that . . . I felt that one wouldn't die from not being able to study. Not being able to study now doesn't mean that I would not have the chance to study ever again. Right?"

Similarly, Margaret, a fourth child in a family who treasured sons over daughters, should have been able to study. Her elder siblings had all been working, and one of her elder brothers had even offered to support her against her parents' wish:

But I said there's no need to. I felt that if Mom didn't let me study, I might as well not. Thinking about this today, I really regret it. Giving up one's study for some pride (*zheng kou qi*). A mere teenage kid, and I was trying to gain pride. Who are you to do that![43]

The gu jia (taking care of the family) daughter: Pride in fulfillment of moral responsibility

In Salaff's dichotomy of the working daughter (the individual) vs. the family (the collective), one takes the former's early contribution to the latter as a form of personal sacrifice.[44] In the same vein, Djao half expected such a daughter to experience a kind of bitterness, and the fact that she didn't testified to her passive acceptance.[45] However, from the women's point of view, being able to support their natal families and their younger siblings could bring them great satisfaction and pride.

One of our younger women, Ling-hoi, for example, didn't have to surrender her whole wage packet as most of her counterparts did.[46] However, she enjoyed treating her younger siblings to snacks, and she took pride in buying new furniture for her home and making it more comfortable. In a follow-up conversation after the interview, she explained that she had got used to being sidelined for "goodies" (whether it was the best piece of mooncake or education) in the family. Having a say in furnishing the home then became a source of great satisfaction.

An older woman, Ping-kin, had started to work at around thirteen. When she was about sixteen or seventeen, her younger brother finished primary school, and their mother had wanted him to learn a trade as a car-repair apprentice. Having worked for three years or so at that time, Ping-kin seemed to have gained some authority at home as she was able to reverse her mother's decision:

> I strongly objected [to my brother quitting school]. Because I felt that I couldn't go on studying, and I regretted it very much. So I didn't agree. I insisted that he went on with his studies. . . . [*And you mom listened to you?*] Because I had money to give her! I gave her all I had earned. . . . I gave him [my brother] money. I said, don't work. I supported him in his studies. So he went on until he finished secondary school.

During her brother's last two years in school, Ping-kin had already got married, but she continued to support her brother, though her contribution to her natal family was reduced.

Another older woman, Yau-lan, described her early days of migration and work as ones "full of sadness" (*qi liang*). Living apart from her family since ten, she had saved every penny, whenever she could, to send home. When she grew older, she had thought of remaining single, so that she could support her younger siblings back in China. She nevertheless got married, but she continued to support her natal family back in China throughout marriage and subsequent motherhood. For this life-long contribution, what she has now gained is authority and respect from her siblings:

> I am one of those daughters [who are] very good and who care very much for her family. [The family] respect me a lot. Now for my younger brothers and sisters — my words count.

Among the working daughters, Yau-lan seems to stand out for her long-term contribution to her natal family, and for the degree of respect and authority she had gained through this. Nevertheless, even for those who felt anger and injustice, like Grace, their contribution towards the family was something that they could still talk about, years later, without a trace of shame. The hard-working daughter who "takes care of the family" is, without doubt, a culturally-prized subject among the working classes in Hong Kong. The pride and self-satisfaction such a daughter gains is perhaps best understood in the Chinese cultural context, where the individual is enmeshed in a web of human relationships rather than standing alone and apart from it. Salaff and Wei Djao, analyzing from a simple dichotomy of self versus the collectivity, could only speak of personal sacrifices and losses, as if the working daughters were mere victims of the patriarchal family.[47] Listening to these women themselves, however, one rediscovers this subtle yet significant cultural agent: the *gu jia* daughter who earns much admiration and self-satisfaction.

Law Kar, a film critic, wrote about the popular actress Chan Po-chu, who had a great following among the young women factory workers of the sixties and seventies. Naming Chan as a representation of the new ideal-typical Cantonese woman, Law said that these young workers, who were the economic mainstay of their families, identified closely with the self-reliant character of Chan Po-chu. Her image as an "untainted but slightly rebellious, candid but slightly conservative" young woman, was appealing because "she was able to protect herself and to fight for her rights under conditions of unfairness."[48] There is no doubt, therefore, about the active agency that had contributed to her appeal.

The Social Construction of the Woman Worker

We now turn to the workplace, where the cultural meanings attached to a girl/woman worker are created and manifested. The most important dimension of the social construction of a worker, regardless of gender, is, of course, discipline. Discipline, or labor control, is the key to the relations of subordination and domination in the capitalist production process, where the labor of the worker is extracted.[49] Gender enters the picture here, being "constitutive of and constituted by power relations in the workplace."[50] In this section, we shall examine this "gendered substructure" of the cultural meanings of work and the female worker, as well as the workplace hierarchy in which she finds herself.

Disciplining the body: Speed and "greed"

Employing the Foucauldian concept of the political technology of the body for economic production, Pun Ngai stated that the regulation of the body and desire began at the very moment of the worker's encounter with the production machine.[51] Looking at the experience of our women participants, one can indeed see how workers', particularly teenagers', bodies, were made to fit into a mechanized production flow to guarantee maximum productivity and minimal resistance.

A description of the work Ling-hoi did in the garment industry reads like some kind of superhuman acrobatics. Starting work at thirteen, Ling-hoi's first job was to iron shirts with a heavy steam iron, weighing several pounds. After some time, she was assigned to the job of turning narrow, pointed shirt-collars inside out. For this, she had to operate a part-manual, part-electrical machine with both hands and both feet. Two needles, one coming down and the other going up, were used to turn the collar inside out, and these were operated by one foot, with both hands holding the collar. Then, the collar had to be slid into a very hot device to be compressed, while the other foot controlled the time of compression: long enough to have the collar well pressed, but not too long to burn it. Accidents were not infrequent, usually with one of the needles piercing into a finger, and sometimes broken inside the flesh. Coworkers would then try to piece the broken bits of the needle together. If they fit into a whole needle, then the worker would be asked to rest for a moment and then start working again. If not, then she would be taken to the hospital to have the broken bit removed. She probably returned to work later in the day, or the following morning. It was a tough, Dickensian environment, typical of garment factories of that time.

The major outstanding feature, however, was speed. For every batch of garments done, a ticket would be torn out and kept by the worker, and the number of tickets would determine her day's wages. The pressure to work fast was very great indeed. In Ling-hoi's words:

> I was only thirteen or fourteen, and there was a lot of pressure. . . . You had to work fast. Every person's speed was different, but each of us was at our maximum speed already. But they [the management] always felt that we were slow. They'd say: you're so slow, and so on. Sometimes, the foreman would even stand behind you to count. One, two, three, like this.

Soon, the teenage worker would graduate to garment making itself, working at the fast, mechanized sewing machines. Wages were calculated at piece rate, and the pace of work was notorious. Many of the workers of the younger generation, like the SCES alumnae, for example, reported having tried their hands at garment making, but had to give up because they were not fast enough. Ling-hoi, a garment-making veteran, described the work process thus:

> It's hard! Digestion problems [were common]. These workers worked like mad. They'd go back to their seats to work once they finished their meal. Even if they were not sewing at their machines, they'd stand there and collect clothes. . . .You'd think they weren't humans, they were machines: *chut, chut, chut.* . . .

Ultimately, the fast pace of work was not due to the speed of the machines (though this probably also played a part), but to the method of remuneration, namely, by piece rate. Payment by the piece encouraged competition and boosted production to the utmost capacity of the workers. Ling-hoi, for example, observed that her coworkers often competed against each other, and even with oneself, for greater income:

> These people were strange — they strove their utmost to earn more. If you earn $220 today, you'd be very happy if you could earn $240 tomorrow. . . . If someone knows that somebody else earns $300, she'd think to herself: No, you could earn $300. I can't let this happen. Then she'd strive harder.

Fanny, who had worked as a sewer of handbags, said: "I had quick hands and feet. I strove to work as fast as possible. I had only one thought: money, money, money!"[52] This heightened concern for money, sometimes designated as "greed" by the workers themselves, became a kind of "built-in" mechanism for body discipline.

There was also a subcontracting system, whereby the owner of a knitwear factory, usually a small-sized one, would contract out part of the production process to an experienced worker. This "contractor" would be paid by the number of batches of goods that passed through her hands. To maximize her income, she would usually do the bulk of the job, while farming out the rest to individual workers only when she could not finish the batch by herself. The pressure of the contractor was to make the shipping dates, balancing out her capacity to go it alone with the taking in of helping hands (*bang gong*), which then cut into her income.

Among my participants, Ah Tim and Yau-lan had been working alternatively as subcontractor and *bang gong* throughout their long years in the garment industry. Ah Tim spoke of the days when she had to go to work despite illness and pain: "We'd only took leave when we almost died."

The shipping dates were deadlines that could never be missed: "Whatever time the goods were due, you had to deliver even if you died in the process!" This, of course, was due to the fact that the Hong Kong garment industry was competing to survive in a highly volatile international market, and so great flexibility in production had to be maintained. This entailed a short production lead time between the placement of orders and delivery, as well as the ability to make extensive use of outworking and subcontracting in order to save on labor costs.[53] It was in this dependent, export-oriented economy that veteran workers like Ah Tim and Yau-lan struggled with extremely long work hours throughout their career:

> [Yau-lan] "Oh, it's really terrible. Every night we worked 'til eleven, followed by several nights when we'd work 'til daybreak. Worked 'til eleven, and in the morning we started at seven, or eight? ([Ah Tim]: Eight!) . . . Actually I didn't have time to sleep at all. . . . No holidays! In those days, there weren't days off! . . . If there was work, we'd work. Come seasons or festivals: no rest anyway. ([Ah Tim]: We worked from the Fourth Day of the New Year to the New Year's Eve! [Laughs])

While it was the method of remuneration (piece rate) and the short production lead time that drove garment workers to work fast and for long hours, speed was built into the production process via the assembly line in the electronics factory. Workers sat at different assembly lines, each forming a "team," and labor control was exerted mainly via pressure from the momentum built up within the team itself. Compared with garment work, the electronics industry demanded less skill from their workers. The most important quality, according to Ah Wah, was "a quick hand" and "being smart" (*sing muk,* in Cantonese). She also had to concentrate on her work, and not talk too much. The worst nightmare for a line worker (known as "line girl") was for products to pile up at her station (*dui ji*), which meant that she was falling far behind the workers in front of her, and leaving those behind her idle. "In any case, when things [goods] flow down, you work on them, and you don't stack up a pile there. Otherwise you'd be scolded." Bonuses were given if the amount of production of the whole line (team) exceeded a certain standard set by management. However, this standard was very high at the outset, and, as workers exceeded it, it would be adjusted upward.

Ah Wah's experience at an "elite line" is illustrative of the high speed of work and concentration that was required of "line girls" at their best. The factory was starting an assembly line for a new TV-radio-cassette tape recorder model for their Japanese producer, and a foreman highly favored by management was asked to handpick the fastest "line girls" from the existing lines. Ah Wah was selected to do part of the quality control work. The line was so quick that within the first month of production, they got the productivity prize. "It was crazy! . . . They pushed us. Those of us who sat at the end of the line had no say. They [the foremen] only had to push those in front, that's the most important — the beginning of the line." In the end, the three workers in the quality control team "took turns to get ill," and in the end, Ah Wah quit the job.

The "body imaginary": The down-to-earth worker vs "the playgirl" (fei nü)

Women workers were not a homogenous group. Among other things, the worker's "body imaginary" created by disciplinary power in the workplace could differ from one industry to another, each holding its respective moral connotations about the worker. In Hong Kong, we find that this was the case for its two major industries: garment and electronics. While the former upheld the down-to-earth, skilled woman worker, the latter was known for its modern, smart girl.

Sectoral differences among the industries were quite real, as in the words of our participants: "Once you enter a trade [industry], you'd remain there." This contradicts England and Rear's speculation that, since skill requirements for operative jobs filled by women were not enterprise nor industry specific, job transfer was relatively easy, which explains their highly instrumentalist attitude.[54] Leaving aside the question of instrumentalism for the time being, the women's experience showed that transfer between industries was not easy nor common. More specifically, in the garment industry, the skill required to master the motorized machine and at the same time fast enough to make a reasonable income on piece rate has to be acquired in the early teenage years.

A careful look at the experience of garment workers showed that they all started very young (around thirteen), and the family or neighborhood network seemed to have played a part in recruitment. Ah Tim, for example, had all her daughters initiated into garment making. In the words of her friend, Yau-lan, "this was the fashion in those days: the mom would teach her whole brood of girls to take up [garment making]." Meanwhile, Ling-hoi, whose mother died young, leaving behind a reputation of a highly skilled and versatile tailor, had no doubt as to which industry she would enter. In her twenty-year career in this industry, Ling-hoi had progressed steadily from a regular garment worker to a sample maker. This latter job was a highly skilled one, involving the making of the first sample product of an upmarket item from paper patterns, in order to decide on the procedure to be followed on the assembly line at a later stage. She had been able to progress to this job through diligent study in tailoring throughout the years, from the time she took up her first job at thirteen. With the restructuring of the garment industry in the mid to late eighties, when fashion production steadily replaced that of ordinary, run-of-the-mill garments, she was able to meet the high demand for sample-making skills.

Ling-hoi was, admittedly, a rather extraordinary worker who aimed not so much at maximizing one's income at work but at self-improvement in her career. However, even for most other garment workers, their vision of themselves in this industry was a long-term one. Ah Tim and Yau-lan had started their career in knitwear in the late 1950s and early 1960s, in its early days, and had soon been promoted to the much-respected job of mender (*bu yi*). In Yau-lan's words:

> I felt that we were already highly skilled workers. There was no need to worry about having nothing to do — I'd stop working only when I didn't want to work. . . . [I]t never occurred to me that I myself would be out of job one day. Absolutely unthinkable!

For a teenage girl to enter a garment-making factory in those days, therefore, it meant that she would acquire a reliable skill that would see her through for a long time to come. By association, the worker herself came to be seen as much more reliable, serious, and down-to-earth, this image being reinforced by the contrast offered by the "modern girl" in electronics. In Ling-hoi's words:

The girls in garment factories behaved themselves better, whereas those in electronics were the most frivolous and distracted (*tan mu xu rong*) . . . The women in our neighborhood would often say: "Ai-ya! Don't go into electronics!" They were afraid that girls would go into bad ways. In fact, they wouldn't really go into bad ways, but [compared to us], they played around much more.

The image of the mature, reliable, down-to-earth garment worker was probably reinforced by the work setting. Because garment factories were mostly run on small, local capital,[55] they were very crammed, dirty, but functional. Yau-lan recounted thus: "It's very dirty under the tables. . . . In those hill-shack factories, there weren't anyone doing the cleaning or tidying up." There was also a much wider age range among the workers in garment making, which gave rise to the impression of the presence of more mature women in this industry. Ah Tim and Yau-lan's experience is a good illustration: they had worked in this industry from their teenage years, through the years of early motherhood, right up to the time when their children reached adulthood. Perhaps because of this wider age range, garment workers were seen to be more "womanly," just as Roberta, a SCES alumna, said:

> I felt I couldn't make friends there [in the garment factory]. I had a more boyish personality. Sewers were very womanly. Also, they were older, and more mature. They shouldered the family's livelihood in a very filial way.[56]

By contrast, the image of the modern and smart girl in electronics had a lot to do with the nature of investment and mode of management employed in this sector. Our participants observed, quite accurately, that most of the electronics factories were set up by foreign investors, armed with much greater capital.[57] The workplace was more spacious, and, for the sake of the equipment and products, these were kept clean and air-conditioned. Workers either dressed in uniforms, or, they could wear more fanciful dress or clothing to work. Ah Wah, for example, recalled that flip-flops or rubber thongs, which were commonly worn by workers in "hill-shack" plastics and garment factories, were never seen in electronics factories.

Another outstanding feature of electronics factories of that time was their style of management. They were more observant of labor laws, according to Ling-hoi, the worker turned trade unionist. Workers worked six day or five-and-half days a week, and, though overtime work was frequent, there were still within reasonable limits (e.g., working until daybreak as in garments would be unheard of). The provision of factory transport, canteens, and low-priced meals was also not uncommon, and though these were catered to boost worker productivity, they were advertised as "factory-provided welfare" and were often perceived as such. So was the short "tea-break" in the morning and afternoon, and though, as Ah Wah commented, the pressure on the daily production quota was never lifted, the tea break did leave workers with a good feeling. Furthermore, as Djao and our participants observed, the management organized occasional social and recreational activities, such as picnics, dances, annual dinners (with lucky draw), personal grooming classes, etc.[58] These were aimed at creating an identity of the active, young, modern woman, thus adding to the attraction of working in this industry.

Because this industry capitalized on low skills but fast-paced, concentrated work on the part of teenage girls, the age range of its workers was much narrower. There was a very short mobility ladder, from line worker to tester, QC worker, to supervisor and foreman,[59] and workers might be promoted from day-rate to monthly salary, but, in reality, only a small minority of those who started out as "line girls" would benefit from it. In Ah Wah's observation, even the minority of the more mature workers, some having been married and had become mothers, were still in their twenties. In other words, unlike the garment worker, the modern, smart girl in electronics probably could not picture herself working in the same industry beyond her twenties. These words of Ah Wah certainly posed as a big contrast to the worldview of garment workers like Ling-hoi, Ah Tim, and Yau-lan: "I didn't think too far into the future. If I could play around for a few years more, I'd do that. . . . No, they [electronics worker] only worked from day to day."

It is interesting to note Ah Wah's switch from the first person singular (I), to the third person plural (they). Towards the last sentence of the quote above, her identity was changing: from that of an electronics worker who lived from day to day, to that of the diligent evening school student preparing for her school-leaving certificate which, in the end, enabled her to leave blue-collar work altogether.

The image of the modern, smart girl working in electronics seemed to be quite prevalent indeed. Even Ah Wah, herself an electronics worker, underlined this danger of "falling into bad ways." At one point, she wondered why she hadn't turned into a "playgirl," commonly thought to be prevalent in this industry. However, elsewhere, she admitted that such "playgirls" were, in fact, a minority. There might be two to three of them in a large factory, though they attracted disproportionately great attention. "At first, I didn't dare talk to them, you know. They sat beside you working, and I just didn't dare speak to them."

What made her, and the majority of "good girls," designate these girls as "playgirls"? According to Ah Wah, they smoked ("Smoking was very bad, very bad indeed, in those days, for girls!"), swore profusely (but only among themselves), wore fashionable clothes (bell-bottomed pants, the fashion of the day), and talked a lot about going to parties. And, what was wrong about going to parties? "Well, in those days, we heard a lot about girls going to parties, taking psychedelic drugs, and then losing their virginity" (*shi shen*, literally, losing their bodies).

So the whole issue boils down to the fear of promiscuity, a moral danger this modern, smart working girl would fall into. The "playgirl" in electronics was a cautionary note, constructed among the working classes, perhaps as a reaction to the rapid increase in the female working population during the high tide of industrialization in Hong Kong. The most outstanding object of this felt need for social control was, of course, the young woman, or, more specifically, her body.

The discipline of the woman worker is, therefore, not only of a social and economic nature, but a moral one. In the case of Ping-kin, the force of moral discipline was probably what had kept her in a worker's position. At the age of sixteen or seventeen, and after having worked for three years or so, Ping-kin left the "hill-shack" factories where she was working and started working in a nightclub in the then fashionable Kowloon City area as a helper. She rather liked the job, particularly because she was able to meet a wide variety of people, including local film people and foreigners. These people, she felt, had a "vision which was not as narrow" as those she had met before, and they were more "high class." However, after two years, she resumed factory work, because she had an uneasy feeling that she was "showing herself" (*pao tou lu mian*) too much. The nightclub was too dangerous a place for young women.

The gender hierarchy in the workplace

We have seen how women workers were subjected to different systems of labor control, each with its corresponding moral and social connotations: e.g., the reliable, down-to-earth garment worker, vs. the modern, smart girl. We have also seen how the young woman's body was disciplined against the backdrop of the dangers of the wider, fast-changing society. Another aspect of the discipline of women workers was the gender hierarchy in the workplace itself, which formed the seemingly "natural" habitat of the woman worker.

David Levin made the general observation that women were relatively disadvantaged compared to men in the factories, and a number of technician and craftsman jobs as well as certain types of shop floor jobs still remained largely or exclusively male preserves.[60]

Gender segregation and hierarchy certainly formed an important backdrop to the working life of our women workers. From what Ah Wah saw in the electronics factories, for example, all the foremen were men, as were some of the QC workers and most of the repairers. Except for a few young men in the packaging department, all the operatives on day rates were young women, mostly teenage girls. Then, there were the male engineers, in their enclosed office, whose task was to design the actual production process on the assembly line. These were so high up in the social ladder that they were almost invisible to the female workers on the shop floor. The occupational hierarchy, when superimposed on the gender hierarchy, became a kind of caste-like structure, emitting an aura of "naturalness" for the low ceiling on pay increment and upward mobility for the women at the bottom.

The gender hierarchy in the factory drew its support, too, from existing social and cultural constructions of "appropriate" male and female attributes. Ah Wah's personal experience of the failure to rise above the ceiling illustrates this very well. While working in a large electronics factory, she was selected by the foreman to be one of the repairers, who, except for her, were all young men. After working together for some time, her "Little Master" (so called because he was a young man assigned to teach her the basic skills of repairing) said she was doing very well, and that she should enroll in an evening electronics course in a government technical college. Only by getting more formal training in technical studies could Ah Wah be more consolidated in her job as repairer.

Ah Wah's response was quite revealing of the tenacity of cultural hegemony:

> I said: "It's so demanding. I'd quit! Can you let me go back [to the assembly line]?" I said, "It looks so odd: girls going to such courses!"... I hated those diagrams and things, so I didn't go . . . He asked me to study again. But I had a headache whenever I saw those circuit diagrams. So, in the end, I told him: I'd quit. And I went with my friend to another factory.

The male prerogative over technical knowledge was a strong cultural factor that buttressed the gender hierarchy in the factory.

Similarly, the gender hierarchy was very much in place in the garment factory. According to Ling-hoi, almost all sewers and other low-level operatives were women, while the men were skilled operatives ("masters"), supervisors, and foremen. A partial reason for this was the slightly higher education qualifications required, especially by larger establishments, for jobs at such levels, and most working class girls in those days did not go beyond primary education. Another reason was straightforward discrimination, which was supported by certain taboos. The most outstanding taboo in a garment factory was that women must not, in any way, go over, under, or on the cutting board. This was a raised platform, sometimes measuring over a hundred yards long, where the master craftsmen (definitely male) cut out stacks of cloth. It had a kind of sacred aura about it, so much so that one could not risk it being polluted by women, who had to make long detours in order to go around it.

The Worker as Wife and Mother

It is the unique contribution of feminist scholarship that makes us realize that the social construction of the worker, male or female, does not take place within the sphere of capitalist production alone. Both the class and gender structures shape and constrain the nature of worker's participation in work, her work relationships, as well as her subjectivities. Earlier in this chapter, we have seen the way in which the relationship of the teenage worker with her natal family shaped her participation in factory work. Here, we shall look into the worker as wife and mother, to see how this gendered position contributes to the shaping of her work and her subjectivities.

Childcare and work demands

Because of the high demand on their work capacity and the urgent need to make ends meet, women workers had to juggle with the conflicting demands of work and childcare, especially when their children were still infants. They would often quit their jobs for childbirth or childcare (maternity leave in factories were unheard of in those days), but would resume when circumstances permitted. In Yau-lin's words:

> I'd work until the baby was almost due — I was rather big by then. After childbirth, I'd rest for some time, and then come back to work. After working for some time, the kid would fall ill, so I'd take care of her for some time. Then, because there's so much work outside, and I was greedy for money — we're so poor! — [so I'd come back to work again].

While the worker resumed work in the factories, babies would often be left in the care of paid child-minders for the day. However, this might not always work out, as in the case of Yau-lin's eldest daughter, who didn't seem to take to child-minders very well and who often fell ill. For about half a year, her baby was cared for by Yau-lin's own mother, back in China, until she strengthened up. As for Ah Tim, she and her husband, who worked nightshifts in a textile factory, would take turns to look after the children at home. This worked out well, except for the fact that the couple hardly saw each other. For both Yau-lin and Ah Tim, they would work as "helping hands" for contractors instead of contracting out work by themselves, when childcare demands were especially great. In this way, and by sacrificing a part of their income, they allowed themselves greater flexibility with the use of time. They would also cut back their working hours, working for twelve hours until 8 p.m., instead of for fifteen hours until 11 p.m., as they did before they had children. When the children reached school age, the workers would resume their long hours of work, and, as in the case of Ah Tim, a kind-hearted neighbor might help to keep an eye on them.

The demand on the worker as a mother was a heavy one, not only in terms of physical labor, but also in psychological terms. Yau-lin, for example, would often get up at three or four in the morning (while going to bed around midnight at the earliest) to put on the broth for the children to feed on when they came in after school in the afternoon. This preparation of broth, within the context of Cantonese food culture, is a signifier of the best culinary care one can get only at home, and at the hands of a woman, usually a wife or a mother. Both Yau-lin and Ah Tim also boasted of the efforts they made to take their children out for recreational activities — swimming, viewing the decorative lights at the harbor at Christmas, etc. — whenever they could squeeze in the time.

These efforts notwithstanding, worker mothers might still have their regrets concerning her contribution as a mother. Yau-lin said, "I'd say: when work was busy, the children were really pitiful. [They're] like a ball, kicked from one child-minder to another. Kicked from left to right, and I had to work myself!" At another point, she said, "The kids' lives were really cheap. Sometimes they didn't get to see the doctor even when they were ill."

At the time of interview, Yau-lin's nineteen-year-old son had just undergone a major surgery to remedy a wide gap between his upper and lower jaws. She was full of blame for herself for not having noticed her son's problem with his jaw, when he was younger. His doctor had told her that even if she had discovered the problem earlier, they would have to wait for this mature age to do the operation. However, she felt that the doctor had probably said this to make her feel "less ashamed" of herself.

To the working mothers, the childcare they could provide was far from ideal, though they acknowledged that they had done the best they could. Yau-lin recalled how her sister-in-law had advised her not to work, because "being able to teach your children yourself is something you can't buy with money. Even when you make lots of money, if your children don't behave, that money is worth nothing at all."

Ah Tim agreed with her long-time coworker and friend. She counted herself "lucky" because, although her children did not get a lot of supervision from her, they nevertheless did not go into bad ways. There was no lack of warning in her neighborhood about the danger of poor parenting. "[Do you see a lot of children in your neighborhood going into bad ways?] Yes, yes. A lot of them! Some became 'playgirls'" Then, she and Yau-lin started a discussion of why several girls of a neighboring family had become "playgirls," and the sons had also gone into bad ways. It turned out that the wife and mother herself did not behave herself properly: "The husband worked in a bus depot. She [the wife] went shopping all day, and chatted with this or that person. Rather improper, you know." (Ah Tim) What is important about this story is not whether Ah Tim's observation was accurate. Rather, it was the moral aspect of parenting that she had emphasized: poor parenting reflects badly on the mother and her morals.

Wife and mother as owner/worker: The case of the "hill-shack factory"

Hsiung's portrayal of "living rooms as factories" and "mother workshops" depicts how women take up multiple roles of worker and co-owner, wife and mother in upholding the satellite factory system during an important phase of economic development in Taiwan. Given the prevalence of small and medium-sized factories in Hong Kong, one would expect this mode of interplay of patriarchy and capitalism to be quite common here too. Among our participants, Ping-kin's experience was most typical.

About three years after her marriage, when her first kid was about two years old, Ping-kin's husband took up the subcontracted job of the finishing of rattan handbags. This involved employing six workers (her husband's former coworkers), renting a small flat from one of Ping-kin's elder sisters at a low rate, and buying a van for transporting the goods. To minimize on the capital, the workshop also doubled as home for this young family, who lived in a cock loft built above the worktables.

Just as what Hsiung had observed about Taiwan's cottage factories, the start-up of the workshop of Ping-kin's husband depended very much on

Ping-kin's own connections. The premise was rented from one of her sisters, and the payment of the rent could be delayed or even forfeited when money was short. Her sister also owned a rice shop and two grocery stores nearby, and Ping-kin and their workers could get food supplies, cigarettes, and even milk powder for babies on loan. This support, as Ping-kin put it, was very important for young families such as theirs.

However, the most important resources were those put in by Ping-kin herself. The factory was first started in 1962 with six workers, and it had its ups and downs as the macro economic situation changed. At its height, the factory had a rented premise in a government industrial complex, and had sixty workers. The practice in that trade was for workers to be offered two meals a day, and Ping-kin was responsible for the buying of the food and the cooking:

> In the early days, I had to cook for more than twenty people. It was hard — there weren't electric cookers those days — you wouldn't know how to cook the rice. With my baby son on my back, I've tried using charcoal, firewood, and kerosene. . . . I had an old lady as helper, but still, it's hard. . . . After you've finished cooking the meal, you [were so tired that you] couldn't eat it.

Apart from cooking, Ping-kin was also responsible for sewing the lining of the handbags (in good times, this would be contracted out as outwork for housewives), delivery of finished goods, purchase of raw materials, and looking after her three children. Ping-kin also had to solicit orders from purchasers and collect payment. At the end of the long day, she still had to clean up the premise before retiring. The factory operated throughout the year, resting only for a few days during the Chinese New Year. "It's hard. Twenty-something hours in a day were not enough for me to finish the work."

Interestingly, Ping-kin's husband seemed to lead a much easier life. "My husband was much more leisurely. [Laughs.] The men usually had tea at three o'clock. Then, very often, they'd play mahjong." It turned out that capital was raised through informal credit unions, and members usually met once a month. These meetings took the form of dinners, preceded by several rounds of mahjong game. As the owner of such factories joined several such credit unions simultaneously, he would attend several such dinner-cum-mahjong meetings each month. "They'd have tea at three, then they'd start playing mahjong until eight or nine. Then they'd have dinner, and after dinner, they'd sometimes move to hotels to play mahjong until daybreak." The major task of the male owner seemed to be social networking and raising of funds, leaving most of the tasks related to factory production in the hands of the owner's wife. Of course, she was also the housewife and mother to the kids.

How did Ping-kin see this unequal division of labor at work and at home? Interestingly, she attributed it to the respective "personality" of her husband and her own. "I don't like to be dependent on others. My husband, on the other hand, was very dependent. . . . I haven't studied a lot, but maybe I've got used to relying on myself."

Women's Voices within Structural Constraints

By inviting women workers to tell their life stories, I hope to discover the meanings they attribute to their own lives and struggles, as these unfolded within the restrictions of the macro structures of gender and class. Following this line of thinking, therefore, I would like to draw this chapter to a close by responding to a core theoretical issue: people's subjectivities and their articulation to larger social and economic structures, i.e., the interplay of agency and structure. In more concrete terms, I would examine our women workers' accommodation to, perceptions of and resistance to the wider context of structural inequality within which they had lived.

Accommodation to class position

A common theme running through the women's stories is their unrelenting efforts at hard work, fuelled by a keen sense of insecurity, which, in turn, had grown out of their perception of the precariousness of their economic situation. Ping-kin, who shouldered the major burden of the work in her husband's "hill-shack factory," had seen the enterprise go through good fortunes and bad, as a result of worldwide economic changes over which they had no control whatsoever. At one point, for example, their factory of sixty workers was forced to close down for lack of orders, and her husband then lost most of his hard-earned capital in stocks and shares when the stock market collapsed in the early 1970s. Ping-kin had to nurse him out of his depression by encouraging him to reactivate his old professional network, and by helping him to start his enterprise from scratch again:

> I worked very hard — that was the hardest time; the hardest time since
> we started our business. Those three to five years. Because you had no
> capital to speak of. And you couldn't even hire a cleaner, so I had to do
> everything.

At this point, the work discipline that she had got used to since her teen years stood her in good stead: "[About work life in her teenage years] you only know about work: work, then go home, eat you meals, and then go to bed. Everyone I came into contact with in our social strata was like that."

Indeed, hard work was the only sure means by which our women workers coped with their economic situation. Ah Wah, for example, explained that all her coworkers in the electronics factory, having gone through a bad period of underemployment and unemployment, would not give up any overtime work. Similarly, Yau-lin explained how she and her coworkers in the garment factory would not give up any chance of making money:

> Everyone was very hard-working. People of our generation were all very hard-working. . . . When work [in the factory] was over, if there was no overtime work, then some of us would take outwork home. They'd just continue to work at home. . . . We didn't even like to take a break. . . . We just thought of work. Apart from work, it's still work! . . . All we could think of was making money.

Behind all this was a sense of insecurity, which Yau-lin was overly sensitive to: "I think the biggest reason for this was — we were afraid that we wouldn't be able to make money — this might happen any time. Our livelihood was unstable, you see. So our biggest concern was making money."

As Ching-kwan Lee said, class domination is a fact of life for these women workers.[61] Their only way of accommodating to this reality was by working hard, making as much money as they could, for as long as they could.

Search for personal space

Even hard-pressed by the sense of insecurity and the need to work hard and long hours, women workers did, however, manifest a quest for personal space outside moneymaking. Such a quest might be rare, or, it might only emerge at certain stages of life, but nevertheless, it was there. Ling-hoi was a good example. She said she was never able to be as single-mindedly money driven as her coworkers in the factory. She felt that "my sense of security came, instead, from how much I have got in myself. I've always felt that once money was made, it'd become an 'outside entity' (*sheng wai wu*), something apart from you. It's not me any more. . . . So, my satisfaction comes from how much I know. This is what is really mine."

This might explain why Ling-hoi had started a serious study of tailoring ever since she started her career as a garment worker at the age of thirteen, and why she had become actively involved in community youth groups as a teenager. After marriage, her in-laws had looked askance at her for insisting on having one evening a week to herself — she usually spent it on evening courses of all sorts. "I don't care. Even if I just go to fold a paper flower for fun, I still feel that the time is mine. That's none of their business. In any case, I'd attend school for one evening."

Djao argued that "allusion to upward social mobility" in the electronics factories in Hong Kong was part of the "socializing" effort of the dominant class to produce structural compliance on the part of the dominated class.[62] This is, no doubt, a top-down view taken by the sociologist. Taking the women's subjectivities more seriously, however, one could see that when workers expended efforts on what seemed to be a "project" of upward mobility, for example, taking up evening studies, it carries a unique meaning for the worker herself. For her, taking up evening studies was more an effort of self-actualization in itself than a mere means for the pursuit of upward mobility. Of course, for some of these women, it turned out that they did experience social mobility afterward, but that was not what they had been certain of, or even aimed at, when they first started. Meanwhile, others might have started evening studies but did not attain any viable qualifications. Yet, to continue to study against all odds amounted to waging a personal struggle against a life script that had been thrust on them. SCES alumnae recalled, for example, the joy of learning and the gratification of friendship built up among schoolmates as they attended evening school for an extended period of time despite the hard toil in factories in the daytime.[63]

Search for personal space seems to come easier for teenage workers, temporarily free of worries for household finances and the various demands of childcare. And, of course, their teen years had coincided with a time of industrial growth, and hence greater availability of working class jobs. By contrast, for the older women workers, their teenage years fell within the 1950s and early1960s. In those days of abject poverty, they had to work all year round, with only a few days' break over the Chinese New Year. Search for personal space for the working classes was thereby highly contingent on the macro economic situation. None of our older workers were able to attend evening schools in their teenage years, much as they had wanted to. It was also a time when they had no Sunday break the whole year round, and, as Ping-kin said, people of their social strata had never questioned why this was so.

For these "mother workers" of the 1970s, the quest for personal space had to come later in life, when their children reached adulthood. Ah Tim and Yau-lin recounted how they would take time off for short holiday trips in the 1980s, when their children had grown up, and when work and money was still forthcoming. As Yau-lin recounted this happiest period of her life, she framed it in spatial terms: "When [the children] grew older, I'd think: space is something that only you can give yourself. Even your husband or anyone [close to you] can't give it to you. Space is something you have to treasure yourself."

At the moment of interview, Yau-ling had lost her job as a skilled mender amidst the macro deindustrialization process, and, with a substantial portion of her savings having evaporated in the stock market, she had to take up the job of a cleaner at a bakery. She described her present job as "demeaning," being ordered around by the much younger shop assistants who had no inkling whatsoever of her earlier status of the respected "Miss *Bu Yi* [Mender]" in the knitwear factory. "What can you do? You have to help yourself get over this [psychological] hurdle," she said. At this point, she spoke about personal dignity instead, which seemed to be less tangible than the personal space she had spoken of earlier, but nevertheless, had just as much tenacity:

> I feel that it doesn't matter what you do. . . . I'm not cheating anybody. I'm making money with my own two hands. The most important thing is that you could face other people without shame, and you could face yourself without shame.

Yau-lin's quest for personal worth at a time when conditions were extremely unfavorable is perhaps not untypical. We see a similar line of thinking in Ping-kin, at a time when she was weighed down heavily by the double burden of household and factory labor. "I prefer working outside [the home]. Ultimately I don't like to stay at home. . . . It'd give me the feeling that I am useless."

Women workers' insight into the gender structure

Class domination is not the only fact of life these women workers have to live with. They have to live with gender domination too. Speaking about the British working class "lads," Paul Willis used the term "penetration" to describe the occasional insight these boys had of the reality of class domination under which they were living.[64] In this chapter, I prefer to use the word "insight," much as one who normally lives in darkness suddenly catches a glimpse of one's situation when a light, however weak, is shed on it.

I have recounted the story of Ah Wah, who gave up the chance to join the technical career path in the electronics factory because she considered taking evening courses in technical institutes an "odd" thing for a girl to do. We have also reviewed the gender hierarchy in factories, as well as misogynist taboos on the shop floor. What kind of insight did women workers have regarding this structure of male hegemony and gender inequality, if any?

While Ah Wah and Ping-kin did not say much about the gender structures they were living in, other women did have such insights of one kind or another. Ling-hoi, for example, readily pointed out the gender hierarchy and misogynist taboos on the shop floor. Concerning the gender hierarchy, she quipped that men were given high-status jobs not because they were more trustworthy. On the contrary, she observed that:

> The men were, in fact, very lazy. They loitered around, had tea, smoked, and talked. The women were much more hardworking. I saw that the women foremen were more diligent. They'd make preparations, organize things well beforehand [for the line girls]. But the men wouldn't. They'd ask others to do it.

Ling-hoi was obviously doubtful about the legitimacy of the gender hierarchy she observed at work.

Throughout her years of participation in trade union activities, she saw many female union members withdraw immediately after marriage. She found this incomprehensible, because it was not that their husbands were unaware of their girlfriends' union activities before marriage. She attributed such withdrawals to the husbands' possessiveness, but she also blamed the women for failing to insist on their own pursuits:

> I think the trade union itself isn't the issue. Rather, it's about whether there is something that you can call your own. Like, if you are learning to make pottery, you'd persist for twenty years, and you'd still be learning. This is you, you see! Hey, you're not telling me that with marriage, you'd lose even this little strain of persistence!

Ling-hoi's insistence on "a room of one's own" has prompted her to "see through" the gendered meanings attached to marriage, together with its restrictions on women's selfhood.

The two older garment workers, Yau-lin and Ah Tim, have more to say about the highly skewed gendered structure of marriage. Just like Ping-kin, who counseled and encouraged her distraught husband to start anew after their business failed, both Yau-lin and Ah Tim showed great tenacity and ingenuity in sustaining the family in dire straits. For example, when Yau-lin's husband was unemployed, it was she who advised him how to start a home-based curtain making service, and how to publicize it. She saw herself transgressing the gender roles in her courage and innovation. "My husband is very shy, but I have very thick skin. I am the man, and he is the woman — that's more like it."

Her friend, Ah Tim, could not agree more. Her own husband did not even dare to go into the pawnshop when the need arose. While they were living in squatter huts, she would raise chickens and hawk them on the streets when these propagated. She asked her husband to help with the transactions, but "he would stand with our son far away, near the public toilets. He really made me angry!"

Similarly, Yau-lin would get some knitwear from factories to sell on the streets when work was not forthcoming, but her husband was not bold enough to do that. She saw this as a reversal of gender roles, and a rather positive one at that:

> That's why, to my husband's family, I'm a rather capable woman. Like, our relatives would see me sitting near the railings [on the curbside], shouting: "Take a look even if you don't buy. Only so much per piece. Really pretty!" I mean, I'm a kind of man-like-woman (*nan ren po*).

Yau-lin thought that, if she were a man, she would try her best to take full responsibility of the family, so that the wife could live comfortably. To this, Ah Tim responded that she had done that already, even as a woman. This triggered off Yau-lin's strong criticism of men whom, she thought, have not lived up to expectations:

> I feel that men nowadays are good for nothing! They feel that they only need to give you some money, and if that is not enough, you'd fix it by whatever means. You'd have to think of ways to make do. I feel that, generally, women in Hong Kong are sort of . . . many of them are really great. . . . They have to do this [fix the finances at home], work outside, do household work, and sleep [with the husband]. [Laughs.]

Having done what she has done for the family, Yau-lin thought that she was not different from a man. As a woman, she has done her best, and heaven knows how blessed her husband was.

Regarding the gender structure, therefore, Yau-lin and Ah Tim held certain conventional conceptions of the respective gender roles, but they perceived themselves to have transgressed them in a positive way. Meanwhile, they also observed that such role reversal as they had experienced it was rather common among the couples around them.

The interesting thing is that Yau-lin went further to state what a woman needed to do in order to maintain an uncharacteristically strong, independent role:

> I feel that, for a woman, the most important thing is to have money. You know, when husbands change [their hearts], women usually say that they'd die and all that. I think that's most stupid. . . . I feel that it's most important to hold onto the money. I don't care if you [the husband] never come back. I don't mind. With money, you'd feel protected. Money gives you the courage. No money, and there's no courage to speak of. Yes, I'm like that since I was young. So, I'm very greedy for money.

Yau-lin's experience of the precariousness of livelihood from childhood onward had indeed brought her to see that economic independence was most important in life. This survival "instinct" and its corresponding emphasis on independence, nurtured in response to her class situation, somehow got transported into the gender sphere.

Conclusion: A Case for a Moral Self

We have seen how class and gender structures interact with each other in defining the life course of working class girls and women, most prominently, in the mobilization of labor of teenage girls via the culturally prized *gu jia* daughter — the filial daughter caring for her family. We have also seen the gender hierarchy in the workplace, and how the worker as daughter, wife, and mother fits into its demands and discipline. On another level, we see how different women attribute meanings to their various choices and experiences in the family and in the workplace, and we see how all this is permeated by some kind of moral and cultural value.

An interesting juxtaposition of the individual versus the family stands out in this discussion of the lives of women workers. Throughout their active working lives, these women had been fulfilling their duties as daughters, wives, and mothers as they spent most of their waking hours in factories. How did their varying subjectivities of being workers, daughters, wives, and mothers interact with one another during this time?

We have seen how the precariousness of existence for working class families drove family heads to make the "natural" decision of sending their daughters to work while they were still in their early teens. Most of our women workers, especially the older cohort among them, had accepted this decision without question because of the gendered construction of familial and filial duty prevalent in those days. At a later stage, these women workers also took up the duties of wife and mother alongside those of skilled and responsible workers at work. These duties include: childcare, which competed for their time and energy that had to be devoted to meeting production deadlines at work; the moral upbringing of their children in case they went into bad ways; and, in the case of the wife of the small factory owner, the overseeing and maintenance of family business.

Our question is: how did these women see themselves amidst their multiple roles of workers, daughters, wives, and mothers? How did they construct their selves as they took up factory work and discharged their daughter and wifely duties?

Listening to the women's stories about their lives, one is struck by the clarity of their agency. In concrete terms, they talked a great deal about how they saw themselves as individuals, even as they were deeply enmeshed in the all-encompassing net of family life. In fact, their independent selves came through unmistakably even as they recounted how they succumbed to circumstances that were often out of their control.

About having to quit school early in life in order to support their families, for example, quite a few women recounted a sense of loss, anger, and injustice which they had experienced as they were forced to quit school at a young age. Paradoxically, we found girls who actually rejected the offer of support from family and relatives for them to stay on in school, precisely because they did not want to be seen as begging (Ling-hoi and Margaret). A similar kind of pride could be found in another woman, Ping-kin, who started work at thirteen, and, a few years later, insisted on supporting her younger brother through school, now that she had gained a much greater say in family decisions with her financial power. This kind of enhanced authority in one's natal family could, as in Yau-lan's case, last several decades, well into middle age. Of course, we have seen that this pride and authority was well supported by the cultural construct of the *gu jia* daughter, which seemed to have existed in the Cantonese region for quite some time.

Apart from pride as a contributing daughter, the women's selfhood also built on one's work and skills in factory production. We have seen how Ling-hoi had set herself high goals as a teenage garment worker, which she achieved as she attained the coveted skills of a sample maker while still in her twenties. Similarly, Yau-lan and Ah Tim, coworkers and good friends, were proud to be menders in a knitwear factory, a position that commanded so much respect that they were addressed politely as "Miss *Bu yi* (mender)" by other workers.

Ultimately, the women's construction of selfhood went beyond their roles as workers, or as daughters, wives, and mothers. As we have seen, they were in search of personal space even amidst economic and cultural strictures. Ling-hoi, for example, talked about the quest for self-improvement, and the importance of having time and space for oneself even as a married woman. Yau-lan and Ah Tim talked about finding their own space in the form of holiday trips in financially better days, and after their children have grown up. Most tellingly, Yau-lan emphasized the importance of having money of one's own so that one could be totally self-reliant. This value placed on self-reliance was also mentioned by another woman, Ping-kin, as an explanation for the much larger share of labor she had put into her husband's small handbag factory.

Listening to the women's voices, one cannot help noticing that the construction of self has a distinct moral dimension. We have seen this in the pride of the *gu jia* daughter as well as the value placed on self-reliance. More interestingly, we can discover this moral dimension in the assertion of one's self when one is placed in the most stringent financial circumstances. Such circumstances were exactly what Yau-lan found herself landed in when she was demoted to the lowly position of a cleaner in her late middle age, after having lost her job as a respected job of a mender. With characteristic boldness and clarity, she stressed that she could still hold her head high, because she was making money with her own hands. Her uprightness and honesty had clearly been the mainstay of her self worth.

Revisiting the question of the individual/self versus family, I would venture to say that selfhood, intricately bound up with and manifested in one's social roles, is always interwoven with morality. That is to say, when one talks about "self," one is always talking about a moral self, as we have seen in these women's accounts of their lives.

Postscript: The Moral Self in the Public Arena

Interestingly but perhaps not surprisingly, the moral self sometimes extends beyond the woman's own immediate life circumstances to leave a mark on the public arena. An outstanding example is Ling-hoi, the veteran garment worker turned full-time unionist. From the time she joined the trade union in the early 1990s as a paid employee (she had been a volunteer executive committee member before that), she had risen in the ranks of the garment worker trade union to become chief executive over the decade, a post that she still held at the time of writing. In the federation of unions to which the garment worker union belonged, she founded the Women's Committee, which according to her, was the most active and closely-knit compared to the other three. Apart from providing a platform for discussion of issues related to the interests of women workers, this committee also became a vehicle for bringing in insights from local feminist groups and the women's movement.[65] Reacting to the economic restructuring in the 1980s and 1990s, as well as to the situation of flux in the post-1997 era, the federation became increasingly active in the political arena. With her rich experience in union activism, Ling-hoi soon became a major organizer and participant in the broader democratic movement.

Another of our workers, Yau-lin, had been a member of the executive committee of the garment workers' union for seven or eights years at the time of interview. By that time she had already lost her job in the knitting industry and was a cleaner in a bakery shop. Unlike most members who took up union membership only after having sought help from the union over pay disputes, Yau-lin joined after she took part in the union's series of protests against the passing of a trade-related ordinance in 1991.[66] She was then invited by the trade union to join their executive committee, contributing through her enthusiastic rallying of fellow workers. She described how she was moved by the organizer of the protest movement, who had cried bitterly when the ordinance went through: "He is literate [meaning he is a university graduate]. Why would he have to struggle like that? Actually I didn't know a thing[67] — I just asked myself why it had gone to this . . . I felt that as a trade unionist, he [the organizer of the protests] had worked so hard for us. So many people supported us, so we should walk the extra step. We should stick together — we should take greater initiative so that the union could become stronger and things would work out better."

About her fellow workers who were much less enthusiastic, Yau-lin had this to say: "I always see these people — they eagerly seek help from the union when something goes wrong [for them], sticking around [the union office] all the time. Then after things get sorted out, and when you ask them to come out for a march, they'd say they're busy or something." She felt this was not right, because "the union people do this and that for you. People work for you, and you should help in whatever way you can." The moral self in her was clearly manifested in these words, and also in her contribution over the years. This contribution, in concrete terms, often meant forgoing a day's pay to join protest or other activities, or attending a meeting after a long day's toil.

Admittedly, Ling-hoi and Yau-lin were a small minority among the women workers we are studying, but this applies to activists drawn from all other populations. The interesting point here is that we do see women whose agency and, in particular, their moral convictions, drive them onto "the road less traveled," despite their restrictive circumstances. Take the example of the founder of the first (and still the only at the time of writing) women workers' union, the Hong Kong Women Workers' Association (HKWWA, 1989). Yim Yuet-lin became a child worker in an electronics factory at the age of twelve. Her first experience of industrial dispute took the shape of support given to a fellow worker in a "minor industrial dispute," out of an urge to "seek justice."[68] After seven years with HKWWA, in 1996, she moved on to found the Zi Teng, the first advocacy group for sex workers' rights.[69] Both the HKWWA and Zi Teng work closely with local feminist groups and with the women's movement in general.[70]

Another example of women from restricted circumstances entering the public arena is Liu Ngan-fung, who, as former resident of an abused women's shelter, helped to found a group advocating for better legislative and judicial protection for victims of domestic violence, the Kwan Fuk Group for Women's Rights, in 1990.[71] A woman with very little formal education and small means, Liu became an active lobbyist, not only for rights of protection for victims of domestic violence, but also for greater democracy.

The stories of women workers are as much about structural constraints as about choice and the construction of meanings (*and* meaningful courses of action) on the part of individuals. This chapter started with a sad note about the economic displacement of these workers, but now it ends with some measure of optimism as we turn our attention to their subjectivity and agency.

Appendix: Biographical notes of the five informants

Name (Pseudonym)	Year of Birth	Year of Entry into Work (Age)	Age at Year of Interview (2001/2002)	Brief Summary of Work Experience
Ah Tim	1936/37	Around 1949 (13 years)	Around 65	• Ironed underwear for small factory as a kid. • Worked as spinner when she was 16/17, for 6–7 years. • Mender of gloves after childbirth, knitwear mender for over 3 decades until 1998/1999. • Helped out with daughter's work, adjusting clothes.
Ping-kin	1941	1954/55 (13/14 years)	60	• Candy wrapping in small factory as a kid. • Worked in shoelace and then towel factory during teenage years. • Assistant in nightclub for 2 years. • Worked in shoe factory, card-box factory, and handbag factory before marriage. • Ran family business in leather and other bags after childbirth. • Retired after husband fell ill and then died in 1995.
Yau-lan	1948	1958 (around 10)	53	• Worked as maid for families after emigrating to Macau as a kid. • Apprentice in garment factory at 13 or 14. • Entered knitwear factory at teenage. • Illegal immigrant to HK at around 20. Became knitwear mender, a job which she kept for over 3 decades, until 1998/1999. • Became cleaner in bakery.
Ling-hoi	1958/1959	Around 1970 (12 years)	43	• Outwork for half a year. • Apprentice in shirt factory. • Knitwear during teenage years. • Shirt-making at around 18, then married. • Started sample-making in her mid-twenties (early 1980s). • Quit factory work and became full time unionist at around 34 (around 1992).

Appendix (*Continued*)

Name (Pseudonym)	Year of Birth	Year of Entry into Work (Age)	Age at Year of Interview (2001/2002)	Brief Summary of Work Experience
Ah Wah	1959	1972 (13 years)	43	• Worked in electronics factory. • Tried her hand at a garment factory, but quit because she found it difficult to catch up. • Experienced unemployment for a month or two in 1975. • Started evening studies in 1976, and took the school leaving exam in 1982. • Changed to white-collar work upon graduation.

10 Half the Sky: Mobility and Late Socialist Reflections

Yan Lijun, with Yang Meijian and Taotao Zhang

Steel Maiden

At the end of the 1950s, during the years of the Great Leap Forward, steelmaking became a nationwide movement in China. "Iron," as a symbol of strength and firmness, was endowed with a special political significance. In this atmosphere, the government promoted the ideal of the "steel maiden," typified by women like Xing Yanzi, who left her comfortable city life to "eat bitterness" and labor work in the countryside for the revolutionary cause. The Chinese Communist Party widely publicized her stories. Song lyrics in her honor provided the justification:

> Xing Yanzi is an excellent role model . . .
> She labors to make grain grow from rocks
> She puts labor first and amusements last
> She labors only for the glory of the Party.[1]

The image of steel maiden forged meticulously in the official rhetoric encouraged Chinese women to bid farewell to femininity and do what had traditionally been done by men. The name "steel maiden" became a symbol of honor for members of female "shock teams" who hauled stones and wielded sledgehammers during the Great Leap Forward campaign in 1958. They were depicted in the popular imagination with certain characteristics: pigtails or short hair, broad shoulders, thick waists, loud voices, and blue uniforms. Strength and stamina came with a lively disposition. They cared little about their looks, and hid their individuality. Promoted along with the ideology of women's emancipation, the steel maiden archetype mobilized wave after wave of Chinese women to join the front lines of industrial labor. The media frequently reported the glorious achievements of women working in male-dominated industries such as petroleum, bridge construction, coal mining, and fishing.

In the 1960s and 1970s, while China was in the throes of the Cultural Revolution, women's equality and empowerment gained a new momentum. "Women hold up half the sky" and "men and women are equal in the new revolutionary era" were two of the era's most common gender equality tropes. In this atmosphere, a wealth of mythologies about women's position in society sprang up. In the eight model Beijing operas praised highly in the official rhetoric, female revolutionary cadres hold up "half the sky" on the stage.[2] In the Red Guard Movement, a large number of women came upon the political stage and exercised leadership over men in the revolution. It was popularly asserted that women in China no longer faced gender discrimination and that the country had pushed the position of women to new heights unknown throughout history. Women, it was believed, were perfectly equal to men and thus encouraged to do everything that men could do.

Each era had its own language of women's liberation, drawing on the language of labor and peasant mobilization. The steel maidens were part of this tradition. In the 1950s, the slogan was "women became the masters of the house," and the Great Leap Forward exhorted women to "leave the home." In the Red Guard Movement during the Cultural Revolution, women fully developed their ability to "hold up half the sky." Scholars like Jin Yihong see the "steel maiden" and associated slogans as the most important conceptualization of gender equality in the 1960s and 1970s.[3]

Although political labels and slogans like these were intended to empower women, many scholars view the decades leading to and after the Cultural Revolution as an era which deprived women of their initiative and individuality.[4] It was their labor and political commitment rather than their gendered selves that were exulted. The impact of these equality campaigns on the lives of women was mixed. In Li Huaiyin's case study of the Qin Village in Jiangsu's Dongtai County in 1977, the work teams had equal numbers of men and women. But according to one villager, the women completed "at least 70% of the team's work." In his words, "if it were not for the women, the work team would have been doomed."[5] On the other hand, Jin Yihong argued that women never received the same encouragement to participate in politics as men, noting that educated young men had the option of joining the army while women did not. Moreover, women only comprised 11% of students who were given educational opportunities based on the "worker-peasant-soldier" status.[6]

These scholars believe that the Maoist revolution pressured both men and women to live according to political labels, thereby preventing them from realizing goals on their own terms. In her study of female Red Guards, Wu Liping argued that:

> Each person was born and lived under a political situation that was as unpredictable as the weather, floating around with no stability. This was even truer for the women of that era. They were forced to attach themselves to the contemporary societal order. They had to become part of the game and play by the rules of the Cultural Revolution. The price they had to pay was to do everything as men did and lose their own tenderness, their own kind nature, their own fragility, and all those other characteristics that constituted "femininity."[7]

Studies in North America and Europe that focus on Chinese women in the Maoist era had their own ideological and analytical perspectives. The pioneering works of Delia Davin, Elizabeth Croll, and Margery Wolf are well known. Wolf has lamented "the unfinished revolution" for Chinese women. Other authors have gone beyond dichotomous perceptions of women's repression and liberation to explore nuanced gender agency.[8] In a broader historical sweep, Helen Siu follows this line of empirical work on women's agency and contextualizes her observations in a complex history of state-making in late imperial China. In her article "Where Were the Women?" she stresses how in indigenous groups in the Pearl River Delta of South China, men and women used their unique cultural experiences and sensibilities to join what they imagined to be the mainstream culture and to find their respective places in an expanding empire.[9]

In substance, marriage practices in South China during the Ming and Qing dynasties as analyzed by Siu might seem far from the turbulence of the Cultural Revolution in the mid-twentieth century. There is, however, a shared agenda to explore women's agency. This chapter uses Siu's analytical framework on regional cultural history to show how women in another significant historical moment of the region's development, the Cultural Revolution, conversed with the state's political rhetoric to further their mobility goals. The rhetoric surrounding the image of the steel maiden demanded conformity, but through the women's individual strategies of using this image, they found fulfillment in their own complicated lives.

In such a framework, the complicated lives of women did not come under total control of the official rhetoric. Regional diversity resulted in the relative multiplicity of their choices. It is exactly on this regional level that the historical experiences of the people in Guangdong Province are to be reconsidered. The Cultural Revolution is characterized by the unusual power of the official rhetoric of revolution, which pushed capitalism to the extreme opposite side of the party line. As a result, Hong Kong, which traditionally had a close relation with Guangdong, was labeled as "a dirty capitalist society." However, the regional archives that we consulted also show that even in this unusual historical moment, Guangdong was able to maintain its long-standing relationship with Hong Kong by way of a reinterpretation of the official rhetoric. Although people of Guangdong could only obey the official rhetoric, they had a more flexible space opened up for them by their special relationship with Hong Kong.

A regional focus is also significant. As described in other chapters in this volume, the historical relationship of Guangdong with Hong Kong granted women a more flexible space. Guangdong had its own version of the "steel maiden," i.e., "*Niunü*".[10] If the steel maiden was a female image idealized in the official rhetoric, *Niunü* was one pregnant with peculiar traits determined by the local historical experiences of Guangdong. *Niunü* was totally different from the degendered steel maiden. She was akin to the fashionable Hong Kong women in the 1960s, wearing large-size sunglasses, tight clothes and jeans, and with curly hair. For this reason, when the Cultural Revolution broke out, *Niunü* was the first image to be attacked by the revolutionary rhetoric for her "bourgeois fantastic garb."[11] Reflecting on these historical documents, one might see that the more harshly *Niunü* was attacked, the greater vitality she proved to possess. She was an image many women in Guangdong were tacitly attracted to and even boldly emulate. Here lay an alternative to the revolutionary rhetoric. If we put aside the uniform label given to women by the revolutionary rhetoric and look at them against the background of the local society of Guangdong and in view of their personal histories, we might see that women indeed had a "flexible space" similar to that of *Niunü*. They were not under total control of the official rhetoric; instead, they had their own resources and could be active participants in the revolutionary movement as well as in the historical constitution of the local society.

The study is based on recent interviews of several women born in the 1950s who lived and worked in Guangdong. The interviews are supplemented by archival research in the Guangdong Archive Museum and newspaper collections in the library of Sun Yat-sen University. Each woman began with different resources, used diverse strategies to succeed, and achieved different results. The fortunate ones among them avoided rural labor, joined the military, and took advantage of educational opportunities to achieve a degree of social mobility. Regional history also became a factor in the women's mobility strategies. Some shrewdly made use of the proximity of Guangdong to Hong Kong to seek illegal entry to a city labeled by the Party rhetoric as "living hell," but popularly imagined as paradise. Their desperate flight from rural Guangdong also showed the added burden of the rural-urban divide for social mobility, especially for the region's women. The following sections explore their various strategies for mobility during the Cultural Revolution. It also hopes to capture some of their emotions and reflections today.

Avoiding Rural Labor

During the ten years in which students and workers were active participants in the Cultural Revolution, the nation's schools and colleges closed and industry was largely paralyzed. In December 1968, Chairman Mao called on the urban intellectual youth to go to the villages by writing in the *People's Daily* that "we have two hands, and we should not idle away in the cities." Afterward, the movement to mobilize the youth to "go to the mountainous and rural areas" (*shang shan xia xiang*) gripped the entire nation. Students who graduated from high schools during the Cultural Revolution settled in the rural villages en masse to learn from the poor and lower middle class peasants.[12] But four of the women whom we interviewed did not join the twelve million members of their age cohort in the countryside.[13] Their family backgrounds played a large role in helping them to avoid the villages, but in some cases, they also had to rely on their own resources to navigate through the state system.

Family background was perhaps the most important social designation during the Cultural Revolution. Officially, family background denoted the social class a person had before obtaining economic independence or entering the work force. In fact, parents transmitted their political status to their children.[14] The Party divided the backgrounds in the so-called "five red categories" and the "five black categories." The former were revolutionary soldiers, revolutionary cadres, industrial workers, poor peasants, and lower middle class peasants. The latter were landlords, rich peasants, counterrevolutionaries, Rightists, and "bad elements." Those who were classified as "red" knew that it implied that they were innately accepted in society as the foundation of the revolution. According to revolutionary ideology, those labeled as black were naturally suspect. Of our four women interviewees, Mrs Ceng and Mrs Fen were children of military families. Mrs Huang was the daughter of an urban worker in Guangzhou, and Mrs

Fang was born into a poor peasant family. Each background required different strategies to migrate to cities or remain in them.

As children of military families, Mrs Ceng and Mrs Fen lived relatively sheltered lives. They also had the easiest time avoiding being sent to the countryside. Moreover, their fathers were fortunately not only in the military, but also had rural backgrounds, giving them solidly "red" roots. As Mrs Ceng explained:

> My parents were both military people. They were born in the impoverished mountainous regions, and enlisted during the war against the Japanese . . . Practically our entire village joined either the Red Army or the United Front Army [the allied forces of the Communists and the Kuomingtang] . . . My father studied at Nanjing Military Academy, and rose to a senior rank when he was very young. My mother also joined up in her teens as a "soldier for the arts" (*wen yi bing*) [female soldiers who performed for the troops].

Mrs Fen's father, on the other hand, was a bright young rural student in 1938 who passed the required examinations to attend the county high school. While there, as she tells it:

> One of the high school teachers was an underground Party member, and he persuaded my father to join the Communist Revolution. My father joined an army unit, and fought from the north all the way down to the south. Because my father had received some secondary education, he rose quickly and easily in the army ranks. When the army reached a city in the south, my father stayed there and became political commissar as well as Party secretary. He became known as the "king" of the province.

Because of their parents' military backgrounds, both women found enlisting almost a natural course in their life and career. Mrs Ceng joined the army in M city and was later assigned to an army unit in H city, where she stayed until she came to G city to enter the civil service.[15] In her words, "I was born into a military family, and my grades were good, so joining the army was the natural thing to do." Like other military children, Mrs Fen began her training early, but unlike many of them, Mrs Fen did not even fear rural labor. She was able to begin firearms training when she was only twelve, after which "all my winter and summer vacations were taken up with military training." During the middle school years, she wanted to "learn from the peasants (*xuenong*)" and briefly joined the rural labor tasks organized by the military residence compound. The conditions were arduous:

We harvested peanuts and sesame under the hot sun — it was so exhausting . . . I still remember very clearly that one time I was cutting grain, and I almost accidentally cut off my finger. Even when the insects got to the turnips, I would still eat them. At that time, I always felt victimized, and I could only cry.

But as difficult as the labor was, it did mean that she "really wasn't afraid of rural life at all," and she was later able to use her experiences to join the prestigious Communist Youth League. Although she did not fear being sent down to the countryside, she joined the military in 1970, after she graduated from middle school at the age of fifteen. As she notes, "I didn't really have any strong emotional reaction to enlisting. But later, when my little sister, who did not want to be a medic in the army, was sent down to a rural village in the mountains, I realized how lucky I was."

Like the two military daughters, Mrs Huang's father's background as an industrial worker figured prominently in her ability to avoid the countryside. Her father held a well-paid job at a hospital's medicine factory, earning about seventy yuan per month. As she explains, "compared to the poverty line at the time, which was set at eight yuan a month, our economic situation was quite good. For fifty cents, you could eat a meal with fish or meat. There were few people who could afford leather shoes, but I was one of them. Raincoats were also luxury goods, but I was able to enjoy them." She arguably had more to lose by going to the countryside than the other two women, but she had the advantage of a "red" background and an urban household registration (*hukou*). With these, she was able to attend the "Old Guangzhou" schools, Xianlong School and Guanya School.[16] Luckily, the middle school she attended only had two grades, and after she graduated, she stayed on as a teacher and managed to avoid being sent to the villages. Eventually, in her second year of high school, she was sent to work at a newspaper publishing factory.

Compared to these three women, Mrs Fang had the least enviable start in life. She was born into a "red" peasant family in the Zhaozhou area.[17] For her, the goal was not to avoid being sent down but to get out of the countryside in the first place. As with the other women, her family background helped, but unlike them, her own abilities and ambition played the decisive role in gaining entry to the city.

Ironically, although gender equality gave her the educational opportunities to leave the village, she left because the same promise of gender equality had been a fallacy in the village. Not only was her family poor, but she also had no older brothers, and as she explained, "the production teams counted men's work and women's work differently. No matter how much or how little a man worked, as long as he put in some work, it would count as enough. But even if a woman worked herself to death, her work would only count as 60% of the work points of a man's work." Because her younger brothers were too young to work, all the labor in her household fell to her and her sisters. Thus, when the work team tallied up the work points, her family always had very few. She remembered that, "whenever grain was portioned out according to work points, my mother would cry. All the other families had working men, so they took the grain away by the basketful, but our family with all our members could only take home a little. It wasn't nearly enough to feed us all." As a result of the village's ill-treatment of her family, she noted that, "very early on, I realized that I had to leave the village. If I had had an older brother, perhaps I wouldn't have left."

There were few opportunities for advancement for peasants during the Cultural Revolution. Mrs Fang did not have enough political connections to join the army, nor could she move to the city to find work without an urban household registration. She could, however, use education as her way out. She, fortunately, had a very liberal-minded father who supported her education. In 1978, the government reinstated the college entrance examinations (*gaokao*), but high school graduates in her year were not yet allowed to take them, so Mrs Fang worked with what little resources the state gave her. She took the exam to enter junior college instead, but as she explains, "I missed the admission cutoff by 1.5 points. The second year, I studied hard to get into college. In order to help my application, I filled in 'Willing to be assigned to any school' on the form. As a result, I was assigned to a railroad engineering college." She was one of the two proud students from her county to be admitted to the college. What excited her most was that "I knew that upon graduation, I would be allocated to a salaried job, and this meant that I could leave the village forever!"

By staying in a city, these women were able to develop careers in the state system. Mrs Ceng and Mrs Fen, for example, worked in government bureaucracies for several decades. Mrs Huang became a journalist in a Party unit after she finished her studies at Peking University as a "worker-peasant-soldier" student. She only recently retired with a comfortable salary. Mrs Fang entered the state railway system after graduation, and rose to be an administrator in property management. Despite the occasional turmoil during the revolutionary decades, they have been able to enjoy some privileges granted by the state system, and by successfully using their own resources to their advantage.

Straddling the Rural-Urban Divide

In 1958, an institution of household registration in favor of the urban population was established in China. Thereafter, urban residents and peasants were in face of two entirely different life opportunities, and a barrier was set up between urban and rural areas. The government took advantage of this to maintain a tight control over people's lives. The government exclusively distributed educational and work opportunities as well as the necessaries of life for urban residents, while peasants were strictly confined to the collective rural economy.[18] As some scholars have observed, in the mid-1960s, the city and the countryside were already two different worlds. As a result, the Cultural Revolution had a varied impact upon urban and rural areas. On the whole, it caused greater disturbances in cities than in the countryside.[19] Our interviews indicate that the revolutionary movement further widened the gap between urban and rural areas. The female interviewees report that what they — whether as educated youth going down to the countryside or as peasants — were most eager for at that time was to shake off the label of peasant.

In 1968, two years after classes were suspended in schools and industry came to a halt, millions of students who had attended high school in the early period of the Cultural Revolution were faced with serious employment problems. Now the policy of "going to the mountainous and rural areas," which had begun in the 1950s, was compulsively implemented. A large number of urban youth were forced to go down to the countryside, and almost every family was affected by the policy. Indeed, there were those who felt that a brave new world was lying ahead.[20] However, most young people had profound feelings of confusion, despair, frustration, and fear.[21] The barrier between urban and rural areas was so impenetrable, and the classification of identities so rigid, that the young people who had lost their identity as urban residents were involved in a process of othering. They considered peasants as the "other," and vice versa, with the consequence that the demarcation of cities from the countryside was further intensified.

For the peasants, the revolution did not bring about the promised "earthly paradise." The barrier between urban and rural areas hindered social mobility. Although the revolutionary slogans repeatedly claimed that peasants were the most worthy revolutionary partners, people tried by all means to avoid the label of peasant, which, as it were, was imposed by the official ideology.[22] Rural women continued to suffer from a double injustice, since they were both women and peasants. In fact, the barrier between urban and rural areas was so formidable that rural women often felt injured in their daily life by this sharp line of demarcation. However, they had their own strategies, which enabled them to obtain as much flexible space as possible.

Although the government promised to provide job opportunities to urban residents, young people actually had no place to shelter themselves in cities in the mid-1960s. With limited resources, the state gave priority to those who had a politically correct family background and who had been educated in its employment program. The three women mentioned above were among the fortunate ones. However, large numbers of less revolutionary youth with a dubious family background were denied access to job opportunities. These young people who were excluded from the revolutionary cause generally felt that there was no way out for them. Mrs Liao's grandfather had come to Hong Kong to do business early in his career and later became a capitalist with a considerable family fortune. Her father, as the eldest son, had been born in Hong Kong. After graduating from the University of Hong Kong, he had returned to his hometown to manage the family business, and for that reason he was later labeled as a "capitalist." Mrs Liao comments that it was her family background that made it difficult for her "to move one inch forward." In 1964, after completing her junior middle school studies, she decided to attend nursing school. Although she passed the entrance examinations, she was deprived of the opportunity for admission because of her dubious family background. As she had no other work to do, she joined in a youth folk art troupe, which was largely composed of unemployed youth.

The slogan "Learn from the peasants" was a beautiful compliment to peasants as well a way out. In 1965, the local neighborhood committees began to create propaganda on the *xia xiang*, which sent a large number of urban school-leavers to the countryside to learn from the peasants. Although it was considered to be a rare opportunity for young people to devote themselves to the revolutionary cause, urban residents did not give up their deep-rooted prejudice against the countryside. There was hesitation on the part of those awaiting employment, because they did not know for sure if they would be able to come back to their native cities in future. Although the countryside was described as a furnace of revolution, urban residents were unwilling to stay there for their entire lives. "It is generally thought that the *xia xiang* policy began to be implemented in 1968," says Mrs Liao. "As a matter of fact, we were the first group. We volunteered to go down to the countryside, while after 1968, people were forced to do so. At that time, it was rumored that we would be trained as potential cadres and were expected to come back to cities in three years."

Before leaving for the countryside, the educated youth had already replaced their prejudice against the countryside with illusions about a brave new world. Mrs Liao expected that her experiences in the countryside would ultimately change people's views about her family background and enable her to be a genuine part of the revolution. "It was a day I will never forget. On March 2, 1965, people held a seeing-off ceremony to the accompaniment of drums and gongs. With a flower on my chest, I proudly started on my way to the countryside. That year I was nineteen. Going with me were my partners in the folk art troupe. We cherished a fervent hope, expecting that we would work in the daytime and play music at night. What an idyllic life!"

After settling down in the countryside, the educated youth began to be keenly aware of the barrier between urban and rural areas. Since they were "people from cities," they could not be cordially accepted by the peasants. They were discriminated by the peasants, whom they in turn discriminated. Mrs Liao found that the peasants were not really good teachers for her. Instead, they were full of contempt and hostility. The village where she labored was on the outskirts of the city. Peasants were familiar with the urban life but it remained well out of their reach. "Seeing the urban youth coming down to the countryside, the peasants were filled with exultation as if a revenge had finally been taken. They thought that we had come down to the countryside because we could no longer muddle along in cities. So they turned up their noses on us. What's more, they felt that we were there to compete with them for bread and thus harmed their economic interests," says Mrs Liao.

The label of "urban resident" implied a superiority granted by the state. Although they lived in the countryside, the educated youth never forgot their identity as urban residents. However, faced with the peasants' attitude of exclusion and the unbearable life conditions, they had to re-examine their own positions in the state's classification system of identities. They became aware of the fact that they had been deprived of their identity as urban residents. As Mrs Liao says, "we were inferior even to the peasants." This perception was further intensified by the arduous working conditions. Mrs Liao could earn three work points per day, and each work point was equal to 0.03 to 0.04 yuan. So she could earn approximately three yuan per month. By contrast, the peasants could develop sideline production in addition to earning work points. "With a pig alone a peasant could earn seventy to eighty yuan, which was twice as much as my yearly income," remembers Mrs Liao. The former "urban resident" began to compare herself with the peasants whom she had previously considered as "people of a different kind": "We work together with the peasants, but why is it that we earn so much less?"

In addition to the tension between urban and rural areas, the female educated youth faced sexual discrimination in the countryside. The archives we consulted show that in the countryside women generally did not receive equal pay for equal work, although the state claimed that they held up "half the sky." This condition even caused some rural young women to commit suicide.[23] For Mrs Liao, this was no less than a double misfortune. She had been deprived of her identity as an urban resident, and as a woman she belonged to a powerless group. Thus she began to compare herself with the male educated youth: "They can earn ten work points, while we can earn only five to six. The educated youth are inferior to the peasants, and the female ones are inferior to the male ones."

If there was still some room for the expression of femininity in cities, the young educated women completely lost their femininity under the heavy burden of farm work. Mrs Liao had secretly brought with her a white silk handkerchief, which had been a gift from her grandfather in Hong Kong. However, overwhelmed by the feeling that "the educated youth being inferior to the peasants," she never dared to show it to others, lest her femininity should add to the peasants' aversion to her. Later, the handkerchief was discovered by the peasants. "They burned it!" This symbolic incident destroyed Mrs Liao's feminine space completely and further deepened her awareness of the unbridgeable gap between urban and rural areas.

The barrier between urban and rural areas resulted in considerable tensions between the educated youth and local peasants, which was most obvious in the young educated women's marriage choices. Local men often made marriage proposals to the girls from cities. Mrs Liao did not wish to get married. "Although I had reached the age for marriage, I did not want to get married. Since I was in such a miserable condition, it made no difference whether I got married or not. What's more, getting married in the countryside would mean that I would remain there all my life. Though I knew I could not go back to my native town in the foreseeable future, there was still a ray of hope," says Mrs Liao. When the girls rejected the local men, their attitude of exclusion towards "people from cities" was sharpened into a hostility, of which there was an extreme example. A team leader was rejected in his marriage proposal. He then revenged himself on the girl by spreading vicious rumors about her. He often deliberately put obstacles in her way by asking her to do the same work over and over again. In the end, the girl was driven mad by all these tortures.[24]

In the mutual "othering" of people from cities and peasants, the urban youth who had come to the countryside in search for a way out were utterly disillusioned. The revolutionary movement put a romantic halo around the countryside, but it did not fundamentally change the inferior position of the countryside compared to the cities. When the "people from cities" found that the countryside was not a sacred place of revolution, they lost their enthusiastic idealism and tried their best to cut off any relationship with the countryside. Not only did the girls refuse to marry local peasants, but they used all means to avoid labor. Mrs Liao had a rheumatic foot, which was a good excuse for her to avoid work. "I found that this was a good excuse. So when I didn't want to work, I just resorted to this excuse," says Mrs Liao. Later, this strategy was widely used and many people pretended to be ill and lay in bed all day long. "Within the institutionally permissible limits, this was the greatest resistance we could put up," concluded Mrs Liao.

The revolutionary movement did not turn the countryside into earthly paradise, not to mention paradise for women. Under the disappointing circumstances, the educated youth were eager to go back to their native towns and the peasants did their utmost to leave the countryside. For the young educated women, there was still a glimmer of hope — however faint it might be, but for the women who were born as peasants, there was little chance. Indeed, the young educated women had their way of resistance, such as being lazy in their work, but this resistance was quite moderate as compared with that of the rural women. According to the archives, there were a consecutive series of incidents of collective suicide in 1974 involving seventeen rural girls in Huilai County, Guangdong Province.[25] Two rural girls often went to the urban areas to buy urine in the morning. After they heard a few urban residents say some "unpleasant words" about them, they began to reflect upon their own life conditions. "We empty urine buckets and carry chamber pots for them. To be a peasant is too insulting. Urban girls wear polyester clothes, while we, barefooted, carry dung tubs on our shoulders every day." They could not figure out why they had to live such difficult lives. Another girl killed herself because her poor educational background barred her from getting a job. On the brink of death, she pledged that she would "lodge a complaint against women with the King of Hell after she died." These incidents of collective suicide made clear the grim realities rural women were faced with under the slogan of "half the sky": mercenary marriages, high rate of illiteracy among young women, unequal pay for equal work, etc. From such an extreme form of resistance it might be clear that these girls were desperate to escape their own situations.

Although the official rhetoric encouraged women to participate in politics, rural women were for the most part confined to household affairs. They had little chance to move out of their homes. Mrs Che, who came from a peasant's family, was not satisfied with the label of peasant, which had accompanied her from her birth. She felt that the production team was just like a reformatory. She knew that very few resources were available to her so that she could change her destiny. "As a peasant, I had no chance to join the army. For me, farm work was a daily routine. How could I spare the time to attend school?" However, she had her own strategy. Within the allowable limits, she was able to break off relations with the countryside and move towards the city. She was aware that a woman must depend on a man to change her fate. The actual strategy she adopted was even more ingenious. She took advantage of her family relationships to come upon the revolutionary stage. But ironically, she took part in the revolution not for the revolution's sake, but in order to cut herself off from the class that claimed to be the most revolutionary.

She relied on her father, an able man in the village, for the first step she took towards her goal of leaving the countryside. After she left primary school in 1966, she did not continue her studies. Instead, she helped her mother, who worked in an embroidery factory, to do embroidery. In 1970, with the help of her father, she became a needle worker in the handicraft plant of the production brigade. She felt how wonderful it was to be a worker. "Though my registered residence was still agricultural, it was a great advantage to work in the handicraft plant. Without my father's assistance, I could not have bid farewell to farm work. I determined never to go back to the production team, which was really a reformatory." In order to consolidate her position in the handicraft plant, she did her utmost to meet the demands of the revolutionary rhetoric. She worked in the plant in the daytime, and at night she joined the brigade propaganda team in its performance of the model operas. She considered it a good opportunity to change her life prospects. "At that time, my greatest wish was to join the Youth League and then to join the Party. If I could obtain some post with the brigade, I would no longer do farm work."

The educated youth did not want to get connected with the countryside through marriage, while peasants tried their best to leave the countryside through marriage. Tamara Jacka notes that there were several possibilities for peasants to become urban residents in the Maoist era and that for women, "marriage is one further strategy that they are able to use to improve their status."[26] Mrs Che was fully aware of the possibility of using this strategy to change her fate. So the second step she took towards the goal of leaving the countryside was to adapt herself to the revolutionary rhetoric and to take advantage of the "red" marriage relationship. She got to know her would-be husband on the propaganda team. At that time, they were both popular in the village. She played the lead female role in the ballet *The Red Detachment of Women*, while he played the lead male role. Their revolutionary position was solid enough for them to continue their cooperation for a long time. Mrs Che married her husband not only out of love, but also out of her appreciation for her husband's "red background." "We got along with each other for a long time on the propaganda team and fell in love. I felt that he was a pretty good guy. He always strove to make progress. At that time, he was leader of the militia."

According to Mrs Che, the marriage rule prevalent at that time once again demonstrated the peasants' disadvantageous position in the social hierarchy. People generally believed that the best option for a girl was to marry a worker. If a worker was unavailable she could marry a man more or less involved in manual labor, like a man whose job was to mend roads. Even if she could not find a husband, she would refuse to marry a peasant. This rule left rural girls with little room to choose. "A girl could hardly decide whom to marry. A man from the poor and lower middle peasant classes would refuse to marry a 'landlord's daughter,' and it was not easy for a girl from a peasant's family to marry a worker," says Mrs Che. Actually, peasants found it extremely difficult to change their status through marriage. In addition to the instinctive prejudice urban residents held against peasants, there were obstacles posed by the state policy. "The policy stipulated that if a rural woman married an urban resident, she must have her residence registration changed within half a year. Yet the reality was that it was almost impossible for her to apply for permanent residence in the city. The problem of residence registration alone would prevent me from marrying a worker," explains Mrs Che.

However, the government gave some peasants who proved to be revolutionary enough the opportunity to improve their status. Mrs Che's husband finally got rid of his identity as a peasant. In 1982, the government made a requisition of land in the village. This gave some villagers an opportunity to change their identities. Her husband made use of various personal relationships and succeeded in applying for a non-agricultural permanent residence. Later he was assigned a job in an automobile company. Mrs Che also became an urban resident and got a job in the city. Mrs Che's case shows how a rural girl skillfully evaded agricultural labor under the pretence of revolution, made use of her marriage to add to her mobile capital and finally got rid of the undesirable label of peasant.

Stowing Away

While the revolutionary movement was raging violently in mainland China, Hong Kong, which is adjacent to Guangdong Province, was on its way to industrialization. As Ching-kwan Lee observes, "South China is a literal borderland of national boundaries, straddling a British colony and a Chinese province, as well as metaphorical borderland of social systems and categories."[27] In the 1960s and 1970s, the debate about whether Hong Kong was paradise or hell, which was provoked by the official rhetoric, never stopped in Guangdong.[28] Hong Kong was described as "paradise for the rich and hell for the poor."[29] During the Cultural Revolution, a fierce attack was launched on capitalist societies. People who had relatives in Hong Kong and Macao were accused of having overseas connections. This dubious background gave them a sense of shame and inferiority.

The fierce criticism of Hong Kong by the official rhetoric reflected yet another fact, namely that Hong Kong had long been a paradise in the imagination of the people in Guangdong. When the country experienced a great famine in 1958–61, Hong Kong became a "granary" for the Guangdong people. In the movie *Close Pursuit* produced by the Pearl River Film Studio in 1963, there was a scene of Hong Kong and Macao compatriots returning to their hometown. They brought back many kinds of goods, including cigarettes and wristwatches as well as sweets, combs, and toys. In her childhood, Mrs Liao never suffered from starvation. Her grandfather sent her family food at regular intervals. Even during the years of the great famine she still had noodles to eat. "Many of my neighbors also had relatives in Hong Kong. The girl who lived next to my house was an example. Each time her father returned from Hong Kong, he would bring back two large baskets of food, usually including two cans of soy-braised pork, which were quite rare on the mainland at that time."

The frequent movement of people between Guangdong and Hong Kong since the 1940s had laid a solid foundation for the imagination of Hong Kong as paradise. Helen Siu discusses the socio-historical origin of the psychological imbalance that gripped the new immigrants from mainland China when they endeavored to merge into the Hong Kong society in the 1970s and 1980s. Her work presents another perspective about the historical origin of the Guangdong people's impression of Hong Kong.[30] There were huge waves of emigrants from Guangdong to Hong Kong during the years before and after 1949 and then at the end of the 1950s. The People of Guangdong who moved to Hong Kong had their relatives and friends on the mainland, so they became a natural link between Guangdong and Hong Kong with respect of the flow of people, materials, money and ideas.

As a matter of fact, the relationship continued into the years of the Cultural Revolution, when the ideological struggle was at its high. Mrs Liao remembers that though her grandfather could no longer send her family food or money, they could still receive letters from Hong Kong. The archives we consulted also show that the overseas remittance service did not cease in Guangdong during the Cultural Revolution. In 1972, Zhongshan County received eleven million dollars in overseas remittance. In the Guzhen Commune alone, forty thousand people received overseas remittances amounting to three hundred thousand yuan.[31] From 1950 to 1972, 93% of total overseas remittances to China came from Hong Kong residents.[32] The government-controlled trade contacts between Guangdong and Hong Kong were not adversely affected by the revolution. From 1966 to 1971, Guangdong continued to export small live animals to Hong Kong. Except for 1968, the supply steadily increased, and in 1970, it increased by a wide margin.[33]

Since the relationship could hardly be tolerated by the revolutionary rhetoric, one might be wondering how it was maintained in Guangdong. In fact, though the central government labeled Hong Kong as "an evil capitalist society" and formulated a policy of isolation, the local government of Guangdong did not execute it in a rigid manner. In the local archives of the 1960s, the attitude towards Hong Kong was expressed very subtly. On the one hand, people in Guangdong appealed to the revolutionary rhetoric in support of the theory of class struggle and criticized capitalism and Revisionism; on the other, they appealed to the theory of "contradictions between ourselves and enemy" and maintained that the various relationships with Hong Kong should be concretely analyzed and dealt with. Undoubtedly, the local government's interpretation of the revolutionary rhetoric more or less legitimized the exchange between Guangdong and Hong Kong.[34] In 1968, the Guangdong Customhouse submitted a report to the Ministry of Foreign Trade asking for direction. The report proposed that a class analysis be conducted of the passengers from Hong Kong and Macao: most of them belonged to the semi-proletariat and petty bourgeoisie and supported the socialist system. The Guangdong Customhouse suggested that some convenience of passage be given to passengers from Hong Kong and Macao. The report shows that the Customhouse did not prohibit the short-term visits of Hong Kong and Macao residents to the mainland. They could even bring back luxury items like watches and cameras.[35]

The local government had to appeal to the revolutionary rhetoric in order to maintain connection with Hong Kong, while in the daily life of common people, the connection became more direct. Though people were forbidden to listen to the broadcasts of the "reactionary radio stations" in Hong Kong, the injunction was often ignored. Mrs Liao speaks about the Guangdong people's attitude towards the injunction. In their view, if one did not listen to the Hong Kong radio in public, one was not really violating the injunction. In Guangdong, especially in the Pearl River Delta area, many people were accustomed to listening to the broadcasts of the "enemy broadcasting stations." According to the statistics of Zhongshan County of Guangdong Province in 1973, in one commune of the county, people possessed 1,509 radio sets and 74.7% of the population listened to the "reactionary radio stations."[36] In one commune of the Nanhai County, a cadre listening to the reactionary radio station was so careless that he forgot to turn off the radio before falling asleep. For this reason, he was taken as a "negative example."[37]

In contrast to the rigid official ideology, the local society of Guangdong took a relatively moderate attitude towards the "evil capitalist society" of Hong Kong. Due to a de facto close relationship with Hong Kong on the nongovernmental level, common people's conception of Hong Kong deviated considerably from the official ideology. In Mrs Liao's words, "if Hong Kong is really a degenerate capitalist society, why is it that those who fled never came back? Since they did not retrace their steps, they must have found a way out there." Many of Mrs Liao's companions shared her view, and some of them even took actions to realize it in spite of the enormous dangers they could possibly encounter.

Why did they so readily run such a risk? Did Hong Kong really promise a way out? People had many different opinions to this point. Mrs Che, who came from a peasant's family, thought that those who fled to Hong Kong were all ambitious. In contrast, Mrs Huang, who came from a worker's family, thought that only those who had a dubious family background and were driven into a corner made such an unwise decision. However, different answers demonstrated one and the same fact, namely that the barrier between urban and rural areas was insurmountable and that the young people who were stranded in the countryside had no opportunity for mobility sanctioned by the state policy. Hong Kong then became a way out for people in a desperate situation. "As a matter of fact, we had no unreasonable expectations. We just wanted to have three meals a day and free ourselves from the toil in the countryside. If one had had a secure job in the city, one would never have thought of fleeing to Hong Kong. The life of the educated youth made us feel that we were really subhuman."

To a certain degree, the act of fleeing the mainland was the result of the conspiracy of the stowaways with the local peasants. Due to the urban and rural barrier, the educated youth were excluded from the social classification system. Their self-exile was exceedingly welcome for the local peasants. "The peasants had always thought that we had come to the countryside to compete with them for bread. So it was all too natural that they hoped to see us leave as quickly as possible, whether by stowing away or by any other means," explains Mrs Liao.

In this sense, the act of fleeing the mainland was not merely a personal choice, but a collective response in a particular historical moment as well. On most occasions, the plan to escape was worked out in a collective manner. Mrs Liao was asked several times by her companions to leave with them. Fellow stowaways usually had a strong collective consciousness. Mrs Liao had rheumatism in her legs, so in the end she had to give up the plan reluctantly for fear that she would become a burden on her companions. Later, stowing away became a common practice. In some places, a large number of cadres and peasants stowed away, so that nobody was left to organize production or care for the land. Classes had to be suspended in schools, and shops and medical stations had to be closed. The stowaways went so far as to assault frontier stations and local police stations.[38] There were frequent reports of emergencies in some areas of Guangdong. In the Bao'an County, there were altogether 1,950 stowaways from July to December 1973.[39] In the Zhongshan County, from January to April 1973, 2,244 people were prepared to stow away. In one production team of the county, all men aged thirty stowed away except one.[40] Many rivers in Guangdong, such as the East River in the Huiyang County and the Pearl River in Guangzhou, became natural training spots. People practiced swimming in preparation for stowing away.

There were a great number of women in the great army of stowaways. In the movie *Swan Song*, one can see a heartbroken girl among the young people who fail in their attempt to stow away because the ringleaders fled with the money.[41] In Bao'an County, of the 1,950 people who stowed away in the latter half of 1973, there were 431 women, including two cadres of the production brigade.[42] According to Mrs Liao's account, "most of the women who stowed away were unmarried. Of course, there were some married women who just abandoned their husbands and children in order to stow away." As young women were healthy and strong, it was easier for them to swim across the border. "One had to swim four or five hours. But if he or she swam slowly, it would take more than ten hours. Besides, it was a long way to the border river. Usually, one had to walk several hours.

At that time, the act of stowing away was under the strict scrutiny of the police. Vehicles leaving the county were often checked, so stowaways had to go on foot. This would take a lot of physical strength. People generally thought that a person who dared to stow away must be a 'master sportsman.'"

As a matter of fact, women took greater risks than men. In addition to the risk of death, there were certain dangers that only affected female stowaways were confronted with. Ringleaders often fled with money, and there were even some rape cases.[43] The strategy of female stowaways was to take action with the help of their male acquaintances. "Almost every small group of stowaways was composed of men and women. Therefore, the success of the action largely depended on the cooperation of each person in the group. Indeed, it was important for female stowaways to be strong physically. But it was even more imperative for them to have strong and reliable male partners. Mrs Liao attributed the success of her three younger sisters to the efficient use of this female strategy: "My younger sister was slight of figure, with a weight of less than forty kilograms, but she managed to swim across the border. Her success was due to the assistance of a few male partners who were quite skillful in swimming. There were even some girls who did not know how to swim but also succeeded. They wore life-belts and were just pushed across the river by their male partners."

The way in which boys helped girls across the border produced some romantic female myths. Now what aroused envy was neither the firm character of the "steel maiden" nor the passion to sacrifice oneself for the revolutionary ideal, but the freedom of love that was unavailable under the actual circumstances. Mrs Liao tells a story: A girl student fell in love with her teacher, who then took the risk to flee with her to Hong Kong. "On the previous day he had told us in class never to leave the mainland. Then he just fled with the girl. Later they got married in Hong Kong and lived together happily."

The official rhetoric described a common fate awaiting female stowaways. "Many females became prostitutes after they fled to Hong Kong because they had no other means of subsistence." However, such frightening warnings did not prevent women from pursuing the long sought-after freedom. Mrs Liao was very happy when she received a letter from her sister telling her that she had arrived safely. Her sister later created a female myth. She worked in a plant during her first year in Hong Kong. Then she was lucky enough to dub television programs and films for the Shaw Brothers Company. She earned a lot of money, which she later invested in real estate. She never got married and is now back in her hometown living with and looking after her elderly mother. She lives a comfortable life on the income from the rents of her real estate in Hong Kong and Shenzhen.

As compared with the one-dimensional myth of the "steel maiden," the myth of female stowaways was varied and diversified. It was not created by the rigid official ideology, but by the women themselves. The myth provided a channel through which the women could express their aspirations for life and give full play to their subjective agency.

Conclusion

In the grand narrative of the Cultural Revolution by Carma Hinton and others, women are described as a group of people victimized in the name of the revolution or as a group of people too powerless to utter their own voices.[44] However, if we look at the women who lived through the Cultural Revolution from the perspective of local history, a different picture will emerge. In an environment where the barrier between urban and rural areas, the various demands of the revolutionary rhetoric, the life aspirations of individuals and the unique local historical experiences interacted with one another, women of different origins tried to improve their lives in their unique ways.

Under a government that was "as unpredictable as the weather," must women "attach themselves to the contemporary societal order"? From the lives of some ordinary women in Guangdong, we can see that there were actually many ways for women to respond to the rhetoric of the Cultural Revolution. Although they could not completely defy the state system, they found space to move around within it and pursue their own interests.

Thirty years after the reform, the "steel maiden" model has left center stage, and the political designation of class status has become less significant. What kind of model do Chinese women have now? There is probably no definitive answer. Instead, women find a wide range of opportunities open to them. There are also diverse career models to inspire. From the stories of the women we interviewed, one thing is certain: regardless of models, young women will always find a way to use their own initiative and pursue life on their own terms.

11 Fantasies of "Chinese-ness" and the Traffic in Women from Mainland China to Hong Kong in Fruit Chan's *Durian Durian*

Pheng Cheah

Following the work of Jean Baudrillard, David Harvey suggested that the flexible accumulation that gives rise to the postmodern condition is characterized by the production of images and sign systems rather than commodities themselves.[1] Such cultural forms and the fantasies they generate in daily experience are integral to the circulation of capital. One of the key fantasies driving and underpinning the East Asian circuit of flexible accumulation is the fantasy of the Chinese diaspora as cosmopolitan capitalist entrepreneur. The Chinese diaspora is fantastic in two senses. Historically, these waves of migration were driven by fantasies of wealth outside the poverty of the mainland. But it is also the subject and object of fantasy today as ideological discourses seek to explain the phenomenon of the East Asian miracle prior to the 1997 financial crisis and in the wake of contemporary Chinese hyperdevelopment.

From this perspective, the economic modernization of the People's Republic of China can be glossed as a rearticulation of Chinese-ness through these fantasies of the diaspora, a rearticulation that is more precisely a repatriation and restoration of certain cultural elements of the migrant business/merchant class back to the mainland. For the mainland wants to model parts of itself, especially the coastal cities of South China, after these diasporic communities and external Chinese cities such as Hong Kong and Singapore. In his famous visit to South China in January 1992, Deng Xiaoping had called for the construction of a few Hong Kongs. After 1992, overseas Chinese investment, which had earlier been concentrated in the South China Economic Periphery, expanded into the interior provinces of Hubei and Sichuan and the northeast beyond Beijing.[2] The global city of

Hong Kong is thus a crucial site and node for this rearticulation and remodeling of Chinese capitalism, of Chinese as capitalist. It was always the gateway to China for Chinese diasporic business networks and the corporate headquarters and eventual place of residence for many overseas Chinese tycoons.[3] From the standpoint of political sovereignty, Hong Kong may have been handed over to the PRC in 1997. But as a synecdoche of the permeability of the mainland's borders to overseas Chinese capital and its enlargement into Greater China, the handover also symbolically marked the irreversible integration of the PRC into the global capitalist system. It is effectively the handover of China to capitalism, its gradual weaning from Communist principles, where Hong Kong itself has become a borderzone for the flow of money, consumer goods, and fantasies, and people. For instance, Disneyland chose to locate itself in Hong Kong as a launchpad for the Disneyfication of China because although its primary intended market is the mainland tourist, the standard of living in the PRC and consumer awareness is not yet high enough to sustain a Disneyland there.[4] Thus, Hong Kong, and its broader economic hinterland in Southern China (especially the Guangdong area and the cities of Guangzhou and Shenzhen) is also a frontier, the source of change and innovation for the mainland. As Xiao Yan/Siew Yin observes in *Durian Durian*, the Fruit Chan film I will be discussing in this chapter, the South (*nanfang*) is where everything foreign, whether it is the exotic Southeast Asian fruit, the durian, or imported cosmetics by Christian Dior, first comes to China.

What seems to me interesting about the post-handover situation is that it leads to the formation of an emergent modality of Chinese migration, what one might call using the current argot, a "subaltern" Chinese diaspora, the study of which can provide resources for a critical understanding of the contemporary articulation of Chinese capitalism because it puts into question the hegemonic fantasy of the triumphal Chinese migrant entrepreneur that has become an important image (*Bild*) for the capitalist *Bildung* of the mainland. The permeability of borders that resulted from the handover also led to a new wave of migration from the mainland to Hong Kong that increased the clandestine and legal migrant worker population. The Shenzhen-Hong Kong border is the busiest border in the entire world. One large component of this migration is the movement and traffic of women for the purpose of sex work from various parts of the mainland to Southern China onward to Macau, Hong Kong, and the rest of the world.[5] What role do they play and what critical light do they shed on the repeated dissolution and rearticulation of Chinese-ness that takes place as a result of these intense cross-border dynamics? It is with this problematic in mind that I wish to offer an exploratory reading of Fruit Chan's *Durian Durian*, a filmic representation of the Chinese woman who returns to the mainland from her sojourn abroad as a sex worker as an alternative figure of Chinese-ness in contemporary global capitalism. *Durian Durian* questions these hegemonic fantasies of Chinese-ness by putting into circulation a set of haunting counter-hegemonic images of the female migrant that exposes the vicissitudes of flexible accumulation and the consumer fantasies it has generated in mainland China.

Situating *Durian Durian* in Fruit Chan's Oeuvre

Let me begin by very briefly positioning *Durian Durian* within Fruit Chan's body of work. Fruit Chan (Chan Guo) is an independent Hong Kong director who was born in Guangdong.[6] He first rose to fame with the release of the first installment of his Hong Kong handover trilogy, *Made in Hong Kong* (1997) (the other two installments are *The Longest Summer* (1998) and *Little Cheung* (2000), which won Best Film, Best Director, and Best Newcomer awards at the Hong Kong Film Awards, and Best Director and Best Original Script awards at the Golden Horse Awards of Taiwan and also the Special Jury Award at the Locarno Film Festival.[7] The handover trilogy depicts and explores the fears and anxieties aroused by Hong Kong's historic transition in sovereignty from British colony to Special Administrative Region of the PRC for marginalized and underrepresented members of Hong Kong society such as its working class, triad members, and legal and clandestine immigrants from China and Southeast Asia. The handover trilogy is therefore primarily concerned with exploring the instabilities, contradictions, and ambivalences of Hong Kong identity and belonging as it is rearticulated both in relation to the departing colonial regime and the influx of "foreign" immigrants from the PRC, the fatherland to which Hong Kong is soon to be repatriated.[8]

   Durian Durian (2000) is the first installment of an unfinished mainland prostitute trilogy whose focus clearly extends beyond Hong Kong to explore the implications of the transnational movement of sex workers on the PRC as well as the position of China within the circuits of global capitalism.[9] One key legal consequence of the handover is important for present purposes. Under British colonial rule, people born in Hong Kong were second-class citizens of the United Kingdom. They had British passports of a restricted kind that did not give them the right of abode in Britain. Under the Basic Law that governs Hong Kong as a Special Administrative Region of China, however, Hong Kongers have special privileges in comparison to other PRC citizens because they (as well as Hong Kong residents who are not new immigrants, i.e. those who have been there for more than seven years) and their children have the right of abode in Hong Kong. Hong Kong identity therefore shifts from being excluded to being excluding, since it is defined after the handover in terms of desirable privileges that new immigrants from the mainland do not have. This distinction is part of a larger discursive construction of migrants from the mainland as economically and culturally backward "others" who threaten to overwhelm Hong Kong either as competitive labor for locals or as a drain on the welfare system.[10] The splitting of Chinese-ness by these deep-seated prejudicial stereotypes is something that the mainland migrant confronts and brings back with her to the mainland despite the rhetoric of ethnic fraternity that figures all Chinese as descendants of the dragon. This emotional and psychological scar is undoubtedly an important component of the critical perspective that the two main characters of *Durian Durian*, Xiao Yan, a mainland prostitute, and Ah Fen, a small girl from Shenzhen who overstays in Hong Kong and becomes an illegal immigrant, develop towards the hegemonic representation of Chinese capitalism as a force for the unification of Greater China.

Durian Durian explores the impact of global consumer capitalism on the mainland. Unlike the handover trilogy, the focus shifts away from Hong Kong to Hong Kong's connection with and impact on the mainland. The second part of the film is set in Mudanjiang, Xiao Yan's hometown in Northeast China, and is sharply distinguished in terms of mood, pace, lighting, and documentary shooting techniques from the frenetic hybridity of cosmopolitan Hong Kong. It offers a scathing critique of the idea of Chinese entrepreneurship through the figure of the migrant sex worker that can be viewed as similar to the social critique of Sixth Generation Chinese film.[11]

Consumption, Money, and Movement

The opening voice-over by the title character of *Little Cheung* had foregrounded the animating power of money. The uncannily savvy child says: "I was already very wise when I was nine. My father runs a teashop because he wants money. The Filipina maid in my household is here because of money. My mother always goes to play mahjong in the mahjong parlor because of money . . . I have known from an early age that in everyone's heart, money is a dream, an ideal fantasy, and also a future. This is why everyone who lives on our street strives so hard." (My translation.) *Durian*

Durian portrays the power of money to move people and things across borders. The durian, a fruit native to Southeast Asia, is an objective correlative of a commodity that moves across borders. The mainland sex worker's name is Xiao Yan/Siu Yin, "little swallow," although in the end her migratory pattern is in reverse since she returns to the Northeast in winter instead of fleeing to warmer climes. A more literal translation of the title (*Liulian Piao Piao*) is "durian adrift" or "floating durian," although the Cantonese pronunciation of "durian" is also a pun and the spoken title in Cantonese can also mean "the lost years that have drifted away."

It is my contention that in *Durian Durian*, the migrant sex worker is a critical parody of the entrepreneurial spirit and the articulation of Chinese-ness in these terms. The film's opening sequence depicts the melding of Hong Kong and the mainland even as it keeps them apart. It begins with a shot of the Hong Kong harbor and the Star Ferry between Tsimshatsui and Hong Kong Island and this shot shades into a scene of Mudanjiang in the Northeast where the river is frozen in winter. The Mandarin voice-over, which is that of Xiao Yan, begins by describing the river in her hometown although the shot is of Hong Kong, and then proceeds to compare the two locations and marks their difference. In the next scene, a Cantonese voice-over by Ah Fen makes a similar contrast between their living conditions in the Hong Kong neighborhood of Mong Kok and their house in Shenzhen. In both cases, therefore, the mainland is yoked to Hong Kong, indicating the porosity of the border between the two, even as a difference is repeatedly marked. But unlike the handover trilogy, the identity in question here is not that of Hong Kong but that of China. At the level of character or the aesthetic representation of personal experience (subjectivity), this difference between Hong Kong and China that is the mechanism for the interrogation of mainland Chinese identity is registered in the two main characters' consciousness of their alien status in Hong Kong. In a scene that occurs roughly in the middle of the film when both Xiao Yan and Ah Fen try to hide from the Hong Kong police, there is a poignant moment of recognition and solidarity where Xiao Yan looks at Ah Fen and also intuitively recognizes herself and identifies her own social position. It is only later that this moment of recognition of herself in solidarity with the other is explicitly thematized. Xiao Yan's Mandarin voice-over in a later scene says that their friendship began in that alley, but it is only much later that she realized that she and Ah Fen are the same. They are both on a three-month visitor's pass. They have both come from the same place, Shenzhen, Ah Fen's hometown, and the location of a brothel where Xiao Yan has been working before moving on to Hong Kong. And they can both only stay for the same limited time period. The only difference, Xiao Yan notes, is that Ah Fen wants to stay in Hong Kong permanently so that she can be with her father, a legal immigrant, even if it means being an illegal immigrant herself.

The paths of the two central characters have been scripted for them by the space of processes and flows that now seamlessly join Hong Kong to south China, a circuit that is ultimately beyond their control. The important role of the sex industry to economic development through global tourism in postcolonial Asia, especially in Thailand and the Philippines, has been well documented in social scientific studies.[12] One witnesses here a gradual transnationalization of migration. The circuit of rural-urban migration, where girls from impoverished rural areas moved to the capital city in search of work, increases the supply of potential sex workers because failure to find adequate income from non-sex work can lead girls to engage in sex work. This circuit has gradually expanded into a genuinely global network. The flow of mainland sex workers to post-handover Hong Kong is a unique case of these cross-border dynamics. Hong Kong is paradoxically part of the Chinese nation but also valued by the PRC as that which is most foreign to it and its bridge to the capitalist world system. This distinctiveness of Hong Kong is also ferociously promoted by the Hong Kong government in its campaign to make it "Asia's world city" and a "global integrator" for the organization of production chains joining China to the rest of the world. Hence, migration to Hong Kong from the mainland is at one and the same time internal migration and quasi-transnational migration.

As such, Hong Kong is an object of deep psychical ambivalence for mainland migrant workers. Xiao Yan and Ah Fen perform tasks and services that are needed for the reproduction of social life in Hong Kong. Yet, as illegal immigrants, they are not offered any hospitality by the Hong Kong government and society. In Xiao Yan's case, although prostitution is not illegal in Hong Kong, Hong Kong laws criminalize the activities related to sex work such as solicitation. Xiao Yan is also violating the conditions of her visitor's pass by working. Her temporary presence in Hong Kong is therefore tolerated at the discretion of the police. She can be arrested at any time and become subjected to human rights violations at the hands of Hong Kong authorities. Much can be said about the approach of the Hong Kong authorities who focus on prosecuting the women instead of investigating whether or not they are victims of trafficking despite the fact that Hong Kong has signed the Bangkok Declaration on Irregular Migration (April 21–23, 1999), which is partly concerned with the trafficking of women in relation to irregular migration, and is also bound by The Convention on the Elimination of All Forms of Discrimination against

Women (CEDAW), which calls on states to suppress all forms of traffic in women and exploitation of women for the purposes of prostitution.[13] For present purposes, what interests me more is the migrant sex worker's permanent estrangement from all forms of legitimate community.

In their different ways, both central characters rearticulate their identity in the mainland through the ways in which they have been defined as "other" during their time in Hong Kong. At the beginning of the film, before she goes to Hong Kong, Ah Fen presents an idealized version of Hong Kong as a place of leisure, consumption, and self-improvement. She speaks of going to the Peak to see the night views of the city, of watching movies, learning English in school, and going to Ocean Park. But her reality is much bleaker. She spends most of her time in an alley, washing dishes with her mother. After she is arrested for having overstayed and is deported back to Shenzhen, Ah Fen tells Xiao Yan in a letter that being sent back is better because she is happier in Shenzhen, which she feels is her real home. This rejection of Hong Kong and identification with the mainland stems from Ah Fen's awareness that she will always be an alien in Hong Kong, someone who will always be rejected for cultural and legal reasons, despite the fact that Cantonese is her mother tongue.

But Ah Fen is at least fortunate enough to be able to achieve repatriation in the mainland in the fullest sense of the word, unlike Xiao Yan, whose time in Hong Kong leaves her permanently dislocated even after she returns to Mudanjiang. Ah Fen is saved from this fate of perpetual limbo and alienation for two reasons. First, her youthful innocence does not permit her to see the infiltration of the mainland by the same materialistic imperatives of consumption and profit-making governing Hong Kong society. Second, and more importantly, her experiences as an illegal immigrant still occur within the relatively safe confines of her family who are there with her and provide her with a support system. In stark contrast, Xiao Yan's experience as an illegal migrant in Hong Kong is more spiritually corrosive because she is a sex worker who must bear the memory of her experience in Hong Kong in utter isolation since it must be forever hidden and kept separate from her life with her family back in Mudanjiang. (The contrast between the innocence of one protagonist and the other's sexual commodification, a veritable pair of Blakean songs of innocence and experience, however, also ominously implies that Xiao Yan's present could be Ah Fen's future). The critical edge that Xiao Yan's experience gives rise to is more biting. First, it exposes the superficiality of transnational Chinese ethnic fraternity. Throughout her time in Hong Kong, Xiao Yan is repeatedly subjected to insulting slurs. Her pimp expresses his disgust at her when he uses her toilet because she does not flush used toilet tissue down the bowl but discards it in an exposed waste bin. Even the illegal Indian immigrants in the alley repeatedly call her a "Pak Ku" (Northern woman). Hence, when a client of hers with a body covered with tattoos of a dragon tells her that all Chinese are descendants of the dragon, the statement rings with hollowness.

Parodying Enterprise

More importantly, Xiao Yan personifies an incisive critique of the myth of the Chinese diasporic entrepreneur. For the migrant sex worker is intimately linked to the opening up of the mainland to economic globalization. It is not only that economic development and the porosity of the border between the mainland and Hong Kong has increased the flow of migrant sex workers because young Chinese women who are adversely affected by modern development resort to prostitution to improve their standard of living. More strikingly, the migrant sex worker embodies many of the traits and characteristics of the savvy and flexible migrant entrepreneur that are celebrated as virtues and ideals both in Hong Kong and in the PRC, at the level of the state and society. As Kevin Ming has argued in his ethnographic work on mainland prostitutes in Hong Kong, the mainland sex worker's "boldness, determination, willingness to cross boundaries…mirror the qualities of the newly imagined, transnational Chinese male entrepreneur extolled in popular and state mainland Chinese media. Such transnational men cross national boundaries, are ambitious and daring, and seek foreign capital for investment in China."[14]

In her decision to become a migrant sex worker and to sell herself as a commodity in order to make money to secure a future for herself back in the mainland, Xiao Yan espouses precisely the values of the old diasporic merchant subject as well as the values of the new Chinese transnational entrepreneurial subject. Xiao Yan's earnings, her bank balance, and the spending power it signifies earn her respect and social status when she returns home. Her family and friends take her for a businesswoman who has taken the initiative and risk and crossed the Southern frontier with success. Her childhood friend, Li Shuang, and her younger cousin both look up to her. They urge her to take them South, show them how to acquire similar business skills, and how to follow her example. Indeed, Xiao Yan intends to start a business with the capital she has accumulated.

It is important to emphasize that Fruit Chan's portrayal of the prostitute as an enterprising subject and an active and consensual agent shatters the widespread discursive representation of mainland women as innocent and naïve victims forced into sex work or as calculative, grasping mercenaries who use their sexuality to defraud Hong Kong men. But Chan also shatters the myth of the entrepreneur through parody. For Xiao Yan is the spirit of enterprise itself. The last segment before the film turns to the mainland includes a montage that shows her working at a frenetic pace to the fevered beat of a Mandarin pop tune. As she rushes through the busy streets of Hong Kong to her next job, we see in the background a poster of a smiling Deng Xiaoping, suggesting the PRC's openness to global capitalism. We are informed through her voice that although she has been in Hong Kong for close to three months, she has been so busy working that she has not visited any of its famous sights. (Earlier, she had told a coworker in a businesslike tone that she has no time for sightseeing because she is here to make money). Even sex workers are allowed four days of rest a month by their pimps, but she has chosen not to rest because one receives a cash bonus as well as a free one-day pass to Ocean Park if one does not take these days off. In the day before she leaves, she has thirty-eight customers, which she proudly proclaims is the highest record in the last six months. She wonders if it will make it into the *Guinness Book of Records*. She may have won the pass to Ocean Park, but she is so tired that she sleeps until the hour before she leaves for the mainland, and even then, she accepts one last "quickie" job before she heads off.

But unlike Ah Fen, Xiao Yan's return home does not involve her felicitous reintegration into the fabric of life in her hometown. We learn that she is in fact married to her old childhood sweetheart, but her absence has so estranged her that she is getting a divorce. The second half of the movie broaches in the most concerted manner the problem of what it means to be mainland Chinese and the different cultural resources available for the articulation of mainland Chinese identity. Three possible resources are presented — Chinese Communist culture, traditional kinship values, and modern capitalist norms — but they seem to be rejected as unfeasible in view of Xiao Yan's personal experience. What the audience witnesses in the film's second half is the crisis of mainland Chinese identity, the fact that no homecoming is possible for Xiao Yan because there is no home to return to in the robust sense of the word, no social or collective substrate in which she can subsist as a member. The first and most obvious resource for such a substrate is Chinese Communist culture, both the revolutionary culture associated with the history of Maoist militant struggle as well as the ethic of communal living and education. In two poignant scenes, Chan shows us the untenability of these values and the economic structures that gave rise to them. Xiao Yan had studied classical Chinese operatic dance as a child and she returns to her old school with her former classmates. As they peer through the window into the dilapidated studio and classroom, they sense the ghostliness of that past even as they are themselves reduced to ghostly shadows that no longer have any effective connection to the disappearing institutional structures of a socialist-collective economy. We learn that Xiao Yan's husband and two other classmates have left the classical dance troupe to form a cabaret show. Towards the end of the film, we see that their show involves precisely a parodic cheesy and tacky rendition of Maoist heroic songs about the internationality of the workers' revolutionary struggle.

The Migrant Sex Worker's Secret and the Aporia of Exile

Capitalist norms are clearly portrayed in a negative light in Xiao Yan's experience of Hong Kong. Her life there is deeply marked by solitude and alienation. She is always performing a role, putting on a mask in front of her clients. She adopts multiple names and tells each client that she is from different parts of China depending on what she thinks they want to hear and what will earn her more tips. She is variously from Sichuan, Hunan, Shanghai, Xinjiang etc. When she has a mainland client, she even pretends to be a local despite her thickly accented Cantonese. One might reasonably expect traditional kinship or familial structures to provide the panacea that can alleviate or soften the experience of alienation and solitude that results from her commodification and her alien status as an illegal sex worker in Hong Kong. In fact, however, these familial structures are also deeply imbricated in market-commodity relations. On the one hand, these familial relations always involve money and profit since this is associated with honor and face. This is precisely the nexus between *guanxi* and capitalism axiomatic to the East Asian capitalist model. Xiao Yan's mother insists that she pay for an elaborate banquet to celebrate her return, with a minimum cost of 200 yuan per table with Western spirits, especially red wine, because she has returned as a successful business woman and it has to "look good" so that they will not "lose face." We see her withdrawing 2,000 yuan from the bank to pay for the dinner, which ends up costing 1,500 yuan and we are given a glimpse of her bank book with the many withdrawals that have been incurred since her return to the mainland, depleting her capital by around 10% to 73,000 yuan.

On the other hand, these familial structures are also marked by a deep societal hypocrisy. They can revel in her newfound wealth and gleefully spend it. But she can never reveal to them its true source, much less seek support or solace for the humiliations and emotional scars that sex work generates because of its stigmatized nature. They can accept capitalism but not the fact that modern capitalism also implies the rationalized or organized commodification of female sexuality. The migrant sex worker is quite literally playing an economic role opened up for her globalization. She is pushed by global economic forces to take up a relatively lucrative form of labor that has emerged as an option for uneducated women in rapidly industrializing China, a form of labor that offers both economic and geographic mobility. This southward migratory path from backward areas to the coastal cities of South China and onward to Hong Kong is so well-trodden that it is increasingly represented even in mainland cinema, for instance, in Li Yu's recent *Dam Street* (*Hong Yan*) (2005). But since this labor is stigmatized, Xiao Yan has to continue playacting. She remains deeply alienated and lonely even when she is back in her hometown and amongst her closest friends and family. Back in Mudanjiang, she may appear to be an integral member of the community — someone's daughter, niece, cousin, daughter-in-law, or close childhood friend. But the fact that she must keep the truth of her profession in the South a secret means that she can never be fully integrated into mainland society and reembedded in a workable support system or *Sittlichkeit* to borrow a Hegelian word.

This sociological fact of being a living secret is repeatedly exploited by Fruit Chan for irony at Xiao Yan's painful expense. For instance, she is repeatedly asked to take her young cousin to the South with her and teach her how to do business. It is also a source of psychical and emotional torture. Xiao Yan repeatedly receives phone calls from the madam at a brothel in Shenzhen where she used to work urging her to go back because business is booming. She receives one such call during her divorce proceeding and she turns off the phone and throws it to the floor in obvious distress. I would like to suggest that Xiao Yan represents the outlines of the sociological type of a new kind of Chinese migrant in the current conjuncture of the integration of China into the global capitalist system. The migrant woman sex worker is someone who is permanently in exile. She can never return to the homeland fully, never be fully repatriated, even if she has returned physically, not because her consciousness has been irreversibly changed and because she doesn't wish to belong, but because there is no abode available that can receive her fully for what she is. As one NGO report puts it:

> although sex work has become a widespread phenomenon in the Mainland
> Chinese society, it is still not accepted by people under the mainstream

social values. People tend to disregard the experience of sex workers and put it into underground, so as to avoid facing the discrepancy between the social reality and moral values. As a result, sex workers have to face many difficulties in their work and lives . . . without receiving desirable concern. The only general discourse on sex workers is negative and in all ways accuses them of chasing for enjoyment but being unwilling to work, or violating the ethics. As sex workers have a stigma attached to them, most of them do not tell their families about their work and problems. Instead, they have to face many conflicts with their families as they try to keep their secrets. . . . It more or less limits their possible change and development. All these problems have been disregarded in society.[15]

This state of permanent dislocation or exile explains why Xiao Yan is always in a state of limbo even after her return home. She has amassed enough capital to start a small business, but she is not sure what she will do next, what kind of business she will start since it cannot be as profitable as her previous work.

For this new type of Chinese diaspora, the true meaning of diasporic movement is permanent dislocation. We commonly associate contemporary economic migration with freedom of movement and passage. But for this particular type of migrant, their very movement leads them to an aporia, literally, "no passage," a road that cannot be crossed, a blockage where there is no passage. There is always some experience of blockage and non-movement because as we see in the case of Xiao Yan, the place of origin no longer provides any repose on return and hence, there is no longer any origin from which to move and no origin to be nostalgically remembered. But it is precisely from this marginal place which is a non-place that the migrant sex worker and other examples of contemporary China-Hong Kong cross-border flows can enable the critic to see the fraying of mainland Chinese society, its cultural identity and the increasing untenability of existing cultural resources for communal support.

Exits?

This is not to say that Fruit Chan does not offer in his film solutions to the dilemma of the new Chinese diaspora. I would like to conclude by looking at these solutions and their limits. We have already seen the solution that Ah Fen personifies: saying "no" to Hong Kong and affirming the mainland. At the end of the film, Xiao Yan performs a similar repudiation. She changes her cell phone number so that she can no longer be reached by contacts from her former profession. But as we have also seen, it is not so easy for Xiao Yan to affirm the mainland because of the secret she cannot disclose. The film seems to offer two solutions to this dilemma. First, at the very end of the film, after she has failed to stop her cousin from going to Shenzhen, Xiao Yan reaches back into her past training and performs a traditional dance. She assumes the role of the Goddess of Mercy in a performance for the New Year festival. But this attempt to find refuge in nostalgia and tradition seems too sentimental and escapist given the film's harsh social realism.

Indeed, it is strongly suggested that we cannot simply say "no" to capitalist consumption. This culture is everywhere: the cell phone that connects Xiao Yan to the brothel keeper in Shenzhen, the cable TV in the apartment that she seeks to rent out has CNN, and all the channels available in a hotel. In an ironic scene at the beauty parlor where Xiao Yan and her friend Li Shuang are having facial treatments, they both emphatically demand to use imported cosmetic products such as Christian Dior instead of inferior local products. Yet, it is precisely this desire for the consumption of imports that leads Xiao Yan to seek work abroad as a prostitute, a job that she would never undertake in the mainland despite the irony of her friend's suggestion that she should do whatever business she did "there" at home. Indeed, the escapism of Xiao Yan's final operatic performance is underscored by the fact that by the end of the film, most of her friends, including her former husband and his dance troupe, have taken the train out of Mudanjiang, leaving the past behind them in search of the new, whereas she chooses nostalgically to stay put, almost in paralysis.

The film, however, offers a second less nostalgic solution although it cannot be taken as a programmatic one. During her time in Hong Kong, the one person that Xiao Yan is able to be genuine with, the one person with whom she doesn't have to play a role, is Ah Fen. Ah Fen does not judge her for being a sex worker. She tells Ah Fen her real name and gives her her address and asks her to write to her. In her moment of despondency in Mudanjiang, she receives a parcel from Ah Fen, which turns out to be the exotic durian of the title, which Ah Fen gives to her in an act of generosity as a New Year gift. This suggests that precious solidarities and subcultures of support can be found in the diasporic space of migrant workers even though they are necessarily transient, felicitous, and chancy and cannot be institutionalized into spaces for the building of permanent communities. Other examples can be found in the film: the comradeship between mainland sex workers, the friendship between the Indian immigrants and Ah Fen. These bonds are like the affective ties between the

Filipina maid and Little Cheung in *Little Cheung,* or the friendship between Tong Tong and the younger Chu son in *Hollywood, Hong Kong* (2002), the second installment of the prostitute trilogy.

But these transient modes of transnational solidarity can no longer be understood under the totalizing sign of China as a political or cultural entity. They indicate the increasing dissolution of the edges of the People's Republic by the circuits of global capitalism. Its sense of its own centrality has become displaced. Indeed, *Hollywood, Hong Kong* shifts its focus away from the mainland. It portrays the mainland sex worker's active grasping of the opportunities conjured in the border-zone of South China and Hong Kong in such a manner that Hong Kong itself is now imagined as a dynamic border-zone between East Asia and the West. This is a veritable aesthetic-cognitive mapping of the sex worker's migratory path within the circuit of global consumerism. *Hollywood, Hong Kong* portrays the mainland sex worker's deep yearning for the West, especially its power to generate desires associated with modern consumer capitalism, as emblematized by the Hollywood of the film's title, whose literal translation is "There is a Hollywood in Hong Kong/Hong Kong has a Hollywood." The film's main theme is consumption: eating, desire, sexual lust, the allure of wealth, and, the illusions and dreams generated by consumption, which are deftly and ingeniously manipulated by the central character, Tong Tong, a Shanghainese prostitute, to fulfill her own dreams. Everything points, in Fukuyama style, to the USA as an apex, a telos, and a final destination. Tong Tong defrauds almost every male character in the film, ends up migrating to Los Angeles, the city of the real Hollywood, and is pictured at the close of the film with a backpack, suggesting that she has become an Americanized college student. The focus is no longer on Hong Kong or China. For her, Hong Kong is only a transit-point for the final destination within the global consumer market. But there are no liberating fantasies. Lest we celebrate too uncritically the agency of the Chinese migrant sex worker to liberate and transform herself in the face of immense hardship, the film repeatedly reminds us of the destruction and violence Tong Tong's path to economic freedom wreaks on almost every other character in the film who desire her. The deployment of sexual fantasies offers no genuine liberation for the female sex worker because all fantasies are part of the limitless web of consumption as a moment of global capitalism.

Notes

Introduction

1   See Susan Brownell and Jeffrey N. Wasserstrom, *Chinese Femininities, Chinese Masculinities: A Reader*, vol. 4, Asia-Local Studies/Global Themes (Berkeley: University of California Press, 2002); Gail Hershatter, "State of the Field: Women in China's Long Twentieth Century," *Journal of Asian Studies* 63, no. 4 (November 2004); Dorothy Ko, *Cinderella's Sisters: A Revisionist History of Footbinding* (Berkeley: University of California Press, 2005); Susan Mann, ed., *Women and Gender Relations: Perspectives on Asia: Sixty Years of the Journal of Asian Studies* (Ann Arbor, M.I.: Association for Asian Studies, Inc., 2004). The exhaustive reviews by Hershatter and Mann are particularly useful. They discuss the issues and substantive works that relate to the social relations of the sexes in the Chinese family, marriage, and kinship (Chinese anthropology in the tradition of Freedman, Cohen, Wolf, Watson), to women's agency and resistance (liberal feminist approaches in the 1970s and 1980s), and nuanced gender subjectivities in different historical and regional cultural contexts (poststructuralist, deconstructionist orientations since the 1980s). The analytical progression corresponds quite well with similar issues and concerns in the literature about other cultures and societies. Beginning with the classic volumes (for example, Michelle Zimbalist Rosaldo, Louise Lamphere, and Joan Bamberger, eds., *Woman, Culture, and Society* [Stanford: Stanford University Press, 1974]; Sherry B. Ortner and Harriet Whitehead, eds., *Sexual Meanings: The Cultural Construction of Gender and Sexuality* [Cambridge; New York: Cambridge University Press, 1981]; Natalie Zemon Davis, *Society and Culture in Early Modern France: Eight Essays* [Stanford: Stanford University Press, 1975]), there have been many critical approaches to gender. They challenge the dichotomy of nature and culture, the material and the symbolic, repression, and resistance. Tracing theoretical genealogy from Foucault, Bourdieu, Butler, and the like, a new generation of ethnographies focuses on power and embodied gender practices in everyday life. These works have taken center stage in academic discourse. Studies that are intellectually useful for the comparative study of gender subjectivities in the Chinese context are those from Islamic and South Asian areas. See Lila Abu-Lughod, *Veiled Sentiments: Honor and Poetry in a Bedouin Society* (Berkeley: University of California Press, 1986); Saba Mahmood, *Politics of Piety: The Islamic Revival and the Feminist Subject* (Princeton, N.J.: Princeton University Press, 2005); Purnima Mankekar, *Screening Culture, Viewing Politics: An Ethnography of Television, Womanhood, and Nation Postcolonial India* (Durham: Duke University Press, 1999).

2 See the following books: Dorothy Ko, *Teachers of the Inner Chambers: Women and Culture in Seventeenth-Century China* (Stanford: Stanford University Press, 1994); Susan Mann, *Precious Records: Women in China's Long Eighteenth Century* (Stanford: Stanford University Press, 1997).

3 Maurice Freedman, *Lineage Organization in Southeastern China*, London School of Economics Monographs on Social Anthropology (London: Athlone Press, 1958); Hugh Baker, *A Chinese Lineage Village: Sheung Shui* (Stanford: Stanford University Press, 1968); James L. Watson and Rubie S. Watson, *Village Life in Hong Kong: Politics, Gender, and Ritual in the New Territories* (Hong Kong: The Chinese University Press, 2004).

4 Marjorie Topley, "Marriage Resistance in Rural Kwangtung," in *Women in Chinese Society*, ed. Margery Wolf, Roxane Witke, and Emily M. Ahern (Stanford: Stanford University Press, 1975); Janice E. Stockard, *Daughters of the Canton Delta: Marriage Patterns and Economic Strategies in South China, 1860–1930* (Stanford: Stanford University Press, 1989); Helen F. Siu, "Where Were the Women? Rethinking Marriage Resistance and Regional Culture History," *Late Imperial China* 11, no. 2 (December 1990); Myron Cohen, "Lineage Development and the Family in China," in *The Chinese Family and Its Ritual Behavior*, ed. Jih-chang Hsieh and Ying-chang Chuang (Taipei: Institute of Ethnology, Academia Sinica, 1985).

5 David Faure and Helen F. Siu, eds., *Down to Earth: The Territorial Bond in South China* (Stanford: Stanford University Press, 1995).

6 Siu, "Where Were the Women? Rethinking Marriage Resistance and Regional Culture History," 32–62.

7 See Gail Hershatter, *Women in China's Long Twentieth Century* (Berkeley: Global, Area, and International Archive, University of California Press, 2007). For a recent challenge to Freedman's lineage paragidm, see David Faure, *Emperor and Ancestor: State and Lineage in South China* (Stanford: Stanford University Press, 2007). A summary can be found in the review by Helen F. Siu, "Review Article: Emperor and Ancestor: State and Lineage in South China by David Faure," *The China Quarterly* 192 (December 2007): 1041–43.

8 Sherry Ortner, "Gender and Sexuality in Hierarchical Societies: The Case of Polynesia and Some Comparative Implications," in *Sexual Meanings: The Cultural Construction of Gender and Sexuality*, ed. Sherry B. Ortner and Harriet Whitehead (Cambridge; New York: Cambridge University Press, 1981).

9 For the rise of gender as a category associated with the body in early modern China, see Tani E. Barlow, "Theorizing Woman: Funü, Guojia, Jiating (Chinese Woman, Chinese State, Chinese Family)," in *Body, Subject and Power in China*, ed. Angela Zito and Tani E. Barlow (Chicago; London: University of Chicago Press, 1994). For women's suffrage movement during the early Republican period, in which Guangdong was one of the provinces featured prominently, see Louise Edwards, "Bourgeois Women and Communist Revolutionaries? De-revolutionizing the Chinese Women's Suffrage Movement," in *Women, Activism, and Social Change*, ed. Maja Mikula (London; New York: Routledge, 2005).

For CCP feminists in Guangdong as the "revolutionary base," see Christina K. Gilmartin, "Gender, Political Culture, and Women's Mobilization in the Chinese Nationalist Revolution, 1924–1927," in *Engendering China: Women, Culture, and the State*, ed. Christina K. Gilmartin, et al. (Cambridge, M.A.: Harvard University Press, 1994).

10   Carl Smith, "The Chinese Church, Labour and Elites and the Mui Tsai Question in the 1920s," *Journal of the Hong Kong Branch of the Royal Asiatic Society* 21 (1981). For the background of Wu Zhimei, a major activist in Guangdong, see Yufa Zhang, "Ershi Shiji Qianbanqi Zhongguo Funu Canzheng Quan De Yanbian" (The Transformation of Women's Election Rights in the First Half of the Twentieth Century), in *Wusheng Zhi Sheng (I): Jindai Zhongguo De Funu Yu Guojia (1600–1950)* (The Sound of Silence [I]): Modern Chinese Women and the State [1600–1950]), ed. Fangshang Lu (Taipei: Zhongyang Yanjiuyuan Jindaishi Yanjiusuo, 2003).

11   Pik-wan Wong, "The Hong Kong Women's Movement in Transition," in *Political Participation in Hong Kong*, ed. Joseph Y. S. Cheng (Hong Kong: City University Press, 1999).

12   Mayfair Mei-hui Yang, "From Gender Erasure to Gender Difference: State Feminism, Consumer Sexuality, and a Feminist Public Sphere in China," in *Spaces of Their Own: Women's Public Sphere in Transnational China*, ed. Mayfair Mei-hui Yang (Minneapolis: University of Minnesota Press, 1999).

13   Eastern No. 66: Hong Kong, Correspondence (June 20, 1899, to August 20, 1900) Respecting the Extension of the Boundaries of the Colony (printed for the use of the Colonial Office: Colonial Office, November, 1900), Enclosure 12 in No. 204, 253–54, Letter from J. Stewart Lockhart, Colonial Secretary, to the Governor, written from Tai Po, April 28, 1899. This reference was kindly provided by Patrick Hase.

14   An informant in Xiangshan who originally came from a "rich peasant" family says that her male family members farmed fields in the sands for long periods. The women took care of pig rearing and helped in the wine-making processes close to home. During the war, she and her women cousins were also sent to collect rent and other debts. They were occasionally accompanied by family laborers. Her reasoning was that during turbulent times, her family hid the male members for fear that warlord armies would snatch them.

15   For examples of women in the Pearl River Delta who were given landed property as dowry, see Siu, "Where Were the Women? Rethinking Marriage Resistance and Regional Culture History." The paper also cites a family division document in Xiangshan County where one of the married daughters was given an annual quota of grain to use whenever she returned to her natal home.

16   See the chapter in this volume by Ching on women's voices. See the chapter in this volume by Liu on lineage rituals and women's sentiments. See also the doctoral dissertation by Wing-hoi Chan, "Writing Women's Words: Bridal Laments and Representations of Kinship and Marriage in South China" (PhD thesis, Department of Anthropology, Yale University, 2000).

17 Philip D. Curtin, *Cross-cultural Trade in World History* (Cambridge: Cambridge University Press, 1984) argues that the region was full of market entrepreneurs skilled in working within the legal fictions of tribute trade and the monopolies of royal courts and colonial powers. Port cities along trade routes were economically competitive and culturally open. Brokers of different ethnic origins rose high in local officialdom.

18 During one of the grand expeditions of the court eunuch Zheng He in the fifteenth century, his entourage had stopped in Quanzhou to collect precious porcelain, silk, and other commodities. Quanzhou had a sizable Muslim population. A Muslim by birth, Zheng allegedly paid his respects at the gravesite of Muslim prophets and was active in preventing Muslims, who had been tax collectors for the Mongols, from being persecuted by Ming officials.

19 See Helen F. Siu, "The Grounding of Cosmopolitans: Merchants and Local Cultures in South China," in *Becoming Chinese: Passages to Modernity and Beyond*, ed. Wen-Hsin Yeh (Berkeley: University of California Press, 2000); Helen F. Siu and Liu Zhiwei, "Lineage, Market, Pirate and Dan: Ethnicity in the Sands of South China," in *Empire at the Margins: Culture, Frontier and Ethnicity in Early Modern China*, ed. Pamela Kyle Crossley, Helen F. Siu, and Donald S. Sutton (Berkeley: University of California Press, 2006).

20 See the works of Jiang Boqin, a noted scholar of Chan Buddhism, on Monk Dashan and his life time of adventures.

21 See the case in Tik-sang Liu's study in the New Territories of Hong Kong ("Becoming Marginal: A Fluid Community and Shamanism in the Pearl River Delta of South China," PhD dissertation, University of Pittsburg, 1995). Siu has encountered numerous similar ones in post-Mao Pearl River Delta, urban Hong Kong and Macao. See Laura Kendall's works on women shaman in Japan and Korea.

22 See *Fan Kwei* on the *hong* merchants in Guangzhou through the eyes of a foreigner. William Maxwell Wood, *Fankwei; or, the San Jacinto in the Seas of India, China, and Japan* (New York: Harper and Brothers, 1859).

23 See the catalogue of the China Trade Museum at Salem, Massachusetts, and the collection of China Trade paintings at the Hong Kong Art Museum. The Hong Kong and Shanghai Bank also has a large collection of these paintings. For more recent catalogues, see Sun Yat-sen University Department of History and Guangzhou Museum, eds., *Views from the West: Collection of Nineteenth Century Pith Paper Watercolours Donated by Mr Ifan Williams to the City of Guangzhou* (Beijing: Zhonghua Book Company, 2001). Ming Wilson and Liu Zhiwei, eds., *Souvenir from Canton: Chinese Export Paintings from the Victoria and Albert Museum* (Shanghai: Shanghai Classics Publishing House, 2003). On cultural interpenetration at home among Guangzhou merchant groups and European traders, see May-bo Ching and Liu Zhiwei, "Shiba, Shijiu Shiji Guangzhou Yangren Jiating Li De Zhongguo Yongren" (Chinese Servants in Foreigners' Families in Eighteenth and Nineteenth Century Guangzhou), *Shilin*, no. 4 (2004).

24 Joseph McDermott, "The Chinese Domestic Bursar," *Asian Cultural Studies* Special issue (1990). Susan Mann initiated similar questions for the Qing, see Mann, *Precious Records: Women in China's Long Eighteenth Century*.

25 In a literary portrayal of Wu Xueyan, a leading merchant in late Qing Jiangnan, his wife consulted with the family business manager to place a new favorite of Wu under a manager in a subsidiary native bank. It could be her way to send off a potential competitor for Wu's attention, but the matter-of-fact portrayal of the negotiations gives one the impression that these roles for women were quite accepted. In a private conversation, David Faure alerted me to such an episode.

26 The traders I encountered in Chaolian xiang near Jiangmen, and in Panyu near Guangzhou were not big-time merchants, but many, to my surprise, had wives and concubines who were economically active. In one case, the concubine of a trader/local boss was a powerful figure in the 1940s. She bore arms and accompanied boatloads of merchandise transported between Guangzhou and Jiangmen. Children from different mothers in these households had their share of conflict and intrigues but seemed able to work closely together in the family enterprises. In private conversations, Elizabeth Sinn, David Faure, and others corroborated this with similar observations of women's active roles in family businesses. Margaret Chu also confirms that among wealthy merchants and scholarly families in the late Qing and Republican periods, when men were away from home for extended periods, women were often entrusted with business decisions and aided by family managers. These women also relied on natal kin to invest their private pocket money.

27 For the cultural strategies of merchants in Republican Guangdong and their demise, see Siu, "The Grounding of Cosmopolitans: Merchants and Local Cultures in South China."

28 For a recent work on Guangzhou's turn of the century city culture, see Ai-dongxi Huang, *Lao Guangzhou (Old Guangzhou)* (Nanjing: Jiangsu meishu chubanshe, 1999). For a Shanghai-Hong Kong comparison, see Leo Ou-fan Lee, *Shanghai Modern: The Flowering of a New Urban Culture in China, 1930–1945* (Cambridge, M.A.; London: Harvard University Press, 1999).

29 In the Republican era, elite women in mainland China's cities gained access to Western education and culture largely through missionary channels. In Hong Kong, the exposure cut across class lines in unusual ways due to interracial relationships. See a paper by Carl Smith, "Ng Akew, One of Hong Kong's 'Protected Women'," *Chung Chi Bulletin* no. 46 (June 1966). Also Peter Hall, *In the Web* (London: Basingstoke Press, 1992).

30 Gail Hershatter, "The Hierarchy of Shanghai Prostitution," *Modern China* 15, no. 4 (1989).

31 See articles in Maria Jaschok and Suzanne Miers, eds., *Women and Chinese Patriarchy: Submission, Servitude and Escape* (Hong Kong: Hong Kong University Press, 1994). See also the investigative reports in a volume of documents compiled by an association against domestic servitude, "Fandui xupi shilue"

(Hong Kong 1934; prefaced by Mai Meisheng 1933) (Mai Meisheng, 1933, *Fandui Xubei Shilue* [A History of the Anti-Mui Tsai Campaign]; Hong Kong: Fuxing zhongxi yinwuju).

32 Louise Edwards, "Bourgeois Women and Communist Revolutionaries? De-revolutionizing the Chinese Women's Suffrage Movement."

33 Zhang Yufa, "Ershi Shiji Qianbanqi Zhongguo Funu Canzheng Quan De Yanbian (The Transformation of Women' Election Rights in the First Half of the Twentieth Century)," in *Wusheng Zhi Sheng (I): Jindai Zhongguo De Funu Yu Guojia (1600–1950)* (The Sound of Silence [I]: Modern Chinese Women and the State [1600–1950]), ed. Fangshang Lu (Taipei: Zhongyang Yanjiuyuan Jindaishi Yanjiusuo, 2003), 55, 57–8.

34 Gilmartin, "Gender, Political Culture, and Women's Mobilization in the Chinese Nationalist Revolution, 1924–1927." See pages 219 to 220 for the case of the child bride's dead body. For the limited mobilization of women workers, see also Michael Tsang-Woon Tsin, *Nation, Governance, and Modernity in China: Canton, 1900–1927* (Stanford: Stanford University Press, 1999).

35 Edwards, "Bourgeois Women and Communist Revolutionaries? De-revolutionizing the Chinese Women's Suffrage Movement," 46. The Society for Citizen's Political Participation (Guomin canzheng hui) sponsored by the government in 1938 had ten to fifteen women members in a total of some two hundred. Of the women members four were from Guangdong and three of those served all three terms. Guo Zhaozhao, "Kangzhan Qijian Guomin Canzhenghui Zhong Nü Canzhengyuan Qunti De Kaocha" (A General Review of the Female Politicians in the National Political Council of the Government of China during the Anti-Japanese War), *Anhui Daxue Xuebao* 30, no. 6 (2006): 102–06.

36 See Margery Wolf, *Revolution Postponed: Women in Contemporary China* (Stanford: Stanford University Press, 1985). If women were not entirely empowered, one needs to explore how the "reversals" in the post-reform era and then the new gendered public sphere may be understood. See Mayfair Mei-hui Yang, ed., *Spaces of Their Own: Women's Public Sphere in Transnational China*; Barlow, "Theorizing Woman: Funü, Guojia, Jiating (Chinese Woman, Chinese State, Chinese Family)"; and Paul Pickowicz and Wang Liping, "Village Voices, Urban Activists: Women, Violence, and Gender Inequality in Rural China," in *Popular China: Unofficial Culture in a Globalizing Society*, ed. E. Perry Link, Richard Madsen, and Paul Pickowicz (Lanham, M.D.: Rowman and Littlefield, 2002).

37 Gar-yin Tsang, "Chronology of Women's Achievements," in *Women in Hong Kong*, ed. Veronica Pearson and Benjamin K. P. Leung (Hong Kong: Oxford University Press, 1995). Wen Zhiqi, "Nannü Tonggong Tongchou Yundong De Canyu Zhe: Mei Meiya" (A Participant in the Equal Pay Movement: Elizabeth Susan Mair), in *Ling Yiban Tiankong: Zhanhou Xianggang Funü Yundong* (The Other Half of the Sky: Post-War Women's Movement in Hong Kong), ed. Zhang Caiyun et al. (Hong Kong: Xin Funü Xiejin Hui, 1992), 9–16.

38 Wong, "The Hong Kong Women's Movement in Transition."

39 See a survey by Citibank showing the wealth of over 200,000 women wielding assets of over HK $10 million. Chun-ho Wong, *Ming Pao Daily News*, May 2, 2007, A11; see also "Who's Worth a Million Dollars in Hong Kong? More Women than Men," *South China Morning Post*, February 14, 2007.

40 See Nicole Constable, *Maid to Order in Hong Kong: Stories of Filipina Workers* (Ithaca, N.Y.; London: Cornell University Press, 1997). In the 1990s, tens of thousands of Indonesian maids have also come to Hong Kong. Many speak rudimentary Cantonese and accept lower than the legal wage. This may mean that lower middle income, non-English speaking, Chinese families are able to hire domestic help.

41 For the history of immigration law in Hong Kong, see Johannes Chan and Bart Rwezura, eds., *Immigration Law in Hong Kong: An Interdisciplinary Study* (Hong Kong: Sweet and Maxwell Asia, 2004). On the history of immigration flow in and out of Hong Kong, see Helen F. Siu, Richard Wong, Faure, David, "Rethinking Hong Kong's Human Resources and Competitiveness: A Pre-Policy Study" (for the 2022 Foundation, 2005).

42 For a history of the "new immigrants" and their changing social profiles, see Helen F. Siu, "Positioning "Hong Kongers" and "New Immigrants"," in *Hong Kong Mobile: Making a Global Population*, ed. Helen F. Siu and Agnes S. Ku (Hong Kong: Hong Kong University Press, 2008), 117–147.

43 See the Hong Kong government's bi-census of 2006 that shows a clear trend of an increase in the number of cross-border unions and that the age difference between spouses has narrowed. See "2006 Population Bi-Census" (Census and Statistics Department, the Government of Hong Kong Special Administrative Region, 2007).

44 Two cases reported by local media gripped public attention in recent years. The first involved a middle-aged woman whose contractor husband took up with an eighteen-year-old mistress in his hometown in northern Guangdong. After numerous family efforts to mediate failed, she killed her husband by stabbing him thirty-one times, one for each year of their marriage, and then jumped to her death. The other highly publicized saga also ended in multiple deaths. Newspapers (October 19, 1998) reported that a young wife was left destitute with her two children because her husband, a laborer, had spent his meager income on "song-and-dance girls" in karaoke bars across the border. Whatever her state of mind that night was, she seemed to have thrown her innocent children from a thirty-story building and jumped off afterwards. The public was infuriated that instead of showing remorse, the husband continued his frolicking in Shenzhen. When he was challenged by the press to show up at the funeral, several passers-by cornered him. A shouting match turned into a beating until he sought help from a policeman. See similar cases described in *Ming Pao Daily News*, June 10, 1999.

45 The post-reform economy in Guangdong has been built on the labor of millions of migrants, most of them women from inland provinces. See Arianne M.

Gaetano and Tamara Jacka, eds., *On the Move: Women and Rural-to-Urban Migration in Contemporary China* (New York: Columbia University Press, 2004). See also "Liudong Renkou Yi Chaoguo 1.2yi, Qizhong Kuasheng Liudong Da 4242Wan, Jinru Guangdong Renshu Ju Quanguo Zhishou" (Floating Population Already Exceeds 120 Million), *Nangfang dushi bao,* October 7, 2002. According to an official estimate, mobile populations reached 120 million, of which 42. 42 million crossed provincial boundaries. Provinces with the most population outflows were Sichuan, Anhui, Hunan, Jiangxi, Henan, and Hubei. Provinces with the most inflows were Guangdong (35.5%), Zhejiang (8.7%), Shanghai (7.4%), Jiangsu (6%), Beijing (5.8%), and Fujian (5.1%).

46 On the cross-border mistress culture between Hong Kong and Guangdong, see Siumi Maria Tam, "Normalization Of "Second Wives": Gender Contestation in Hong Kong," *Asian Journal of Women Studies* 2 (1996); Graeme Lang and Josephine Smart, "Migration and The 'Second Wife' in South China: Toward Cross-Border Polygyny," *International Migration Review* 36, no. 2 (2002). See also Carolyn Cartier, "Symbolic City-Regions and Gendered Identity Formation," *Provincial China* 8, no. 2 (2003). Numerous magazines focus on the migrant women workers in south China. They supposedly report personal stories, but some of the stories verge on the pornographic. Web sites have sprung up for participants to exchange information about the range of "services" available for men seeking sexual adventure.

47 Liu Li, "Guangdong Nüxing Jiuye Renkou De Zhiye Zhuangkuang He Jingji Shouru Fenxi" (Analysis of the Occupational Condition and Incomes of Guangdong Women in Employment), *Ningbo Dangxiao Xuebao*, no. 5 (2003): 77–80. Zuo Waiqing, "Guangdong Shehui Xingbie Diaocha Yu Bijiao Fenxi" (Survey and Comparative Analysis of Gender in Guangdong), *Tequ Lilun yu Shijian*, no. 6 (2003): 57–60.

48 Sun Hailong, Gong Dejia, and Li Bin, "Chengshihua Beijing Xia Nongcun 'Waijianü' Quanyi Jiufen Jiqi Jiejue Jizhi De Sikao" (Reflections on Disputes over the Rights of Rural "Married Daughter" amid Urbanization and Mechanism for Their Resolutions), *Falü Shiyong*, no. 3 (2004): 26–30. The obstacles include gender biases embedded in some provincial provisions on the protection of women's rights, the highest court's restriction on individuals' civil litigation against rural collectives as well as the courts' reluctance to "inconvenience" themselves and relevant administrative units by a kind of case anticipated to come in overwhelming numbers if accepted.

49 See Liu Zhiwei, "Lineage on the Sands: The Case of Shawan," in *Down to Earth: The Territorial Bonds in South China*, ed. David Faure and Helen F. Siu (Stanford: Stanford University Press, 1995).

50 Ritual focus on women is not unique. It is well known that a number of the Tang (Deng) surnamed lineages in the New Territories of Hong Kong attributed their wealth and good fortune to an ancestress, "the emperor's paternal aunt." The worship of legendary mothers of focal ancestors (*bopo*) is also found among lineages in the region. See *Chen Lineage Genealogy of Xinhui*, for example (1923).

For works that have acknowledged the indigenous origins of Lingnan's populations and their gender implications, see Qu Dajun, *Guangdong Xinyu* (New Items Relating to Guangdong, 1700) (reprint, Beijing: Zhonghua Shuju, 1985); Wolfram Eberhard, *The Local Cultures of South and East China* (Leiden: E. J. Brill, 1968); Herold J. Wiens, *Han Chinese Expansion in South China* (Hamden: Shoe String Press, 1967); David Faure, "The Lineage as a Cultural Invention: The Case of the Pearl River Delta," *Modern China* 15, no. 1 (1989); Siu, "Where Were the Women? Rethinking Marriage Resistance and Regional Culture History."; Wing-hoi Chan, "Ordination Names in Hakka Genealogies: A Religious Practice and Its Decline," in *Down to Earth: The Territorial Bond in South China*, ed. David Faure and Helen F. Siu (Stanford: Stanford University Press, 1995).

51 On the rise of a particular kind of lineage formation in the Ming and Qing dynasties, and the implications for kinship and gender relationships, see Faure, *Emperor and Ancestor: State and Lineage in South China.*

52 Wing-hoi Chan, on the other hand, explores the linguistic strategies of bridal and funeral laments among Cantonese women in the New Territories of Hong Kong to appreciate the infinite improvisations of meaning and style in regional dialects and genres. He argues that despite the formalized language and literati images in these laments, the strategies continue to allow women to express their sentiments and to assert their agency, see Chan, "Writing Women's Words: Bridal Laments and Representations of Kinship and Marriage in South China."

53 The late Carl Smith also explored a great deal of legal cases involving women and their inherited properties in Hong Kong's early colonial history.

54 See Elizabeth Sinn, *Power and Charity: The Early History of the Tung Wah Hospital, Hong Kong*, East Asian Historical Monographs (Hong Kong; New York: Oxford University Press, 1989).

55 See the work of the Japanese scholar Hiroaki Kani; see also Elizabeth Sinn and Hong-ming Yip on the Po Leung Kuk archives.

56 See Elizabeth Sinn, "Women at Work: Chinese Brothel Keepers in Nineteenth-Century Hong Kong," *Women's History* 19, no. 3 (2007). The similarity of these women's enterprises to some sworn spinsters in the Pearl River delta raising girls to become prostitutes or to engage in other forms of servitude might be worth noting.

57 See chapters in Jaschok and Miers, eds., *Women and Chinese Patriarchy: Submission, Servitude and Escape;* Susanne Hoe, *The Private Life of Old Hong Kong: Western Women in The British Colony, 1841–1941* (Hong Kong: Oxford University Press, 1991); see also Watson's chapter in Rubie S. Watson and Patricia Buckley Ebrey, eds., *Marriage and Inequality in Chinese Society* (Berkeley: University of California Press, 1991). See also Barbara-Sue White, ed., *Hong Kong: Somewhere Between Heaven and Earth* (Hong Kong: Oxford University Press, 1996).

58 See Irene Cheng, *Clara Ho Tung: A Hong Kong Lady, Her Family and Her Times* (Hong Kong: The Chinese University Press, 1976). The books mentioned that

Lady Ho Tung's father, a Eurasian, considered Hong Kong his native place. When he died during an assignment in Guangdong, Clara's mother transported him back to Hong Kong for burial.

59 Wai-ching Wong, "Negotiating Gender Identity: Postcolonialism and Christianity in Hong Kong," in *Gender and Change in Hong Kong: Globalization, Postcolonialism, and Chinese Patriarchy*, ed. Eliza W. Y. Lee (Vancouver: University of British Columbia Press, 2004).

60 Wong, "Negotiating Gender Identity: Postcolonialism and Christianity in Hong Kong," 162.

61 See Hall, *In the Web*. See also Cheng, *Clara Ho Tung: A Hong Kong Lady, Her Family and Her Times*. Both books are personal accounts of their families.

62 Women who at a young age devoted themselves to life in a Buddhist monastery is a well-known custom in the region (Patrick Hase, and David Faure, personal communications). For many sworn spinsters who migrated to Hong Kong before and after the Second World War to look for employment often ended up in Buddhist vegetarian halls after retirement, see Stockard, *Daughters of the Canton Delta: Marriage Patterns and Economic Strategies in South China, 1860–1930*. Tung Lin Kok Yuen under Lady Clara, however, was a much more public institution.

63 See Timothy Brook, *Praying for Power: Buddhism and the Formation of Gentry Society in Late-Ming China*, Harvard-Yenching Institute Monograph Series (Cambridge, M.A.: Council on East Asian Studies Distributed by Harvard University Press, 1993).

64 See Elizabeth Sinn, "Lesson in Openness: Creating a Space of Flow in Hong Kong," in *Hong Kong Mobile: Making a Global Population* (Hong Kong: Hong Kong University Press, 2008), 13–43.

65 Among the voluminous literature on the coming of age of this home-grown Hong Kong generation, see the works of sociologists Tai-lok Lui, Agnes Ku, Thomas Wong, and cultural scholars Koon-chung Chan, Stephen Chan, and Chun-hung Ng.

66 From Siu's fieldwork experiences in Guangdong, she observes that there are women in high positions, but they are few and far between, especially in rural areas and the boomtowns.

67 According to a survey on businesses, described by "Eighty-three percent Gangqi Ping Nü Gaoceng Lie Quanqiu Diwu" (83% Hong Kong Businesses Hired Senior Women Executives, Ranking Number Five in the World), *Ming Pao Daily News*, March 8, 2007. The number of Japanese women professionals taking up senior management positions in the business sector are low, 25%, compared to the 83% indicated for Hong Kong. The low number in Japan is confirmed by a recent report made by Claire Chino, senior lawyer, activist, and a World Fellow visiting Yale University. On Hong Kong, see also *South China Morning Post*, February 23, 2007.

68 See Veronica Pearson and Benjamin K. P. Leung, eds., *Women in Hong Kong* (Hong Kong; New York: Oxford University Press, 1995). See also a

comprehensive collection on the topic by Anita Kit-wa Chan and Wai-ling Wong, eds., *Gendering Hong Kong* (Hong Kong: Oxford University Press, 2004).

69 Sam Ho, "Licensed to Kick Men: The Jane Bond Films," in *The Restless Breed: Cantonese Stars of the Sixties*, ed. the Urban Council (Hong Kong: Urban Council, 1996).

70 Lisbeth Ku, "Mass-Mediated Images of Women: Connie Chan Po-Chu and Josephine Siao Fong-Fong as Desired Cultural Images," *Hong Kong Cultural Studies Bulletin* 8–9 (Spring/Summer 1998).

71 See Po-king Choi, ed. *Wan Wan Liudianban: Qishi Nindai Shang Yexiao De Nügong* (Every Night at Six-Thirty: Women Workers Who Attended Evening Schools in the Seventies) (Hong Kong: Stepforward Multimedia Co.Ltd., 1998). See also Tai-lok Lui, *Waged Work at Home: The Social Organization of Industrial Outwork in Hong Kong* (Aldershot, England: Avebury, 1994). See also Ching-kwan Lee, *Gender and the South China Miracle: Two Worlds of Factory Women* (Berkeley: University of California Press, 1998).

72 For a more comprehensive treatment of the topic, see Ngai Pun, *Made in China: Women Factory Workers in a Global Workplace* (Durham: Duke University Press; Hong Kong: Hong Kong University Press, 2005).

73 See an excellent portrayal of karaoke hostesses in Dalian and their aspirations to become "modern" in Tiantian Zheng, "From Peasant Women to Bar Hostesses: Gender and Modernity in Post-Mao Dalian," in *On the Move: Women in Rural-to-Urban Migration in Contemporary China*, ed. Arianne Gaetano and Tamara Jacka (New York: Columbia University Press, 2004); Tiantian Zheng, *Red Lights: The Lives of Sex Workers in Postsocialist China* (Minneapolis: University of Minnesota Press, 2009).

74 On how recent decades of reform translate into the lives of a generation desperate to move ahead and to catch up with the world, see Helen F. Siu, "China's Century: Fast Forward with Historical Baggage," *American Anthropologist* 108, no. 2 (2006).

Chapter 1

1 The practice of reconstituting women's image as reflected in Chinese literature can clearly be proven in the following paragraph, written by Gu Jiegang: "Mr Xu Shenyu told me that he had once proofread the *Siku Quanshu* in the Song edition of Lou Yue's *Gongkui ji*. He noticed that all of the stories about women recorded as having remarried in the biographies and epitaphs written by Lou were rewritten in Siku Quanshu as if they had never married a second time." See Gu Jiegang, *Mao Xue Congji*, Vol. 1. In *Gu Jiegang Dushu biji* (Reading Notes of Gu Jiegang), Vol. 10 (Taipei: Lianjing Chuban Shiye Gongsi, 1990), 7802.

2 See Makino Tatsumi, "Koto Genju Minzoku Ko" (An Investigation of the Indigenous Population of Guangdong), in *Makino Tatsumi Chokikushu*, ed. Makino Tatsumi (Tokyo: Ochanomizu Shoba 5, 1985).

3 Liu Wanzhang, *Guangzhou Minjian Gushi* (Folk Stories of Canton) (Guangzhou: Zhongshan Daxue Yuyan Lishi Yanjiusuo, 1929).

4   Throughout this study, the genealogical record of the Shawan Hes, from which I quote, refers to the extracts handcopied by members of the contemporary He family.

5   An "auspicious tomb" (*jimu*) actually refers to an empty tomb (*kongmu*). Because the character *kong* is pronounced the same way as *xiong* (meaning unfortunate) in Cantonese, Cantonese people usually substitute it with the character *ji* (meaning fortunate) to avoid speaking ill-fated words.

6   Judging from the brick pattern and composition, we speculate that they were not constructed on the same occasion.

7   Interview with Mr He Rugen, June 30, 1989.

8   Interview with Mr He Rugen, June 30, 1989. See also the letter written by the Shawan Chongxiu Gusaofen Choubei xiaozu to the Guangzhoushi wenwu guanli weiyuanhui, dated January 5, 1994.

9   *Guangdong Tongzhi* (Guangdong Provincial Gazetteer), *juan* 18 (1561).

10 See Liu Zhiwei, "Lineage on the Sand: The Case of Shawan," in *Down to Earth: The Territorial Bond in South China*, ed. David Faure and Helen F. Siu (Stanford: Stanford University Press, 1995).

11 Ma Duanlin, *Wenxian Tongkao* (General Study of the Literary Remains), *juan* 64, *zhiguan* 18 (Beijing: Zhonghua Shuju, rep. 1986).

12 *Guangdong Tongzhi* (Guangdong Provincial Gazetteer), *juan* 20 (1561), 55b.

13 For a detailed study of the Nanxiong zhujixiang legend, see David Faure, "The Lineage as a Cultural Invention: The Case of the Pearl River Delta," *Modern China*, Vol. 15, no. 1 (January, 1989): 4–36.

14 The genealogical record of the Hes in Shawan.

15 *Panyu Xianzhi* (Panyu County Gazetteer), *juan* 24 (1870), 5b.

16 See Makino Tatsumi (1985).

17 Zhang Zi, "Guangzhou Fu Yixue Ji" (An Account of Moving the Guangzhou Prefectural School), in *Yuan Dade Nanhaizhi Canben* (An Incomplete Copy of Nanhai Gazetteer Compiled in the Yuan Dynasty), ed. Guangzhoushi Difangzhi Bianzuan Weiyuanhui Bangongshi (Guangzhou: Guangdong Renmin Chubanshe, 1991 reprint), 160–61.

18 Zhu Yu, *Pingzhou Ketan* (Talks on Pingzhou), *juan* 2, 6a. *Siku Quanshu* ed. (Shanghai: Shanghai Guji Chubanshe, 1982).

19 Professor Xu Songshi, an expert on Lingnan culture, once pointed out that "even today, the society of the Zhuang ethnic group is still centered on women activities." See Xu Songshi, *Yuejiang Liuyu Renmin Shi* (A History of the People Residing along the Pearl River) (Shanghai: Zhonghua Shuju, 1929), 162.

20 Wang Sen, *Yuexi Congzai* (Collected Records on Guangxi), *juan* 18, 16a–b.

21 See Luo Xianglin, "Guangdong Minzu Gailun" (A General Discussion of the Ethnic Groups in Guangdong), in *Minsu (Folklores)*, no. 63 (Guangzhou: Guoli Zhongshan Daxue, 1929). Lin Yutang accurately summarizes the culture of the Guangdong people in one sentence: "where beneath the Chinese culture a snake-eating aborigines tradition persists." See Lin Yutang, *My Country and My People* (New York: The John Day Company, 1939), 18.

22 For a general description of the local customs of Guangdong, see 1561 and 1602 editions of *Guangdong Tongzhi* (*juan* 20 and *juan* 14 respectively). The direct citation is from *Guangdong Tongzhi* (Guangdong Provincial Gazetteer), *juan* 20 (1561), 13a–b.

23 See Helen F. Siu, "The Reconstitution of Brideprice and Dowry in South China," in *Chinese Families in the Post-Mao Era*, ed. Deborah Davis and Stevan Harrell (Berkeley: University of California Press, 1993).

24 *Panyu Xianzhi* (Panyu County Gazetteer), *juan* 16 (1774), 1b.

25 *Xinhui Xianzhi* (Xinhui County Gazetteer), *juan* 15 (*lienu*) (Beijing: Shumu Wenxian Chubanshe, 1690; reprint, 1991), 368.

26 See Helen F. Siu, "Where Were the Women? Rethinking Marriage Resistance and Regional Culture History," *Late Imperial China* 11, no. 2 (1990): 32–62.

27 *Shunde Xianzhi* (Shunde County Gazetteer) (1750), *juan* 3, *fengsu*, Zhongguo shudian, Hanjian Zhongguo difangzhi huikan, rep. 1992, vol. 45, 852. Qianlong edition of *Guangzhou Fuzhi* (Guangzhou Prefectural Gazetteer) has the same entry and notes that are quoted from the "old gazetteer," which should be the Kangxi edition of *Guangzhou Fuzhi*.

28 One may suggest "uxorilocal marriage" for translating the Chinese term "*ruzhui*." However, while uxorilocality implies matrilocality and is thus matrifocal, "*ruzhui*," at least within the historical context of the Pearl River Delta region, is a means through which outsiders could acquire settlement rights.

29 Zhang Qu, *Yuedong Wenjian Lu* (An Account of What [I] Hear and Observe in Guangdong) (Guangzhou: Guangdong Gaodeng Jiaoyu Chubanshe, 1990), 59.

30 (Xinhui) *Waihai Chenshi Zupu Gao* (The Geneaology of the Chens of Waihai Township in Xinhui County) (n.p., n.d.), 11–20.

31 Interview with Mr Wang Su, July 21, 1989.

32 See the field notes that Helen Siu and I recorded for the interviews conducted in Chakeng and Tianma townships in Xinhui county, July 1, 1987. See also (Xinhui) *Chenzu Shipu*, "Tianma kaiji shilue" (A Record of the History of Settlement at Tianma).

33 *Panyu Xianzhi* (Panyu County Gazetteer), *juan* 16 (1774), 3a, *juan* 5 (1774), 28a.

34 Interview with Mr He Jinhua and Mr He Yin, June 24, 1989.

35 *Panyu Xianzhi* (Panyu County Gazetteer), *juan* 5 (1774), 26a.

36 Liang was a lecturer of classics colloquium in the Southern Study while appointed the vice minister of the Ministry of Revenue. For the official career of Liang, see Qian Yiji, *Beizhuanji* (A Collection of Biographies), *juan* 28, *Qingdai Beizhuan Quanji* (A Complete Collection of Biographies of the Qing Dynasty) (Shanghai: Shanghai Guji Chubanshe, 1987), 182.

37 Liang also mentioned in the inscription that when he "undertook the appointment to supervise the civil service examinations in Guangdong" in 1756, he had already seen the accounts of the Sisters-in-Law Tomb in a local gazetteer. Because the Qianlong edition of *Panyu Xianzhi* was published in 1774, the gazetteer that Liang saw must have been the Kangxi edition of *Panyu Xianzhi*. Liang's inscription was re-inscribed by the Hes in 1994 and was inlaid adjacent to the newly repaired Sisters-in-Law Tomb.

38 Long Tinghuai, *Jingxue Xuan Wenji* (Collected Essays of Jingxue xuan), *juan* 7, 10b (1842).
39 The county record only notes the close relationship between the sisters-in-law, but it certainly is not complete.
40 I would like to thank the Guangzhou Shi Wenwu Guanli Weiyuanhui for allowing me to read this and the subsequent letters.
41 Liu Wanzhang (1928). Another version says that the site of the tomb land directed by the Earth Goddess is for He Renjian, not for the pair of sisters-in-law.

Chapter 2

1   I have in mind the essays of Gui Youguang (1506–1571) on members of his family as I write this essay, but have not found anything in the Pearl River Delta record to match his sensitivities.
2   Chen Baisha, "Qi Zhongyang Shu," in *Chen Xianzhang ji* (The Collected Works of Chen Xianzhang) (Beijing: Zhonghua, 1987), 2.
3   Huang Zuo, *Taiquan Xiangli*, Siku edition ed., vol. 3 (preface of 1549).
4   Li Suiqiu, *Lianxu Ge Wenchao* (Essays of the Lianxu Pavilion), *Preface of 1638, Guangdong congshu* edition of 1940 ed., vol. 8, 9b–10.
5   Ibid., vol. 8, 10b–11b.
6   Ibid., vol. 17, 4b–5b; vol. 4, 1a–2a.
7   Margery Wolf, *Women and the Family in Rural Taiwan* (Stanford: Stanford University Press, 1972).
8   *Huoshi zupu* 1848, vol. 9, 37a–39a, 55b–56a, and 68b–72b.
9   Ibid., vol. 9, 69a.
10 Dorothy Ko, *Teachers of the Inner Chambers: Women and Culture in Seventeenth-Century China* (Stanford: Stanford University Press, 1994).
11 The biography of Luo Tianchi's father, Shiju, may be found in the 1750 *Shunde Xianzhi*. vol. 13, 19a–20a. His essay, "Jiabei quanyan" is reproduced in the *Shunde Beimen Luoshi Zupu* (1882), vol. 21, 24a–25b.
12 Luo Tianchi, *Wushan Jilin* (Shunde shizhi bangongshi preface of 1761; reprint, 1986), 41.
13 Luo Tianchi, "Weizi Xunfu" (Sacrificing One's Life for the Husband before Wedding Is Completed), in *Wushan Jilin* (Shunde shizhi bangongshi, 1761; reprint, 1986), 40–41.
14 This account may be found in the *Shunde Beimen Luoshi Zupu*, vol. 21, 27b–30b.
15 Untitled correspondence in D. Faure's holding, manuscript, 2b–3a.
16 Ibid., 8b–9a.
17 Ibid., 13b–14a.
18 Helen F. Siu, "Where Were the Women? Rethinking Marriage Resistance and Regional Culture History," *Late Imperial China* 11, no. 2 (December 1990): 32–62.

Chapter 3

1 For a critical review of studies on marriage resistance in South China, see Helen F. Siu, "Where Were the Women? Rethinking Marriage Resistance and Regional Culture History," *Late Imperial China* 11, no. 2 (December 1990).

2 *Liugu Huimen* (Sixth Aunt Returning to Her Natal Home) (Hong Kong: Wuguitang, n.d.), *juan* 3, 2b.

3 Ibid.

4 *Sangu Huimen* (Third Aunt Returning to Her Natal Home), n.p. (probably Hong Kong and Guangzhou: Wuguitang, n.d.), *juan* 1, 2b.

5 Ibid., *juan* 1, 4a.

6 Sai-shing Yung, "Mu-Yu Shu and the Cantonese Popular Singing Arts," *The Gest Library Journal* 2, no. 1 (1987).

7 See Tan Zhengbi and Tan Xun, *Muyuge, Chaozhouge Xulu* (An Annotated Catalogue of Wooden-fish Songs and Chaozhou Songs) (Beijing: Shumu Wenxian Chubanshe, 1982); Yung.

8 Kuang Lu, *Qiaoya* (A Collection of Poems) (n.p., n.d., the poem selected was written in 1694), *juan* 1, 29b–30b; Tan and Tan; Wang Shizhen, *Nanhai Ji* (A Collection of Essays on the South, n.p., n.d., preface dated 1684), *juan* 2, 3b.

9 Qu Dajun, *Guangdong Xinyu* (New Accounts of Guangdong), preface dated 1700 (Hong Kong: Zhonghua Shuju; reprint, 1974).

10 Zheng Zhenduo, *Bali Guojia Tushuguan Zhong Zhi Zhongguo Xiaoshuo Yu Xiqu* (Chinese Novels and Opera Scripts Collected at Bibliothèque nationale de France in Paris) (1927; reprint, in his *Zhongguo Wenxue Yanjiu* [Studies of Chinese Literature], Hong Kong: Guwen Shuju, 1961), 1275–313. See also Tan and Tan.

11 See Tan and Tan.

12 Wing-hoi Chan, "Traditional Folksongs and Rural Life in Hong Kong," in *"Overall Report on the General Context of Local Folksongs" for the Project on the Recording of Local Traditional Folksongs of the Hong Kong Region* (Hong Kong: Hong Kong Museum, 1984 [unpublished]).

13 I have seen only the editions collected in the University of Hong Kong, which are exactly the same as the copies personally owned by Mr Zhou Chuqi. I am grateful to Mr Zhou for generously showing me his personal *muyushu* collection.

14 Pui-chee Leung, *Xianggang Daxue Suocang Muyushu Xulu Yu Yanjiu* (Wooden-fish Books: Critical Essays and Annotated Catalogue Based on the Collection in the University of Hong Kong) (Hong Kong: Centre of Asian Studies, The University of Hong Kong, 1978).

15 For a careful documentation of the case, see Luo Ergang, "Jiuming Qiyuan De Benshi" (The Original Story of Jiuming Qiyuan), and "Jiuming Qiyuan Xiongfan Chuansaiqi Dang'an Zhi Faxian" (The Discovery of the Archives Concerning the Murderer, Chuansaiqi, in Connection with the Story Entitled Jiuming Qiyuan), both in *Wu Jianren Yanjiu Ziliao* (Materials for Studying Wu Jianren), ed. Wei Shaochang (Shanghai: Shanghai Guji Chubanshe, 1980).

16 According to Leung.

17   The edition of the *muyushu* that I read is collected at the University of Hong Kong. Judging from the printing style and cover, it is probably a late Qing or early Republican edition.

18   An example of Cantonese opera adapted from the story of Liang Tianlai is *Huoshao shishi* (Setting fire to a stone house, performed in the mid-1920s; the script was published in Guangzhou). See Shiu-hon Wong, *Xianggang Daxue Yazhou Yanjiu Zhongxin Suocang Yueju Juben Mulu* (A Catalogue of Cantonese Opera Scripts Collected at the Centre of Asian Studies, The University of Hong Kong) (Hong Kong: Centre of Asian Studies, The University of Hong Kong, 1990), Item 15. A copy of this opera script is available at the Chinese Opera Information Centre, the Department of Music, The Chinese University of Hong Kong.

19   For other *muyushu* that have their stories or narratives originating in Guangdong, see Tan and Tan.

20   I would like to thank Dr Wing-hoi Chan and the Hong Kong Museum for allowing me to read the report on folksong traditions of Hong Kong, written by Chan himself in 1984, and to listen to the tapes that he recorded during the study.

21   See Fred Blake, "Death and Abuse in Marriage Laments: The Curse of Chinese Brides," *Studies in Asian Folklore* 37, no. 1 (1978); Elizabeth Johnson, "Grieving for the Dead, Grieving for the Living: Funeral Laments of Hakka Women," in *Death Ritual in Late Imperial and Modern China*, ed. James L. Watson and Evelyn S. Rawski (Berkeley: University of California Press, 1988); Liu Wanzhang and Gu Jiegang, *Su Yue De Hunsang* (The Marriage and Funeral Rite of Soochow [Suzhou] and Canton [Guangzhou]) (Guangzhou: Guoli Zhongshan Daxue Yuyan Lishi Yanjiusuo, 1928); Emily Martin, "Gender and Ideological Difference in Representation of Life and Death," in *Death Ritual in Late Imperial and Modern China*, ed. James L. Watson and Evelyn S. Rawski (Berkeley: University of California Press, 1988); Zhang Zhengping, *Ku Gezi Ci* (Hong Kong New Territories Folk-literature Study), vol. 1 (Hong Kong: Youhua Publisher, 1969). See also Wing-hoi Chan for his review of the studies of Fred Blake and Emily Martin: Wing-hoi Chan, "Locating Women's Voice: Chinese Bridal Songs in Its Social Context," in *Conference on Merchants and Local Cultures* (Hong Kong: Division of Humanities, Hong Kong University of Science and Technology, 1994).

22   The Dan fishermen are usually called "Tanka." They are roughly categorized as those coming from the "Eastern side" and those from "Western side." Some tunes of the bridal laments from both sides are different, and some are the same. See Chan, "Traditional Folksongs and Rural Life in Hong Kong."

23   Ibid., 81.

24   Ibid., 74. He notes that exceptions are found among the Punti populations in the Yuen Long–Sheung Shui–Fanling area of the New Territories in Hong Kong.

25   Wing-hoi Chan, *Local Traditional Folksongs: Transcriptions* (Hong Kong: Hong Kong Museum, 1984 [unpublished]).

26   Ibid., 311, 43.

27   Chan, "Traditional Folksongs and Rural Life in Hong Kong," 83.

28   Chan, *Local Traditional Folksongs: Transcriptions*.

29 Chan, "Locating Women's Voice: Chinese Bridal Songs in Its Social Context."

30 There are three occasions on which bridal laments appear in the text. They are, namely, *shangtou kaimian* (pinning and making up the face), *zhuqin songjia* (various relatives seeing off the bride), and *tongxin kubie* (lamenting the separation by [sisters] with the same heart).

31 *Liugu Huimen, juan* 1, 10a.

32 Blake, 25–27; Chan, "Traditional Folksongs and Rural Life in Hong Kong," 69.

33 *Hunyin Sangji Hanshu* (A Book of Marriage and Funeral Laments), manuscript collected at Guangdong Provincial Library, Guangzhou (n.p., n.d.).

34 *Liugu Huimen, juan* 2, 6b.

35 Ibid.

36 Ibid., *juan* 3, 7b.

37 *Zishunu* refers to those women who remained spinsters and took vows, usually before a deity and in front of witnesses, never to wed. Their vows are preceded by a hairdressing ritual that resembles the one traditionally performed before marriage to signal a girl's arrival at social maturity. *Buluojia* refers to those women who were formally married but did not live with their husbands. For discussions on both topics, see Siu; Janice E. Stockard, *Daughters of the Canton Delta: Marriage Patterns and Economic Strategies in South China, 1860–1930* (Stanford: Stanford University Press, 1989); Marjorie Topley, "Marriage Resistance in Rural Kwantung," in *Women in Chinese Society*, ed. Margery Wolf, Roxane Witke, and Emily M. Ahern (Stanford: Stanford University Press, 1975).

38 See Tan and Tan; Zhou Chuqi, "Jiebai Jinlan Zhen Yewei: Muyushu Zhong Zishunu Tongxinglian Jingguan" (How Scrumptious Knotting a "Golden-orchid" Relationship Is: The Homosexual Outlook of the Zishunu as Reflected in the Wooden-Fish Song Books), *Jiushi Niandai*, no. 7 (1994).

39 See *Tongxin Shangbannian* ([Thinking about] My "Same Heart" [As I Think about the Things and Events Occurring in] the First Half of the Year) (n.p., n. d.); *Wuxiang Tongxin* (Five Times I Think about My Sisters with the "Same Heart") (Guangzhou: Wuguitang, n.d.).

40 *Chuixiao Yiyou* (Playing the Flute [She] Misses [Her] Friend) (Guangzhou: Yiwentang, n.d.), 2b.

41 *Menglan Yiyou* (Menglan Missing Her Friend) (n.p., n.d.), 6b.

42 *Riye Shichen* (Hours through Days and Nights) (n.p., n.d.), 4b.

43 See *Jiexielan* (Untying the Carrying Basket) (n.p. [probably Guangzhou: Wuguitang], n.d.); *Yuchan Fujian* (Yuchan Sending a Letter [to Her "Golden-orchid" Sister]) (n.p. [probably Guangzhou: Wuguitang], n.d.); *Yuchan Wenxi* (Yuchan Inquiring the Sorcerer) (n.p. [probably Guangzhou: Wuguitang], n.d.).

44 *Shi'er Shichen* (Twelve [Chinese] Hours) (Hong Kong: Xingji Shuju, n.d.), *juan* 2, 6.

45 See *Chai Waimu Wu* (Tearing down the Mother-in-law's House) (Guangzhou: Yiwentang, n.d.).

46 See *Jinxiu Shizhai* (Jiuxiu Eating Vegetarian Feast) (Guangzhou: Zuijingtang, n.d.). The text is personally possessed by Mr Zhou Chuqi.

47 *Mei Li Zeng Hua* (Mr Mei and Mr Li Competing with Each Other for Miss Hua) (Guangzhou: Zuijingtang, n.d.), *juan* 3, 12a.

48 *Xinchu Husinu Zitan* (A Woman Silk Worker Lamenting on Her Own) (n.p., n.d.).

49 *Yejian Jinlan* (Warning Jinlan at Night) (n.p., n.d.), *juan* 1, 1a.

50 For a review of modern intellectuals' attitude towards local customs and practices, see Chang-tai Hung, *Going to the People: Chinese Intellectuals and Folk Literature, 1918–1937*, Harvard East Asian Monographs (Cambridge, M.A.: Council on East Asian Studies Distributed by Harvard University Press, 1985); Zhao Shiyu, *Yanguang Xiangxia De Geming: Zhongguo Xiandai Minsuxue Sixiangshi Lun (1918–1937)* (A Revolution Towards the Masses: A History of Folklore Studies in Modern China 1918–1937) (Beijing: Beijing Shifan Daxue Chubanshe, 1999).

51 For a similar argument, see Wu Ruiqing, "Guangfuhua Shuochangben Muyushu De Yanjiu" (A Study on Cantonese Wooden-fish Song Books) (PhD dissertation, The Chinese University of Hong Kong, 1989).

52 A similar argument can be found in Wu Ruiqing, 209. Men are also consumers of *muyushu*, although they may not be as enthusiastic as women. Chan Wing-hoi's study on the Hakka region shows that the *Huajian ji* is one of the favorites of men. See Chan, "Traditional Folksongs and Rural Life in Hong Kong," Chapter 4.

53 See Wu Ruiqing.

54 These examples showing the ways of addressing parents come from the Punti song texts collected by Wing-hoi Chan as well as the oral account of my grandmother, who was born in and married in the Zhongshan–Zhuhai region.

55 See *You Yinghua Qianxue Qimeng Shu Yi* (Translating from an English Primer of Enlightenment), collected at Cambridge University (n.p., 1873).

56 Pui-chee Leung records the number of publishing houses that produce *muyushu* in Hong Kong, Chaozhou, and other counties in the Pearl River Delta region, and as far as the United States as fifty. See Leung; Evelyn S. Rawski, "Economic and Social Foundations of Late Imperial Culture," in *Popular Culture in Late Imperial China*, ed. David G. Johnson, et al. (Berkeley: University of California Press, 1985).

Chapter 4

1 For other kinds of criticism, see "Introduction" in this volume and, for example, Allen Chun, *Unstructuring Chinese Society: The Fictions of Colonial Practice and the Changing Realities of "Land" in the New Territories of Hong Kong* (Amsterdam: Harwood Academic, 2000).

2 Margery Wolf, *Women and the Family in Rural Taiwan* (Stanford: Stanford University Press, 1972).

3 Rubie Watson, *Inequality among Brothers: Class and Kinship in South China* (Cambridge [Cambridgeshire]; New York: Cambridge University Press, 1985).

4 D. K. Feil, "Beyond Patriliny in the New Guinea Highlands," *Man* n.s. 19, no. 1 (1984): 53.

5   Emily Ahern and James Watson study the symbolism of pigs in rural Hong Kong and Taiwan respectively, without paying much attention to the place of swine in local economy.

6   See Wing-hoi Chan, "Writing Women's Words: Bridal Laments and Representations of Kinship and Marriage in South China" (PhD thesis, Department of Anthropology, Yale University, 2000).

7   Not that Freedman ignores exploitation. He observes that even as the poor in a lineage "were exploited they enjoyed privileges important enough" to make them stay in the lineage, see Maurice Freedman, *Lineage Organization in Southeast China* (New York: Humanities Press, 1965), 127.

8   This usage is significantly different from the meaning of the same term in models of "segmentary lineage" in Africa.

9   After referring to reports from other parts of China that intra-lineage tenants enjoy secure tenancy and lower rent than outsiders, Potter acknowledges that "this economic benefit for poorer members of a lineage should not be overemphasized. . . ." In Ping Shan, the village he studied, intralineage tenants mostly rented from "branches of which they were not members" and were "charged the same rate as outsiders." Moreover, some lineages had rules against leasing to their own members (Jack M. Potter, "Land and Lineage in Traditional China," in *Family and Kinship in Chinese Society*, ed. Maurice Freedman [Stanford: Stanford University Press, 1970]).

10   Ibid., 128.

11   Elizabeth L. Johnson, "Hakka Women: Great Aunt Yeung: A Hakka Wage Laborer," in *Lives: Chinese Working Women*, ed. Mary Sheridan and Janet W. Salaff (Bloomington: Indiana University Press, 1984).

12   Rubie S. Watson, *Inequality among Brothers: Class and Kinship in South China*, (Cambridge [Cambridgeshire]; New York: Cambridge University Press, 1985), 80–81.

13   Ibid., 78–79.

14   Ibid., 65.

15   Ibid., 80–81.

16   Myron Cohen, "Lineage Development and the Family in China," in *The Chinese Family and Its Ritual Behavior*, ed. Jih-chang Hsieh and Ying-chang Chuang (Taipei: Institute of Ethnology, Academia Sinica, 1985), 210.

17   Ibid., 212.

18   Watson, *Inequality among Brothers: Class and Kinship in South China*, 77.

19   James L. Watson, *Emigration and the Chinese Lineage: The Mans in Hong Kong and London* (Berkeley: University of California Press, 1975), 60–61, 63. San Tin men also worked outside their lineage in more traditional forms of employment. One of my informants at Ho Sheung Heung mentioned that during the prewar period in his village there were always some male annual farm helpers hired from San Tin.

20   On sailors, see Watson, *Inequality among Brothers: Class and Kinship in South China*, 80. For the number of households see Watson, *Inequality among Brothers*, 65–66.

21 Watson, *Emigration and the Chinese Lineage: The Mans in Hong Kong and London*, 60–64.

22 Micaela di Leonardo, "The Female World of Cards and Holidays: Women, Families, and the Work of Kinship," *Signs* 12, no. 3 (1987).

23 For some of the circumstances of the rise of local lineage, see Gompertz, "Some Notes on Land Tenure in the New Territory," in *Report on Operations in the New Territories During 1900* (London: His Majesty's Stationery Office, 1901).

24 See a tenancy contract dated 1733 cited by David Faure, *The Structure of Chinese Rural Society: Lineage and Village in the Eastern New Territories* (Hong Kong: Oxford University Press, 1986), 36–37.

25 Hugh Baker, *A Chinese Lineage Village: Sheung Shui* (London: Frank Cass and Co., 1968), 32–36.

26 The trust by the same name appeared in a document dated 1733. See Faure, 36–37.

27 One female informant attended the banquet for elders held in Wanshi *tang*, for which women became eligible in recent years. Before then some women recalled participating in the grave worship of the founding ancestor, but only as laborers.

28 Baker, 21–22. There Baker also mentions "Selling . . . high quality rice to buy cheap grain and other goods," where probably alleviated the problem of land shortage. But that was probably a relatively late development because the "cheap grain" was broken in the process of machine milling, which was probably introduced in the early 1930s according to one informant.

29 Three *danzhong*, "gross" assumed here.

30 Although many plots in the core area are much closer to other villages than they are to Sheung Shui and some of those were mostly likely rented to outsiders, most of the plots were probably farmed by the Lius. Baker has drawn attention to the lineage's ownership of three irrigation dams in the core area, and has linked that to a pattern that "land near the village was not only owned by [Lius], but, where rented out, it was leased to [Lius] too." See Baker, 166.

31 As Baker has suggested, it would be difficult for a Liu family to farm isolated plots or clusters of plots amidst fields farmed by outsiders, as irrigation disputes often caused serious conflicts when the parties belonged to different communities. Other factors include perpetual tenancy (ibid., 166–67). See, for example, John Kamm, "Two Essays on the Ch'ing Economy of Hsin-An," *Journal of the Royal Asiatic Society Hong Kong Branch* 17 (1977). Or Michael Palmer, "The Surface-Subsoil Form of Divided Ownership in Late Imperial China: Some Examples from the New Territories of Hong Kong," *Modern Asian Studies* 21, no. 1 (1987); James L. Watson, "Hereditary Tenancy and Corporate Landlordism in Traditional China: A Case Study," *Modern Asian Studies* 11, no. 2 (1977): 161–82. Moreover, tenant communities often participated in local coalitions that allowed them to unite and resist their common enemies (see, for example, John Brim, "Village Alliance Temples in Hong Kong," in *Religion and Ritual in Chinese Society*, ed. Arthur Wolf [Stanford: Stanford University Press, 1974]). The power of dominant lineages was also limited by the fact that they were far

from being united. See, for example, Hugh Baker, "The Five Great Clans of the New Territories," *Journal of the Royal Asiatic Society Hong Kong Branch* 6 (1966).

32 One informant at Ho Sheung Heung born in the 1910s consistently used the term *caizhu* for such men only.

33 In nearby Ho Sheung Heung, well-to-do men who farmed their own paddy fields owned about four acres of rice land. Those in Sheung Shui probably had similar holdings.

34 *Shangshui Xiang Wenxian* (Historical documents from Sheung Shui Village), vol. 6 (n.p., n.d.), 76. A list on p. 26 indicates that each descendant received two taels (about 2.66 oz.) of pork. See Baker, *A Chinese Lineage Village: Sheung Shui*, 92.

35 Some of these subgroups had their own ancestral halls and some have "study halls" that served as the venues of traditional education and banquets.

36 This is an estimate based on the fact that at the time the poorer families belonging to Yunsheng tang, the trust in the name of the wealthiest Yimou tang's father, was in the eighteenth generation and after according to Baker, *A Chinese Lineage Village: Sheung Shui*, 127. The descriptions on pages 110 and 126 suggest some confusion about the generation numbers of these Liu ancestors, but the information quoted here should be a good approximation.

37 This was after losses suffered during the land registration exercise at the beginning of British rule when some tenants in other communities successfully claimed ownership. Information from the comparable lineage of Kam Tin suggests that the land lost in the event probably had not generated very significant income for average lineage members (ibid., 113–15). The proportion of double-crop paddy land is derived from Baker's samples data on the composition of trust holdings on p. 170, which reflects the overall composition of all trust holdings taken together.

38 Ibid., 108.

39 A Wanshi *tang* document bearing no dates named tenants who were also house owners in the House Block Crown Lease of 1904, suggesting that the tenancy existed before the transformations that took place after the Second World War. Three of the six tenants of rice land owned 1.17, 1.34 and 0.51 acres of first-class land respectively, all at or above the 20% percentile in terms of first-class holdings. Given the moderate size of the tenants' own holdings, it is likely that they do not sublet to others. If they do, the extra rent they charge will significantly reduce the benefit to the cultivator. There is another list for pieces of land with much lower total rent suggesting much smaller total acreage and involving many more tenants, who seem to be of a younger generation than those on the Block Crown Lease of 1904, making it harder to trace their economic backgrounds.

40 We were unable to identify contiguous lots using maps. Instead, we made a heuristic assumption that contiguous lots, taking together, bear consecutive lot numbers. There is corroboration for the validity of the numbers: the total acreage found is very close to Baker's 635.23 (Baker, *A Chinese Lineage Village: Sheung Shui*, 165).

41 Fei's estimate for a rural population in southwestern China is equivalent to an average of 437 catties after allowance for variations by age and gender (Fei Hsiao-tung and Chang Chih-i, *Earthbound China: A Study of Rural Economy in Yunnan* [Chicago: University of Chicago Press, 1945], 51). He gives the total estimated for a rural population of 694 persons in terms of the smaller new picul (for conversion into pound, see Fei and Chang, 50, note 3). Faure uses 400 catties as "a narrowly defined minimum" in his study of rural economy in Guangdong and Jiangsu provinces during a comparable period (David Faure, *The Rural Economy of Pre-Liberation China: Trade Expansion and Peasant Livelihood in Jiangsu and Guangdong* [Hong Kong: Oxford University Press, 1989], 227, note 29). The Hong Kong government's standard budget for urban workers during 1930–49 translates to 375 catties per year. The rural diet was likely to include much less meat, peanut oil, and bean curd, which are included in the standard budget. For the government figures, see, for example, "Hong Kong Statistics 1947–1967" (Hong Kong: Census and Statistics Department, 1969), 215.

42 Faure uses a conversion ratio of 70% (Faure, *The Rural Economy of Pre-Liberation China: Trade Expansion and Peasant Livelihood in Jiangsu and Guangdong*, 52–54). Hase reports a lower ratio of 60% (Patrick Hase, "A Note on Rice Farming in Sha Tin," *Journal of the Royal Asiatic Society Hong Kong Branch* 21 [1981]: 197).

43 For productivity figures, see Charles J. Grant, "The Soils and Agriculture of Hong Kong" (Hong Kong: Hong Kong Government Press, 1960), figure VI(p). Grant's own translation is 20% lower (expressed in pounds, p. 18). This may be attributed to the conversion of a *douzhong* to 1/5 acres. J. Watson translates a *douzhong* (*tou*) to approximately 1/6 acre, which corresponds to the Chinese *mu* (Watson, *Emigration and the Chinese Lineage: The Mans in Hong Kong and London*, ix). Potter mentions that the *douzhong* was the equivalent of *mu* in some local usage but the ratio varied according to fertility. He also noted that there can be a large variation in yield between a normal year and one in which there was insufficient spring rain (Jack M. Potter, *Capitalism and the Chinese Peasant: Social and Economic Change in a Hong Kong Village* [Berkeley: University of California Press, 1968], 62, 82). Grant's productivity figures could be considerably higher than their counterparts in prewar years (Grant, 116). He observes with respect to Tai Hong Wai in another part of the New Territories that the current productivity represented a 40% increase due to newly introduced seeds, insecticides and fertilizers.

44 This is similar to Grant's report from a hamlet in the dominant lineage in Kam Tin that three piculs were paid out of a harvest of up to six piculs (Grant, 115). Similarly, Potter reports from another wealthy and powerful lineage in the New Territories that lineage members and outsiders paid rent at the same rate (Potter, "Land and Lineage in Traditional China," 128).

45 In term of *douzhong* each *dou* (about ten catties) produced between 200 and 300 catties per crop. The percentage of seed implied would be around 4%. As

already explained, a *douzhong* normally took considerably less than a *dou* to plant. Therefore, an allowance of 3% should be closer to reality.

46 While actual family size should not be independent of landholding, averaging approximates family ideals.

47 Consumption need is assumed to be the same as the one presented above. Productivity is according to Grant, Figure VI(I), 101–3. Second-class land was assumed to be as productive as first-class and the inferiority of the rice it produced is ignored. Other data are from Watson, *Inequality among Brothers: Class and Kinship in South China*. The hamlet's share of rental land is estimated as proportional to its 1911 population adjusted by taking into account the fraction of houses whose owners were not lineage members in 1906. Of landlord holdings in the *xiang*, including 183 first-class and fifty second-class acres, 41% is in the "core area" Watson has defined as "the land that is located within a half mile radius of Ha Tsuen Market" (77). That overall ratio is used to estimate the smaller "core area" acreage for each class. The second-class portion of non-first-class land owned by trusts and residents of the hamlet is optimistically estimated at the higher ratio known for landlords. The ancestral-trust-owned first-class and second-class land acreages are 207 and sixty-one respectively in the larger *xiang*. Of those 30% to 88% is said to be in the core area. The higher percentage is used for an optimistic estimate. "A few" reported the rent to be 50% to 60% of yield and "others" 30% to 40% according to Watson. The middle of the lower range, 35% is used here.

48 Freedman, 9–10.

49 Potter, "Land and Lineage in Traditional China," 135.

50 This is based on informant descriptions, which is corroborated by Grant, 122.

51 This is somewhat different from the situation recorded by Johnson, where the mother-in-law was responsible (Johnson, 88).

52 Quoted in Potter, *Capitalism and the Chinese Peasant: Social and Economic Change in a Hong Kong Village*, 33.

53 Reports in *Guangdong Nongye Gaikuang Diaocha Baogaoshu* provides relevant information during the early 1920s (*Guangdong Nongye Gaikuang Diaocha Baogaoshu* [Guangdong Agriculture Survey Report] [Guangzhou: Guoli Guangdong Daxue Nongke Xueyuan, 1925]). Hogs were sold when they reached 120 catties in Xinhui County (Chen Zelin, "Xinhui Xian Nongye Diaocha Baogao" [Agriculture Survery Report for Xinhui County], in *Guangdong Nongye Gaikuang Diaocha Baogaoshu,* ed. Guangdong Sheng Difang Nonglin Shiyanchang Diaochake [Guangzhou: Guoli Guangdong Daxue Nongke Xueyuan] [Guangdong Agriculture Survey Report, 1925], 287). In Boluo pigs were sold at weights between 100 and 160 (Zheng Zhenzhou, "Buolo Xian Nongye Diaocha Baogao" [Agriculture Survey Report for Boluo County], in *Guangdong Nongye Gaikuang Diaocha Baogaoshu* [Guangdong Agriculture Survey Report], ed. Guangdong Sheng Difang Nonglin Shiyanchang Diaochake [Guangzhou: Guoli Guangdong Daxue Nongke Xueyuan, 1925], 27–28). In Heyuan county, under a different kind of operation, the typically weight was 150 (Qiaofang Li, "Heyuan

Xian Nongye Diaocha Baogao" [Agriculture Survey Report for Heyan County], in Guangdong Nongye Gaikuang Diaocha Baogaoshu [Guangdong Agriculture Survey Report], ed. Guangdong Sheng Difang Nonglin Shiyanchang Diaochake [Guangzhou: Guoli Guangdong Daxue Nongke Xueyuan, 1925], 52).

54 "Evidence of J. T. Cotton, Given before the Food Commission," in Edward Osborne, et al., *Food Commission Report, 1900* (n.p., 1900), 9. But the Hongkong Government Gazette shows that 22,727 imported swine weighted 1,345 (long) tons, which imply an average weight of very close to 100 catties. See "The Hongkong Government Gazette, 6 July" (Hong Kong 1901), 1192.

55 The estimate is made by John Brim, "Local Systems and Modernizing Change in the New Territories of Hong Kong" (PhD thesis, Stanford University, 1970), 151. He uses the average price of imported swine in 1934 and the price of rice in 1937. The estimate ignores changes over a three-year period and possible effects of short-term variations on the numbers.

56 In parts of Guangdong for which data are available, the average price ratio was about 35% higher during the 1920s. There were considerable volatility in the prices of hog and paddy. Reports in *Guangdong Nongye Gaikuang Diaocha Baogaoshu* provides information on prices in different localities of Guangdong Province during the early 1920s (*Guangdong Nongye Gaikuang Diaocha Baogaoshu*, 27–8, 36–7, 52, 62–3, 95, 108–9, 149–50, 287, 245, 252, 390). Around 1933 the price fell due to an economic decline ultimately caused by world depression and the related import of cheap foreign rice (Faure, *The Rural Economy of Pre-Liberation China: Trade Expansion and Peasant Livelihood in Jiangsu and Guangdong*, 128–31). According to Chen Hansheng, within a year the price of pigs in Canton dropped from 34 to 15 taels (about 43 to 19 dollars) per hundred catties (Chen Han-seng, *Agrarian Problems in Southernmost China* [Shanghai: Kelly and Walsh, 1936], 86).

57 A government survey in 1941 reports that there were 43,000 pigs in the New Territories. The most detailed figure appears in "Xinjie de Yangzhu Shiye" (Pig Farming in the New Territories), in *Xinjie Nianjian* (Yearbook of the New Territories) (Hong Kong: Yu Nong Chu [Agriculture and Fisheries Department], 1971), 14. See the rounded-off figure in "Colonial Annual Reports, Hong Kong, 1948" (London: His Majesty's Stationery Office, 1949), 45. In 1938, the New Territories population, excluding recent refugee immigrants, was estimated at 109,028 ("Annual Report on the Social and Economic Progress of the People of Hong Kong, 1938" [London: His Majesty's Stationery Office, 1939], 18). The regional breed was likely to take about 10 months to raise for the market (N. L. Smith, et al. "Report of the Committee Appointed to Consider the Breeding of Pigs and Poultry in the New Territories," [1934], 127). However, *Zhongguo Zhu Pinzhong Zhi* suggests that it was shorter at 9 months (*Zhongguo Zhu Pinzhong Zhi* [A Description of Breeds of Pig in China] [Shanghai: Shanghai Kexue Jishu Chubanshe, 1986], 87–88).

58 Orme writes, "No Chinese village in the Territory is complete without its complements of pigs . . . all of which cost nothing to keep . . ." (G. N. Orme,

Report on the New Territories, 1899–1912 [n.p., 1912], 52). Fei and Chang reports from a different region a similar feature of small-scale pig raising. "The materials used for feed need not be purchased, and there is little market for them, since pigs are not raised with purchased feed" (Fei and Chang, 49–50, 166–67).

59 Improved communication with urban areas of the colony probably increased profitability for the farmer. By 1919, the road from Kowloon links many villages in different parts of the New Territories. By 1921 a road extension reached the outskirts of Sheung Shui. See "Hong Kong, Annual Report for 1921" (London: His Majesty's Stationery Office, 1922), 19; S. G. Davis, *Hong Kong in Its Geographical Setting* (London: Collins, 1949), 129. But comparative data from parts of Guangdong cited earlier suggests that the New Territories situation was far from unique.

60 Baker, *A Chinese Lineage Village: Sheung Shui*, 124, n30.

61 Freedman already mentions women's labor in rice farming (G. William Skinner, ed., *The Study of Chinese Society: Essays by Maurice Freedman* (Stanford: Stanford University Press, 1979).

62 See, for example, Ping-ti Ho, *Studies on the Population of China, 1368–1953* (Cambridge: Harvard University Press, 1959), 186–87.

63 See Chen Shuping, "Yumi He Fanshu Zai Zhongguo Chuanbo Qingkuang Yanjiu" (A Study of the Spread of Corn and Sweet Potato in China), *Zhongguo shehui kexue jikan*, no. 3 (1980): 193–95, 201–4.

64 The acreage is estimated on the basis of information relating to the sale of one of the two parcels of land: (1) the purchase price of a house site and construction costs of the house, both paid for with the proceed from the sale, and (2) the sale price per square foot.

65 Hase, 196–97. Brim quoted another Hong Kong source giving a very similar figure (Brim, "Local Systems and Modernizing Change in the New Territories of Hong Kong," 150). Based on three cycles per year, the production figure is comparable to that mentioned by a source from the mid-eighteenth century referred to by Chen: (probably annual) of three to four thousand catties per *mu* 畝 (roughly a *douzhong*) (Chen, "Yumi He Fanshu Zai Zhongguo Chuanbo Qingkuang Yanjiu," 195). Hase also reports that each person ate 3 to 4 catties of sweet potato a day if the individual did not eat rice at all (196).

66 Watson, *Inequality among Brothers: Class and Kinship in South China*, 81.

67 Between 1928 and 1933, the crop fetched a price between 23% to 18% that of rice in a county very near Canton according to Chan, *Agrarian Problems in Southernmost China*, 86. Writing in 1935, the author reports that "recently the prices [of taro, potato, carrots, and peanuts] have fallen to a level which barely covers the transportation charges."

68 Watson, *Inequality among Brothers: Class and Kinship in South China*, 77.

69 See also Baker, *A Chinese Lineage Village: Sheung Shui*, 153. Baker also reports a Sheung Shui legend in which the strength of one male member of the community who supposedly lived in the 1700s was expressed in these terms: he was "capable of leaping [over] seven rows of sweet potato at once" (79).

The crop must have been very commonplace for it to be used as a yardstick of physical prowess in the tale.

70 Davis, 138–40.

71 An informant account suggests that the crop was grown in part for its good effects on land productivity. Palmer mentions the peanut-oil-press factory set up at the nearby Shek Wu Hui market in the 1920s (Michael Palmer, "Lineage and Urban Development in a New Territories Town," in *An Old State in New Settings: Studies in the Social Anthropology of China in Memory of Maurice Freedman*, ed. Hugh Baker and Stephan Feuchtwang [Oxford: JASO, 1991], 74).

72 Ping Shan and Tun Mun were noted for their production. See Oral History Project interview at Lung Yeuk Tau, July 9, 1982. Even at nearby Ha Tsuen, where there were peanut and sugar cane processing factories, the local peasants never had much involvement in growing the two crops according to Watson, *Inequality among Brothers: Class and Kinship in South China*, 80.

73 Baker, *A Chinese Lineage Village: Sheung Shui*, 92.

74 J. Watson covers "dry land" in San Tin and states, "Some of the dry fields produced crops of groundnuts, but many were used only to grow rough brush for fuel." (Watson, *Emigration and the Chinese Lineage: The Mans in Hong Kong and London*, 36–37, 46.) The author also suggests that catching "fish and shrimp from the river" was an important economic activity for members of the community (46). That no mention is made of growing sweet potatoes in the lineage is probably the result of omission. It seems that in Ha Tsuen a large portion of ancestral trust holdings was third-class land. Out of about 470 acres, only about 207 (44%) were first-class land. This is in part the effect of an atypical trust that consisted mostly of about 100 acre of third-class land. (If the 100 acres are excluded from the denominator, the first-class portion would be 56%.) The anomaly may be the result of accumulation of third-class land for some unusually profitable cash crop, which may also explain why an estimated 55% of Ha Tsuen villagers of the Sik Kong Wai hamlet owned no land at all. On the trust holdings and Sik Kong Wai holdings, see Watson, *Inequality among Brothers: Class and Kinship in South China*, 68, 65–66.

75 Lockhart's report on the land registration exercise mentions this factor in the case of a nearby area that was among the first to be dealt with (J. H. S. Lockhart, "New Territories Report for 1901" [1902], 7). About 13% of lots found to be under current or recent cultivation remained unclaimed, and they could be attributed to "poor cultivation in the occupation of mere squatters who are in no hurry to assume the burdens of ownership." C. M. Messer in Land Court states, "It was also decided to exclude from leases and rent rolls, sloping dry cultivation of a shifting nature to which the occupiers had no valid titled" ("New Territories: Land Court, Report on Work from 1900 to 1905" [Land Court], 1905, 149).

76 Helen F. Siu, "Where Were the Women? Rethinking Marriage Resistance and Regional Culture History," *Late Imperial China* 11, no. 2 (December 1990).

77   Ibid.
78   Most informants acknowledged considerable variation in the relationship. But there was an expectation that a mother-in-law would be harsh. They tended to have to rely on the mother-in-law for cooking and childcare during busy agricultural seasons.
79   The quality of a woman's relationship with her husband was obviously a factor in her predicament as a young wife. This complex issue is taken up elsewhere.
80   Some of the elderly women collect paper cartons, newspaper, and aluminum cans to sell for a few Hong Kong dollars. One woman has been admonished by her children, but would refrain from doing so only when they are in Hong Kong briefly.
81   This is contrary to some influential accounts in the literature, see below.
82   Chan, "Writing Women's Words: Bridal Laments and Representations of Kinship and Marriage in South China."
83   Rubie Watson, "Class Differences and Affinal Relations in South China," *Man* n.s. 16, no. 4 (December 1984): 593–613; Watson, *Inequality among Brothers: Class and Kinship in South China*, Chapter 7.
84   Martin King Whyte, "Revolutionary Social Change and Patrilocal Residence in China," *Ethnology* 18, no. 3 (1979): 211–27.
85   Ibid., 211.
86   Baker, *A Chinese Lineage Village: Sheung Shui*, 161.
87   Palmer, "The Surface-Subsoil Form of Divided Ownership in Late Imperial China: Some Examples from the New Territories of Hong Kong."
88   Interview at Sheung Shui Wai, November 4, 1981.
89   Ho Sheung Heung had a population of 580 in 1955 according to *A Gazetteer of Place Names in Hong Kong, Kowloon and the New Territories* (1969, 2–6). There were only about ten seamen during the prewar period, suggesting that sailors could be found in not much more than 10% of families in the same period.
90   Palmer, "Lineage and Urban Development in a New Territories Town," 74, 76.
91   Among them, Liu Hei Ting was, according to an interviewee of the Oral History Project, a *xiucai*'s son who worked as a teacher in the village and later as a "secretary" in a business firm based in metropolitan Hong Kong. See the project's notes for the interview at Sheung Shui, November 4, 1981. For Liu's involvement in the trucking business see Palmer (ibid., 77, note 19).
92   Compare Brim, "Local Systems and Modernizing Change in the New Territories of Hong Kong", 103–05. After the end of Japanese occupation in 1945, the husband of one of my informants in Sheung Shui obtained a job in the clinic at the nearby village of Kam Tsin.
93   One Ho Sheung Heung informant mentions that when his son emigrated around 1960, the family needed to raise three thousand Hong Kong dollars, and he borrowed part of the money from two married sisters.
94   Feil, 58–60.
95   Wolf, 36.
96   Feil, 58–60.

97   The argument is made with additional cases and in much more detail in Chan, "Writing Women's Words: Bridal Laments and Representations of Kinship and Marriage in South China."

Chapter 5

1   Margery Wolf, Roxane Witke, and Emily M. Ahern, eds., *Women in Chinese Society* (Stanford: Stanford University Press, 1975), 23–24 and 27. See also Dorothy Ko, *Teachers of the Inner Chambers: Women and Culture in Seventeenth-Century China* (Stanford: Stanford University Press, 1994).

2   Noboru Niida, "Chugoku Shufu No Chii to Kagi No Ken (Status of the Chinese Women and the Right of the Key)," in *Chugoku Noson Kazoku* (Chinese Rural Family) (Tokyo: Tokyo Daigaku Toyo Bunka Kenkyujo, 1952); Myron Cohen, "Family Management and Family Division in Contemporary Rural China," *China Quarterly*, no. 130 (1992); Joseph McDermott, "The Chinese Domestic Bursar," *Ajia Bunka Kenkyu* (Asian Cultural Studies), no. 2 (1990).

3   Myron Cohen, "Family Management and Family Division in Contemporary Rural China," *China Quarterly*, no. 130 (1992).

4   For example, Wang Xifeng, the very capable daughter-in-law, was manager of the family in *Hong Lao Meng* (The Dream of the Red Chamber). As for Zeng Zifan, see Thomas L. Kennedy and Micki Kennedy, eds., *Testimony of a Confucian Woman: The Autobiography of Mrs. Nie Zeng Jifen, 1852–1942* (Athens, G.A.; London: University of Georgia Press, 1993), 69, 90.

5   See Chi-cheung Choi, "Settlement of Chinese Families in Macau," in *Macau: City of Culture and Commerce,* ed. R. D. Cremer (Hong Kong: API Press, 1991).

6   For example, see C. R. Boxer, *South China in the Sixteenth Century* (Nendeln/ Liechtenstein: Kraus Reprint Limited, 1953 and 1967), 149ff.

7   See Elizabeth Perry, *Shanghai on Strike: The Politics of Chinese Labor* (Stanford: Stanford University Press, 1993); Alvin Y. So, *The South China Silk District: Local Historical Transformation and World-System Theory* (Albany: State University of New York Press, 1986).

8   Their power came unless they were in the inner chamber of the imperial court and exercised through their emperor son or grandson or through the eunuch.

9   "Special Resolution of Kin Tye Lung Co. Ltd," Company Registry (Hong Kong, 1988), Company no. 14575.

10   In this year, fifteen female members inherited 62,132 shares (11% of the total) of the company. See Company Registry (Hong Kong, 1992), Company no. 14575.

11   Since the death of Chen Sou-yan, proprietor and managing director of the family enterprise, decision making has been under his daughter's control. For the history of the company, see Chi-cheung Choi, "Competition among Brothers: The Kin Tye Lung Company and Its Associate Companies," in *Chinese Business Enterprise in Asia*, ed. Rajeswary Brown (London; New York: Routledge, 1995), 96–114.

12 Ta Chen, *Emigrant Communities in South China, a Study of Overseas Migration and Its Influence on Standards of Living and Social Change* (New York: Secretariat, Institute of Pacific Relations, 1940), 59.

13 Xiao Guanying, *Liushi Nian Lai Zhi Lingdong Jilue* (Accounts of Eastern Guangdong in the Recent Sixty Years) (Guangdong: Guangdong Renmin Chubanshe, 1996 [reprint of 1925]), 96.

14 Chen, 123.

15 Refer to Chi-cheung Choi, ed., *Business Documents and Land Deeds Collected by Dr. James Hayes: Kin Tye Lung Document*, vol. 1: *Land Deeds of the Chaoshan Region* (Tokyo: The Institute of Oriental Culture, Tokyo University, 1995).

16 For example, ibid., Land deed no. L35-1-1, 55.

17 Ibid., Land deed no. L10-2-2, 25.

18 *Chenghai Xianzhi* (Gazetteer of the Chenghai County) (Guangdong: Guangdong Renmin Chubanshe, 1991), 155.

19 Ta Chen, *Nan Yang Huaqiao Yu Minyue Shehui* (Southeast Asian Chinese and the Society of Fujian and Guangdong) (Changsha: Shangwu Publishing House, 1938), 130.

20 For example, refer to Choi, ed., *Business Documents and Land Deeds Collected by Dr. James Hayes: Kin Tye Lung Document*, vol. 1: *Land Deeds of the Chaoshan Region*. Land deed no. L27-1-1, L48-1-1, L99-1 and L125-1-1, 45, 71–2, 143–44, 201.

21 Chen, *Nan Yang Huaqiao Yu Minyue Shehui*, 35, 37.

22 Ibid., 36–37.

23 Ibid., 129.

24 Ibid., 31. Refer also to Shishun Chou, ed., *Chaozhou Fuzhi* (Gazetteer of Chaozhou Prefecture), vol. 3, book 12 (u.p., 1893), 5.

25 J. Dyer Ball, *Things Chinese: Or Notes Connected with China*, 5th ed. (Hong Kong and Shanghai: Kelly and Walsh, 1925), 718.

26 The story was widely reported in local literatures and retold by Chen Chunsheng. See Chen Chunsheng, "Tianhou Gushi Yu Shequ Lishi Zhuanbian: Zhanglin Sige Tianhou Miao De Yanjiu" (Stories of the Goddess of Heaven and the Historical Development of Local Communities: Study of Four Tianhou Temples in Zhanglin), *Chaoxue Yanjiu*, no. 8 (2000): 167–69.

27 Akira Suehiro, *Capital Accumulation in Thailand, 1855–1985* (Tokyo: UNESCO [The Centre for East Asian Cultural Studies], 1989), 84–87, 110ff.

28 For a comparison of these two companies, see Chi-cheung Choi, "Kinship and Business: Paternal and Maternal Kin in Chaozhou Chinese Family Firms," *Business History* 40, no. 1 (1998). For details of the development of Kin Tye Lung company, see Choi, "Competition among Brothers: The Kin Tye Lung Company and Its Associate Companies."

29 For example, Wanglee, founder of the Wanglee company in Bangkok and son of the founder of Kin Tye Lung in Hong Kong, enjoyed his retirement in their hometown as village and lineage head in the late nineteenth century. His eldest natal son, Limei, was born in Bangkok by his Thai Chinese wife, came "home"

in a coffin in the early 1920s. See Chi-cheung Choi, "Hometown Connection and the Chaozhou Business Networks: A Case Study of the Chens of Kintyelung, 1850–1950," in *the XIV International Economic Congress* (Session #71) (Helsinki, 2006).

30   For example, in Chen Limei's wills, pledged in 1927 in the Supreme Court in Hong Kong and Singapore, stated that after his death, his second concubine should go back to his home town, adopted a son and lived there until the end of her life. See "Hkrs No. 144, D&S No.4/3020 and 4/3792," Hong Kong Public Records Office.

31   There were three coffin houses (*guancai wu*) in the village, one for Wanglee (*Cihong*), one for Wanglee's Thai Chinese wife, and one for Wanglee's eldest natal son, Limei. The latter two were sent back from Bangkok. All three coffins were rested in the houses waiting for a graveyard of good geomancy. They were buried hastily in 1939 when the district was alarmed by the threats of the Japanese army.

32   The Chens as well as the Gaos of Yuanfa hang were famous of having many adopted sons. This can also be reflected in local proverbs "Chen Jia you Yangzi" (the Chen family has adopted sons) or "Gao jia you Yangzi." The Chens had four major housekeepers before 1949. Besides the adopted son, the other three were an affinal kin and two remote clan relatives who did not live in the village.

33   Peishen Yin, *Fengshan Jixu* (Accounts on Chenghai county) (u.p., n.d. [c.1810–1820]), 38b–39a. Before its establishment as a treaty port, Shantou area was under the jurisdiction of Chenghai county.

34   Ibid., 38–39.

35   Liang Tingnan, ed. *Yue Hai Guan Zhi* (Gazetteer of the Guangdong Maritime Customs), vol. 6 (u.p., c.1874).

36   *Shantou Bainian Dashiji, 1859–1959* (Major Events in Shantou from 1858 to 1959) (Shantou: Shantou Shi Zhi Bianxie Weiyuan Hui, 1960).

37   *Shantou Gaikuang* (General Survey of Shantou) (Shantou: Shantou Shi Defang Zhi Bianzuan Weiyuan Hui Bangong Shi, 1987), 6ff.

38   *Xin Shantou* (New Swatow) (Shantou: Shantou Shi Shizhengting Bianji Gu, 1928), 2.

39   *Chaohai Guanshiliao Huibian* (Collected Archives of Chaozhou Maritime Customs) (Zhongguo haiguan xuehui Shantou haiguan xiaozu and Shantou shi difangzhi bianzuan weiyuanhui bangong shi 1988), 23–24, 27. Refer also to Zongyi Rao, ed. *Chaozhou Zhi Huibian* (Gazetteers of Chaozhou Prefecture) (Xianggang: Longmen Shudian, 1965), 875.

40   Julean Arnold, ed., *Commercial Handbook of China*, vol. 1, Miscellaneous (Washington: Government Printing Office, Department of Commerce, 1919), no. 84, 600–10.

41   Rao, ed., 835–877.

42   See advertisements in Xie Xueying, ed., *Chao Mei Xianxiang* (Conditions in the Chaozhou Mei xian area) (Guangdong: Shantou Shi Tongxun She, 1935), 82, 83, 87, 90, 134ff.

43 Pan Xinlong, *Malaiya Chaoqiao Tongjian* (Gazetteer of the Chaozhou Chinese in Malaya) (u.p., 1950), 20; Xia Chenghua, *Jindai Guangdong Sheng Qiaohui Yanjiu (1862–1949): Yi Guang, Chao, Mei, Qiong Diqu Wei Li* (Study of Remittance of Guangdong Province in the Modern Period: Using Guangzhou, Chaozhou, Meizhou and Qiongzhou Districts as Examples) (Singapore: Xinjiapo Nanyang Xue Hui, 1992), 27.

44 Xie, ed., 44.

45 Sharon M. Lee, "Female Immigrants and Labor in Colonial Malaya: 1860–1947," *International Migration Review* 23, no. 2 (1989).

46 The sources Lee used are: Annual Reports of the Chinese Protectorate, Strait Settlements, 1881–1932, the Annual Reports of the Immigration Department, Strait Settlements and Federated Malay States, 1922–1938 and the Malayan Statistics Monthly digest, Singapore, 1939–1940.

47 "Zai Langhua Guanfan Zhong De Chaoshan Fun v (1)" (Chaoshan Wemen in the Turmoil of Waves), *Huazhi Ribao*, 2.18, 1935, 2.

48 "Zai Langhua Guanfan Zhong De Chaoshan Fun v (2)" (Chaoshan Wemen in the Turmoil of Waves), *Huazhi Ribao*, 2.19, 1935, 3.

49 Ibid.

50 It should also be noted that many women in the city worked as prostitutes serving the men of the business sector. It was said that, in the 1930s, there were many brothels in the Shantou city. Xie, ed., 35.

51 This can be found in some private accounting papers of the Tan Guan Lee company, an associate company of Kin Tye *Lung* in Singapore (private collection).

52 Interview, mother of vice-mayor Xu of Chenghai county. Xu was a descendant of the Gaos of Yuanfa hang. He was adopted by his uncle (his mother's brother) in the 1950s and thereby changed his surname.

53 Frank H. H. King, *The Hong Kong Bank between the Wars and the Bank Interned, 1919–1945: Return from Grandeur* (Cambridge: Cambridge University Press, 1988), 496–97.

54 Rao, ed., 868.

55 Suehiro, 83.

56 The Gaos had trading companies in Singapore (Yuan Fa Chan), Kobe, Japan (Wen Fa Hang) and Canton (Cheng Fa Hang), a trading enterprise (Yuan Fa Sheng Hang, or Koh Mah Wah and companies as it was known in Bangkok) including five rice mills in Bangkok, a plantation in Johor, Malaysia and in Shantou several public utilities companies (water, electricity), a textile factory, and Chinese banks. They also owned warehouses in Hong Kong and Canton. See Lin Xi, "Cong Xianggang Di Yuanfa Hang Tanqi" (Talking from Yuan Fat Hong in Hong Kong), *Da Cheng*, no. 117–121 (1983); Lin Xi, "Gao Zizheng Gong Qianbiao Yu Gao Chuxiang Jia Zhuan" (Obituary and Biography of Gao Chuxiang), *Da Cheng*, no. 121 (1983). Lin Xi is the pseudonym of Gao Zhenbai, a grandson of Gao Chuxiang. See also K. C. Fok, "Lineage Ties, Business Partnership and Financial Agency: The Many Roles of a Hong Kong Commercial Network," in *the Preliminary Workshop for the 11th International Economic History Congress* (Milan, Atami, Japan, 1994).

57 See Zhang Y. Q., "Taiguo Huaqiao Gao Chuxiang Yu Hongli Jiazu Di Yeji" (Achievements of the Thai Chinese Gao Chuxiang and Chen Hongli Families), in *Shantou Wenshi* (1990), 31–3.

58 As suggested by Wellington Chan, in order to minimize risk and maximize opportunities, many Chinese businesses tend to have their shares and directors intertwined with each other. See W. K. K. Chan, "Chinese Business Networking and the Pacific Rim: The Family Firm, Roles Past and Present," *Journal of American-East Asian Relations* 1, no. 2.

59 For instance, the "common company," the forth and fifth branch of the family had shares in the Yuan Zhang Sheng rice mill in Bangkok. The "common company" also had shares in the Yu De Sheng, a Nanbei *hang* company owned by Chen Chunquan, his son and Shunqin.

60 For example, the Yu De Sheng and Fu Tai Xiang in Hong Kong, and Cheng Fa Hang in Canton. Lin, "Cong Xianggang Di Yuanfa Hang Tanqi" (Talking from Yuan Fat Hong in Hong Kong), no. 117: 52; no. 118: 48.

61 See Chi-cheung Choi, "Dongnan Ya Huaren Jiazu Qiye De Jiegou: Qiantai Long Yu Yuanfa Hang De Bijiao Yanjiu" (Structure of Southeast Asian Chinese Family Firms: A Comparative Study of the Kin Tye Lung and Yuanfa Hang), in *Southeast Asian Chinese and Chinese Economy and Society*, ed. Hou-seng Lim (Singapore: Singapore Society of Asian Studies, 1995), 98–99.

62 "Lugang Chaozhou Shanghui Sanshi Zhounian Jinian Tekan" (Special Bulletin Commemorating the Thirtieth Anniversary of the Chaozhou Chamber of Commerce) (Hong Kong: Lugang Chaozhou Shanghui [Hong Kong Chaozhou Chamber of Commerce], 1951), 2.

63 Ibid.

64 See Lin, "Cong Xianggang Di Yuanfa Hang Tanqi" (Talking from Yuan Fat Hong in Hong Kong), no. 118: 47, 50.

65 Ibid., 48–49.

66 Ibid., 50.

67 Ibid., no. 119: 35–6.

68 Lin Xi, "Yijiu Sansan Nian Shantou Jinrong Fengchao" (The 1933 Financial Crisis in Shantou), *Da Cheng*, no. 22 (1967): 4.

69 See "Special Resolution of Kin Tye Lung Co. Ltd."

70 G. William Skinner, *Chinese Society in Thailand: An Analytical History* (Ithaca, N.Y.: Cornell University Press, 1957), 127.

71 Ibid., 128.

72 Chi-cheung Choi, "Cong Yizhu Kan Jindai Chaoshan Jiazu Qiye De Fazhan: Yi Xianggang Qiantai Longji Mangu Hongli Chen Shi We Li" (Development of Family Business in Modern Chaoshan Area: A View from Wills, Using the Chens of Kinn Tye *Lung* in Hong Kong and Wanglee in Bangkok as Example), *Journal of Resources for Hong Kong Studies*, no. 1 (1998).

73 Suehiro and Nanbara, *Tai No Zaibatsu* (Thai's financial tycoons) (Tokyo: Tongbun kan, 1991).

74 "Text Book of Documentary Chinese: Selected and Designed for the Special Use of Members of the Civil Services of the Straits Settlements and the Protected Native States" (Singapore, 1894).

75 See discussions in Ko (1994), So (1986), and Wolf and Witke (1975).

Chapter 6

1 *Hongkong Telegraph,* September 24, 1895, 289–90.

2 *Hong Kong Government Gazette,* October 25, 1879.

3 The spelling of the name has been inconsistent. The Portuguese use "Macau", but "Macao" has been used in English-language literature. The editor has left the term the way Carl Smith has used it.

4 Carl T. Smith, "A Comparative Study of Eurasians in Macau and Hong Kong," in *Meeting Point of Cultures: Macau and Ethnic Diversity in Asia* (Macau: Instituto Cultural de Macau, 1993).

5 For a discussion of the word "Tanka," see Carl Smith, "Protected Women in 19th-Century Hong Kong," in *Women and Chinese Patriarchy: Submission, Servitude, and Escape,* ed. Maria Jachok and Suzanne Miers (London: Zed Books Ltd., 1994), 236.

6 "The half-caste population of Hongkong were . . . almost exclusively the offspring of these Tan-ka women." E. J. Eitel, *Europe in China, the History of Hongkong from the Beginning to the Year 1882* (Taipei: Chen-Wen Publishing Co., originally published in Hong Kong by Kelly and Walsh, 1895, 1968), 169.

7 Charles Toogood Downing, *The Fan-Qui in China 1836–37,* vol. 1 (1838), 28–29.

8 William Maxwell Wood, *Fankwei; or, the San Jacinto in the Seas of India, China, and Japan* (New York: Harper and Brothers, 1859), 289–90. See also the images of boatwomen drawn by George Chinnery in Patrick Conner, *George Chinnery: 1774–1852: Artist of India and the China Coast* (Woodbridge, Suffolk: Antique Collectors' Club, 1993). Color Plates 70, 71, Plate 126, 127, 199–200. A 1984 edition of Conner's book was not found.

9 Conner quote from Wood, see Conner, *George Chinnery: 1774–1852: Artist of India and the China Coast,* 202; Wood, *Fankwei; or, the San Jacinto in the Seas of India, China, and Japan,* 290.

10 Conner quote from Downing. See Conner, *George Chinnery: 1774–1852: Artist of India and the China Coast,* 202; Downing, *The Fan-Qui in China 1836–37,* 28–9.

11 In an early document, Memorial 77, one of these lots records their original designation: number 3 in row 5 of the Bazaar Lots.

12 This is a term for Indian seamen employed in European ships. The term is rarely used today.

13 Chinese names and designations of grantor and grantee are given in English in the Memorials. They are accompanied by Chinese characters, which do not

always correspond to the English. My reference to the name of the grantor/ grantee is given as it appears in English. The version following "otherwise" is a Cantonese romanization of the Chinese characters given in the record.

14 "Hong Kong Land Registry," Memorial 559.

15 Ibid., Memorial 956.

16 A *serang* or *ghaut serang* was a recruiter and contractor of lascar seamen to man vessels plying the eastern seas.

17 "Hong Kong Land Registry," Memorial 714.

18 Ibid., Memorials 555, 626.

19 Ibid., Memorials 526, 563.

20 K. J. P. Lowe, "Hong Kong, 26 January 1841: Hoisting the Flag Revisited," *Journal of the Hong Kong Branch of the Royal Asiatic Society,* vol. 29 (1989). In my opinion, some of the data in this article should be used with caution.

21 *Probate File,* No. 1132 of 878 (4/365).

22 "Hong Kong Land Registry," Memorial 571.

23 Ibid., Memorials 516, 591.

24 Ibid., Memorial 728.

25 Ibid., Memorial 77.

26 Ibid., Memorial 1835.

27 Ibid., Memorials 459, 3058, 5291.

28 Barbara-Sue White, *Turbans and Traders, Hong Kong's Indian Communities* (Hong Kong: Oxford University Press, 1994), 66.

29 Peter Hall, *In the Web* (London: Basingstoke Press 1992), 32, Appendix, Genealogical Charts No. 3: Anderson/Overbeck, 167, No. 29: Overbeck, 93, No. 35: Tyson, 99, No. 36: Tyson, 200. I have been unable to identify a person named Bartou as resident on the China coast. Could the man have been Dr George Kingston Barton, a partner of Dr Thomas Hunter? They had a dispensary at Macau and Hong Kong in the 1840s. Dr Barton married Rhoda Dobbs in Hong Kong in 1850.

30 "Hong Kong Land Registry," Memorial 4320.

31 The date of death of Lam A-shui is left blank in Memorial 18,631. Her daughter, Chan Quay Neo (a Malaysian romanization) married Choa Lap-chee, a member of an old Malacca Chinese family, who moved to Hong Kong. See Hall, *In the Web.* Genealogical Chart No 35: Tyson/Chan, 199; and Genealogical Chart No. 9: Choa, 173.

32 These facts are recited in Memorial 18,631, dated April 1, 1891 for the conveyance of sub-section 1 of Section A of Inland Lot 110. In the 1871 and 1876 Rate lists, E.C. Ray is named as the agent for the owner of the lot. He succeeded Gustav Overbeck as the protector of Lam Tsat-tai.

33 There are difficulties in interpretation of records of Lam Fong-kew and Lam Kew-fong. "Mother" Chan, of the Lam family, otherwise Chan mo Lam, is buried at the Chiu Yuen Cemetery, Mount Davis Road, Pokfulam. Her gravestone records her birth as 1843, her death as 1925, and her sons as Kai-ming and Kai-cheung. Chan Kai-ming was also known as George Tyson. However, the land

records indicate that the woman who died in 1925 was Lam Kew-fong was protected by Albert Farley Heard and Lam Fong-kew, who died in 1871 was protected by George Tyson. It is possible that George Tyson was the first protector of Lam Fong-kew, and Albert Farley Heard her second protector.

34   "Hong Kong Land Registry," Memorial 17, 281.

35   Ibid., Memorial 5724, dated May 3, 1873. The property was section B of Inland Lot 94. Lot 94 was a large tract extending from Caine Road to Staunton Street owned by Augustine Heard, the younger. Section B was on the farthest corner from the Heard mansion on Caine Road. Before Albert F. Heard conveyed the lot to Lam Kew-fong, the property had been occupied by "Miss Li Kiu." Her name appears on the Rates lists from 1869 to 1872 and was replaced in 1873 by that of Lam Kew-fong. In 1869 the owner of this small lot was A. Heard and Co, but it had been crossed out, and the name Lee Kee was written in. In the official title for the lot there is no record of a transfer to Lee Kiu/Li Kiu, although she is listed as occupant and owner until 1873. Augustine Heard, the younger, in 1866 sold the whole of lot 94 to a consortium of six of its Chinese employees (Memorials 4032, 4033). The consortium sold Section B, the small corner lot, in February 1867 to Albert Farley Heard for $500 (Memorial 4199). As mentioned above, it was occupied by Li Kiu. She may have died in 1872, and perhaps was protected by A. F. Heard. The circumstances suggest that he had a similar relationship with Lam Kew-fong, who may, in turn, have been previously protected by George Tyson.

36   "Macau Land Registry," B-1, 211, No. 193, dated July 10, 1873. The lot was No. 8 (otherwise No. 17) Travessa Matre Tigre in the Bazarinho section of S. Lourenco parish. I have not found any record of the disposal of this property. An adjoining house belonged to John Heard.

37   "Hong Kong Land Registry," Memorial 5689, dated May 7, 1873, Inland Lot 110, remaining part. "Hong Kong Land Registry," Memorial 8459, dated October 1, 1879.

38   "Hong Kong Land Registry." Memorials 7788, 7892, 7893, and 18,632. Lots 183 and 184 were bounded south by Gage Street, east by Graham Street, and west by Peel Street.

39   Ibid., Memorial 4870, dated October 26, 1869, Inland Lots 491 and 490. Section A. Memorial 6261, dated May 15, 1875.

40   Ibid., Memorial 5688, dated May 7, 1873, Inland Lot 110, Section D. The vendor was the Parsee merchant, Dadabhoy Cowasjee Tata, Memorial 22,681, dated September 27, 1896. The purchaser was Lung Lin-hin.

41   Ibid., Memorial 6774, dated August 29, 1876, Inland Lot 110, sub-section 2 of Section A. The lot had been purchased by William Hammond Foster, junior, in of Russell and Co. in 1867. "For diverse considerations and good causes" he conveyed it in 1873 to Kwok A-cheong, single woman. She died the following year and her father, Kwok Foon Tuck, was appointed administrator of her estate. In 1875 he conveyed it to John Murray Forbes, Jr., as trustee for Kwok A-cheong's children. Memorials 4321, 5564, 6113, and 6114.

42 Ibid., Memorial 14,899, dated February 12, 1887. The two properties were leased for $1,440 per annum.

43 Her name is given as Akew in the newspaper accounts of the "Cumsingmun Affair" in *China Mail*, September 27, November 1, 1849. and *The Friend of China*, October 13, 1849. In 1875 she is called Hung Mow (red haired) Akew, "a stout Chinese woman."

44 Account in *China Mail*, October 13, 1849: "Several years ago Captain J. B. Endicott, now of the American opium receiving ship *Ruparell*, purchased (as was then common with foreigners) a Chinese girl named Akeu; she has lived with him since and is the mother of several children. Akeu is a shrewd, intelligent woman, without any of those feelings of degradation which Europeans attach to females in her condition."

45 "Hong Kong Land Registry," Memorial 662, dated October 18, 1852.

46 Ibid., Memorial 663.

47 James Bridges Endicott, in his will stated, "Sensible of unceasing care and devotion she [his wife Sarah Anne Russell Endicott] has at all times displayed toward myself and all my children, as well as those who stand in relationship of step-children as of her own, she having made no distinction in the treatment of them, and I trust when I am no more my three children, Henry, James and Sarah, will be aware of obligation which they are under to her and always display a true sense of gratitude for the unceasing care and attention she has bestowed on them from our marriage to the present time, through which they have been mainly enabled to hold the position they now enjoy, and anxious to requite the love and attention they have received of her, they will unite with her own children, Sarah Anne, Lucy Russell and Robert Russell, my said sons Henry and James will contribute to their support." Hong Kong Public Records Office, "Probate File," No. 104 of 1870 (4/227).

48 *The Friend of China*, December 6, 1856. Fung/Foong Aching, a native of Shun-te District, Guangdong Province, bought land in Hong Kong in 1845. He died in 1881. Letters of administration on his estate were granted to his son, Foong Chi. "Hong Kong Land Registry," Memorial 10,764.

49 James Norton-Kyshe, *The History of the Laws and Courts of Hong Kong*, vol. 2, 317. Does this may mean that Akew was actively engaged in the brothel business or that she owned property that was rented to brothel keepers?

50 "Hong Kong Land Registry." Memorials 56,759, 60,958, 61066. If Akew lived until 1914, she would have been aged about ninety-four years.

51 Susanna Hoe, *The Private Life of Old Hong Kong: Western Women in the British Colony, 1841–1941* (Hong Kong: Oxford University Press, 1991), 111–19.

52 *China Mail*, February 27, 1872.

53 *Daily Advertiser*, July 4, 1872.

54 *Daily Press*, August 25, 1876.

55 John Olsen was a Swede and a tavern keeper. He also had a Chinese wife. She was Mrs Ellen Olsen, otherwise Au Chung Ah-fung, who was baptized in 1891 at To Tsai Church, Hong Kong. They had three children, baptized by the Rev. Mr Ost of the Anglican Church.

56 *Probate File* No. 1035 of 1876 (4/334).

57 January 21, 1880.

58 *China Mail,* March 8, 1881.

59 The child may be the George McBreen who was enrolled at the Diocesan Home and Orphanage in 1889.

60 At the time Mrs McBreen lived there, North Bridge Street, Singapore was occupied by brothels catering to Europeans. See James Francis Warren, "Chinese Prostitution in Singapore: Recruitment and Brothel Organisation," in *Women and Chinese Patriarchy: Submission, Servitude, and Escape*, ed. Maria Jaschok and Suzanne Miers (Hong Kong: Hong Kong University Press; London; Atlantic Highlands, N.J.: Zed Books, 1994), 92–94.

61 *China Mail,* May 21, 1889, *Daily Press,* September 16, 1889. In 1898, a Mr McBreen gave information about the brothel business to Singapore authorities, Watson, op. cit., 90, 101. John Francis Webber was a disreputable character who left Hong Kong for Singapore under a cloud in 1891. Perhaps the McBreens went with him.

62 An exception would have been the Hong Kong Macaenese and "local" Muslim communities, although among some individuals, they may have had reservations.

Chapter 7

1 See Peter Hall, *In the Web* (London: Basingstoke Press 1992), 99, 112–14.

2 Florence Yeo, *My Memories* (Pittsburgh, P.A.: Dorrance Publishing Co., Inc, 1994), 12.

3 Irene Cheng, *Lady Clara Ho Tung: A Hong Kong Lady, Her Family and Her Times* (Hong Kong: Chinese University of Hong Kong, 1980, first published 1976), 7.

4 For more details on Lady Margaret Ho Tung, Mak Sau Ying, see Xiaohong Lee et al., eds., *Biographical Dictionary of Chinese Women* (New York: M.E. Sharpe, 1998), 69–71.

5 Robert Ho Tung (1862–1956). Born on December 22, 1862 in Hong Kong with the original name as He Qidong and the style name as Xiao Sheng, Robert was the first generation of Eurasians but took his Chinese identity seriously. "Little is known of his father except that he was a British of Dutch descent and his name was Bosman" (*South China Morning Post,* January 27, 1991). His Chinese mother's native place could be traced back to Guangdong Baoan. Robert was the second child of the family, but the eldest son, after a sister and was followed by four brothers and two sisters. He was educated at the Central School (later Queen's College) and graduated in 1878. He then worked as pupil teacher at the School before entering the Chinese Imperial Maritime Customs in Canton in 1878. Starting from 1880, he became the compradore for the Messrs. Jardine, Matheson & Co and was a millionaire before the age of thirty, which won him both fortune and reputation in the colony. He then invested widely in Hong

Kong and elsewhere. Due to sickness, he retired from his compradore position in 1900, but was still very active in the colony's economy, politics, and philanthropy. "He was always involved with public matters relating to Chinese population. He was the chief founder and the first President of the Chinese Club in 1899" (quoting Peter Hall. He was made Justice of Peace in 1889, knighted by King George V in 1915 and by Queen Elizabeth II in 1955, and received honors from many other countries. He sat on a number of boards of directors, including Tung Wah Hospital and Po Leung Kuk, and represented Hong Kong at the British Empire Exhibition at Wembley in 1924–25. He helped the Hong Kong government settle strike disputes in 1922 and 1925. He proposed the famous "Round Table Conference" among warlords in China. He made huge donations to the colony's war effort during the two world wars, and financed Generalissimo Chiang Kai-shek of the Kuomintang [Guomindang] on the mainland. Education and hospitals were two main items of his philanthropic contributions in Hong Kong and Macau. He died on April 26, 1956 at the age of ninety-four and earned the title of "The Grand Old Man of Hong Kong." For more details on Robert, see Cheng, *Lady Clara Ho Tung: A Hong Kong Lady, Her Family and Her Times*, 1, 2, 7–9, 86, 112, 42–57, 85; Sing-lim Woo, *Xianggang Huaren Mingren Shilue* (Hong Kong: Wuchou Publishing, 1937); Wen Xiang He, *Xianggang Jiazu Shi* (Hong Kong: Capital Communications Corporation Limited, 1989), 5–55; Hall, *In the Web*, 118–19, 80–82. (See also, the personal account of two or her children, Florence and Jean.)

6   For the original letter, see Cheng, *Lady Clara Ho Tung: A Hong Kong Lady, Her Family and Her Times*, 12; He, *Xianggang Jiazu Shi*, 22–23.

7   For more details on Lady Clara's life, see her own biographical notes in Jingrong Zhang, *Mingshan Youji* (Hong Kong: Private publication, 1935); Cheng, *Lady Clara Ho Tung: A Hong Kong Lady, Her Family and Her Times*; Irene Cheng, *Intercultural Reminiscences* (Hong Kong: David C. Lam Institute for East-West Studies, Hong Kong Baptist University, 1997); Jean Gittins, "Eastern Windows – Western Skies" (Hong Kong: South China Morning Post, 1969; Yeo, *My Memories*; Shai-lai Ho, *Xianci Hemu Zhang Taifuren Lianjue Jushi Shengping Yixing Buyi* (Hong Kong: Private publication, 1954); Shai-lai Ho, *Hemu Zhang Taifuren Bazhi Mingshou Jilian Ji* (Hong Kong: Private publication, 1954); Susanna Hoe, "Clara Ho Tung, 1875–1938," in *Chinese Footprints* (Hong Kong: Roundhouse Publications, 1997).

8   For more examples, see Cheng, *Lady Clara Ho Tung: A Hong Kong Lady, Her Family and Her Times*, 4, 6, 9, 50, 66, 75, 73–4, 98, 153; Gittins, "Eastern Windows – Western Skies" 86, 71. Yeo, *My Memories*. See also Ho, *Xianci Hemu Zhang Taifuren Lianjue Jushi Shengping Yixing Buyi*, 6.

9   Cheng, *Lady Clara Ho Tung: A Hong Kong Lady, Her Family and Her Times*, 4, 179. See also Cheng, *Intercultural Reminiscences*, 51–52.

10 Keeping the vegetarian vow is a common Buddhist practice. It means that the practitioner is willing to abstain his or her pleasure for food to transfer the merit onto the loved ones. In this case, Clara kept the vow for her mother's

next life and probably also for her husband's health and longevity. For more details on the religious roots of vegetarianism, see Holmes Welch, *The Practice of Chinese Buddhism 1900–1950* (Cambridge, M.A.: Harvard University Press, 1973, first published 1967), 112, 365.

11 Cheng, *Lady Clara Ho Tung: A Hong Kong Lady, Her Family and Her Times*, 99, 112–14. Zhang, *Mingshan Youji*, 92; Ho, *Hemu Zhang Taifuren Bazhi Mingshou Jilian Ji*, 4.

12 Cheng, *Lady Clara Ho Tung: A Hong Kong Lady, Her Family and Her Times*, 17, 99.

13 Gittins, "Eastern Windows – Western Skies"; Cheng, *Intercultural Reminiscences*, 70.

14 Lin Lengzhen (1899–1966) née Lin Shunqun was born in Japan. She was a distant relative of the Ho Tung family and she and Lady Clara addressed each other as cousins; and others simply called her Cousin Lin (Lin *biaogu*). She received her education in Japan until the age of fifteen when her father died, and she returned Hong Kong. Influenced by Lady Clara, she became interested in Buddhism, took refuge vows under two monks, and assumed two more Buddhist names, Lengzhen and Guanzhen. To assist Lady Clara in her Buddhist business, Lin decided not to marry. She was not only a central figure of the Yuen, but also an active member who earned respect in the local Buddhist community. For more information on Lin, see Cheng, *Lady Clara Ho Tung: A Hong Kong Lady, Her Family and Her Times*, 8; Cheng, *Intercultural Reminiscences*, 21. *Dayushan Zhi* (Lantau Gazetteer) (Hong Kong, 1958), 37, 67; *Baojue Liankan* (Baojue Annual) Vol.11 (1966); *Xianggang Fojiao Lianhehui Huikan Ji Chuangli Wushi Zhounian Jinxi Jinian Tekan* (Hong Kong: Hong Kong Buddhist Association, 1995), 141.

15 Cheng, *Lady Clara Ho Tung: A Hong Kong Lady, Her Family and Her Times*, 125.

16 In Buddhism, there are different sets of rules and ceremonies to define and differentiate common laity, such as being refuge disciples or tonsure disciple. Lay Buddhists who hope to be admitted as refuge disciples must keep the Three Jewels Refuges (the Buddha, the Buddhist truth, and the congregation of clergy) and the Five Vows (promise not to kill, steal, lie, drink alcoholic beverages, or commit any immoral sexual act), and to learn from a master ordained Buddhist. One can follow more than one Buddhist masters. For more details, see Welch, *The Practice of Chinese Buddhism 1900–1950*, 317, 58, 64.

17 Interview with Irene Cheng, November 18, 1996: the Buddhist name for Victoria was Lian Jie; Daisy was Lian Hui; Eva was Lian Jing; and Irene was Lian Sheng. Daisy, the second daughter who eventually suffered from mental instability, did not go on the trip, but Lady Clara took the refuge vow in her daughter's stead, probably for the blessing of her health.

18 The interpretation of the May Fourth Movement has been a controversial one. Vera Schwarz attempts to downplay the movement as an "unfinished business" whose main significance was its legacy as only an allegory for generations to

come, see Vera Schwarz, *The Chinese Enlightenment: Intellectuals and the Legacy of the May Fourth Movement of 1919* (Berkeley: University of California Press, 1986).

19 Cheng, *Lady Clara Ho Tung: A Hong Kong Lady, Her Family and Her Times*, 122.

20 Sir Robert Ho Tung's involvement in the political arena during the Republican period can also be found in *Zhonghua Minguo Shishi Rizhi: 1922–1926*, vol. 3 (Taipei: u.d.).

21 Zhang Lianjue, *Mingshan Youji*, 70.

22 That was the Qixia Si, which needed restoration because of the damage done during the Taiping Rebellion. The restoration was also aimed at reviving and reforming the Monastery. For more details of the Ho Tung couple's visit, their donation, their long-term patronage, the inscription of the plaque, and the personal relationship between Clara and the abbot, see Zhu Jiexuan, *Qixia Shan Zhi* (*The Gazetteer of Qixiashan*) (unknown published place, 1962), 73, 97, 117, 139–41; Shi Dong Chu, *Zhonghua Fojiao Jindai Shi*, 738.

23 Cheng, *Lady Clara Ho Tung: A Hong Kong Lady, Her Family and Her Times*, 137.

24 Ibid., xii and 121. The first draft of the travelogue was prepared by Chiu Kutum (Zhao Jian) and later revised by Lady Clara's Buddhist friend and tutor, Ting-yuk Leung (Liang Tingyu). For more details on Lady Clara's 1916 pilgrimage, see her travelogue, *Mingshan Youji* and Cheng, *Lady Clara Ho Tung: A Hong Kong Lady, Her Family and Her Times*, 120–21.

25 On Lady Clara's observations about Buddhism in Guangdong, see *Mingshan Youji*, 54, 80–84.

26 Zhang Lainjue, *Mingshan Youji,* 80.

27 Zhang Lianjue, *Mingshan Youji*, 83–84.

28 The relationship between monk Shi Ai Ting and Lady Clara will be elaborated in the chapter. For a detailed background of the monk, see *Ai Ting Fashi Jinian Kan* (Commemorative Issue on Master Ai Ting) (Hong Kong: Private publication, 1948).

29 Ai Ting Shi, "Wosuo Renshi Di Lianjue Jushi-2" (What I Knew about Laywoman Lin-Kok – Part II), *Huanan Jueyin* 29: 32, 1941.

30 Ibid., 36.

31 Ai Ting Shi, "Wosuo Renshi Di Lianjue Jushi-1" (What I Knew about Laywoman Lin-Kok – Part I) *Huanan jueyin* 27 and 28: 36–37. 1941. See also Zhang Lainjue, *Mingshan Youji*, 40–42.

32 Zhang Lianjue, *Mingshan Youji,* 3–4.

33 Zhang Lianjue, *Mingshan Youji*, 104.

34 Cheng, *Lady Clara Ho Tung: A Hong Kong Lady, Her Family and Her Times*, 83, 101.

35 Gittins, "Eastern Windows – Western Skies," 105.

36 Susanna Hoe, "Clara Ho Tung, 1875–1938," 234.

37 For references to Clara's public and social engagements, see *Hong Kong Government Administrative Report* (*1916, 1927, 1928, 1931, 1932, 1935*); *Royal Society for the Prevention of Cruelty to Animals: 75 Anniversary Commemorative Issue* (1996). *Huazi Ribao,* December 9, 1938; also see Lady Clara's obituary, *South China Morning Post,* January 6, 1938, p. 10, which described her as a "prominent Social Worker the Colony loses."

38 Cheng, *Lady Clara Ho Tung: A Hong Kong Lady, Her Family and Her Times,* 3–4, 100.

39 For more details on the visit, see Zhang Jingrong, *Mingshan Youji,* 97; words quoted in the paragraph are from ibid., 100.

40 Zhang Jingrong, *Clara Ho Tung,* 101–5.

41 For information on monk Shi Bao Jing, see *Baojing Dashi Quanji* (The Collection on Master Bao Jing) (Hong Kong: Private publication, 1979). Monk Shi Yuan Can (1873–1967) was from Guangdong and among the first group of clergy coming to Hong Kong in 1911. Ordained at the age of fifteen, he was once a student disciple of another famous monk, Miao Can (refer to the previous chapter for background information). He was well-known for his extensive travels and public lectures. Besides Hong Kong, he had been to Japan and other Southeast Asian countries. Because of his radical and strong opinions towards Tai Xu's reformation ideas, he was a controversial figure in the Chinese Buddhist circle. In time, he settled down in Hong Kong and founded a Buddhist institution in Causeway Bay called Weixin foxueshe. He also bought the hermitage on Lantau Island, Bayan ge, from a nun for his retirement. The two-story hermitage was initially founded in 1926. His funeral was an occasion in Hong Kong with days of newspaper coverage. For more information on Yuan Can, see Ming Hui, *Dayushan Zhi,* op. cit., 36, 52; Shi Ming Hui, *Yuan Can Laofashi Jilian Ji* (The Commemorate Issue on the Old Master Yuan Can) (Hong Kong: Private publication, 1967); Man-yee Ip, "Xianggang Zaoqi Zhi Fojiao Fazhan" (The Early Development of Buddhism in Hong Kong), *The Dharmalakshana Buddhist Institute Buddhist Journal* III (November 1992): 49.

42 Zhang Jing Rong, *Mingshan Youji,* 103–4.

43 Cheng, *Lady Clara Ho Tung: A Hong Kong Lady, Her Family and Her Times,* 100–1.

44 For example, Lady Clara and some of her Buddhist friends organized the visit of a Japanese monk to Hong Kong. For details, see Ip, "Xianggang Zaoqi Zhi Fojiao Fazhan" (The Early Development of Buddhism in Hong Kong), 37.

45 Jinglin Wang, *Zhongguo Gudai Siyuan Shenghuo* (Xian: Shanxi Renmin Chubanshe, 1991).

   The "Water and Land" ritual service is the largest activity and "festival" celebrated in Chinese Buddhist monasteries and lasts from a minimum of seven to forty-nine days, depending on the request of patrons. Usually, the service could mobilize the entire monastery, or on some larger occasions, the combined efforts of several monasteries would be employed. The main purpose of the ritual service is to say prayers for the dead, the ghosts, and spirits of all sides and all levels. The reputation and status of clergy and monasteries taking part is closely related to the effectiveness of the service. The venue could be at one of the monasteries, a patron's residence, or in the open space near the monastery. The service was not inherited from Indian Buddhism, but was formulated by a devoted Buddhist Chinese Emperor in AD 505. The complication level of the ritual and setting again depend on the scale of the service, which could include chanting different Buddhist scriptures day and night, specifically those for the dead, specially chanted by 108 monks. There are also elaborate food offering rituals to ghosts and spirits.

46 For more background information of Qixia Si, and its restoration project, see Zhu Jiexuan, *Qixia Shan Zhi*.

47 Zhang Jingrong, *Mingshan Youji*, 97–98.

48 Ip, "Xianggang Zaoqi Zhi Fojiao Fazhan" (The Early Development of Buddhism in Hong Kong), 27.

49 For more details on the activity, see ibid., 21, 27.

50 Zhang Jingrong, *Mingshan Youji*, 100–1.

51 For more details of the assassination, see Vivienne Poy, *A River Named Lee* (Scarborough, Ont.: Calyan Publishing Ltd. , 1995), 1, 2, 59–63.

52 Ibid., 45, 52, 58.

53 Zhang Jingrong, *Mingshan Youji*, 105.

54 Poy, *A River Named Lee*, 63.

55 For background on the Lee Gardens and Lee Theatre, see ibid., 40–41; Vivienne Poy, *Building Bridges: The Life and Times of Richard Charles Lee, Hong Kong: 1905–1983* (Canada: Calyan Publishing Ltd., 1998).

56 He, *Xianggang Jiazu Shi*, 113. The Lee family has been a patron of local Buddhist development, even in recent times, for example, the HK$1,000,000 donation to the Bronze Buddha project finished in 1992.

57 Tung Lin Kok Yuen was founded on May 10, 1935 (the 8th day of the fourth month in the Chinese lunar calendar). There are different dates to commemorate Buddhism. These dates also differ among Buddhist countries in northern and southern Asia. In China, for example, Buddhists commemorate Buddha's death on the 15th day of the second month, Buddha's birthday on the 8th day of the fourth month, Buddha's enlightenment on the 8th day of the twelfth month. These dates are based on the Chinese lunar calendar; according to which the year of Buddha began in 486 BC when the year was believed to be Buddhist death. In many Southeastern Asian Buddhist countries, Buddhists celebrate Buddha's birthday, death, and enlightenment on the same day, April 15. For these countries, the year of Buddha began 59 years later than in the North, in 545 BC. For more details on the Yuen's opening, see *Renhaideng* (The Lamp of the Sea of Man), vol. 2, no. 13 (June 1935): 207–9.

58 The Enlightened Voice, 1941, vol. 29, 32.

59 For more information on the layout and function of the chamber, see Cheng, *Lady Clara Ho Tung: A Hong Kong Lady, Her Family and Her Times*, 104–5.

60 Zhang Jingrong, *Mingshan Youji*, 107–8.

61 Yong Ming Shi, *Xianggang Fojiao Yu Fosi* (Hong Kong: Po Lin Monastery, 1992), 49.

62 Zhang Jingrong, *Mingshan Youji*, 108.

63 Ho, *Hemu Zhang Taifuren Bazhi Mingshou Jilian Ji*, 5, 21.

64 Zhang Jingrong, *Mingshan Youji*, 107–8.

65 Mantao Zhang, ed., *Xiandai Fojiaoxueshu Congkan 86: Mingguo Fojiao Pian* (Taipei: Dasheng wenhua chuban she, 1978), 333. The year 1937 was a turning point in the Buddhist Reformation movement in China, as marked by the Japanese invasion, the shifting of the agenda among reformist Buddhists from a religious to a patriotic cause. In the 1930s, there were clergy fleeing to Hong Kong first and mainly as refugees. Later some reformist Buddhists transplanted their ideals to Hong Kong. In this case, Tung Lin Kok Yuen was very much a place for both refugees and reformist idealists.

66 Cheng, *Lady Clara Ho Tung: A Hong Kong Lady, Her Family and Her Times*, 140–41.

67 Cheng, *Intercultural Reminiscences*, 225.

68 Ibid., 231.

69 For a more detailed reference, see Irene Cheng, "Women Students and Graduates," in *University of Hong Kong: The First 50 Years, 1911–1961*, ed. Harrison B (Hong Kong: Cathay Press, 1962), 148–58.

70 For some explanation on the *mui-tsai* system, see Cheng, *Lady Clara Ho Tung: A Hong Kong Lady, Her Family and Her Times*, 177.

71 Ibid., 60, 65–66.

72 Ibid., 66.

73 Ibid., 145, Ho, *Xianci Hemu Zhang Taifuren Lianjue Jushi Shengping Yixing Buyi*, 3.

74 Extracted and translated from Zhang Jingrong, *Mingshan Youji*, 106–7.

75 Ibid.

76 Cheng, *Intercultural Reminiscences*, 188.

77 The two free schools are referred differently in different contexts, see Fang Meixian, *Xianggang Zaoqi Jiaoyu Fazan Shi: 1841–1941*, 150. Po Kok Free School in Hong Kong is named as Baojue Nuyixue.

78 He, *Xianggang Jiazu Shi*, 99–100. In the 1930s, the entire Percival Street was Lee Hysan family's property, and Lady Clara was a good friend of the Lee family. Her travelogue recorded Lee Haysan's death and her involvement in arranging the Buddhist funeral for the Lee family. It would be interesting to know if there was any connection between Lady Clara's friendship with the Lee family and her successful search for the free school's premises in Percival Street.

79 Zhang Jingrong, *Mingshan Youji*, 106.

80 Shi, *Xianggang Fojiao Yu Fosi*, 49.

81 Bao-qiong Mai, "Xiaoyou Yanjiang" (A Speech from a Former Graduate), *Baojue Tongxue* (Baojue Students) no. 1 (1953): 2, Jin Ping, "Xianggang Fojiao Xuexiao Gaikuang" (The General Situation of Buddhist Schools in Hong Kong), *Xianggang fojiao* (Hong Kong Buddhism), no. 36 (1963): 36.

82 Wai-ying Shi, "Zhanqian Guhou Yicien: Zhuinian Lin Yuanchang Zhen Jushi" (In Memory of Mother Superior Lin, Laywoman Zhen), *Po Kok Annual Journal* 11, no. 27 (1966): 3. The account was written by Shi Wai Yin, a former student of the seminary and the subsequent Po Kok School and now a Buddhist nun.

83 Zhang Jing Rong, *Mingshan Youji*, 106. The other two were Mr Xie Mengbo and "the fourth auntie" with unknown background.

84 Cheng, *Lady Clara Ho Tung: A Hong Kong Lady, Her Family and Her Times*, 130. See also Susanna Hoe, "Clara Ho Tung, 1875–1938," in *Chinese Footprints: Exploring Women's History in China, Hong Kong and Macau* (Hong Kong: Roundhouse Publication, 1997), 239.

85 Ibid., 18, 73, 150. In October 1902, Lady Clara took her son Eddie to Macau for medical retreat because the climate there seemed better for the sick baby. Due to her interest in Chinese theatre, Lady Clara "became acquainted with one of the owners of the Tsing Ping Theatre in Macao." During the Japanese occupation, Sir Robert Ho Tung took refuge in Macau to avoid being forced to cooperate with the Japanese. In time, the Ho Tung family contributed much to Macau, including a donation to the Macau Government of a Chinese Library worth $25,000, funding Macau's Keng Wu Hospital, and many other charitable organizations, including Lady Clara's efforts to promote Buddhist education in Macau.

86 Tanxu Shi, "Wuyu Guanben Heshang Zhi Yinyuan" (My Relation with Monk Guan Ben), *Wujindeng* 5, no. 2 (November 1955): 18–19, 30; Tanxu Shi, "Wuyu Guanben Heshang Zhi Yinyuan" (My Relation with Monk Guan Ben), *Wujindeng* 5, no. 3 (December 1955): 15–17. Zhang Xiubo (1868–1946) was born in 1868, and his native place was Guangdong Xiangshan. He passed several levels of imperial examinations in 1886, 1890, and 1891. He married twice in 1887 and 1892 and had three daughters and one son. In the 1890s, with his friends, he organized a study society and a free school in Macau to promote social reforms such as anti-footbinding and anti-smoking. He fled to Japan and studied there after the failure of the Hundred Days Reform. Later, he was involved in a publishing business, in running schools, and in the Sino-Japanese trade and railway in Shanghai. He first learned about Buddhism in 1914 from a lay friend. In 1915, he took his family members and moved to Macau where he headed two schools and ran a Buddhist institution, *Fosheng she* to promote vegetarianism and Buddhist studies. From time to time, he returned to Shanghai to take laymen vows. In 1928, he initiated his Buddhist tours to southeastern countries, including staying in Hong Kong for four months to give lectures in Shatin. In 1931, at the age of sixty-four, with most of his senior family members dead, he took the final step to become an ordained monk and returned to China to receive monastic training. He headed Gongde Lin in 1933, but he continued to travel to Hong Kong, Macau, and China for Buddhist lectures and proposed updating Buddhist ritual songs. After the fall of Canton in 1937, he took refuge in Hong Kong and stayed in Shatin Baoling Dong. He then moved back to China when Hong Kong fell to the Japanese. He returned to Canton after the war, and, by that time, he already had more than 10,000 disciples. He died in Canton in 1946, at the age of seventy-eight. His son was also an ordained monk, much earlier in 1920, but died a year later; one of his daughters remained single throughout her life and took charge of Gongde Lin.

87 Tan Xu Shi and Tai Guang Shi, *Yingchen Huiyi Lu* (1991), 220, 56. *Xianggang Fojiao* (Buddhism in Hong Kong) vol. 170, 21: July 1974. The term "Gongde Lin" comes from mixed Taoist and Buddhist backgrounds. *Gongde* is a Taoist concept that means to count and balance one's good and bad deeds. *Lin* in Buddhism is a metaphoric word used to describe different organizations, for example, *jushi lin* and *conglin* meaning a lay organization and a common monastic organization. The term is used widely by different Buddhist institutions and vegetarian restaurants. For example, there were Buddhist institutions named Gongde Lin in Shanghai and Tianjin.

88 Cheng, *Lady Clara Ho Tung: A Hong Kong Lady, Her Family and Her Times*, 150.

89 Shi, "Wuyu Guanben Heshang Zhi Yinyuan" (My Relation with Monk Guan Ben), no. 2: 18–19, 30; no. 3: 15–17.

90 Shi, "Zhanqian Guhou Yicien: Zhuinian Lin Yuanchang Zhen Jushi" (In Memory of Mother Superior Lin, Laywoman Zhen), 3. The author described the seminary as *conglin*, that is, the traditional Buddhist monastic style, though no further details are given about how the seminary was run as such with fewer than one hundred inmates.

91 Ibid., 4, Shi, "Wosuo Renshi Di Lianjue Jushi-2" (What I Knew about Laywoman Lin-Kok – Part II), 36.

92 *Aomen Youlan Zhinan* (Macau: Private Publication, 1939), 58–59.

93 Please note that the seminary has different names in Lady Clara's travelogue and on the photograph taken on the opening day. The photograph's caption shows the name of the seminary as Qingshan foxue yanjiushe. There is also confusion about whether Lady Clara bought or rented the venue at *Haiyun lanruo*. Monk Ai Ting recalled that Lady Clara rented the place, whereas nun Wai-ying suggested otherwise.

94 Zhang Jingrong, *Mingshan Youji*, 106.

95 Ai Ting Shi, "Wosuo Renshi Di Lianjue Jushi-1" (What I Knew about Laywoman Lin-Kok – Part I), *Huanan Jueyin* (The Enlightened Voice for South China), 27–28, 36.

96 Shi, "Zhanqian Guhou Yicien: Zhuinian Lin Yuanchang Zhen Jushi" (In Memory of Mother Superior Lin, Laywoman Zhen), 4; Shi, "Wosuo Renshi Di Lianjue Jushi-1" (What I Knew about Laywoman Lin-Kok – Part I), 36.

97 Shi, *Xianggang Fojiao Yu Fosi*, 61.

98 For more details of the funeral, see Cheng, *Lady Clara Ho Tung: A Hong Kong Lady, Her Family and Her Times*, 153–64.

99 Cheng, *Intercultural Reminiscences*, 217–18, 301.

100 For more details, see *Memorandum and Articles of Association of Tung Lin Kok Yuen*.

101 See Annual Report of Tung Lin Kok Yuen in 1952, and Amendment of the Yuen's Articles of Association in 1957.

102 Cheng, *Intercultural Reminiscences*, Chapter 20, 12.

103 See booklet produced by Tung Lin Kok Yuen, Canada Society, 1; see also its website: www.tunglinkok.ca.

104 Cheng, *Lady Clara Ho Tung: A Hong Kong Lady, Her Family and Her Times*, 164.

105 *South China Morning Post*, January 6, 1938, 10; see also ibid., 181.

106 Tai Xu Shi, "Sanshi Nianlai Zhi Zhongguo Fojiao" (Buddhism in China in the Thirty Years), in *Xiandai Fojiaoxueshu Congkan 86: Mingguo Fojiao Pian*, ed. Mantao Zhang (Taipei: Dasheng Wenhua Chubanshe, 1978), 324–5.

107 Zhu Kong Shi, "Mingguo Fojiao Nianji" (The Chronology of Buddhism during the Republican Period), in *Xiandai Fojiaoxueshu Congkan 86: Mingguo Fojiao Pian*, ed. Mantao Zhang (Taipei: Dasheng Wenhua Chubanshe, 1978), 199, 213.

108 Shi Ai Ting, "Wosuo renshi di Lianjue jueshi," 32–33.

109 Le Guan Shi, "Wosuo Renshi Di Yiwei Lupusa" (A Female Bodhistattva as I Knew Her), in *Hemu Zhang Taifuren Bazhi Mingshou Jilian Ji*, ed. Shai-lai Ho (Hong Kong: Private publication, 1954), 13.

110 See Bicheng Lu, "Zhang Lianhue Jushi Chuan" (A Biographical Sketch on Zhang Lianjue), in *Guangdong Fojiaoshi*, ed. Yongkang Liang (Hong Kong: Zhonghua Fojiao Tushu Guan, 1984), 108–10.

111 Susanna Hoe, *Chinese Footprints*, 234.

112 Siu-lun Wong, "Gender and Trust: The Dynamism of Chinese Family Enterprise Revisited," in *Chinese Sociology and Anthropology in the Twenty First Century*, ed. Chiao Chien, Rance Lee, and Ma Rong (Kaohsiung: Liwen Cultural Enterprise Ltd., 2001).

Chapter 8

1   A survey of doctoral dissertations written in the last twenty years at the University of Hong Kong produces only a few that are remotely related to the topic. See Priscilla Pue Ho Chu, *The Making of Women Entrepreneurs in Hong Kong* (Hong Kong: Hong Kong University Press, 2003).

2   Some notable biographies include one on Lady Clara Ho-tung by her daughter Irene Cheng, but she belonged to a different era. Although she was respected for her public service and charity, she was by no means seen as "professional." Ellen Li (born 1907), a pioneer professional woman, produced her own autobiography that summarizes her life and work over eight decades. Although recognized for her tremendously high profile record of public service and her push for legislation to advance the rights of women in Hong Kong, she is seen as a woman of privilege who engaged in charity and "do-goodism." In her self-perception, she juxtaposed familial ties and duties of a wife and mother with her extremely progressive record of public involvement in women's causes. I interviewed her in 1993.

3   A leading journalist in Hong Kong volunteered these impressions during a conversation I had with him. Similarly, an academic who was active in public service once confessed that when Chief Secretary Anson Chan stared him in the eye, his legs turned weak; when she smiled, his heart melted.

4   See Elizabeth Sinn, "Lesson in Openness: Creating a Space of Flow in Hong Kong," in *Hong Kong Mobile: Making a Global Population*, ed. Helen F. Siu and Agnes S. Ku (Hong Kong: Hong Kong University Press, 2008), 13–43.

5   See summary in the introduction of this volume. See also Zhaoxing Li and Zeng Fan, eds., *Xianggang 101: Ai Hen Xianggang De 101 Ge Li You* (Hong Kong 101: One Hundred and One Reasons to Love and Hate Hong Kong) (Hong Kong: Feel Company Ltd., 2000). On the likes and dislikes of a postwar Hong Kong generation (born between 1955 and 1975), Chan portrayed the diligent factory girls of working class families, and members of her fan clubs identified with her movie images. Siu Fong Fong played the upwardly mobile, middle-class girl going through secondary school and local university, and captured another class of fans. The images and the fans' experiences characterized Hong Kong in the postwar decades.

6   See Karen Kelsky, *Women on the Verge: Japanese Women, Western Dreams*, (Durham: Duke University Press, 2001).

7   See Norma Connolly and Martin Wong, "Scales Tip as Women Outnumber Men," *South China Morning Post*, February 23, 2007.

8   See Chun-ho Wong "Who's Worth a Million Dollars in Hong Kong? More Women Than Men," *South China Morning Post*, February 14, 2007. See also articles "Nü Dagong Guizu Shinian Zeng Wucheng,Gang Zui Gaoxin 1% Ren Shuikuan Zhan Zong'e 36%" (Female Working Aristocrats Increased Fifty Percent in Ten Years; Top One Percent Income Earners Paid Thirty-six Percent of Total Hong Kong Taxes), *Ming Pao Daily News*, May 2, 2007, A11, and "83% Gangqi Ping Nü Gaoceng Lie Quanqiu Diwu" (83% Hong Kong Businesses Hired Senior Women Executives, Ranking Number Five in the World), *Ming Pao Daily News*, March 8, 2007.

9   This occurs across political lines for public figures, such as Audrey Eu (Civic Party), and Rita Fan (convener for LegCo).

10   See interviews of these women in *Xianggang Funü Nianbao Bianji Weiyuanhui*, ed. *Xianggang Funü Nianbao* (Hong Kong Women's Annual Book) (Hong Kong: Xianggang Xinwen Chubanshe, 1975–).

11   These are leading social magazines in Hong Kong that highlight elite women and their styles.

12   See Betty Yau, Kit Chun Au, and Fanny M. Cheung, "Women's Concern Groups in Hong Kong" (Hong Kong: Hong Kong Institute of Asia-Pacific Studies, 1992). See also Xiaoyun Fang, *Xianggang Nü Fuhao Liejuan* (Wealthy Women in Hong Kong) (Hong Kong: Chinshiyuan Chubanshe, 1993). The author examines the background and family ties of five wealthy women in Hong Kong who are the wives of prominent businessmen. See also Liu Su, *Xianggang, Xianggang* . . . (Hong Kong, Hong Kong . . .)(Hong Kong: Zhongguo Tu Shu Kan Xing She, 1987).

13   David Faure, *Colonialism and the Hong Kong Mentality* (Hong Kong: Centre of Asian Studies, The University of Hong Kong, 2003).

14   See Liu, *Xianggang, Xianggang* . . .

15   See media reports on the campaigns of the two candidates since the death of Ma Li, a Legislative Councilor who died in August 2007.

16 See Fan Zuoyun "Shengguan zhiri huixiang zhizu" (High Official Returning to Native Place to Pay Respect to Ancestors), *Hong Kong Economic Journal,* October 1, 1993, 5.

17 See Luo Di, "Buzhengsi Chen Fang Ansheng Renzhong Daoyuan" (Chief Secretary Anson Chan Shoulders Heavy Responsibilities), *Nanbeiji,* December 1993, 8–9.

18 See "Buzhengsi Anson Chan Changtan Danren Lingdaoren Suoxu Pinzhi: Gui Yi Shen Zuo Ze Geng Xu Duidezhu Liangxin" (Chief Secretary Discusses Necessary Quality of Leadership: Be a Model for Society and Act with a Conscience). *Shing Pao,* December 5, 1993, 10.

19 See Dorinda Elliot, "The Iron Lady Is on the Spot," *Newsweek,* June 9 1997, 11–15.

20 See Margaret Ng, "And Now, the Real Tung Administration," *South China Morning Post,* January 16, 2001.

21 See Weng Yuxiong, "Fendai Guanchang Yingxiong Shise" (Heroes Pale in a Female-dominated Officialdom), *Apple Daily,* June 25, 2000. A figure in September 2004 puts it at 24.6%. See "Nü Jiao Nan Duo 25 Wan, Yue Lai Yue Chihun, Nan 31 Nü28," *Ming Pao Daily News,* July 29, 2005 (Women Outnumber Men by 250,000. Rising Trend for Late Marriages, Men 31 Women 28) on a rise in the percentage of women civil servants at the directorate level and above. See also "Ben Gang Nüxing Cangxuan Bilü Di" (The Ratio of Political Participation among Hong Kong Women is Low), *Ming Pao Daily News,* April 7, 2005, in which Fang Minsheng, a social services activist, lamented the low participation rate and success rate of women in electoral politics (less than 20%).

22 See Weng, "Fengdai Guanchang, Yingxiong Shishe" (Heroes Pale in a Female-dominated Officialdom).

23 See *Ming Pao Daily News,* November 13, 1998.

24 See Ma Zhenping, *Gangren Da Xieyi: Yige Beijing Ren Yanzhong De Xianggang Ren* (An Overall Description of Hong Kong People Through the Eyes of a Beijing Person) (Beijing: Qunyan Chubanshe, 1998).

25 I heard the comments in a morning radio program in Hong Kong during the year 2000, when citizens called in to express their views on current public affairs. For the comment on Cheung, see Ma, *Gangren Da Xieyi:Yige Beijing Ren Yanzhong De Xianggang Ren* on Hong Kong women.

26 See the comic book: Lai Yifu, *Saobatou* (Broomhead) (Hong Kong: Subculture Publisher, 2001). The TV program in which Ip was interviewed was "James Wong Xianggang Qing Zhi Zongyou Chutou Tian, episode 10–11" (Program by James Wong on Unveiling Hong Kong Moods, episode 9–10), broadcast on February 7 and 8, 2002 at 10:35 p.m. See also http://www.mingpaoweekly.com/htm/1810/bb01_8.htm on popular comments on Ip.

27 As Secretary for Security, she was given the task to "persuade" the public to accept a rather tough national securities legislation (known locally as the Article 23 legislation in the Basic Law of Hong Kong). She and the government were

accused by an alliance of liberal democrats of not seeking enough public consultation, yielding to political pressure from China, and being high-handed. The attempts triggered a mass demonstration of more than half a million people on July 1, 2003, which took China completely by surprise. Ip resigned soon after, although friends have argued that her resignation was not related to the episode. See HKU POP Site (http://hkupop.hku.hk/) and Archive-POP Polls, there is "Ratings of Secretary for Security Regina Ip Lau Suk-yee." The first poll was conducted in July 2002 (five months after the TV program) and the ratings still showed a downward trend.

28 Emily Lau, a legislator, asked the universities in Hong Kong to be vigilant in their hiring. She pointed to the low ratio of female faculty (23%) — especially in the Chinese University of Hong Kong (CUHK) and the Hong Kong University of Science and Technology. The pro-Vice Chancellor of CUHK, Professor Kenneth Young, denied any sex discrimination, but noted that a few decades before, there had been fewer opportunities for women to receive higher education. Hence, there is a lack of female academics today. See "Jiaoshi Yangcheng Yin Shuai" (Male Dominance in Number of Academics), *Ming Pao Daily News,* March 11, 1999.

29 The report in Weng, "Fen Dai Guanchang, Yingxiong Shi Se" (Heroes Pale in a Female-dominated Officialdom), quotes Chi-chiu Leung, chair of the Senior Civil Servants Association, who attributes the high numbers of women administrative officers to the particular demands of the British colonial service and the subsequent localization in preparation for 1997.

30 I interviewed a dozen or so women professionals with law degrees. The oldest generation of women lawyers is now in their sixties and mostly retired. The active political figures are in their fifties and forties.

31 Interview with Elsie Leung in 1994. Among the recent chairs of the Hong Kong Bar Association are Gladys Li, Jacqueline Leung, and Audrey Eu. The late Helen Lo was the territory's first women magistrate, followed by others. See most recent figures for junior counsels at the Hong Kong bar Association, in http://barlist.hkba.org/hkba/SeniorityJunior/JuniorCounsel.htm. As of 2008, the total number of junior counsels is 975, including 712 male and 263 female, i.e. around 30%.

32 It was December 18, 2001. I was invited by a graduate of the university to attend the dinner, held at the Hong Kong Convention Centre.

33 Faure (2003), 48–49.

34 See an autobiography by Patrick Shuk-siu Yu, *A Seventh Child and the Law* (Hong Kong: Hong Kong University Press, 1998).

35 See *Ming Pao Daily News,* January 6, 1988 (excerpted in Dr Li's autobiography, *Life's Journey,* July 1993, 108).

36 "Tai tai" is a term that refers to a wealthy but dependent spouse.

37 The quote is taken from Ellen Li's autobiography, 113.

38 Lydia Dunn, Rita Fan, Audrey Eu, Emily Lau, Rosanna Wong, Selina Chow, and Laura Cha are all remarkable examples across a political spectrum who, at

one time or another, were appointed to the Executive Council or elected to the Legislative Council.

39 I interviewed her in Hong Kong in November and December 2000. We have had many other opportunities to discuss her life and career.

40 This quote is taken from "Wu Hung Yuk Zai Xiang Hushan Xing" (Hu Hongyu Heads towards the Tiger Mountain Again), *Ming Pao Daily News,* July 25, 1999. In response to the news that she had been appointed by the government as the new chair of the Equal Opportunities Commission.

41 See the statement mounted on Equal Opportunity Commission's website (www. eoc.org.hk).

42 Two years later, with public support, the government renewed her contract although they downgraded the position. See "Ping Ji Hui Gao Zhengfu Minjian Kong Chunu Gaoguan, Tuanti Fen Han Teshou Bao Hu Hongyu" (The Equal Opportunities Commission's Lawsuit against the Government might have Offended officials. Organizations appealed to the Chief Executive to Retain Hu Hongyu), *Ming Pao Daily News,* June 29, 2002 and "Gangfu Shunying Minjian 'Bao Yu Xingdong', Xianshi Zunzhong Renquan, Hu Hongyu Xuyue Ping Ji Hui Yinian" (The Hong Kong Government Accommodates Public Efforts to Retain Hu. Showing Respect for Human Rights, Hu's Contract in Equal Opportunity Commission Is Renewned for a Year), *Ming Pao Daily News,* July 28, 2002.

43 Her father was a cotton commodity merchant from Shanghai. Her maternal grandmother and mother have been managers of the high-end English department store, Lane Crawford. They came from a family of old wealth. Generations of its male members had served on the board of the Tung Wah Hospital. (Interview with her mother and maternal grandmother in 1996.)

44 See a document by the Citizens Party, "Claiming the Hong Kong Advantage: Future Based and Ambition Driven" (Hong Kong: Citizens Party, 1999).

45 See "Lu Gonghui Shinian Jiu Yige Wei Gang" (Christine Loh Took Ten Years to Save a Victoria Harbour), *Ming Pao Daily News,* April 16, 2000. During a newspaper interview after she announced her intention not to run for a third term. The interview focused on her work on Hong Kong's environment.

46 See "Tian Shao Zhi Lu Gonghui Guofen Duli" (Master Tian Accuses Christine Loh of Being Too Independent), *Sing Tao Daily,* April 13, 2000.

47 See an interview "Bu Shi Danchu, Ershi Chongxin Touru: Christine Loh Zhuanhuan Kongjian 'Chong Dian' (Not a Retreat, but Re-engagement: Christine Loh Changes an Environment to 'Recharge') by Yuk-man Wong, a talk show host and political commentator, published in *Oriental Daily,* May 14, 2000, downloaded from www.orisun.com on July 22, 2000.

48 See, for example, a report done in partnership with CLSA, "Hong Kong Strategy," focusing on Hong King's relationship with Guangdong (October 2002), and a follow-up report in March 2003. On the environment front, she has been active in publicizing and mobilizing the public against further harbor reclamation. Earlier, Civic Exchange conducted a joint survey report with the China Development Institute in Shenzhen on "Zhujiang sanjiaozhou jumin

huanbao shehui diaocha baogao" (A Social Survey Report on Community Environmental Practices in the Pearl River Delta) (December 2002).

49 See "Guihua Yuanjing Wenjian Duanshi" ("Document on Strategic Planning Vision" Short-sighted), *Taiyang bao* (Sun), March 1, 2001.

50 See Kaishan Yang and Xue Yike, "Xuni Shequ Ninju Shimin Liliang, Lu Gonghui Tuidong Wangshang Canzheng" (Virtual Community to Gather Citizen's Strength. Christine Loh Pushes for Internet Political Participation), *Sing Tao Daily*, July 19, 2000.

51 See a special bulletin put out by the Hong Kong General Chamber of Commerce in November 2006 and speeches made by David Eldon, former chairman of the Hong Kong and Shanghai Banking Corporation, in November 2006, on the Clean Air Charter. See corresponding publications by Christine Loh in Civic Exchange.

52 She was once criticized by a women's organization for her "lack of empathy." In a meeting with legislators, women's advocates were not pleased to hear Christine's analysis of why uneducated middle-aged women in Hong Kong would face chronic structural unemployment and need government assistance. See "Christine Loh Beima 'Shi Li Nü Ren'" (Christine Loh Accused of Disappointing Her Gender), *Apple Daily*, February 5, 1999, A16, downloaded from Wiser Information Ltd.

53 See debates in the local newspapers in that period for in-depth reporting of the process and outcome.

54 See "Da Xuesheng Xiang Jian Emily Lau Christine Loh" (University Students Eager to Meet Emily Lau and Christine Loh), *Ming Pao Daily News*, August 24, 2000, A12 on the details of the survey of over 900 university students.

55 See "Zhengtan 'Athena Chu' De Jingcai Zhengzhi Xiu" (The "Athena Chu' in Politics Staging a Political Show), *Sing Tao Daily News*, April 12, 2000, A09, and "Fei Peng Tiba Ruju Renqi Ya Martin Lee Zhengtan 'Guimei' Minwang Di Er" (Fatty Patten LegCo Appointee Overtakes Martin Lee in Popularity. "Foreign Little Devil" comes Second in Poll), *Apple Daily*, April 12, 2000, A01.

56 See "Xin Jiyuan Renlei Xi Gang, Yin Shui Du Jiang Zhihui" (New Century Beings Descend upon Hong Kong, Oozing Wisdom Even in Water-Drinking), *Sing Dao Daily*, November 30, 2000.

57 After she was appointed a board member of the Hong Kong University of Science and Technology, she decided to stay at a dormitory a night each semester to experience and to listen to student views.

58 Although the legal profession is sharply divided between barristers and solicitors, with the latter outnumbering the former by a ratio of 5 to 1, Margaret Ng, a barrister, has won over two-thirds of the votes in all the elections. In the 1998 election immediately after the political return of Hong Kong to China, she received 1,741 votes in a three-way competition. The other two candidates received 394 and 138 respectively (see Hong Kong Government Announcements, May 25, 1998).

59 See her book of essays on her year in Cambridge. Margaret Ng, *Jianqiao Guilu* (Home from Cambridge) (Hong Kong: Mingbao Chubanshe, 1987).

60   See Elsie Leung's defense as published in a government news item on March 11, 1999, http://www.info.gov.hk/gia/general/199903/11/0311102.htm, accessed on June 23, 2008.

61   See Johannes Chan and Bart Rwezura, eds., *Immigration Law in Hong Kong: An Interdisciplinary Study* (Hong Kong: Sweet and Maxwell Asia, 2004).

62   Article 45 of the Basic Law in Hong Kong involves the constitutional basis for universal suffrage in the reelection of the Chief Executive and the Legislative Council. The possibilities were ruled out by Beijing through another reinterpretation in 2004. For more on the July 1 march and the issues, see Margaret Ng, *23 Tiao Lifa Rizhi* (A Dairy on the Legislation of Article 23) (Hong Kong: Next Publications, 2004).

63   Audrey Eu, a former chair of the Hong Kong Bar Association, made her political debut when she campaigned and won handsomely against her pro-China opponent in a bi-election in 2000. Educated in a missionary school in Hong Kong and then in England, she is known for her elegance, articulation, and quality brain power through her work in the Legislative Council. She also runs a popular radio talk show on public affairs and continues to be ranked by public opinion polls as one of the most popular political figures. She is a core member of the Article 45 Concern Group.

64   See documents and newspaper reporting on the party during its establishment. For details of the party and Margaret Ng's role in it, see www.margaretng.com, and www.civicparty.hk.

65   She has published a highly entertaining book on her food ventures. Margaret Ng, *Chi He Wan Le* (Eat, Drink, and Be Merry) (Hong Kong: Mingbao Chubanshe Youxian Gongsi, 1997).

66   The flood of pornography, prostitution, and the short-term keeping of "second wives" in these boomtowns has been quite alarming.

67   See the tabloid by *Beijing qingnian bao* during the Hong Kong Tools Exhibition.

68   See Wendy Tam, "Chuzou Hou Leyuan" (Venturing out for Happier Circumstances), *Ming Pao Daily News* (May 14, 2007, A14) on interviews of Hong Kong men who have chosen to find spouses across the border. On the changing profiles of mainland spouses, see Hei-wah Ho, "Chengqing Dui Xinyimin De Jige Mouwu" (Clarifying a Few Misunderstandings towards New Immigrants), *Ming Pao Daily News*, September 17, 2007.

Chapter 9

1   E. H. Phelps Brown, "The Hong Kong Economy: Achievements and Prospects," in *Hong Kong: The Industrial Colony*, ed. Keith Hopkins (Hong Kong; London; New York: Oxford University Press, 1971); Siu-lun Wong, *Emigrant Entrepreneurs: Shanghai Industrialists in Hong Kong* (Hong Kong; New York: Oxford University Press, 1988); Graham Johnson, "Hong Kong, from Colony to Territory: Social Implications of Globalization," in *25 Years of Social and Economic Development*

in Hong Kong, ed. Benjamin K. P. Leung and Teresa Y. C. Wong (Hong Kong: Centre of Asian Studies, The University of Hong Kong, 1994).

2   Stephen Wing-kai Chiu and Ching-kwan Lee, *Withering Away of the Hong Kong Dream? Women Workers under Industrial Restructuring* (Hong Kong: Hong Kong Institute of Asia-Pacific Studies, The Chinese University of Hong Kong, 1997).

3   Tak-wing Ngo, ed., *Hong Kong's History State and Society under Colonial Rule*, Routledge Studies in Asia's Transformations (London; New York: Routledge, 1999).

4   David A. Levin, "Women and the Industrial Labour Market in Hong Kong," in *Status Influences in Third World Labor Markets*, ed. James G. Scoville (Berlin; New York: W. de Gruyter, 1991).

5   Levin, "Women and the Industrial Labour Market in Hong Kong," 190.

6   Tai-lok Lui, "Waged Work at Home: Married Women's Participation in Industrial Outwork in Hong Kong," in *Selected Papers of Conference on Gender Studies in Chinese Societies*, ed. Fanny M. Cheung, et al. (Hong Kong: Hong Kong Institute of Asia-Pacific Studies, The Chinese University of Hong Kong, 1991).

7   Kim-ming Lee, "Flexible Manufacturing in a Colonial Economy," in *Hong Kong's History State and Society under Colonial Rule*, ed. Tak-wing Ngo (London; New York: Routledge, 1999).

8   Stephen Wing-kai Chiu and David A. Levin, "The World Economy, State, and Sectors in Industrial Change: Labor Relations in Hong Kong's Textile and Garment-Making Industries," in *Industrialization and Labor Relations: Contemporary Research in Seven Countries*, ed. Stephen Frenkel and Jeffrey Harrod (Ithaca, N.Y.: ILR Press, 1995); Lee, "Flexible Manufacturing in a Colonial Economy," 166.

9   Lee, "Flexible Manufacturing in a Colonial Economy."

10 Eliza W. Y. Lee, ed., *Gender and Change in Hong Kong: Globalization, Postcolonialism, and Chinese Patriarchy* (Vancouver: University of British Columbia Press, 2003).

11 Ping-chun Hsiung, *Living Rooms as Factories: Class, Gender, and the Satellite Factory System in Taiwan = [Ke Ting Ji Gong Chang]* (Philadelphia: Temple University Press, 1996).

12 Hsiung did her fieldwork in 1989, while Lee did hers in 1992–93.

13 Ching-kwan Lee, "Engendering the Worlds of Labor: Women Workers, Labor Markets, and Production Politics in the South China Economic Miracle," *American Sociological Review* 60, no. 3 (1995); Ching-kwan Lee, *Gender and the South China Miracle: Two Worlds of Factory Women* (Berkeley: University of California Press, 1998).

14 Ngai Pun, "Becoming Dagongmei: Politics of Identities and Differences," in *Made in China: Women Factory Workers in a Global Workplace*, ed. Ngai Pun (Durham: Duke University Press, 2005); Ngai Pun, "Am I the Only Survivor? Global Capital, Local Gaze, and Social Trauma in China," *Public Culture* 14, no. 2 (2002): 341–47.

15 Read also Siumi Maria Tam, "The Structuration of Chinese Modernization: Women Workers of Shekou Industrial Zone" (PhD dissertation, University of Hawai'i, 1992).

16 Tamara Jacka, *Rural Women in Urban China: Gender, Migration, and Social Change* (Armonk, N.Y.: M.E. Sharpe, Inc., 2006); Shulamit Reinharz and Lynn Davidman, *Feminist Methods in Social Research* (New York: Oxford University Press, 1992); Patricia Ann Lather, *Getting Smart: Feminist Research and Pedagogy with/in the Postmodern* (New York: Routledge, 1991).

17 A good example is Lisa Rofel's skilful attention to the voices of different generations of women workers in the mid-eighties in China. Due to the different social and political contexts in which they had entered factory work, middle-aged and young women workers held widely diverse views of what constituted personal freedom and autonomy as women. As a result, Rofel argued for the deconstruction of a unitary "Chinese woman" and standard of feminism and liberation, in favor of "situated feminisms." See Lisa Rofel, "Liberation Nostalgia and a Yearning for Modernity," in *Engendering China: Women, Culture, and the State*, ed. Christina K. Gilmartin, et al. (Cambridge, M.A.: Harvard University Press, 1994).

18 Lee, *Gender and the South China Miracle: Two Worlds of Factory Women.*

19 Joan Acker, Kate Barry, and Joke Esseveld, "Objectivity and Truth: Problems in Doing Feminist Research," *Women's Studies International Forum* 6, no. 4 (1983): 423–35.

20 Reinharz and Davidman, *Feminist Methods in Social Research.*

21 Jacka, *Rural Women in Urban China: Gender, Migration, and Social Change.*

22 Reinharz and Davidman, *Feminist Methods in Social Research*; Jacka, *Rural Women in Urban China: Gender, Migration, and Social Change.*

23 Dorothy E. Smith, "Institutional Ethnography: A Feminist Method," *Resources for Feminist Research* 15, no. 1 (1986): 6–13.

24 Smith, "Institutional Ethnography: A Feminist Method," 6.

25 Ibid., 8.

26 Jacka, *Rural Women in Urban China: Gender, Migration, and Social Change.*

27 The names of these five women are pseudonyms.

28 Hsiung, *Living Rooms as Factories: Class, Gender, and the Satellite Factory System in Taiwan* = [Ke Ting Ji Gong Chang].

29 *Ye-Ye Sheng-Ge: Wo Zai Jianuosha De Rizi* (Music and Songs Every Evening: My Days At the Canossian School) (Hong Kong: Publishing Committee for the School History of the Shaukiwan Canossian Evening School, 1998). Comprising original essays written by the alumnae of this school, this was a desktop publication for private circulation only. It preceded the publication of a book for public circulation: Po-king Choi, ed., *Wan Wan Liudianban: Qishi Nindai Shang Yexiao De Nugong* (Every Night at Six-Thirty: Women Workers Who Attended Evening Schools in the Seventies) (Hong Kong: Stepforward Multimedia Co. Ltd., 1998).

30 Choi, ed., *Wan Wan Liudianban: Qishi Nindai Shang Yexiao De Nugong*, 17–18.

31 This was the common fate of most of the SCES alumnae. See *Ye-Ye Sheng-Ge: Wo Zai Jianuosha De Rizi*, 6, 21; Choi, ed., *Wan Wan Liudianban: Qishi Nindai Shang Yexiao De Nugong.*

32 Choi, ed., *Wan Wan Liudianban: Qishi Nindai Shang Yexiao De Nugong*.

33 See the stories of Brenda, Betty and Winnie, in Choi, ed., *Wan Wan Liudianban: Qishi Nindai Shang Yexiao De Nugong*, 16–17.

34 Choi, ed., *Wan Wan Liudianban: Qishi Nindai Shang Yexiao De Nugong*, 17–18.

35 Transcription of group discussion among SCES alumnae on evening school life (July 12, 1997).

36 Janet W. Salaff, *Working Daughters of Hong Kong: Filial Piety or Power in the Family?* (Cambridge; New York: Cambridge University Press, 1981).

37 Lee, *Gender and the South China Miracle: Two Worlds of Factory Women*, 34.

38 This was recounted by three SCES alumnae, Cecilia, Wendy, and Emily, in the group discussion on evening school life. (See Choi, ed., *Wan Wan Liudianban: Qishi Nindai Shang Yexiao De Nugong*, 22–25.) However, in one or two years' time, they started taking evening classes. All three worked hard at their studies and got their secondary school leaving qualifications.

39 Choi, ed., *Wan Wan Liudianban: Qishi Nindai Shang Yexiao De Nugong*, 20.

40 Ibid.

41 Ibid., 31.

42 Ibid., 19–20, 28–31.

43 Ibid., 53.

44 Salaff, *Working Daughters of Hong Kong: Filial Piety or Power in the Family?*

45 A. Wei Djao, "Public Issues and Private Troubles: The Government and the Working Class in Hong Kong," in *Poverty and Social Change in Southeast Asia*, ed. Ozay Mehmet (Ottawa: University of Ottawa, 1979), 109–10.

46 It was a common practice for a working daughter to surrender her whole pay packet to the family, while keeping the wages they got for overtime work. At a time when overtime work was abundant and almost mandatory, it could fetch a rather good sum.

47 Kit-mui Wong criticized Salaff for simply casting these working daughters in the role of victims of traditional ideologies. Such a view is not only a great insult to these women, but also a lame excuse on the part of the researcher for not trying to understand them. See Choi, ed., *Wan Wan Liudianban: Qishi Nindai Shang Yexiao De Nugong*, 50.

48 Kit-wah Man, "Hong Kong Films of the Sixties and Woman's Identity," in *Hong Kong Sixties: Designing Identity*, ed. Matthew Turner and Irene Ngan (Hong Kong: The Hong Kong Arts Centre, 1995), 76–77.

49 Lee, *Gender and the South China Miracle: Two Worlds of Factory Women*, 15.

50 Ibid., 27.

51 Pun, "Am I the Only Survivor? Global Capital, Local Gaze, and Social Trauma in China," 345.

52 Choi, ed., *Wan Wan Liudianban: Qishi Nindai Shang Yexiao De Nugong*, 84.

53 Chiu and Levin, "The World Economy, State, and Sectors in Industrial Change: Labor Relations in Hong Kong's Textile and Garment-Making Industries," 159; Lee, "Flexible Manufacturing in a Colonial Economy," 166.

54 England and Rear, in Levin, "Women and the Industrial Labour Market in Hong Kong," 204.

55 Chiu and Levin, "The World Economy, State, and Sectors in Industrial Change: Labor Relations in Hong Kong's Textile and Garment-Making Industries," 149.

56 Transcription of group discussion among SCES alumnae in work life, July 1997.

57 Djao, "Public Issues and Private Troubles: The Government and the Working Class in Hong Kong," 278.

58 Ibid., 285–82.

59 Levin, "Women and the Industrial Labour Market in Hong Kong," 208.

60 Levin, ibid., 183–214.

61 Lee, *Gender and the South China Miracle: Two Worlds of Factory Women*, 166.

62 Djao, "Public Issues and Private Troubles: The Government and the Working Class in Hong Kong," 281–82.

63 Choi, ed., *Wan Wan Liudianban: Qishi Nindai Shang Yexiao De Nugong*, 39–42.

64 Paul E. Willis, *Learning to Labor: How Working Class Kids Get Working Class Jobs* (New York: Columbia University Press, 1981).

65 Choi, 1997, 335.

66 In 1991, on the eve of the passing of the "Trade Descriptions Ordinance," the garment union rallied for the support of workers in their massive protests outside the Legislative Council. Yau-lin joined a number of sit-ins, the hunger strike, and then an overnight vigil, after which she witnessed the defeat of their side when the ordinance was passed. With the passing of the ordinance, relocation of garment factories over the border intensified, as garment products could now legitimately bear the "Made in Hong Kong" label even when only an insignificant proportion of the production work is done in Hong Kong.

67 Yau-lin said when she was invited to join the executive committee, she tried to decline by saying that she was illiterate, but then she was convinced when she was told that she could contribute by networking among her fellow workers.

68 Wai-fong Chan, Shun-hing Chan, and Yuen-yee Law, "Pioneers in Women's Rights: Fung-ying Lee, Wai-ming Leung and Yuet-lin Yim," in *The Other Half of the Sky: Women's Movement in Post-War Hong Kong*, ed. Cheung Choi Wan, et al. (Hong Kong: Association for the Advancement of Feminism, 1992), 33–34.

69 For a detailed report on Yim's work in the sex workers' rights movement, see Yuet-lin Yim and Yan-yan Chan, "The Enlightenment Age of the Hong Kong Sex Workers' Rights Movement," in *Xing Gongzuo Yanjiu* (The Study of Sex Work), ed. Ho Chuen Juei (Taipei: The Centre for the Study of Sexualities, National Central University, 2003), 59–94.

70 See Mei-lin Wu, "Drifting between the Women's Movement and the Workers' Movement," in *Chayi Yu Pingdeng: Xianggang Funu Yundong De Xin Tiaozhan* (Differences and Equality: New Challenges to the Hong Kong Women's Movement), ed. Kam-wah Chan, et al. (Hong Kong: Association for the Advancement of Feminism, in collaboration with the Centre for Social Policy Studies, Department of Applied Social Studies, Hong Kong Polytechnic University, 2001), 71–76. Wu is a full-time executive of the HKWWA. See also Kit-sum Yim and Wai-yi Lee, "Realize Women's Sex Rights, Support Sex Workers: The Rights of Sexual Minorities as a Feminist Issue," in *Chayi Yu*

Pingdeng: Xianggang Funu Yundong De Xin Tiaozhan (Differences and Equality: New Challenges to the Hong Kong Women's Movement), ed. Kam-wah Chan, et al. (Hong Kong: Association for the Advancement of Feminism, in collaboration with the Centre for Social Policy Studies, Department of Applied Social Studies, Hong Kong Polytechnic University, 2001), 133–56.

71 See a report on Ngan-fung Liu's talk given on the fifteen anniversary of Kwan Fook, in which she made known her convictions and political stance as a grassroots activist, in http://www.inmediahk.net/node/62438. See also her contribution to a conference on women's movement in Hong Kong held in 2000: Ngan-fung Liu, "Family Violence and Sexual Self-Determination," in *Chayi Yu Pingdeng: Xianggang Funu Yundong De Xin Tiaozhan* (Differences and Equality: New Challenges to the Hong Kong Women's Movement), ed. Kam-wah Chan, et al. (Hong Kong: Association for the Advancement of Feminism, in collaboration with the Centre for Social Policy Studies, Department of Applied Social Studies, Hong Kong Polytechnic University, 2001), 109–14.

Chapter 10

1 Luo Mu, "Jiqing Ranshao 'Tie Guniang'" (Burning Passion: The Steel Maidens), *Shenghuo Yuekan* (Life Monthly), no. 4 (2005).

2 In the eight model operas, many heroines are revolutionary cadres, e.g., Fang Haizhen in "Seaport," Jiang Shuiying in "Ode to the Dragon River," and Ke Xiang of "The Mountain of Cuckoos." Each of them is either a Party secretary or a Party representative.

3 Jin Yihong, "Tie Gunian Zaisikao – Zhongguo Wenhua Dageming Qijian De Shehui Xingbie Yu Laodong" (Rethinking the Steel Maidens: Gender roles and Labor in the Cultural Revolution), *Shehuixue Yanjiu* (Sociology Research), no. 1 (2006).

4 See Margery Wolf, *Revolution Postponed: Women in Contemporary China* (Stanford: Stanford University Press, 1985); Kay Ann Johnson, *Women, the Family and Peasant Revolution in China* (Chicago and London: The University of Chicago Press, 1983).

5 Hu Yukun, "Guojia, Shichang Yu Zhongguo Nongcun Funü De Jingji Canyu" (Nation, the Market, and Peasant Women's Economic Participation), in Jianshe Shehui Zhuyi Xinnongcun Yu Xingbie Pingdeng – Duoxueke He Kuaxueke De Yanjiu (Multi-Disciplinary Studies in Creating Socialist Villages and Gender Equality), ed. Zhongguo Funü Yanjiuhui (The Association for Chinese Women's Studies) (Beijing: Zhongguo Funü Chubanshe, 2007).

6 Jin Yihong, "Tie Guniang Zaisikao – Zhongguo Wenhua Dageming Qijian De Shehui Xingbie Yu Laodong" (Rethinking the Steel Maidens: Gender roles and Labor in the Cultural Revolution).

7 Wu Liping, "Wenhua Dageming Zhong De Nühongweibing" (Female Red Guards in the Culture Revolution), *Ershiyi Shiji* (Twenty-First Century

Bimonthly) 68, no. 11 (2007). For web version, see http://www.cuhk.edu.hk/ics/21c/.

8   See works by Wolf, *Revolution Postponed: Women in Contemporary China.* Elisabeth J. Croll, *Women and Rural Development in China: Production and Reproduction* (Geneva: International Labour Office, 1985). Johnson, *Women, the Family, and Peasant Revolution in China,* and Delia Davin, *Woman-Work: Women and the Party in Revolutionary China* (Oxford: Clarendon Press, 1976). For a later work, focusing on the Federation of Chinese Women in rural China in the early reform period, Ellen R. Judd provides a nuanced picture. See Ellen R. Judd, *The Chinese Women's Movement between State and Market* (Stanford: Stanford University Press, 2002). Portrayal of women's complicated predicaments in the Maoist period can also be gleaned from personal memoirs and literature published in the post-Mao period. Famous women writers of the post-Mao period who stress the conflicts between private emotions and revolutionary sacrifices include Zhang Jie, Shen Rong, Wang Anyi, Shu Ting, Yang Jian. See Helen F. Siu and Zelda Stern, eds., *Mao's Harvest: Voices of China's New Generation* (New York: Oxford University Press, 1983).

9   Helen F. Siu, "Nianzai Huanan Yanjiu Zhilu" (A Twenty-Year Journey through South China), *Qinghua shehuixue pinglun* (Tsinghua Sociological Review) 1, no. 3 (2001). See "Where Were the Women? Rethinking Marriage Resistance and Regional Culture History," *Late Imperial China* 11, no. 2 (1990).

10   See the picture: Zhuo "niu" (Capture 'Cows'), *Yangcheng Wanbao* (Yangcheng Evening News), August 30, 1966.

11   According to a news report at that time, in order to resist the unhealthy life style of *niu nü*, a hairdresser in Guangzhou proposed that all hairdressers refuse to design the hair style of *niu nü* for customers. See "Da Mie Te Mie Kuai Mie Zichanjieji Guai Faxing"(Get Rid of Strange Bourgeois Hairstyles Extensively, Thoroughly, and Promptly), *Yangcheng Wanbao* (Yangcheng Evening News), August 27, 1966.

12   Shou Beibei, "Renkou Liudong Wushi Nian" (Fifty Years of Migration), *Nanfang Zhoumo* (Nanfang Weekly), November 6, 1998.

13   There are different statistics on the number of people who went down to the countryside. The data here come from Tamara Jacka, *Women's Work in Rural China: Change and Continuity in an Era of Reform,* 38.

14   Li Ruojian, "Cong Shuzui Dao Tizui: 'Si Lei Fenzi' Jieji Chutan" (From Atonement to Scapegoats: A Class Analysis of the "Four Kinds of Elements" in the Initiate Period of the People's Republic of China), *Kaifang Shidai* (Open Times), no. 5 (2006).

15   To protect the identities of the interviewees, we use M, H, and G to represent three different cities.

16   Pseudonyms are used here.

17   A pseudonym is used here.

18   Zhong Dajun, *Guomin Daiyu Bu Pingdeng Shenshi: Eryuan Jiegou Xia De Zhongguo* (Examining the Inequality of National Treatment: The Urban-Rural Dual Structure in China) (Beijing: Zhongguo Gongren Chubanshe, 2002).

19 See Huang Shumin, *Lincun De Gushi: 1949 Nian Hou De Zhongguo Nongcun Bianqe* (The Spiral Road: Change in a Chinese Village through the Eyes of a Communist Party Leader) (Beijing: Sanlian Shudian, 2002), 68–110; Jacka, *Women's Work in Rural China: Change and Continuity in an Era of Reform*.

20 Some artists acquired a new artistic life through their experiences in the countryside. See Documentary by Hu Jie and Ai Xiaoming, "Red Art" (China, 2007).

21 The difficult situation in which the educated youth found themselves is described in many literary works. See, for example, Wang Anyi, *Zhiqing Xiaoshuo* (Novels about Educated Youth) (Chengdu: Sichuan Wenyi Chubanshe, 1992).

22 For a recent analysis of the restrictive rural-urban divide, see Helen Siu, "Grounding Displacement: Uncivil Urban Spaces in Postreform South China," *American Ethnologist* 34, no. 2 (2007). The quote is taken from p. 330 of the article.

23 According to a government document, which analyses the cause of the collective suicide of some young women at a certain place, unequal pay for equal work was an important factor. See Guangdong sheng Fulian, "Guanyu Huilaixian Lianxu Fasheng Nüqingnian Jiti Toushui Zisha Shijian De Qingkuang Diaocha" (An Investigation on Recent Mass Suicides by Self-drowning among Young Women in Huilai County), November 13, 1974 (Guangzhou: Guangdong Sheng Dang'an Guan), (Guangdong Provincial Archives), 233-3-20.

24 Guangdong sheng Fulian (Women's Federation, Guangdong Province), "Jieji Douzheng Zhuyao Fanying Zai Yixia Jige Fangmian" (Class Struggle Included the Following Aspects), November 30, 1973. Guangzhou: Guangdong sheng Dang'an Guan, 233-3-9.

25 Guangdong sheng Fulian (Women's Federation, Guangdong Province), "Guanyu Huilaixian Lianxu Fasheng Nüqingnian Jiti Toushui Zisha Shijian De Qingkuang Diaocha" (An Investigation on Recent Mass Suicides by self-drowning among Young Women in Huilai County).

26 Jacka, *Women's Work in Rural China: Change and Continuity in an Era of Reform*, 133.

27 Ching-kwan Lee, *Gender and the South China Miracle: Two Worlds of Factory Women* (Berkeley; Los Angeles; London: University of California Press, 1998), 14.

28 Liwan Quwei (the District Party Committee of Liwan), "Huanan Jinbi Chang Jinxing 'Xianggang Hao Haishi Guangzhou Hao' Jiaoyu De Zuofa" (The Patriotic Education by the South China Pen Factory: 'Which is better, Hong Kong or Guangzhou?'), August 6, 1962. Guangzhou: Guangdong Sheng Dang'an Guan (Guangdong Provincial Archives), 214-1-293.

29 Zhonggong Guangdong Shengwei Xuanchuanbu (The Propaganda Department of Guangdong Provincial Party Committee), "Guangzhou Shi Yixie Zhongxuesheng Qu Xianggang Hou De Zaoyu" (The Experiences of Some High School Students fleeing to Hong Kong from Guangzhou), July 30, 1963. Guangzhou: Guangdong Sheng Dang'an Guan (Guangdong Provincial Archives), 214-1-300.

30 Helen F. Siu, "Immigrants and Social Ethos: Hong Kong in the Nineteen-Eighties," *Journal of The Hong Kong Branch of the Royal Asiatic Society* 26 (1986).

31 Guangdong sheng Nong Lin Shui Bangongshi Diaochazu (The Investigation Team of Guangdong Department of Agriculture, Forestry, and Water Resources), "Zhongshan Xian Toudu Waitao Qingkuang Zonghe" (A Summary Report of Massive Fleeing from Zhongshan County), May 31, 1973. Guangzhou: Guangdong sheng Dang'an Guan (Guangdong Provincial Archives), 229-4-298.

32 Lee, *Gender and the South China Miracle: Two Worlds of Factory Women*, 39.

33 Xianggang Wu Feng Hang (Ng Fung Hong Limited), "Xianggang Shichang Xiao Huo Dongwu Gongxiao Qingkuang" (The Supply and Marketing of Live Game in Hong Kong), September 1972. Guangzhou: Guangdong Sheng Dang'an Guan (Guangdong Provincial Archives), 296-A2.1-5.

34 Liwan Quwei (The District Party Committee of Liwan), "Huanan Jinbi Chang Jinxing 'Xianggang Hao Haishi Guangzhou Hao' Jiaoyu De Zuofa" (The Patriotic Education by the South China Pen Factory: 'Which is better, Hong Kong or Guangzhou?').

35 Guangzhou Haiguan Junguan Xiaozu (The Military Control Commission of Guangzhou Customs), "Guanyu Gaige Haiguan Dui Laizi Xianggang Aomen Duanqi Lüke Xingli Wupin Guanli Guiding De Qingshi Baogao" (The Request for Instructions to Pilot Customs Departments on Administration of the Baggage Carried by Short-term Visitors from Hong Kong and Macao), August 24, 1968. Guangzhou: Guangdong Sheng Dang'an Guan (Guangdong Provincial Archives), 229-4-11.

36 Guangdong sheng Nong Lin Shui Bangongshi Diaochazu (The Investigation Team of Guangdong Department of Agriculture, Forestry, and Water Resources), "Zhongshan Xian Toudu Waitao Qingkuang Zonghe" (A Summary Report of Massive Fleeing from Zhongshan County).

37 Da Li Gongshe Dangwei Bangongshi (The CPC Committee Office of Dali). "Da Li Gongshe Hong Feng Dadui Dangqian Jieji Douzheng De Yixie Qingkuang" (Current Situations of Class Struggle in Hongfeng Brigade of Dali Commune), May 13, 1973. Guangzhou: Guangdong Sheng Dang'an Guan (Guangdong Provincial Archives), 229-4-298.

38 Guowuyuan, Zhongyang Junwei (The State Council, and the Military Commission of the Central Committee), "Guowuyuan, Zhongyang Junwei Guanyu Jianjue Zhizhi Guangdongsheng Daliang Qunzhong Toudu Waitao De Zhishi" (The Directive by the State Council and the CMC to Stop Massive Fleeing from Guangdong Province), June 14, 1979. Guangzhou: Guangdong sheng Dang'an Guan (Guangdong Provincial Archives), 235-2-287.

39 Guangdong sheng Fulian (Women's Federation, Guangdong Province), "Jieji Douzheng Zhuyao Fanying Zai Yixia Jige Fangmian"(Class Struggle Included the Following Aspects).

40 Guangdong sheng Nong Lin Shui Bangongshi Diaochazu (The Investigation Team of Guangdong Department of Agriculture, Forestry, and Water Resources), "Zhongshan Xian Toudu Waitao Qingkuang Zonghe" (A Summary Report of Massive Fleeing from Zhongshan County).

41 See a film by Zhang Zeming, "Jue Xiang" (Swan Song). China, 1985.

42 Guangdong sheng Fulian (Women's Federation, Guangdong Province), "Jieji Douzheng Zhuyao Fanying Zai Yixia Jige Fangmian"(Class Struggle Included the Following Aspects).

43 Guangdong sheng Fulian (Women's Federation, Guangdong Province), "Gei Zhongshan Xian Fulian Liaojie Nüqingnian Toudu De Quxin" (A Letter to the Women's Federation of Zhongshan County Concerning Young Female Fleeing), June 26, 1977. Guangzhou: Guangdong Sheng Dang'an Guan (Guangdong Provincial Archives), 233-3-94.

44 See the documentary by Carma Hinton, Geremie Barme, and Richard Gordon, *Morning Sun*, 2003.

Chapter 11

1 David Harvey, *The Condition of Postmodernity: An Enquiry into the Origins of Cultural Change* (Oxford, UK; Cambridge, M.A.: B. Blackwell, 1989), Chapter 2.

2 See Gungwu Wang, "Greater China and the Chinese Overseas," *The China Quarterly*, no. 136 (1993): 930–31.

3 For instance, the movie studio tycoons, the Shaw Brothers, are Singaporean, the Kuok family that heads the Shangri-la group is from Penang, and the Haw Par brothers of Tiger Balm are Burmese Chinese.

4 There is an elaborate plan for developing Disney consumerism in China through a spectacular program of English-language education from kindergarten onward that is infused with Disney characters.

5 See the report by Zi Teng (a Hong Kong-based NGO), "Research Report on Mainland Chinese Sex Workers: Hong Kong, Macau, and Town B in Pearl River Delta," Hong Kong, 2000.

6 For a fuller biography and study that positions Fruit Chan's work within Hong Kong film, see Wendy Gan, *Fruit Chan's Durian Durian* (Hong Kong: Hong Kong University Press, 2005).

7 *Little Cheung* received the Silver Leopard at the Locarno Film Festival. *Durian Durian* won awards for Best Original Screenplay and Best New Performer (for Qin Hailu) at the 2001 Hong Kong Film Awards and won Best Film, Best Actress, Best New Performer, and Best Original Screenplay at the Golden Horse Awards in 2002.

8 For a fuller study of the handover trilogy, see Ka-fai Yau, "Cinema 3: Towards a 'Minor Hong Kong Cinema'," *Cultural Studies* 15, no. 3/4 (2001). I do not necessarily agree with the details of Yau's interpretations of the films.

9 *Little Cheung* already strains at transnationalism in the centrality it accords to the Filipina maid, and the illegal immigrant girl, who also appears as Ah Fen in *Durian, Durian*.

10 For a fuller discussion, see especially Agnes S. Ku, "Hegemonic Construction, Negotiation and Displacement," *International Journal of Cultural Studies* 4, no. 3 (2001); Helen F. Siu, "Immigrants and Social Ethos: Hong Kong in the

Nineteen-Eighties," *Journal of the Hong Kong Branch of the Royal Asiatic Society* 26 (1986).

11 Wendy Gan suggests that Chan adopts a different mode of social realism when he goes back to China and enters the world of China's Sixth Generation filmmakers, who are interested in low-key realist explorations of contemporary Chinese life that is devoid of ideals, certainty and hope of a future "and filled instead with the worship of money as China embraces money-making." See Gan, 40.

12 See, for instance, Ryan Bishop and Lillian S. Robinson, *Night Market: Sexual Cultures and the Thai Economic Miracle* (New York; London: Routledge, 1998); Phongpaichit Pasuk, *From Peasant Girls to Bangkok Masseuses* (Geneva: International Labour Office, 1982); Ara Wilson, *The Intimate Economies of Bangkok: Tomboys, Tycoons, and Avon Ladies in the Global City* (Berkeley: University of California Press, 2004), Chapter 2. All these studies deal with Thailand.

13 See Robyn Emerton, "Trafficking of Women into Hong Kong for the Purpose of Prostitution: Preliminary Research Findings" (Centre for Comparative and Public Law, Faculty of Law, The University of Hong Kong: 2001). On the violation of sex workers rights, see Carolina Ng, "Policemen Humiliate and Hurt Us, Prostitutes Claim," *Sunday Morning Post*, July 24, 2005.

14 Kevin D. Ming, "Cross-Border 'Traffic': Stories of Dangerous Victims, Pure Whores and Hiv/Aids in the Experiences of Mainland Female Sex Workers in Hong Kong," *Asia Pacific Viewpoint* 46, no. 1 (2005): 44–45.

15 Zi Teng, "Research Report on Mainland Chinese Sex Workers: Hong Kong, Macau, and Town B in Pearl River Delta," 4–5.

Glossary

a ba 阿爸
a bo 阿伯
a die 阿爹
a ei 阿嫣
a jie 阿姐
a mu 阿母
a nai 阿奶
a niang 阿娘
a shu 阿叔
a ye 阿爺
Ai Ting Fashi Jinian Kan 靄亭法師紀念刊
Ailou yizhi 靄樓逸志
Ap Chau 鴨州

Baiyun (Mountain) 白雲(山)
bang gong 幫工
Baoan 寶安
Baojing Dashi Quanji 寶靜大師全集
Baojue foxue yanjiushe 寶覺佛學研究社
Baojue foxueshe 寶覺佛學社
Baojue Nuyixue 寶覺女義學
Baoling Dong 寶靈洞
Bayan ge 芭嚴閣
Beidi 北帝
Bilan 碧蘭
bingzi 丙子
Bobbie Ho Hongyi 何鴻毅
bopo 伯婆
bu yi 補衣
buluojia 不落家

caizhu 財主
caizi jiaren 才子佳人
Chai waimu wu 拆外母屋
Chakeng xiang 茶坑鄉
Chan 禪
Chan Po Chu 陳寶珠

chang san gong 長散工
changgong 長工
Chao'an 潮安
Chaoshan 潮汕
Chaoyang 潮陽
Chaozhou 潮州
Chaozhou Chousha 潮州抽紗
Chau Tau 洲頭
Chen 陳
Chen Chunquan 陳春泉
Chen Cihong 陳慈黌
Chen Dianchen 陳殿臣
Chen Guijie 陳圭姐
Chen Jia you yangzi 陳家有養子
Chen Limei 陳立梅
Chen Shouming 陳守明
Chen Souyan 陳守炎
cheng fu 承父, 承夫
cheng zu 承祖
cheng zu yingfen ji fen 承祖應分己份
cheng zu zhifeng ji fen 承祖支分己份
Chengfa hang 成發行
Chenghai 澄海
Cheung 張
Chiu Kut-um 趙吉庵
Chuixiao yiyou 吹簫憶友
ci 慈
conglin 叢林
conglin zhi 叢林制

da po 大婆
dagongmei 打工妹
dai mi shi shui 帶米食水
dakai tancheng 打開炭埕
Dalan laopo gui 打爛老婆櫃
Dan 疍
Daoguang 道光
Dashan 大汕
Di Qing 狄青

diegui 疊櫃
Dongguan 東莞
douzhong 斗種
dui ji 堆機
dushu wei chuanjia shiye 讀書為傳家
　　世業

egupo 惡姑婆
Enping 恩平
Er/San mei tuanyuan/tonghuan
　　二／三美團圓／同歡
ernai cun 二奶村
erxi 兒媳

fan kwai 番鬼
Fan Ling 粉嶺
Fandui Xubei Shilue 反對蓄婢史略
fang 房
fei nü 飛女
fenjia 分家
Foshan 佛山
Fosheng she 佛聲社
fourth auntie 梁四姑
Fu Tai Xiang 福泰祥
Fupan gong 府判公
fuqin 父親
Furu xige buqiuren 婦孺習歌不求人

Gao 高
Gao Bo'ang 高伯昂
Gao Chenglie 高誠烈
Gao Chuxiang 高楚香
Gao Huishi 高暉石
Gao jia you yangzi 高家有養子
Gao Rixi 高日熙
Gao Shengzhi 高繩芝
Gao Shunqin 高舜琴
Gao Wenju zhenzhu ji 高文舉珍珠記
Gao Zhenbai 高貞白
gaokao 高考
getang 歌堂
Gongde 功德
Gongde Lin 功德林
gongjia 公家

gu 姑
gu jia 顧家
guancai wu 棺材屋
Guangdong 廣東
Guangdong Tongzhi 廣東通志
Guangdong Xiangshan 廣東香山
Guangdong Xinyu 廣東新語
Guangxu 光緒
Guangzhou 廣州
Guangzhoufu yixue ji 廣州府移學記
Guanhua Si 觀華寺
guanxi 關係
Guanzhen 觀真
gui mui tsai 鬼妹仔
guijian xushu, renze yi ye 貴賤雖殊，
　　人則一也
gumu 姑母
Guomindang 國民黨
guren 古人
gusaofen 姑嫂墳
guzhang 姑丈

Ha Tsuen 廈村
hai ye 亥爺
Haiyun lanruo 海雲蘭若
Han 韓
hang shuen 行船
Hanlin 翰林
He 何
He Chang 何昶
He Chen 何琛
He Cize 何慈澤
He Ding 何鼎
He Ji 何集
He Li 何栗
He Mi 何秘
he niangeng 合年庚
He Qidong 何啟東
He Qu 何渠
He Quanxing 何全興
He Renduo 何人鐸
He Renjian 何人鑒
He Ruji 何汝楫
He Shaoda 何紹達

He Shaogui　何紹圭
He Shaopu　何紹溥
He Yuanchong　何元崇
He Ze　何澤
He Zhilin　何志麟
He Zhiteng　何志騰
He Zhiyi　何志一
He Zhiyong　何志庸
He Zhizhong　何志中
He Zihai　何子海
hengxing dianzou　橫行掂走
heung shan yan　香山人
Hiroaki Kani　可兒弘明
Ho Cheung Lin-kok　何張蓮覺
Ho Hung Ki Fan　何洪奇芬
Ho Lo Yee Man　何羅綺文
Ho Qidong　何啟東
Ho Sheung Heung　河上鄉
Ho Tung　何東
Hong Lao Meng　紅樓夢
Hongwu　洪武
Hu　胡
Huajian ji　花箋記
Huang Shouxing　黃受興
Huang Zuo　黃佐
Hui-Chao-Jia　惠潮嘉
huidui　匯兌
huimen　回門
hukou　戶口
Hunan　湖南
Hunyin sangji hanshu　婚姻喪祭喊書
Husinu zitan　護絲女自歎

Ji　姬
jia　嫁
Jiajing　嘉靖
Jiangnan　江南
Jiangsu　江蘇
Jiangxi　江西
jiao　醮
jiaolai　轎來
Jiaoshan Si　焦山寺
Jiaqing　嘉慶
Jie xielan　解攜籃

Jieyang　揭陽
jimu　吉墓
Jin Yuchan　金玉蟬
Jingfu qishu　警富奇書
Jinxiu shizhai　錦繡食齋
jiu　舅
Jiujiang　九江
Jiuming qiyuan　九命奇冤
Jueyin　覺音
juren　舉人
jushi lin　居士林

Kaiping　開平
Kang Youwei　康有為
Keng Wu Hospital　鏡湖醫院
Kevin Ho Yuan Kwong　何猶廣
Kin Tye Lung　乾泰隆
Ko Lau Wan　高流灣
Koh Man Wah　高滿華
Kuang Lu　鄺露

Lady Clara, Cheung Lin-kok　張蓮覺
Leung Ting-yuk　梁廷玉
Li Guanwang　李觀旺
Li Maoying　李昴英
Lian Hui　蓮慧
Lian Jie　蓮戒
Lian Jing　蓮敬
Lian Sheng　蓮聖
Liang　梁
Liang Guozhi　梁國治
Liang Shanbo　梁山伯
Liang Shanbo yu Zhu Yingtai
　梁山伯與祝英台
Liang Tianlai　梁天來
Liang Tianlai gao yuzhuang
　梁天來告御狀
Liang Tianlai jingfu qishu
　梁天來警富奇書
Liao　廖
Lin　林
Lin biaogu　林表姑
Lin Lengzhen　林楞真
Lin Shunqun　林舜群

Ling Guiqing　凌貴卿
Lingnan　嶺南
Lingnan University　嶺南大學
Linji sect　臨濟宗
Lin-Kok　蓮覺
Liu Quan jingua　劉全進瓜
Liu Wanzhang　劉萬章
Liu Xueshi　六學士
Liu　廖
Liu　劉
Liugeng Tang　留耕堂
Liugu　六姑
Liugu huimen　六姑回門
liupo　六婆
Lo Man Kam　羅文錦
Lo Tak Shing　羅德承
Long Tinghuai　龍廷槐
Longdu　隆都
longzhou　龍舟
Luk Keng　鹿頸

Ma Fok Hing-tong　馬霍慶棠
ma laili　媽來里
ma　媽
Mai Meisheng　麥梅生
Margaret Madam Ho Min Kwan
　　何勉君
Margaret Mak Sau Ying　麥秀英
mawu　麻屋
Mayu　媽嶼
Mei Li zheng hua　梅李爭花
Menglan yiyou　夢蘭憶友
Ming　明
ming　命
Mingshan youji　名山遊記
mou men mou shi　某門某氏
mou mou shi　某某氏
moyuge　摸魚歌
mu　母
Mu Guiying　穆桂英
muitsai　妹仔
muqin　母親
muyushu　木魚書

nan　男
nan ren po　男人婆
nanbei gang hang　南北港行
Nanbei hang　南北行
nanfang　南方
Nanxiong　南雄
Nanyang　南洋
nanyin　南音
nao xinfang　鬧新房
nianfohui　念佛會
niang laili　娘來里
niang shiji　娘十幾
Niansan Chengshilang　念三承事郎
Niantian　奫田
Nie　聶
Ningbo　寧波
niu nü　牛女
nü　女
nü qiangren　女強人
nui yan　女人

O-Mun yan　澳門人

Pak Ku　北姑
Panyu　番禺
Panyu Xianzhi　番禺縣志
pao tou lu mian　拋頭露面
Percival Street　波斯富街
ping qi　平妻
Po Ko Free School　寶覺義學校
　　First and Second Po Kok
　　Free School
　　寶覺第一、第二義學
Po Kok　寶覺
Po Leung Kuk　保良局
Pujian　蒲澗
Punti　本地
putu　譜圖
Putuo Si　普陀寺

qi　妻
Qianlong　乾隆
qianzhuang　錢莊

Qianmei　前美
Qianpan gong　僉判公
Qiantai long　乾泰隆
qiao pi　僑批
qiliang　淒涼
qing　情
Qing　清
Qingdao　青島
Qingshan foxue yanjiushe　青山佛學
　研究社
Qingyu　清玉
qipao　旗袍
Qiu　邱
Qixia Shan Zhi　棲霞山誌
Qixia Si　棲霞寺
Qu Dajun　屈大均
Quanzhou　泉州
Qufu　曲阜

Raoping　饒平
Renhaideng　人海燈
Rita Lo　羅佩賢
Riye shichen　日夜時辰
Rua Central　龍嵩街
Rua St. Jose　三巴仔街
ruzhui　入贅

San Tin　新田
Sangu huimen　三姑回門
Sanjiu Chengshilang　三九承事郎
Santai (Mountain)　三台嶺
sanzai　山寨
sao　嫂
Sha Shantou　沙汕頭
Sha Tau Kok　沙頭角
Shandong　山東
shang shan xia xiang　上山下鄉
shangtou kaimian　上頭開面
shanlin fojiao　山林佛教
Shantou　汕頭
Shawan　沙灣
Shek　石
sheng wai wu　身外物
Sheung Shui　上水

shi　市
Shi　施
Shi Ai Ting　釋藹亭
Shi Bao Jing　釋寶靜
Shi Chao Lin　釋朝林
Shi Ding Fo　釋定佛
Shi Guan Ben　釋觀本
Shi Hai Yen　釋海仁
Shi Le Guan　釋樂觀
Shi Miao Shan　釋妙善
Shi Ming Hui　釋明慧
Shi Ruo Shun　釋若舜
shi shen　失身
Shi Tai Xu　釋太虛
Shi Yong Ming　釋永明
Shi Yuan Can　釋遠參
Shi'r shichen　十二時辰
Shijiu wenlu　士九問路
Shikuan hanshu　時款喊書
shinuanfangfan　食暖房飯
shiqu fojiao　市區佛教
Shisiqi　十思起
shoudai dong　手袋黨
shuen-nui　船女
shui dang di　水蕩弟
shuike　水客
Shunde　順德
Shunji　舜記
shuqi　梳起
Sik King Wai　錫降圍
sing muk　醒目
siren　私人
Siu Fong Fong　蕭芳芳
Siu Lik Yuen　小瀝源
Siyi　四邑
Song　宋
songjia　送嫁
sui　歲
sun　孫
Suzhou　蘇州

taigong　太公
taipo　太婆
Taiquan xiangli　泰泉鄉禮

Taishan　臺山
Tan Guan Lee　陳元利
tan mu xu rong　貪慕虛榮
Tang　唐
tanqing　歎情
Tanka (danjia)　蜑家
Tianhou　天后
Tianma xiang　天馬鄉
Tianshun　天順
tongxin　同心
Tsang　曾
Tsuen Wan　荃灣
Tsung Pak Long　松柏塱
tuanyuan　團圓
Tung Lin Kok Yuen　東蓮覺苑
Tung Tau Tsuen　東頭村
Tung Wah　東華
Tuopu si　鮀浦司

Vera Lo　羅佩堅

Waihai　外海
Wang　王
Wang Shen　汪森
Wang Shizhen　王士禎
wanji　綰髻
Wanshi tang　萬石堂
Weixin foxueshe　維新佛學社
wen yi bing　文藝兵
Wo (Mountain)　喎(山)
Wo Hang　禾坑
Wong Siu-lun　黃紹倫
Wu Jianren　吳趼人
Wu Ruiqing　吳瑞卿
Wu Zhenliang　吳貞良
Wu Zhimei　伍智梅
Wuguitang　五桂堂
Wuhui nianfo xinsheng　五會念佛新聲
Wushan jilin　五山志林
Wuzhou　梧州

xi　媳
Xi'an　璽庵
Xiamen　廈門

Xianggang Fojiao　香港佛教
Xiangshan　香山
Xiangshan xianzhi　香山縣志
xiangzhi　相知
Xianqing jushi　閒情居士
Xianyan　仙岩
Xiao Sheng　曉生
Xie Mengbo　謝孟博
Xinhui　新會
Xiqiao　西樵
Xiyouji　西遊記
xizhuang　西裝
xuenong　學農

Yang　楊
yehu　椰胡
Yejian Jinlan　夜薦金蘭
Yeung　楊
yewei　野味
yima　姨媽
yipin guan　一品官
yiyu jiangun　異域奸棍
yongjiu genben jiguan　永久根本機關
Yongle　永樂
You yinghua qianxue qimeng shu yi　由英話淺學啟蒙書譯
Yu (Mountain)　庾嶺
yuan　元
Yuan Can Laofashi Jilian Ji　遠參老法師紀念集
Yuan Fat Hong (Yuanfa hang)　元發行
Yuan Qingchan　袁青嬋
Yuan Zhang Sheng　元章盛
yuanpei　元配
Yuchan fujian jinlan　玉蟬附薦金蘭
Yuchan tan wugeng　玉蟬歎五更
Yuchan wenxi　玉蟬問覡
Yude Sheng　裕德盛
Yue　粵
yunkai xuehen　雲開雪恨

Zeng Zhifen　曾芷芬
zhaitang　齋堂
Zhang Dehui　張德輝

Zhang Jingrong　張靜蓉
Zhang Qu　張渠
Zhang Xiubo　張秀波
Zhang Zi　章篆
Zhanglin　樟林
Zhao　趙
Zhejiang　浙江
zheng kou qi　爭口氣
Zhengtong　正統
zhenjie　貞潔
Zhilian Jingyuan　志蓮靜苑
zhongyuan　中原
Zhou (dynasty)　周(代)

Zhu Jiexuan　朱潔軒
Zhu Yingtai　祝英台
zhugong lanlu　豬公攔路
zhuhua　豬花
zhuji jiali　朱子家禮
Zhuji xiang　珠璣巷
Zhulin Si　竹林寺
zi　子
zishunu　自梳女
Ziteng　紫藤
ziye　子夜
zumu　祖母
zuzhi　竹枝

Bibliography

Introduction

"83% Gangqi Ping Nü Gaoceng Lie Quanqiu Diwu" (83% Hong Kong Businesses Hired Senior Women Executives, Ranking Number Five in the World). *Ming Pao Daily News*, March 8, 2007, A28.

"2006 Population Bi-Census." Census and Statistics Department, the Government of Hong Kong Special Administrative Region, 2007.

Abu-Lughod, Lila. *Veiled Sentiments: Honor and Poetry in a Bedouin Society*. Berkeley: University of California Press, 1986.

Baker, Hugh. *A Chinese Lineage Village: Sheung Shui*. Stanford: Stanford University Press, 1968.

Barlow, Tani E. "Theorizing Woman: Funü, Guojia, Jiating" (Chinese Woman, Chinese State, Chinese Family). In *Body, Subject and Power in China*, edited by Angela Zito and Tani E. Barlow, 253–89. Chicago; London: University of Chicago Press, 1994.

Brook, Timothy. *Praying for Power: Buddhism and the Formation of Gentry Society in Late-Ming China*, Harvard-Yenching Institute Monograph Series. Cambridge, M.A.: Council on East Asian Studies, distributed by Harvard University Press, 1993.

Brownell, Susan, and Jeffrey N. Wasserstrom. *Chinese Femininities, Chinese Masculinities: A Reader*, vol. 4, Asia-Local Studies/Global Themes. Berkeley: University of California Press, 2002.

Cartier, Carolyn. "Symbolic City-Regions and Gendered Identity Formation." *Provincial China* 8, no. 2 (2003): 60–77.

Chan, Anita Kit-wa, and Wai-ling Wong, eds. *Gendering Hong Kong*. Hong Kong: Oxford University Press, 2004.

Chan, Johannes, and Bart Rwezura, eds. *Immigration Law in Hong Kong: An Interdisciplinary Study*. Hong Kong: Sweet and Maxwell Asia, 2004.

Chan, Wing-hoi. "Ordination Names in Hakka Genealogies: A Religious Practice and Its Decline." In *Down to Earth: The Territorial Bond in South China*, edited by David Faure and Helen F. Siu, 65–82. Stanford: Stanford University Press, 1995.

———. "Writing Women's Words: Bridal Laments and Representations of Kinship and Marriage in South China." PhD thesis, Department of Anthropology, Yale University, 2000.

Cheng, Irene. *Clara Ho Tung: A Hong Kong Lady, Her Family and Her Times*. Hong Kong: Chinese University of Hong Kong, 1976.

Ching, May-bo, and Liu Zhiwei. "Shiba, Shijiu Shiji Guangzhou Yangren Jiating Li De Zhongguo Yongren" (Chinese Servants in Foreigners' Families in Eighteenth and Nineteenth Century Guangzhou). *Shilin*, no. 4 (2004): 2–11.

Choi, Po-king, ed. *Wan Wan Liudianban: Qishi Nindai Shang Yexiao De Nügong* (Every Night at Six-Thirty: Women Workers Who Attended Evening Schools in the Seventies). Hong Kong: Stepforward Multimedia Co. Ltd., 1998.

Cohen, Myron. "Lineage Development and the Family in China." In *The Chinese Family and Its Ritual Behavior,* edited by Jih-chang Hsieh and Ying-chang Chuang, 210–18. Taipei: Institute of Ethnology, Academia Sinica, 1985.

Constable, Nicole. *Maid to Order in Hong Kong: Stories of Filipina Workers.* Ithaca, N.Y.; London: Cornell University Press, 1997.

Curtin, Philip D. *Cross-cultural Trade in World History.* Cambridge: Cambridge University Press, 1984.

Davis, Natalie Zemon, *Society and Culture in Early Modern France: Eight Essays.* Stanford: Stanford University Press, 1975.

Department of History, Sun Yat-sen University, and Guangzhou Museum, eds. *Views from the West: Collection of Nineteenth Century Pith Paper Watercolours Donated by Mr Ifan Williams to the City of Guangzhou.* Beijing: Zhonghua Book Company, 2001.

Eberhard, Wolfram. *The Local Cultures of South and East China.* Leiden: E. J. Brill, 1968.

Edwards, Louise. "Bourgeois Women and Communist Revolutionaries? De-revolutionizing the Chinese Women's Suffrage Movement." In *Women, Activism, and Social Change,* edited by Maja Mikula, 29–48. London; New York: Routledge, 2005.

Faure, David. *Emperor and Ancestor: State and Lineage in South China.* Stanford: Stanford University Press, 2007.

———. "The Lineage as a Cultural Invention: The Case of the Pearl River Delta." *Modern China* 15, no. 1 (1989): 589–627.

Faure, David, and Helen F. Siu, eds. *Down to Earth: The Territorial Bond in South China.* Stanford: Stanford University Press, 1995.

Freedman, Maurice. *Lineage Organization in Southeastern China,* London School of Economics Monographs on Social Anthropology. London: Athlone Press, 1958.

Gaetano, Arianne M., and Tamara Jacka, eds. *On the Move: Women and Rural-to-Urban Migration in Contemporary China.* New York: Columbia University Press, 2004.

Gilmartin, Christina K. "Gender, Political Culture, and Women's Mobilization in the Chinese Nationalist Revolution, 1924–1927." In *Engendering China: Women, Culture, and the State,* edited by Christina K. Gilmartin, Gail Hershatter, Lisa Rofel and Tyrene White, 195–225. Cambridge, M.A.: Harvard University Press, 1994.

Guo, Zhaozhao. "Kangzhan Qijian Guomin Canzhenghui Zhong Nü Canzhengyuan Qunti De Kaocha" (A General Review of the Female Politicians in the National Political Council of the Government of China during the Anti-Japanese War). *Anhui Daxue Xuebao* 30, no. 6 (2006): 102–06.

Hall, Peter. *In the Web.* London: Basingstoke Press, 1992.

Hershatter, Gail. "The Hierarchy of Shanghai Prostitution." *Modern China* 15, no. 4 (1989): 463.

———. "State of the Field: Women in China's Long Twentieth Century." *Journal of Asian Studies* 63, no. 4 (November 2004): 991.

———. *Women in China's Long Twentieth Century*. Berkeley: Global, Area, and International Archive, University of California Press, 2007.

Ho, Sam. "Licensed to Kick Men: The Jane Bond Films." In *The Restless Breed: Cantonese Stars of the Sixties*, edited by the Urban Council, 40–52. Hong Kong: Urban Council, 1996.

Hoe, Susanne. *The Private Life of Old Hong Kong: Western Women in The British Colony, 1841–1941*. Hong Kong: Oxford University Press, 1991.

Huang, Ai-dongxi. *Lao Guangzhou (Old Guangzhou)*. Nanjing: Jiangsu meishu chubanshe, 1999.

Jaschok, Maria, and Suzanne Miers, eds. *Women and Chinese Patriarchy: Submission, Servitude and Escape*. Hong Kong and London; Atlantic Highlands, N.J.: Hong Kong University Press; Zed Books, 1994.

Ko, Dorothy. *Cinderella's Sisters: A Revisionist History of Footbinding*. Berkeley: University of California Press, 2005.

———. *Teachers of the Inner Chambers: Women and Culture in Seventeenth-Century China*. Stanford: Stanford University Press, 1994.

Ku, Lisbeth. "Mass-Mediated Images of Women: Connie Chan Po-Chu and Josephine Siao Fong-Fong as Desired Cultural Images." *Hong Kong Cultural Studies Bulletin* 8–9 (Spring/Summer 1998): 31–40.

Lang, Graeme, and Josephine Smart. "Migration and The 'Second Wife' in South China: Toward Cross-Border Polygyny." *International Migration Review* 36, no. 2 (2002): 546–69.

Lee, Ching Kwan. *Gender and the South China Miracle: Two Worlds of Factory Women*. Berkeley: University of California Press, 1998.

Lee, Leo Ou-fan. *Shanghai Modern: The Flowering of a New Urban Culture in China, 1930–1945*. Cambridge, M.A.: London: Harvard University Press, 1999.

Li, Liu. "Guangdong Nüxing Jiuye Renkou De Zhiye Zhuangkuang He Jingji Shouru Fenxi" (Analysis of the Occupational Condition and Incomes of Guangdong Women in Employment). *Ningbo Dangxiao Xuebao*, no. 5 (2003): 77–80.

Liu, Zhiwei. "Lineage on the Sands: The Case of Shawan." In *Down to Earth: The Territorial Bonds in South China*, edited by David Faure and Helen Siu, 21–43. Stanford: Stanford University Press, 1995.

"Liudong Renkou Yi Chaoguo 1.2yi, Qizhong Kuasheng Liudong Da 4242Wan, Jinru Guangdong Renshu Ju Quanguo Zhishou" (Floating Population Already Exceeds 1,20 Million). *Nangfang Dushi Bao*, October 7, 2002, A11.

Lui, Tai-lok. *Waged Work at Home: The Social Organization of Industrial Outwork in Hong Kong*. Aldershot, England: Avebury, 1994.

Liu Tik-sang. "Becoming Marginal: A Fluid Community and Shamanism in the Pearl River Delta of South China." PhD dissertation, University of Pittsburg, 1995.

Mahmood, Saba. *Politics of Piety: The Islamic Revival and the Feminist Subject*. Princeton, N.J.: Princeton University Press, 2005.

Mankekar, Purnima. *Screening Culture, Viewing Politics: An Ethnography of Television, Womanhood, and Nation Postcolonial India.* Durham, N.C.: Duke University Press, 1999.

Mann, Susan. *Precious Records: Women in China's Long Eighteenth Century.* Stanford: Stanford University Press, 1997.

———, ed. *Women and Gender Relations: Perspectives on Asia: Sixty Years of the Journal of Asian Studies.* Ann Arbor, M.I.: Association for Asian Studies, Inc., 2004.

McDermott, Joseph. "The Chinese Domestic Bursar." *Asian Cultural Studies,* special issue (1990): 13–30.

Ortner, Sherry. "Gender and Sexuality in Hierarchical Societies: The Case of Polynesia and Some Comparative Implications." In *Sexual Meanings: The Cultural Construction of Gender and Sexuality,* edited by Sherry B. Ortner and Harriet Whitehead, 359–409. Cambridge; New York: Cambridge University Press, 1981.

Ortner, Sherry B., and Harriet Whitehead, eds. *Sexual Meanings: The Cultural Construction of Gender and Sexuality.* Cambridge; New York: Cambridge University Press, 1981.

Pearson, Veronica, and Benjamin K. P. Leung, eds. *Women in Hong Kong.* Hong Kong; New York: Oxford University Press, 1995.

Pickowicz, Paul, and Wang Liping. "Village Voices, Urban Activists: Women, Violence, and Gender Inequality in Rural China." In *Popular China: Unofficial Culture in a Globalizing Society,* edited by E. Perry Link, Richard Madsen and Paul Pickowicz, 57–87. Lanham, M.D.: Rowman and Littlefield, 2002.

Pun, Ngai. *Made in China: Women Factory Workers in a Global Workplace.* Durham: Duke University Press, 2005.

Rosaldo, Michelle Zimbalist, Louise Lamphere, and Joan Bamberger, eds. *Woman, Culture, and Society.* Stanford: Stanford University Press, 1974.

Sinn, Elizabeth. "Lesson in Openness: Creating a Space of Flow in Hong Kong." In *Hong Kong Mobile: Making a Global Population,* edited by Helen F. Siu and Agnes S. Ku, 13–43. Hong Kong: Hong Kong University Press, 2008.

———. *Power and Charity: The Early History of the Tung Wah Hospital, Hong Kong,* East Asian Historical Monographs. Hong Kong; New York: Oxford University Press, 1989.

———. "Women at Work: Chinese Brothel Keepers in Nineteenth-Century Hong Kong." *Women's History* 19, no. 3 (2007): 87–111.

Siu, Helen F. "China's Century: Fast Forward with Historical Baggage." *American Anthropologist* 108, no. 2 (2006): 389–92.

———. "The Grounding of Cosmopolitans: Merchants and Local Cultures in South China." In *Becoming Chinese: Passages to Modernity and Beyond,* edited by Wenhsin Yeh, 191–227. Berkeley: University of California Press, 2000.

———. "Positioning 'Hong Kongers' and 'New Immigrants'." In *Hong Kong Mobile: Making a Global Population,* edited by Helen Siu and Agnes S. Ku. Hong Kong: Hong Kong University Press, 2008.

———. "Review Article: Emperor and Ancestor: State and Lineage in South China by David Faure." *The China Quarterly* 192 (December 2007): 1041–43.

———. "Where Were the Women? Rethinking Marriage Resistance and Regional Culture History." *Late Imperial China* 11, no. 2 (December 1990): 32–62.

Siu, Helen F., and Liu Zhiwei. "Lineage, Market, Pirate and Dan: Ethnicity in the Sands of South China." In *Empire at the Margins: Culture, Frontier and Ethnicity in Early Modern China*, edited by Pamela Kyle Crossley, Helen F. Siu and Donald S. Sutton, 285–310. Berkeley: University of California Press, 2006.

Siu, Helen F., Richard Wong, David Faure. "Rethinking Hong Kong's Human Resources and Competitiveness: A Pre-Policy Study" for the 2022 Foundation, 2005.

Smith, Carl. "The Chinese Church, Labour and Elites and the Mui Tsai Question in the 1920s." *Journal of the Hong Kong Branch of the Royal Asiatic Society* 21 (1981): 91–113.

———. "Ng Akew, One of Hong Kong's 'Protected Women'." *Chung Chi Bulletin* no. 46 (June 1966): 13–17, 27.

Stockard, Janice E. *Daughters of the Canton Delta: Marriage Patterns and Economic Strategies in South China, 1860–1930*. Stanford: Stanford University Press, 1989.

Sun, Hailong, Gong Dejia, and Li Bin. "Chengshihua Beijing Xia Nongcun 'Waijianü' Quanyi Jiufen Jiqi Jiejue Jizhi De Sikao" (Reflections on Disputes over the Rights of Rural "Married Daughter" amid Urbanization and Mechanism for their Resolutions). *Falü Shiyong*, no. 3 (2004): 26–30.

Tam, Siumi Maria. "Normalization of 'Second Wives': Gender Contestation in Hong Kong." *Asian Journal of Women Studies* 2 (1996): 113–32.

Topley, Marjorie. "Marriage Resistance in Rural Kwangtung." In *Women in Chinese Society*, edited by Margery Wolf, Roxane Witke and Emily M. Ahern, 67–88. Stanford: Stanford University Press, 1975.

Tsang, Gar-yin. "Chronology of Women's Achievements." In *Women in Hong Kong*, edited by Veronica Pearson and Benjamin K.P. Leung. Hong Kong: Oxford University Press, 1995.

Tsin, Michael Tsang-woon. *Nation, Governance, and Modernity in China: Canton, 1900–1927*. Stanford: Stanford University Press, 1999.

Watson, James L., and Rubie S. Watson. *Village Life in Hong Kong: Politics, Gender, and Ritual in the New Territories*. Hong Kong: The Chinese University Press, 2004.

Watson, Rubie S., and Patricia Buckley Ebrey, eds. *Marriage and Inequality in Chinese Society*. Berkeley: University of California Press, 1991.

Wen, Zhiqi. "Nannü Tonggong Tongchou Yundong De Canyu Zhe: Mei Meiya" (A Participant in the Equal Pay Movement: Elizabeth Susan Mair). In *Ling Yiban Tiankong: Zhanhou Xianggang Funü Yundong* (The Other Half of the Sky: Post-War Women's Movement in Hong Kong), edited by Zhang Caiyun et al., 9–16. Hong Kong: Xin Funü Xiejin Hui, 1992.

White, Barbara-Sue, ed. *Hong Kong: Somewhere Between Heaven and Earth*. Hong Kong: Oxford University Press, 1996.

"Who's Worth a Million Dollars in Hong Kong? More Women Than Men." *South China Morning Post*, February 14, 2007, 3.

Wiens, Herold J. *Han Chinese Expansion in South China*. Hamden, CT: Shoe String Press, 1967.

Wilson, Ming, and Liu Zhiwei, eds. *Souvenir from Canton: Chinese Export Paintings from the Victoria and Albert Museum*. Shanghai: Shanghai Classics Publishing House, 2003.

Wolf, Margery. *Revolution Postponed: Women in Contemporary China*. Stanford: Stanford University Press, 1985.

Wong, Pik-wan. "The Hong Kong Women's Movement in Transition." In *Political Participation in Hong Kong*, edited by Joseph Y.S. Cheng, 207–48. Hong Kong: City University Press, 1999.

Wong, Wai-ching. "Negotiating Gender Identity: Postcolonialism and Christianity in Hong Kong." In *Gender and Change in Hong Kong: Globalization, Postcolonialism, and Chinese Patriarchy*, edited by Eliza W. Y. Lee, 151–76. Vancouver: University of British Columbia Press, 2004.

Wood, William Maxwell. *Fankwei; or, the San Jacinto in the Seas of India, China, and Japan*. New York: Harper and Brothers, 1859.

Yang, Mayfair Mei-hui. "From Gender Erasure to Gender Difference: State Feminism, Consumer Sexuality, and a Feminist Public Sphere in China." In *Spaces of Their Own: Women's Public Sphere in Transnational China*, edited by Mayfair Mei-hui Yang, 35–67. Minneapolis: University of Minnesota Press, 1999.

———, ed. *Spaces of Their Own: Women's Public Sphere in Transnational China*. Minneapolis: University of Minnesota Press, 1999.

Zhang, Yufa. "Ershi Shiji Qianbanqi Zhongguo Funü Canzheng Quan De Yanbian." (The Transformation of Women's Election Rights in the First Half of the Twentieth Century). In *Wusheng Zhi Sheng (I): Jindai Zhongguo De Funü Yu Guojia (1600–1950)* (The Sound of Silence [I]: Modern Chinese Women and the State [1600–1950]), edited by Fangshang Lu, 39–71. Taipei: Zhongyang Yanjiuyuan Jindaishi Yanjiusuo, 2003.

Zheng, Tiantian. "From Peasant Women to Bar Hostesses: Gender and Modernity in Post-Mao Dalian." In *On the Move: Women in Rural-to-Urban Migration in Contemporary China*, edited by Arianne Gaetano and Tamara Jacka, 80–108. New York: Columbia University Press, 2004.

———. *Red Lights: The Lives of Sex Workers in Postsocialist China*. Minneapolis: University of Minnesota Press, 2009.

Zuo, Waiqing. "Guangdong Shehui Xingbie Diaocha Yu Bijiao Fenxi" (Survey and Comparative Analysis of Gender in Guangdong). *Tequ Lilun yu Shijian* no. 6 (2003): 57–60.

Chapter 1

Chenzu Shipu (The Genealogy of the Chens).

Faure, David. "The Lineage as a Cultural Invention: The Case of the Pearl River Delta." *Modern China* Vol. 15, no. 1 (January, 1989): 4–36.

Gu, Jiegang. *Mao Xue Congji*. Vol. 1. In *Gu Jiegang Dushu biji* (Reading Notes of Gu Jiegang), Vol. 10. Taipei: Lianjing Chuban Shiye Gongsi, 1990.

Guangdong Tongzhi (Guangdong Provincial Gazetteer), 1561.

Lin, Yutang. *My Country and My People*. New York: The John Day Company, 1939.

Liu, Wanzhang. *Guangzhou Minjian Gushi* (Folk Stories of Canton). Guangzhou: Zhongshan Daxue Yuyan Lishi Yanjiusuo, 1929.

Liu, Zhiwei. "Lineage on the Sand: The Case of Shawan." In *Down to Earth: The Territorial Bond in South China*, edited by David Faure and Helen F. Siu. Stanford: Stanford University Press, 1995.

Long, Tinghuai. *Jingxue Xuan Wenji* (Collected Essays of Jingxue xuan), 1842.

Luo, Xianglin. "Guangdong Minzu Gailun" (A General Discussion of the Ethnic Groups in Guangdong). In *Minsu* (Folklores), No. 63. Guangzhou: Guoli Zhongshan Daxue, 1929.

Ma, Duanlin. *Wenxian Tongkao* (General Study of the Literary Remains). Beijing: Zhonghua Shuju, reprint, 1986.

Makino, Tatsumi. "Koto Genju Minzoku Ko " (An Investigation of the Indigenous Population of Guangdong). In *Makino Tatsumi Chokikushu*, edited by Makino Tatsumi. Tokyo: Ochanomizu Shoba 5, 1985.

Panyu Xianzhi (Panyu County Gazetteer), 1870.

Qian, Yiji. *Beizhuanji* (A Collection of Biographies), *Qingdai Beizhuan Quanji* (A Complete Collection of Biographies of the Qing Dynasty). Shanghai: Shanghai Guji Chubanshe, 1987.

Siu, Helen F. "The Reconstitution of Brideprice and Dowry in South China." In *Chinese Families in the Post-Mao Era*, edited by Deborah Davis and Stevan Harrell, 165–88. Berkeley: University of California Press, 1993.

———. "Where Were the Women? Rethinking Marriage Resistance and Regional Culture History. " *Late Imperial China* 11, no. 2 (1990): 32–62.

Wang, Sen. *Yuexi Congzai* (Collected Records on Guangxi).

Xinhui Xianzhi (Xinhui County Gazetteer). Beijing: Shumu Wenxian Chubanshe, 1690, reprint, 1991.

Xu, Songshi. *Yuejiang Liuyu Renmin Shi* (A History of the People Residing along the Pearl River). Shanghai: Zhonghua Shuju, 1929.

Zhang, Qu. *Yuedong Wenjian Lu* (An Account of What [I] Hear and Observe in Guangdong). Guangzhou: Guangdong Gaodeng Jiaoyu Chubanshe, reprint, 1990.

Zhang Zi. "Guangzhou Fu Yixue Ji" (An Account of Moving the Guangzhou Prefectural School). In *Yuan Dade Nanhaizhi Canben* (An Incomplete Copy of Nanhai Gazetteer Compiled in the Yuan Dynasty), edited by Guangzhoushi Difangzhi Bianzuan Weiyuanhui Bangongshi. Guangzhou: Guangdong Renmin Chubanshe, reprint, 1991.

Zhu, Yu. *Pingzhou Ketan* (Talks on Pingzhou). Siku Quanshu ed. Shanghai: Shanghai Guji Chubanshe, 1982.

Chapter 2

Chen, Baisha. "Qi Zhongyang Shu." In *Chen Xianzhang ji* (The Collected Works of Chen Xianzhang). Beijing: Zhonghua, 1987.

Huang, Zuo. Taiquan Xiangli. Siku edition ed. Vol. 3, preface of 1549.

Huoshi zupu 1848. Guangzhou: Guangdong Provincial Library; K/0.189/470.2.

Ko, Dorothy. *Teachers of the Inner Chambers: Women and Culture in Seventeenth-Century China.* Stanford: Stanford University Press, 1994.

Li, Suiqiu. *Lianxu Ge Wenchao* (Essays of the Lianxu Pavilion), Preface of 1638. Guangdong congshu edition of 1940 ed.

Luo Tianchi. Wushan Jilin. Shunde shizhi bangongshi. Preface of 1761. Reprint, 1986.

Shunde Beimen Luoshi Zupu. 1882.

Shunde Xianzhi. 1750.

Siu, Helen F. "Where Were the Women? Rethinking Marriage Resistance and Regional Culture History." *Late Imperial China* 11, no. 2 (December) (1990): 32–62.

Wolf, Margery. *Women and the Family in Rural Taiwan.* Stanford: Stanford University Press, 1972.

Chapter 3

Blake, Fred. "Death and Abuse in Marriage Laments: The Curse of Chinese Brides." *Studies in Asian Folklore* 37, no. 1 (1978): 13–33.

Chai Waimu Wu (Tearing down the Mother-in-law's House). Guangzhou: Yiwentang, n.d.

Chan, Wing-hoi. *Local Traditional Folksongs: Transcriptions.* Hong Kong: Hong Kong Museum, 1984 (unpublished).

———. "Locating Women's Voice: Chinese Bridal Songs in Its Social Context." In *Conference on Merchants and Local Cultures.* Division of Humanities, Hong Kong University of Science and Technology, 1994.

———. "Traditional Folksongs and Rural Life in Hong Kong." In *"Overall Report on the General Context of Local Folksongs" for the Project on the Recording of Local Traditional Folksongs of the Hong Kong Region.* Hong Kong: Hong Kong Museum, 1984 (unpublished).

Chuixiao Yiyou (Playing the Flute [She] Misses [Her] Friend). Guangzhou: Yiwentang, n.d.

Hung, Chang-tai. *Going to the People: Chinese Intellectuals and Folk Literature, 1918–1937,* Harvard East Asian Monographs. Cambridge, M.A.: Council on East Asian Studies; distributed by Harvard University Press, 1985.

Hunyin Sangji Hanshu (A Book of Marriage and Funeral Laments), manuscript collected at Guangdong Provincial Library, Guangzhou: n.p., n.d.

Jiexielan (Untying the Carrying Basket). n.p. (probably Guangzhou: Wuguitang), n.d.

Jinxiu Shizhai (Jiuxiu Eating Vegetarian Feast). Guangzhou: Zuijingtang, n.d.

Johnson, Elizabeth. "Grieving for the Dead, Grieving for the Living: Funeral Laments of Hakka Women." In *Death Ritual in Late Imperial and Modern China*, edited by James L. Watson and Evelyn S. Rawski, 135–63. Berkeley: University of California Press, 1988.

Kuang, Lu. *Qiaoya* (A Collection of Poems). n.p., n.d.

Leung, Pui-chee. *Xianggang Daxue Suocang Muyushu Xulu Yu Yanjiu* (Wooden-fish Books: Critical Essays and Annotated Catalogue Based on the Collection in the University of Hong Kong). Hong Kong: Centre of Asian Studies, The University of Hong Kong, 1978.

Liu, Wanzhang, and Gu Jiegang. *Su Yue De Hunsang* (The Marriage and Funeral Rite of Soochow [Suzhou] and Canton [Guangzhou]). Guangzhou: Guoli Zhongshan Daxue Yuyan Lishi Yanjiusuo, 1928.

Liugu Huimen (Sixth Aunt Returning to Her Natal Home). Hong Kong: Wuguitang, n.d.

Luo, Ergang. "Jiuming Qiyuan De Benshi" (The Original Story of Jiuming Qiyuan). In *Wu Jianren Yanjiu Ziliao* (Materials for Studying Wu Jianren), edited by Wei Shaochang, 99–105. Shanghai: Shanghai Guji Chubanshe, 1980.

———. "Jiuming Qiyuan Xiongfan Chuansaiqi Dang'an Zhi Faxian" (The Discovery of the Archives Concerning the Murderer, Chuansaiqi, in Connection with the Story Entitled Jiuming Qiyuan). In *Wu Jianren Yanjiu Ziliao* (Materials for Studying Wu Jianren), edited by Wei Shaochang, 105–10. Shanghai: Shanghai Guji Chubanshe, 1980.

Martin, Emily. "Gender and Ideological Difference in Representation of Life and Death." In *Death Ritual in Late Imperial and Modern China*, edited by James L. Watson and Evelyn S. Rawski, 164–79. Berkeley: University of California Press, 1988.

Mei Li Zeng Hua (Mr Mei and Mr Li Competing with Each Other for Miss Hua). Guangzhou: Zuijingtang, n.d.

Menglan Yiyou (Menglan Missing Her Friend): n.p., n.d.

Qu, Dajun. *Guangdong Xinyu* (New Accounts of Guangdong), preface dated 1700. Hong Kong: Zhonghua Shuju. Reprint, 1974.

Rawski, Evelyn S. "Economic and Social Foundations of Late Imperial Culture." In *Popular Culture in Late Imperial China*, edited by David G. Johnson, Andrew J. Nathan, Evelyn S. Rawski and Judith A. Berling, 3–33. Berkeley: University of California Press, 1985.

Riye Shichen (Hours through Days and Nights). n.p., n.d.

Sangu Huimen (Third Aunt Returning to Her Natal Home). n.p. (probably Hong Kong and Guangzhou: Wuguitang), n.d.

Shi'er Shichen (Twelve [Chinese] Hours). Hong Kong: Xingji Shuju, n.d.

Siu, Helen F. "Where Were the Women? Rethinking Marriage Resistance and Regional Culture History." *Late Imperial China* 11, no. 2 (December 1990): 32–62.

Stockard, Janice E. *Daughters of the Canton Delta: Marriage Patterns and Economic Strategies in South China, 1860–1930*. Stanford: Stanford University Press, 1989.

Tan, Zhengbi, and Tan Xun. *Muyuge, Chaozhouge Xulu* (An Annotated Catalogue of Wooden-fish Songs and Chaozhou Songs). Beijing: Shumu Wenxian Chubanshe, 1982.

Tongxin Shangbannian ([Thinking about] My "Same Heart" [As I Think about the Things and Events Occurring in] the First Half of the Year). n.p., n.d.

Topley, Marjorie. "Marriage Resistance in Rural Kwantung." In *Women in Chinese Society*, edited by Margery Wolf, Roxane Witke and Emily M. Ahern, 67–88. Stanford: Stanford University Press, 1975.

Wang, Shizhen. *Nanhai Ji* (A Collection of Essays on the South). n.p., n.d. (preface dated 1684).

Wong, Shiu-hon. *Xianggang Daxue Yazhou Yanjiu Zhongxin Suocang Yueju Juben Mulu* (A Catalogue of Cantonese Opera Scripts Collected at the Centre of Asian Studies, The University of Hong Kong). Hong Kong: Centre of Asian Studies, The University of Hong Kong, 1990.

Wu, Ruiqing. "Guangfuhua Shuochangben Muyushu De Yanjiu" (A Study on Cantonese Wooden-fish Song Books). PhD dissertation, The Chinese University of Hong Kong, 1989.

Wuxiang Tongxin. (Five Times I Think about My Sisters with the "Same Heart"). Guangzhou: Wuguitang, n.d.

Xinchu Husinu Zitan (A Woman Silk Worker Lamenting on Her Own). n.p., n.d.

Yejian Jinlan (Warning Jinlan at Night). n.p., n.d.

You Yinghua Qianxue Qimeng Shu Yi (Translating from an English Primer of Enlightenment), collected at Cambridge University: n.p., 1873.

Yuchan Fujian. (Yuchan Sending a Letter [to Her "Golden-orchid" Sister]). n.p. (probably Guangzhou: Wuguitang), n.d.

Yuchan Wenxi (Yuchan Inquiring the Sorcerer). n.p. (probably Guangzhou: Wuguitang), n.d.

Yung, Sai-shing. "Mu-yu Shu and the Cantonese Popular Singing Arts." *The Gest Library Journal* 2, no. 1 (1987): 16–30.

Zhang, Zhengping. *Ku Gezi Ci* (Hong Kong New Territories Folk-literature Study). Vol. 1. Hong Kong: Youhua Publisher, 1969.

Zhao, Shiyu. *Yanguang Xiangxia De Geming: Zhongguo Xiandai Minsuxue Sixiangshi Lun (1918–1937)* (A Revolution Towards the Masses: A History of Folklore Studies in Modern China, 1918–1937). Beijing: Beijing Shifan Daxue Chubanshe, 1999.

Zheng, Zhenduo. *Bali Guojia Tushuguan Zhong Zhi Zhongguo Xiaoshuo Yu Xiqu* (Chinese Novels and Opera Scripts Collected at Bibliothèque nationale de France in Paris), 1927. Reprint, in his *Zhongguo Wenxue Yanjiu* (Studies of Chinese Literature), Hong Kong: Guwen Shuju, 1961.

Zhou, Chuqi. "Jiebai Jinlan Zhen Yewei: Muyushu Zhong Zishunu Tongxinglian Jingguan" (How Scrumptious Knotting a "Golden-orchid" Relationship Is: The Homosexual Outlook of the Zishunu as Reflected in the Wooden-fish Song Books). *Jiushi Niandai*, no. 7 (1994): 82–83.

Chapter 4

"Annual Report on the Social and Economic Progress of the People of Hong Kong, 1938." London: His Majesty's Stationery Office, 1939.

Baker, Hugh. *A Chinese Lineage Village: Sheung Shui*. London: Frank Cass and Co., 1968.

———. "The Five Great Clans of the New Territories." *Journal of the Royal Asiatic Society Hong Kong Branch* 6 (1966): 25–48.

Brim, John. "Local Systems and Modernizing Change in the New Territories of Hong Kong." PhD thesis, Stanford University, 1970.

———. "Village Alliance Temples in Hong Kong." In *Religion and Ritual in Chinese Society*, edited by Arthur Wolf. Stanford: Stanford University Press, 1974.

Chan, Han-seng. *Agrarian Problems in Southernmost China*. Shanghai: Kelly and Walsh, 1936.

Chan, Wing-hoi. "Writing Women's Words: Bridal Laments and Representations of Kinship and Marriage in South China." PhD thesis, Yale University, 2000.

Chen, Shuping. "Yumi He Fanshu Zai Zhongguo Chuanbo Qingkuang Yanjiu" (A Study of the Spread of Corn and Sweet Potato in China), *Zhongguo shehui kexue jikan*, no. 3 (1980): 187–204.

Chen, Zelin. "Xinhui Xian Nongye Diaocha Baogao" (Agriculture Survey Report for Xinhui County). In *Guangdong Nongye Gaikuang Diaocha Baogaoshu*, edited by Guangdong Sheng Difang Nonglin Shiyanchang Diaochake. Guangzhou: Guoli Guangdong Daxue Nongke Xueyuan (Guangdong Agriculture Survey Report), 1925.

Chun, Allen. *Unstructuring Chinese Society: The Fictions of Colonial Practice and the Changing Realities of "Land" In the New Territories of Hong Kong*. Amsterdam: Harwood Academic, 2000.

Cohen, Myron. "Lineage Development and the Family in China." In *The Chinese Family and Its Ritual Behavior*, edited by Jih-chang Hsieh and Ying-chang Chuang, 210–18. Taipei: Institute of Ethnology, Academia Sinica, 1985.

"Colonial Annual Reports, Hong Kong, 1948." London: His Majesty's Stationery Office, 1949.

Davis, S. G. *Hong Kong in Its Geographical Setting*. London: Collins, 1949.

di Leonardo, Micaela. "The Female World of Cards and Holidays: Women, Families, and the Work of Kinship." *Signs* 12, no. 3 (1987): 440–53.

Faure, David. *The Rural Economy of Pre-Liberation China: Trade Expansion and Peasant Livelihood in Jiangsu and Guangdong*. Hong Kong: Oxford University Press, 1989.

———. *The Structure of Chinese Rural Society: Lineage and Village in the Eastern New Territories*. Hong Kong: Oxford University Press, 1986.

Fei, Hsiao-tung, and Chang Chih-i. *Earthbound China: A Study of Rural Economy in Yunnan*. Chicago: University of Chicago Press, 1945.

Feil, D. K. "Beyond Patriliny in the New Guinea Highlands." *Man* n.s. 19, no. 1 (1984): 50–76.

Freedman, Maurice. *Lineage Organization in Southeast China*. New York: Humanities Press, 1965.

Gompertz. "Some Notes on Land Tenure in the New Territory." In *Report on Operations in the New Territories During 1900*, 16–20. London: His Majesty's Stationery Office, 1901.

Grant, Charles J. "The Soils and Agriculture of Hong Kong." Hong Kong: Hong Kong Government Printer, 1960.

Guangdong Nongye Gaikuang Diaocha Baogaoshu (Guangdong Agriculture Survey Report). Edited by Guangdong Sheng Difang Nonglin Shiyanchang Diaochake. Guangzhou: Guoli Guangdong Daxue Nongke Xueyuan, 1925.

Hase, Patrick. "A Note on Rice Farming in Sha Tin." *Journal of the Royal Asiatic Society Hong Kong Branch* 21 (1981): 196–206.

Ho, Ping-ti. *Studies on the Population of China, 1368–1953*. Cambridge: Harvard University Press, 1959.

"Hong Kong Statistics 1947–1967." Hong Kong: Census and Statistics Department, 1969.

"Hong Kong, Annual Report for 1921." London: His Majesty's Stationery Office, 1922.

Johnson, Elizabeth L. "Hakka Women: Great Aunt Yeung: A Hakka Wage Laborer." In *Lives: Chinese Working Women*, edited by Mary Sheridan and Janet W. Salaff, 76–91. Bloomington: Indiana University Press, 1984.

Kamm, John. "Two Essays on the Ch'ing Economy of Hsin-An." *Journal of the Royal Asiatic Society Hong Kong Branch* 17 (1977): 55–84.

Li, Qiaofang. "Heyuan Xian Nongye Diaocha Baogao" (Agriculture Survey Report for Heyuan County). In *Guangdong Nongye Gaikuang Diaocha Baogaoshu* (Guangdong Agriculture Survey Report), edited by Guangdong Sheng Difang Nonglin Shiyanchang Diaochake. Guangzhou: Guoli Guangdong Daxue Nongke Xueyuan, 1925.

Lockhart, J. H. S. "New Territories Report for 1901." 1902.

"New Territories: Land Court, Report on Work from 1900 to 1905." Land Court.

Orme, G. N. *Report on the New Territories, 1899–1912*: n.p., 1912.

Osborne, Edward, et al. *Food Commission Report, 1900*: n.p., 1900.

Palmer, Michael. "Lineage and Urban Development in a New Territories Town." In *An Old State in New Settings: Studies in the Social Anthropology of China in Memory of Maurice Freedman*, edited by Hugh Baker and Stephan Feuchtwang, 70–106. Oxford: JASO, 1991.

———. "The Surface-Subsoil Form of Divided Ownership in Late Imperial China: Some Examples from the New Territories of Hong Kong." *Modern Asian Studies* 21, no. 1 (1987): 1–119.

Potter, Jack M. *Capitalism and the Chinese Peasant: Social and Economic Change in a Hong Kong Village*. Berkeley: University of California Press, 1968.

———. "Land and Lineage in Traditional China." In *Family and Kinship in Chinese Society*, edited by Maurice Freedman, 121–38. Stanford: Stanford University Press, 1970.

Shangshui Xiang Wenxian (Historical Documents from Sheung Shui Village). Vol. 6: n.p., n.d.

Siu, Helen F. "Where Were the Women? Rethinking Marriage Resistance and Regional Culture History." *Late Imperial China* 11, no. 2 (December) (1990): 32–62.

Skinner, G. William, ed. *The Study of Chinese Society: Essays by Maurice Freedman.* Stanford: Stanford University Press, 1979.

Smith, N. L., et. al. "Report of the Committee Appointed to Consider the Breeding of Pigs and Poultry in the New Territories." 1934.

"The Hongkong Government Gazette, 6 July." Hong Kong 1901.

Watson, James L. *Emigration and the Chinese Lineage: The Mans in Hong Kong and London.* Berkeley: University of California Press, 1975.

———. "Hereditary Tenancy and Corporate Landlordism in Traditional China: A Case Study." *Modern Asian Studies* 11, no. 2 (1977): 161–82.

Watson, Rubie. "Class Differences and Affinal Relations in South China." *Man* n.s. 16, no. 4 December (1984): 593–613.

———. *Inequality among Brothers: Class and Kinship in South China.* Cambridge [Cambridgeshire]; New York: Cambridge University Press, 1985.

Watson, Rubie S. *Inequality among Brothers: Class and Kinship in South China.* Cambridge [Cambridgeshire]; New York: Cambridge University Press, 1985.

Whyte, Martin King. "Revolutionary Social Change and Patrilocal Residence in China." *Ethnology* 18, no. 3 (1979): 211–27.

Wolf, Margery. *Women and the Family in Rural Taiwan.* Stanford: Stanford University Press, 1972.

"Xinjie De Yangzhu Shiye" (Pig Farming in the New Territories). In *Xinjie Nianjian* (Yearbook of the New Territories). Hong Kong: Yu Nong Chu (Agriculture and Fisheries Department), 1971.

Zheng, Zhenzhou. "Buolo Xian Nongye Diaocha Baogao" (Agriculture Survey Report for Boluo County). In *Guangdong Nongye Gaikuang Diaocha Baogaoshu* (Guangdong Agriculture Survey Report), edited by Guangdong Sheng Difang Nonglin Shiyanchang Diaochake. Guangzhou: Guoli Guangdong Daxue Nongke Xueyuan, 1925.

Zhongguo Zhu Pinzhong Zhi (A Description of Breeds of Pig in China). Shanghai: Shanghai Kexue Jishu Chubanshe, 1986.

Chapter 5

Arnold, Julean ed. *Commercial Handbook of China.* Vol. 1, *Miscellaneous.* Washington: Government Printing Office, Department of Commerce, 1919.

Ball, J. Dyer. *Things Chinese: Or Notes Connected with China.* 5th ed. Hong Kong and Shanghai: Kelly and Walsh, 1925.

Boxer, C. R. *South China in the Sixteenth Century.* Nendeln/Liechtenstein: Kraus Reprint Limited, 1953 and 1967.

Chan, W. K. K. "Chinese Business Networking and the Pacific Rim: The Family Firm, Roles Past and Present." *Journal of American-East Asian Relations* 1, no. 2: 171–90.

Chaohai Guanshiliao Huibian (Collected Archives of Chaozhou Maritime Customs). Zhongguo Haiguan Xuehui Shantou Haiguan Xiaozu and Shantou Shi Difangzhi Bianzuan Weiyuanhui Bangong Shi, 1988.

Chen, Chunsheng. "Tianhou Gushi Yu Shequ Lishi Zhuanbian: Zhanglin Sige Tianhou Miao De Yanjiu" (Stories of the Goddess of Heaven and the Historical Development of Local Communities: Study of Four Tianhou Temples in Zhanglin). *Chaoxue Yanjiu* no. 8 (2000): 159–71.

Chen, Ta. *Emigrant Communities in South China, a Study of Overseas Migration and Its Influence on Standards of Living and Social Change.* New York: Secretariat, Institute of Pacific Relations, 1940.

———. *Nan Yang Huaqiao Yu Minyue Shehui* (Southeast Asian Chinese and the Society of Fujian and Guangdong). Changsha: Shangwu Publishing House, 1938.

Chenghai Xianzhi. (Gazetteer of the Chenghai County). Edited by Chenghai xian difang zhi bianji weiyuanhui. Guangdong: Guangdong Renmin Chubanshe, 1991.

Choi, Chi-cheung, ed. *Business Documents and Land Deeds Collected by Dr. James Hayes: Kin Tye Lung Document* Vol. 1: *Land Deeds of the Chaoshan Region.* Tokyo: The Institute of Oriental Culture, Tokyo University, 1995.

———. "Competition among Brothers: The Kin Tye Lung Company and Its Associate Companies." In *Chinese Business Enterprise in Asia,* edited by Rajeswary Brown, 96–114. London; New York: Routledge, 1995.

———. "Cong Yizhu Kan Jindai Chaoshan Jiazu Qiye De Fazhan: Yi Xianggang Qiantai Longji Mangu Hongli Chen Shi We Li" (Development of Family Business in Modern Chaoshan Area: A View from Wills, Using the Chens of Kinn Tye Lung in Hong Kong and Wanglee in Bangkok as Example). *Journal of Resources for Hong Kong Studies* no. 1 (1998): 70–79.

———. "Dongnan Ya Huaren Jiazu Qiye De Jiegou: Qiantai Long Yu Yuanfa Hang De Bijiao Yanjiu" (Structure of Southeast Asian Chinese Family Firms: A Comparative Study of the Kin Tye Lung and Yuanfa Hang). In *Southeast Asian Chinese and Chinese Economy and Society,* edited by Hou-seng Lim, 91–108. Singapore: Singapore Society of Asian Studies, 1995.

———. "Hometown Connection and the Chaozhou Business Networks: A Case Study of the Chens of Kintyelung, 1850–1950." In *the XIV International Economic Congress (Session #71).* Helsinki, 2006.

———. "Kinship and Business: Paternal and Maternal Kin in Chaozhou Chinese Family Firms." *Business History* 40, no. 1 (1998): 26–49.

———. "Settlement of Chinese Families in Macau." In *Macau: City of Culture and Commerce,* edited by R. D. Cremer, 61–80. Hong Kong: API Press, 1991.

Chou, Shishun, ed. *Chaozhou Fuzhi* (Gazetteer of Chaozhou Prefecture). Vol. 3, book 12: u.p., 1893.

Cohen, Myron. "Family Management and Family Division in Contemporary Rural China." *China Quarterly* no. 130 (1992): 357–77.

Fok, K.C. "Lineage Ties, Business Partnership and Financial Agency: The Many Roles of a Hong Kong Commercial Network." In *the Preliminary Workshop for the 11th International Economic History Congress.* Milan, Atami, Japan, 1994.

Hare, G.T. "Text Book of Documentary Chinese: Selected and Designed for the Special Use of Members of the Civil Services of the Straits Settlements and the Protected Native States." Singapore: Government Printing Office, 1894.

"Hkrs No.144, D&S No.4/3020 and 4/3792." Hong Kong Public Records Office.

Kennedy, Thomas L., and Micki Kennedy, eds. *Testimony of a Confucian Woman: The Autobiography of Mrs. Nie Zeng Jifen, 1852–1942*. Athens, G.A.; London: University of Georgia Press, 1993.

King, Frank H. H. *The Hong Kong Bank between the Wars and the Bank Interned, 1919–1945: Return from Grandeur*. Cambridge: Cambridge University Press, 1988.

Ko, Dorothy. *Teachers of the Inner Chambers: Women and Culture in Seventeenth-Century China*. Stanford: Stanford University Press, 1994.

Lee, Sharon M. "Female Immigrants and Labor in Colonial Malaya: 1860–1947." *International Migration Review* 23, no. 2 (1989): 313–14.

Liang, Tingnan, ed. *Yue Hai Guan Zhi* (Gazetteer of the Guangdong Maritime Customs). Vol. 6: u.p., ca.1874.

Lin, Xi. "Cong Xianggang Di Yuanfa Hang Tanqi" (Talking from Yuan Fat Hong in Hong Kong). *Da Cheng* no. 117–121 (1983).

———. "Gao Zizheng Gong Qianbiao Yu Gao Chuxiang Jia Zhuan" (Obituary and Biography of Gao Chuxiang). *Da Cheng* no. 121 (1983): 50–59.

———. "Yijiu Sansan Nian Shantou Jinrong Fengchao" (The 1933 Financial Crisis in Shantou). *Da Cheng* no. 22 (1967): 4.

"Lugang Chaozhou Shanghui Sanshi Zhounian Jinian Tekan" (Special Bulletin Commemorating the Thirtieth Anniversary of the Chaozhou Chamber of Commerce). Hong Kong: Lugang Chaozhou Shanghui (Hong Kong Chaozhou Chamber of Commerce), 1951.

Pan, Xinlong. *Malaiya Chaoqiao Tongjian* (Gazetteer of the Chaozhou Chinese in Malaya). u.p., 1950.

Perry, Elizabeth. *Shanghai on Strike: The Politics of Chinese Labor*. Stanford: Stanford University Press, 1993.

Rao, Zongyi, ed. *Chaozhou Zhi Huibian* (Gazetteers of Chaozhou Prefecture). Xianggang: Longmen Shudian, 1965.

Shantou Bainian Dashiji, 1859–1959 (Major Events in Shantou from 1858 to 1959). Shantou: Shantou Shi Zhi Bianxie Weiyuan Hui, 1960.

Shantou Gaikuang (General Survey of Shantou). Shantou: Shantou Shi Defang Zhi Bianzuan Weiyuan Hui Bangong Shi, 1987.

Skinner, G. William. *Chinese Society in Thailand: An Analytical History*. Ithaca, N.Y.: Cornell University Press, 1957.

So, Alvin Y. *The South China Silk District: Local Historical Transformation and World-System Theory*. Albany: State University of New York Press, 1986.

"Special Resolution of Kin Tye Lung Co. Ltd." Company Registry. Hong Kong, 1988.

Suehiro, Akira. *Capital Accumulation in Thailand, 1855–1985*. Tokyo: UNESCO (The Centre for East Asian Cultural Studies), 1989.

Suehiro, Akira and Makoto Nanbara. *Tai No Zaibatsu* (Thai's financial tycoons). Tokyo: Tongbun Kan, 1991.

Wolf, Margery, Roxane Witke, and Emily M. Ahern, eds. *Women in Chinese Society.* Stanford: Stanford University Press, 1975.

Xia, Chenghua. *Jindai Guangdong Sheng Qiaohui Yanjiu (1862–1949): Yi Guang, Chao, Mei, Qiong Diqu Wei Li* (Study of Remittance of Guangdong Province in the Modern Period: Using Guangzhou, Chaozhou, Meizhou and Qiongzhou Districts as Examples). Singapore: Xinjiapo Nanyang Xue Hui, 1992.

Xiao, Guanying. *Liushi Nian Lai Zhi Lingdong Jilue* (Accounts of Eastern Guangdong in the Recent Sixty Years). 1925. Reprint, Guangdong: Guangdong Renmin Chubanshe, 1996.

Xie, Xueying, ed. *Chao Mei Xianxiang* (Conditions in the Chaozhou Mei Xian Area). Guangdong: Shantou shi tongxun she, 1935.

"*Xin Shantou*" (New Swatow). Shantou: Shantou shi shizhengting bianji gu, 1928.

Yin, Peishen. *Fengshan Jixu* (Accounts on Chenghai County). U.p., n.d., ca.1810–1820.

"Zai Langhua Guanfan Zhong De Chaoshan Fun v (1)" (Chaoshan Wemen in the Turmoil of Waves). *Huazhi Ribao*, 2.18, 1935, 2.

"Zai Langhua Guanfan Zhong De Chaoshan Fun v (2)" (Chaoshan Wemen in the Turmoil of Waves). *Huazhi Ribao*, 2.19, 1935, 3.

Zhang, Y. Q. "Taiguo Huaqiao Gao Chuxiang Yu Hongli Jiazu Di Yeji" (Achievements of the Thai Chinese Gao Chuxiang and Chen Hongli Families). In *Shantou Wenshi*, 26–41, 1990.

Chapter 6

China Mail. March 8, 1881.

Conner, Patrick. *George Chinnery: 1774–1852: Artist of India and the China Coast.* Woodbridge, Suffolk: Antique Collectors' Club, 1993.

Daily Advertiser.

Daily Press.

Downing, Charles Toogood. *The Fan-Qui in China 1836–37.* Vol. 11838.

Eitel, E. J. *Europe in China, the History of Hongkong from the Beginning to the Year 1882.* Taipei: Chen-Wen Publishing Co., 1968, originally published 1895 by Kelly and Walsh.

Hall, Peter. *In the Web.* London: Basingstoke Press 1992.

Hoe, Susanna. *The Private Life of Hong Kong.* Hong Kong: Oxford University Press, 1991.

Hong Kong Government Gazette, October 25, 1879.

"Hong Kong Land Registry."

Lowe, K. J. P. "Hong Kong, 26 January 1841: Hoisting the Flag Revisited." *Journal of the Hong Kong Branch of the Royal Asiatic Society* v.29 (1989): 13.

"Macau Land Registry," 211.

Norton-Kyshe, James. *The History of the Laws and Courts of Hong Kong.* Vol. 2.

Smith, Carl T. "A Comparative Study of Eurasians in Macau and Hong Kong." In *Meeting Point of Cultures: Macau and Ethnic Diversity in Asia*. Macau: Instituto Cultural de Macau, 1993.

———. "Protected Women in 19th-Century Hong Kong." In *Women and Chinese Patriarchy: Submission, Servitude, and Escape*, edited by Maria Jachok and Suzanne Miers, 221–37. London: Zed Books Ltd., 1994.

The Friend of China.

The Hong Kong Telegraph. September 24, 1895.

The Public Records Office of Hong Kong. *Probate File*.

Warren, James Francis. "Chinese Prostitution in Singapore: Recruitment and Brothel Organisation." In *Women and Chinese Patriarchy: Submission, Servitude, and Escape*, edited by Maria Jaschok and Suzanne Miers, 77–107. Hong Kong: Hong Kong University Press; London; Atlantic Highlands, N.J.: Zed Books, 1994.

White, Barbara-Sue. *Turbans and Traders, Hong Kong's Indian Communities*. Hong Kong: Oxford University Press, 1994.

Wood, William Maxwell. *Fankwei; or, the San Jacinto in the Seas of India, China, and Japan*. New York: Harper and Brothers, 1859.

Chapter 7

Baojue liankan (Baojue Annual), Vol. 11 (1966).

Aomen Youlan Zhinan, Macau, 1939.

Cheng, Irene. *Intercultural Reminiscences*. Hong Kong: David C. Lam Institute for East-West Studies, Hong Kong Baptist University, 1997.

———. *Lady Clara Ho Tung: A Hong Kong Lady, Her Family and Her Times*. Hong Kong: The Chinese University of Hong Kong Press, 1980. First published 1976.

———. "Women Students and Graduates." In *University of Hong Kong, the First 50 Years, 1911–1961*, edited by Harrison B, 148–58. Hong Kong: Cathay Press, 1962.

Dayushan Zhi (Lantau Gazetteer) Hong Kong, 1958.

Gittins, Jean. "Eastern Windows – Western Skies." *South China Morning Post* 1969.

Hall, Peter. *In the Web*. London: Basingstoke Press, 1992.

He, Wen Xiang. *Xianggang Jiazu Shi*. Hong Kong: Capital Communications Corporation Limited, 1989.

Ho, Shai-lai. *Hemu Zhang Taifuren Bazhi Mingshou Jilian Ji*. Hong Kong: Private publication, 1954.

———. *Xianci Hemu Zhang Taifuren Lianjue Jushi Shengping Yixing Buyi*. Hong Kong: Private publication, 1954.

Hong Kong Government Administrative Report (1916, 1927, 1928, 1931, 1932, 1935).

Ip, Man-yee. "Xianggang Zaoqi Zhi Fojiao Fazhan" (The Early Development of Buddhism in Hong Kong). *The Dharmalakshana Buddhist Institute Buddhist Journal* III (November 1992).

Lee, Xiaohong, et al., eds. *Biographical Dictionary of Chinese Women*. Armonk, N.Y.: M. E. Sharpe, 1998.

Lu, Bicheng. "Zhang Lianhue Jushi Chuan" (A Biographical Sketch on Zhang Lianjue). In *Guangdong Fojiaoshi*, edited by Yongkang Liang. Hong Kong: Zhonghua Fojiao Tushu Guan, 1984).

Mai, Bao-qiong. "Xiaoyou Yanjiang" (A Speech from a Former Graduate). *Baojue tongxue* (Baojue Students) no. 1 (1953).

Ping, Jin. "Xianggang Fojiao Xuexiao Gaikuang" (The General Situation of Buddhist Schools in Hong Kong). *Xianggang fojiao* (Hong Kong Buddhism), no. 36 (1963): 36.

Poy, Vivienne. *Building Bridges: The Life and Times of Richard Charles Lee, Hong Kong: 1905–1983*. Scarborough, Ont.: Calyan Publishing Ltd., 1998.

———. *A River Named Lee*. Scarborough, Ont.: Calyan Publishing Ltd., 1995.

Royal Society for the Prevention of Cruelty to Animals: 75 Anniversary Commemorative Issue. 1996.

Schwarz, Vera. *The Chinese Enlightenment: Intellectuals and the Legacy of the May Fourth Movement of 1919*. Berkeley: University of California Press, 1986.

Shi, Ai Ting. "Wosuo Renshi Di Lianjue Jushi-1" (What I Knew about Laywoman Lin-Kok – Part I). *Huanan jueyin* (The Enlightened Voice for South China 1941), 27–28.

———. "Wosuo Renshi Di Lianjue Jushi-2" (What I Knew about Laywoman Lin-Kok – Part II). *Huanan jueyin*, 1941, 29.

———. "Wosuo Renshi Di Lianjue Jushi-1." *Huanan jueyin*, 1941, 27–28.

Shi, Le Guan. "Wosuo Renshi Di Yiwei Lupusa" (A Female Bodhistattva as I Knew Her). In *Hemu Zhang Taifuren Bazhi Mingshou Jilian Ji*, edited by Shai-lai Ho. Hong Kong: Private publication, 1954.

Shi, Tai Xu. "Sanshi Nianlai Zhi Zhongguo Fojiao" (Buddhism in China in the Thirty Years). In *Xiandai Fojiaoxueshu Congkan 86: Mingguo Fojiao Pian*, edited by Mantao Zhang. Taiwan, 1978.

Shi, Tan Xu, and Tai Guang Shi. *Yingchen Huiyi Lu*, 1991.

Shi, Tanxu. "Wuyu Guanben Heshang Zhi Yinyuan" (My Relation with Monk Guan Ben). *Wujindeng* 5, no. 2 (November 1955).

———. "Wuyu Guanben Heshang Zhi Yinyuan" (My Relation with Monk Guan Ben). *Wujindeng* 5, no. 3 (December 1955).

Shi, Wai-ying. "Zhanqian Guhou Yicien: Zhuinian Lin Yuanchang Zhen Jushi" (In Memory of Mother Superior Lin, Laywoman Zhen). *Po Kok Annual Journal* 11, no. 27 (1966).

Shi, Yong Ming. *Xianggang Fojiao Yu Fosi*. Hong Kong: Po Lin Monastery, 1992.

Shi, Zhu Kong. "Mingguo Fojiao Nianji (The Chronology of Buddhism during the Republican Period)." In *Xiandai Fojiaoxueshu Congkan 86: Mingguo Fojiao Pian*, edited by Mantao Zhang. Taipei: Dasheng Wenhua Chubanshe, 1978).

Wang, Jinglin. *Zhongguo Gudai Siyuan Shenghuo*, 1991.

Welch, Holmes. *The Practice of Chinese Buddhism 1900–1950*. Cambridge, M.A.: Harvard University Press, 1973. First published 1967.

Wong, Siu-lun. "Gender and Trust: The Dynamism of Chinese Family Enterprise Revisited." In *Chinese Sociology and Anthropology in the Twenty First Century*, edited by Chiao Chien, Rance Lee and Ma Rong, 257–76. Kao Ksiong: Liwen Cultural Enterprise Ltd., 2001.

Woo, Sing-lim. *Xianggang Huaren Mingren Shilue.* Hong Kong, 1937.

Xianggang Fojiao Lianhehui Huikan Ji Chuangli Wushi Zhounian Jinxi Jinian Tekan. Hong Kong: Hong Kong Buddhist Association, 1995.

Yeo, Florence. *My Memories.* Pittsburgh, P.A.: Dorrance Publishing, 1994.

Zhang, Jingrong. *Mingshan Youji.* Hong Kong: Private publication, 1935.

Zhang, Mantao, ed. *Xiandai Fojiaoxueshu Congkan 86: Mingguo Fojiao Pian.* Taipei: Dasheng Wenhua Chubanshe, 1978).

Zhonghua Minguo Shishi Rizhi: 1922–1926. Vol. 3. Taipei, u.d.

Chapter 8

"83% Gangqi Ping Nü Gaoceng Lie Quanqiu Diwu." (83% Hong Kong Businesses Hired Senior Women Executives, Ranking Number Five in the World). *Ming Pao Daily News*, March 8, 2007, A28.

"Ben Gang Nüxing Cangxuan Bilü Di" (The Ratio of Political Participation among Hong Kong Women Is Low). *Ming Pao Daily News*, April 7, 2005, A15.

Chan, Johannes, and Bart Rwezura, eds. *Immigration Law in Hong Kong: An Interdisciplinary Study.* Hong Kong: Sweet and Maxwell Asia, 2004.

Chu, Priscilla Pue Ho. *The Making of Women Entrepreneurs in Hong Kong.* Hong Kong: Hong Kong University Press, 2003.

Connolly, Norma, and Martin Wong. "Scales Tip as Women Outnumber Men." *South China Morning Post*, February 23, 2007.

Di, Luo. "Buzhengsi Chen Fang Ansheng Renzhong Daoyuan" (Chief Secretary Anson Chan Shoulders Heavy Responsibilities). *Nanbeiji*, December 1993, 8–9.

Elliot, Dorinda. "The Iron Lady Is on the Spot." *Newsweek*, June 9, 1997, 11–15.

Fang, Xiaoyun. *Xianggang Nü Fuhao Liejuan* (Wealthy Women in Hong Kong). Hong Kong: Chinshiyuan Chubanshe, 1993.

Faure, David. *Colonialism and the Hong Kong Mentality.* Hong Kong: Centre of Asian Studies, The University of Hong Kong, 2003.

"Fengdai Guanchang, Yingxiong Shishe" (Heroes Pale in a Female-dominated Officialdom). *Apple Daily*, June 25, 2000, A12.

"Gangfu Shunying Minjian 'Bao Yu Xingdong', Xianshi Zunzhong Renquan, Hu Hongyu Xuyue Ping Ji Hui Yinian" (The Hong Kong Government Accommodates Public Efforts to Retain Hu. Showing Respects for Human Rights, Hu's Contract in Equal Opportunity Commission Is Renewed for a Year). *Ming Pao Daily News*, July 28, 2002, A06.

"Guihua Yuanjing Wenjian Duanshi" ("Document on Strategic Planning Vision" Short-sighted). *Taiyang Bao* (Sun), March 1, 2001, D08.

Ho, Hay Wah. "Chengqing Dui Xinyimin De Jige Mouwu" (Clarifying a Few Misunderstandings towards New Immigrants). *Ming Pao Daily News*, September 17, 2007.

"Jiaoshi Yangcheng Yin Shuai" (Male Dominance in Number of Academics). *Ming Pao Daily News*, March 11, 1999, B14.

Kelsky, Karen. *Women on the Verge: Japanese Women, Western Dreams*. Durham: Duke University Press, 2001.

Lai, Yifu. *Saobatou* (Broomhead). Hong Kong: Subculture Publisher, 2001.

Li, Zhaoxing, and Zeng Fan, eds. *Xianggang 101: Ai Hen Xianggang De 101 Ge Li You* (Hong Kong 101: One Hundred and One Reasons to Love and Hate Hong Kong). Hong Kong: Feel Company Ltd., 2000.

Liu, Su. *Xianggang, Xianggang . . .* (Hong Kong, Hong Kong . . .) Hong Kong: Zhongguo Tu Shu Kan Xing She, 1987.

"Lu Gonghui Shinian Jiu Yige Wei Gang" (Christine Loh Took Ten Years to Save a Victoria Harbour). *Ming Pao Daily News*, April 16, 2000, A06.

Ma, Zhenping. *Gangren Da Xieyi:Yige Beijing Ren Yanzhong De Xianggang Ren* (An Overall Description of Hong Kong People Through the Eyes of a Beijing Person). Beijing: Qunyan Chubanshe, 1998.

"Nü Jiao Nan Duo 25 Wan, Yue Lai Yue Chihun, Nan 31 Nü28." (Women Outnumber Men by 250,000. Rising Trend for Late Marriages, Men 31 Women 28) *Ming Pao Daily News*, July 29, 2005, A10.

Ng, Margaret. "And Now, the Real Tung Administration." *South China Morning Post*, January 16, 2001.

Ng, Margaret. *Chi He Wan Le* (Eat, Drink, and be Merry). Hong Kong: Mingbao, Chubanshe Youxian Gongsi, 1997.

———. *Jianqiao Guilu* (Home from Cambridge). Hong Kong: Mingbao Chubanshe, 1987.

Ng, Margaret. *23 Tiao Lifa Rizhi* (A Dairy on the Legislation of Article 23). Hong Kong: Next Publications, 2004.

"Ping Ji Hui Gao Zhengfu Minjian Kong Chunu Gaoguan, Tuanti Fen Han Teshou Bao Hu Hongyu" (The Equal Opportunities Commission's Lawsuit against the Government Might Have Offended Officials. Organizations Appealed to the Chief Executive to Retain Hu Hongyu). *Ming Pao Daily News*, June 29, 2002, A06.

Sinn, Elizabeth. "Lesson in Openness: Creating a Space of Flow in Hong Kong." In *Hong Kong Mobile: Making a Global Population*, edited by Helen F. Siu and Agnes S. Ku, 13–43. Hong Kong: Hong Kong University Press, 2008.

"Tian Shao Zhi Lu Gonghui Guofen Duli" (Master Tian Accuses Christine Loh of Being Too Independent). *Sing Tao Daily*, April 13, 2000, A13.

Weng, Yuxiong. "Fendai Guanchang Yingxiong Shise" (Heroes Pale in a Female-dominated Officialdom). *Apple Daily*, June 25, 2000, A12.

"Who's Worth a Million Dollars in Hong Kong? More Women Than Men." *South China Morning Post*, February 14, 2007, 3.

"Wu Hung Yuk Zai Xiang Hushan Xing" (Hu Hongyu Heads towards the Tiger Mountain Again). *Ming Pao Daily News*, July 25, 1999.

Xianggang Funü Nianbao Bianji Weiyuanhui, ed. *Xianggang Funü Nianbao* (Hong Kong Women's Annual Book). Hong Kong: Xianggang Xinwen Chubanshe, 1975–.

"Xin Jiyuan Renlei Xi Gang, Yin Shui Du Jiang Zhihui" (New Century Beings Descend upon Hong Kong, Oozing Wisdom Even in Water-drinking). *Sing Dao Daily*, November 30, 2000, D01.

Yang, Kaishan, and Xue Yike. "Xuni Shequ Ninju Shimin Liliang, Lu Gonghui Tuidong Wangshang Canzheng" (Virtual Community to Gather Citizen's Strength. Christine Loh Pushes for Internet Political Participation). *Sing Tao Daily*, July 19, 2000, A13.

Yau, Betty, Kit Chun Au, and Fanny M. Cheung. "Women's Concern Groups in Hong Kong." Occasional paper No. 15. Hong Kong: Hong Kong Institute of Asia-Pacific Studies, 1992.

Yu, Patrick Shuk-siu. *A Seventh Child and the Law*. Hong Kong: Hong Kong University Press, 1998.

Chapter 9

Acker, Joan, Kate Barry, and Joke Esseveld. "Objectivity and Truth: Problems in Doing Feminist Research." *Women's Studies International Forum* 16, no. 4 (1983): 423–35.

Brown, E. H. Phelps. "The Hong Kong Economy: Achievements and Prospects." In *Hong Kong: The Industrial Colony*, edited by Keith Hopkins, 1–20. Hong Kong, London, New York: Oxford University Press, 1971.

Chan, Wai-Fong, Shun-hing Chan, and Yuen-yee Law. "Pioneers in Women's Rights: Lee Fung Ying, Leung Wai Ming and Yim Yuet Lin." In *The Other Half of the Sky: Women's Movement in Post-War Hong Kong*, edited by Choi-wan Cheung, Yuen-yee Law, Chi-kei Wan and Ka-yin Tsang, 33–44. Hong Kong: Association for the Advancement of Feminism, 1992.

Chiu, Stephen Wing-kai, and Ching-kwan Lee. *Withering Away of the Hong Kong Dream? Women Workers under Industrial Restructuring*. Hong Kong: Hong Kong Institute of Asia-Pacific Studies, The Chinese University of Hong Kong, 1997.

Chiu, Stephen Wing-kai, and David A. Levin. "The World Economy, State, and Sectors in Industrial Change: Labor Relations in Hong Kong's Textile and Garment-Making Industries." In *Industrialization and Labor Relations: Contemporary Research in Seven Countries*, edited by Stephen Frenkel and Jeffrey Harrod, 143–75. Ithaca, N.Y.: ILR Press, 1995.

Choi, Po-king. "The Women's Movement in Hong Kong: The Construction of Identity and Its Contradictions." In *Praxis a La Hong Kong*, edited by Man Si-wai and Leung Mei-yee, 318–59. Hong Kong: Ching Man Publishers, 1997.

Choi, Po-king, ed. *Wan Wan Liudianban: Qishi Nindai Shang Yexiao De Nugong* (Every Night at Six-Thirty: Women Workers Who Attended Evening Schools in the Seventies). Hong Kong: Stepforward Multimedia Co.Ltd., 1998.

Djao, A. Wei. "Dependent Development and Social Control: Labour-Intensive Industrialization in Hong Kong." *Social Praxis* V, no. 3/4 (1978): 275–93.

————. "Public Issues and Private Troubles: The Government and the Working Class in Hong Kong." In *Poverty and Social Change in Southeast Asia*, edited by Ozay Mehmet, 100–22. Ottawa: University of Ottawa, 1979.

Fung, Liu-ngan. "Family Violence and Sexual Self-Determination." In *Chayi Yu Pingdeng: Xianggang Funu Yundong De Xin Tiaozhan* (Differences and Equality: New Challenges to the Hong Kong Women's Movement), edited by Kam-wah Chan, Kit-mui Wong, Lai-ching Leung, Wai-yi Lee and Chi-kwan Ho, 109–14. Hong Kong: Association for the Advancement of Feminism, in collaboration with the Centre for Social Policy Studies, Department of Applied Social Studies, Hong Kong Polytechnic University, 2001.

Hsiung, Ping-chun. *Living Rooms as Factories: Class, Gender, and the Satellite Factory System in Taiwan = [Ke Ting Ji Gong Chang]*. Philadelphia: Temple University Press, 1996.

Jacka, Tamara. *Rural Women in Urban China: Gender, Migration, and Social Change*. Armonk, N.Y.: M.E. Sharpe, Inc., 2006.

Johnson, Graham. "Hong Kong, from Colony to Territory: Social Implications of Globalization." In *25 Years of Social and Economic Development in Hong Kong*, edited by Benjamin K. P. Leung and Teresa Y. C. Wong, 660–88. Hong Kong: Centre of Asian Studies, The University of Hong Kong, 1994.

Lather, Patricia Ann. *Getting Smart: Feminist Research and Pedagogy with/in the Postmodern*. New York: Routledge, 1991.

Lee, Ching-kwan. "Engendering the Worlds of Labor: Women Workers, Labor Markets, and Production Politics in the South China Economic Miracle." *American Sociological Review* 60, no. 3 (1995): 378–97.

————. *Gender and the South China Miracle: Two Worlds of Factory Women*. Berkeley; Los Angeles: University of California Press, 1998.

Lee, Eliza W. Y., ed. *Gender and Change in Hong Kong: Globalization, Postcolonialism, and Chinese Patriarchy*. Vancouver: University of British Columbia Press, 2003.

Lee, Kim-ming. "Flexible Manufacturing in a Colonial Economy." In *Hong Kong's History State and Society under Colonial Rule*, edited by Tak-wing Ngo, 162–79. London; New York: Routledge, 1999.

Levin, David A. "Women and the Industrial Labor Market in Hong Kong." In *Status Influences in Third World Labor Markets*, edited by James G. Scoville, 183–214. Berlin; New York: W. de Gruyter, 1991.

Lui, Tai-lok. "Waged Work at Home: Married Women's Participation in Industrial Outwork in Hong Kong." In *Selected Papers of Conference on Gender Studies in Chinese Societies*, edited by Fanny M. Cheung, Po-san Wan, Hang-keung Choi and Lee-man Choy, 1–42. Hong Kong: Hong Kong Institute of Asia-Pacific Studies, The Chinese University of Hong Kong, 1991.

Luk, Hung-kay. *Cong Rongshu Xia Dao Diannao Qian – Xianggang Jiaoyu De Gu Shi* (From the Banyan Tree to The Computer – The Story of Hong Kong Education). Hong Kong: Stepforward Multimedia, 2003.

Man, Kit-wah. "Hong Kong Films of the Sixties and Woman's Identity." In *Hong Kong Sixties: Designing Identity*, edited by Matthew Turner and Irene Ngan, 76–77. Hong Kong: The Hong Kong Arts Centre, 1995.

Ngo, Tak-Wing, ed. *Hong Kong's History State and Society under Colonial Rule*, Routledge Studies in Asia's Transformations. London; New York: Routledge, 1999.

Pun, Ngai. "Am I the Only Survivor? Global Capital, Local Gaze, and Social Trauma in China." *Public Culture* 14, no. 2 (2002): 341–47.

———. "Becoming Dagongmei: Politics of Identities and Differences." In *Made in China: Women Factory Workers in a Global Workplace*, edited by Ngai Pun, 109. Durham: Duke University Press, 2005.

Reinharz, Shulamit, and Lynn Davidman. *Feminist Methods in Social Research*. New York: Oxford University Press, 1992.

Rofel, Lisa. "Liberation Nostalgia and a Yearning for Modernity." In *Engendering China: Women, Culture, and the State*, edited by Christina K. Gilmartin, Gail Hershatter, Lisa Rofel and Tyrene White, 226–49. Cambridge, M.A.: Harvard University Press, 1994.

Salaff, Janet W. *Working Daughters of Hong Kong: Filial Piety or Power in the Family?* Cambridge; New York: Cambridge University Press, 1981.

Smith, Dorothy E. "Institutional Ethnography: A Feminist Method." *Resources for Feminist Research* 15, no. 1 (1986): 6–13.

Tam, Siumi Maria. "The Structuration of Chinese Modernization: Women Workers of Shekou Industrial Zone." PhD dissertation, University of Hawai'i, 1992.

Willis, Paul E. *Learning to Labor: How Working Class Kids Get Working Class Jobs*. Morningside ed. New York: Columbia University Press, 1981.

Wong, Kit-mui. "One Family, One Story." In *Wan Wan Liudianban: Qishi Nindai Shang Yexiao De Nugong* (Every Night at Six-Thirty: Women Workers Who Attended Evening Schools in the Seventies), edited by Choi Po-king, 48–78. Hong Kong: Stepforward Multimedia Co. Ltd, 1998.

Wong, Siu-lun. *Emigrant Entrepreneurs: Shanghai Industrialists in Hong Kong*. Hong Kong; New York: Oxford University Press, 1988.

Wu, Mei-lin. "Drifting between the Women's Movement and the Workers' Movement." In *Chayi Yu Pingdeng: Xianggang Funu Yundong De Xin Tiaozhan* (Differences and Equality: New Challenges to the Hong Kong Women's Movement), edited by Kam-wah Chan, Kit-mui Wong, Lai-ching Leung, Wai-yi Lee and Chi-kwan Ho, 71–76. Hong Kong: Association for the Advancement of Feminism, in collaboration with the Centre for Social Policy Studies, Department of Applied Social Studies, Hong Kong Polytechnic University, 2001.

Ye-Ye Sheng-Ge: Wo Zai Jianuosha De Rizi (Music and Songs Every Evening: My Days At the Canossian School). Hong Kong: Publishing Committee For the School History of the Shaukiwan Canossian Evening School, 1998.

Yim, Kit-sum, and Wai-yi Lee. "Realize Women's Sex Rights, Support Sex Workers: The Rights of Sexual Minorities as a Feminist Issue." In *Chayi Yu Pingdeng: Xianggang Funu Yundong De Xin Tiaozhan* (Differences and Equality: New Challenges to the Hong Kong Women's Movement), edited by Kam-wah Chan, Kit-mui Wong, Lai-ching Leung, Wai-yi Lee and Chi-kwan Ho, 133–56. Hong Kong: Association for the Advancement of Feminism, in collaboration with the Centre for Social Policy Studies, Department of Applied Social Studies, Hong Kong Polytechnic University, 2001.

Yim, Yuet-lin, and Yan-yan Chan. "The Enlightenment Age of the Hong Kong Sex Workers' Rights Movement." In *Xing Gongzuo Yanjiu* (The Study of Sex Work), edited by Ho Chuen Juei, 59–94. Taipei: The Centre for the Study of Sexualities, National Central University, 2003.

Chapter 10

Croll, Elisabeth J. *Women and Rural Development in China: Production and Reproduction*. Geneva: International Labour Office, 1985.

Da Li Gongshe Dangwei Bangongshi (The CPC Committee Office of Dali). "Da Li Gongshe Hong Feng Dadui Dangqian Jieji Douzheng De Yixie Qingkuang" (Current Situations of Class Struggle in Hongfeng Brigade of Dali Commune), May 13, 1973. Guangzhou: Guangdong Sheng Dang'an Guan (Guangdong Provincial Archives), 229-4-298.

"Da Mie Te Mie Kuai Mie Zichanjieji Guai Faxing" (Get Rid of Strange Bourgeois Hairstyles Extensively, Thoroughly, and Promptly) in *Yangcheng Wanbao* (Yangcheng Evening News), August 27, 1966, 2.

Davin, Delia. *Woman-Work: Women and the Party in Revolutionary China*. Oxford: Clarendon Press, 1976.

Guangdong sheng Fulian (Women's Federation, Guangdong Province). "Gei Zhongshan Xian Fulian Liaojie Nüqingnian Toudu De Quxin" (A Letter to the Women's Federation of Zhongshan County Concerning Young Female Fleeing), June 26, 1977. Guangzhou: Guangdong Sheng Dang'an Guan (Guangdong Provincial Archives), 233-3-94.

———. "Guanyu Huilaixian Lianxu Fasheng Nüqingnian Jiti Toushui Zisha Shijian De Qingkuang Diaocha" (An Investigation on Recent Mass Suicides by self-drowning among Young Women in Huilai County), November 13, 1974. Guangzhou: Guangdong Sheng Dang'an Guan (Guangdong Provincial Archives), 233-3-20.

———. "Jieji Douzheng Zhuyao Fanying Zai Yixia Jige Fangmian" (Class Struggle Included the Following Aspects), November 30, 1973. Guangzhou: Guangdong Sheng Dang'an Guan (Guangdong Provincial Archives), 233-3-9.

Guangdong sheng Nong Lin Shui Bangongshi Diaochazu (The Investigation Team of Guangdong Department of Agriculture, Forestry, and Water Resources). "Zhongshan Xian Toudu Waitao Qingkuang Zonghe" (A Summary Report of Massive Fleeing from Zhongshan County), May 31, 1973. Guangzhou: Guangdong Sheng Dang'an Guan (Guangdong Provincial Archives), 229-4-298.

Guangzhou Haiguan Junguan Xiaozu (The Military Control Commission of Guangzhou Customs). "Guanyu Gaige Haiguan Dui Laizi Xianggang Aomen Duanqi Lüke Xingli Wupin Guanli Guiding De Qingshi Baogao" (The Request for Instructions to Pilot Customs Departments on Administration of the Baggage Carried by Short-term Visitors from Hong Kong and Macao), August 24, 1968. Guangzhou: Guangdong Sheng Dang'an Guan (Guangdong Provincial Archives), 229-4-11.

Guowuyuan, Zhongyang Junwei (The State Council, and the Military Commission of the Central Committee). "Guowuyuan, Zhongyang Junwei Guanyu Jianjue Zhizhi Guangdongsheng Daliang Qunzhong Toudu Waitao De Zhishi" (The Directive by the State Council and the CMC to Stop Massive Fleeing from Guangdong Province), June 14, 1979. Guangzhou: Guangdong Sheng Dang'an Guan (Guangdong Provincial Archives), 235-2-287.

Hinton, Carma, Geremie Barme, and Richard Gordon. "Morning Sun." 117 minutes. 2003.

Huang, Shumin. *Lincun De Gushi: 1949 Nian Hou De Zhongguo Nongcun Biange* (The Spiral Road: Change in a Chinese Village through the Eyes of a Communist Party Leader). Beijing: Sanlian Shudian, 2002.

Hu, Jie, and Ai Xiaoming. "Red Art". 70 minutes. China, 2007.

Hu, Yukun. "Guojia, Shichang Yu Zhongguo Nongcun Funü De Jingji Canyu" (Nation, the Market, and Peasant Women's Economic Participation). In *Jianshe Shehui Zhuyi Xinnongcun Yu Xingbie Pingdeng — Duoxueke He Kuaxueke De Yanjiu* (Multi-Disciplinary Studies in Creating Socialist Villages and Gender Equality), edited by Zhongguo Funü Yanjiuhui (The Association for Chinese Women's Studies). Beijing: Zhongguo Funü Chubanshe, 2007.

Jacka, Tamara. *Women's Work in Rural China: Change and Continuity in an Era of Reform.* Cambridge: Cambridge University Press, 1997.

Jin, Yihong, "Tie Guniang Zaisikao — Zhongguo Wenhua Dageming Qijian De Shehui Xingbie Yu Laodong"(Rethinking the Steel Maidens: Gender roles and Labor in the Cultural Revolution). *Shehuixue Yanjiu* (Sociology Research), no. 1 (2006): 169–96.

Johnson, Kay Ann. *Women, the Family and Peasant Revolution in China.* Chicago and London: The University of Chicago Press, 1983.

Judd, Ellen R. *The Chinese Women's Movement between State and Market.* Stanford: Stanford University Press, 2002.

Lee, Ching-kwan. *Gender and the South China Miracle: Two Worlds of Factory Women.* Berkeley, Los Angeles, London: University of California Press, 1998.

Li, Ruojian. "Cong Shuzui Dao Tizui: 'Si Lei Fenzi' Jieji Chutan" (From Atonement to Scapegoats: A Class Analysis of the "Four Kinds of Elements" in the Initiate Period of the People's Republic of China). *Kaifang Shidai* (Open Times), no. 5 (2006): 113–30.

Liwan Quwei (the District Party Committee of Liwan). "Huanan Jinbi Chang Jinxing 'Xianggang Hao Haishi Guangzhou Hao' Jiaoyu De Zuofa" (The Patriotic Education by the South China Pen Factory: 'Which is better, Hong Kong or Guangzhou?') , August 6, 1962. Guangzhou: Guangdong Sheng Dang'an Guan (Guangdong Provincial Archives), 214-1-293.

Luo, Mu. "Jiqing Ranshao 'Tie Guniang'" (Burning Passion: The Steel Maidens). *Shenghuo Yuekan* (Life Monthly), no. 4 (2005).

Pun, Ngai. *Zhongguo Nügong* (Made in China). Hong Kong: Mingbao Chubanshe Youxian Gongsi, 2007.

Shou, Beibei. "Renkou Liudong Wushi Nian" (Fifty Years of Migration). *Nanfang Zhoumo* (Nanfang Weekly), November 6, 1998.

Siu, Helen F. "Grounding Displacement: Uncivil Urban Spaces in Postreform South China." *American Ethnologist* 34, no. 2 (2007): 329–50.

———. "Immigrants and Social Ethos: Hong Kong in the Nineteen-Eighties." *Journal of The Hong Kong Branch of the Reyal Asiatic Society* 26, (1986): 1–16.

———. "Nianzai Huanan Yanjiu Zhilu" (A Twenty-Year Journey through South China). *Qinghua shehuixue pinglun* (Tsinghua Sociological Review) 1, no. 3 (2001): 181–90.

———. "Where Were the Women? Rethinking Marriage Resistance and Regional Culture History." *Late Imperial China* 11, no. 2 (1990): 32–62.

Siu, Helen F., and Zleda Stern, eds. *Mao's Harvest: Voices of China's New Generation.* New York: Oxford University Press, 1983.

Wang, Anyi. *Zhiqing Xiaoshuo* (Novels about Educated Youth). Chengdu: Sichuan Wenyi Chubanshe, 1992.

Wolf, Margery. *Revolution Postponed: Women in Contemporary China.* Stanford: Stanford University Press, 1985.

Wu, Liping. "Wenhua Dageming Zhong De Nühongweibing" (Female Red Guards in the Culture Revolution). *Ershiyi Shiji* (Twenty-First Century Bimonthly) 68, no. 11 (2007). (web version) http://www.cuhk.edu.hk/ics/21c/.

Xianggang Wu Feng Hang (Ng Fung Hong Limited). "Xianggang Shichang Xiao Huo Dongwu Gongxiao Qingkuang" (The Supply and Marketing of Live Game in Hong Kong), September 1972. Guangzhou: Guangdong Sheng Dang'an Guan Guangdong Provincial Archives), 296-A2.1-5.

Zhong, Dajun. *Guomin Daiyu Bu Pingdeng Shenshi: Eryuan Jiegou Xia De Zhongguo* (Examining the Inequality of National Treatment: The Urban-Rural Dual Structure in China). Beijing: Zhongguo Gongren Chubanshe, 2002.

Zhonggong Guangdong Shengwei Xuanchuanbu (The Propaganda Department of Guangdong Provincial Party Committee). "Guangzhou Shi Yixie Zhongxuesheng Qu Xianggang Hou De Zaoyu"(The Experiences of Some High School Students fleeing to Hong Kong from Guangzhou), July 30, 1963. Guangzhou: Guangdong Sheng Dang'an Guan (Guangdong Provincial Archives), 214-1-300.

Zhang, Zeming. "Jue Xiang" (Swan Song). China: Pearl River Film Studio, 1985.

Chapter 11

Bishop, Ryan, and Lillian S. Robinson. *Night Market: Sexual Cultures and the Thai Economic Miracle.* New York; London: Routledge, 1998.

Emerton, Robyn. "Trafficking of Women into Hong Kong for the Purpose of Prostitution: Preliminary Research Findings." Occasional Paper No. 3. Centre for Comparative and Public Law, Faculty of Law, The University of Hong Kong, 2001.

Gan, Wendy. *Fruit Chan's Durian Durian.* Hong Kong: Hong Kong University Press, 2005.

Harvey, David. *The Condition of Postmodernity: An Enquiry into the Origins of Cultural Change.* Oxford, UK; Cambridge, M.A.: B. Blackwell, 1989.

Ku, Agnes S. "Hegemonic Construction, Negotiation and Displacement." *International Journal of Cultural Studies* 4, no. 3 (2001): 259–78.

Ming, Kevin D. "Cross-Border 'Traffic': Stories of Dangerous Victims, Pure Whores and Hiv/Aids in the Experiences of Mainland Female Sex Workers in Hong Kong." *Asia Pacific Viewpoint* 46, no. 1 (2005): 35–48.

Ng, Carolina. "Policemen Humiliate and Hurt Us, Prostitutes Claim." *Sunday Morning Post,* July 24, 2005, 5.

Pasuk, Phongpaichit. *From Peasant Girls to Bangkok Masseuses.* Geneva: International Labour Office, 1982.

Siu, Helen F. "Immigrants and Social Ethos: Hong Kong in the Nineteen-Eighties." *Journal of the Hong Kong Branch of the Royal Asiatic Society* 26 (1986): 1–16.

Wang, Gungwu. "Greater China and the Chinese Overseas." *The China Quarterly,* no. 136 (1993): 926–48.

Wilson, Ara. *The Intimate Economies of Bangkok: Tomboys, Tycoons, and Avon Ladies in the Global City.* Berkeley: University of California Press, 2004.

Yau, Ka-fai. "Cinema 3: Towards a 'Minor Hong Kong Cinema'." *Cultural Studies* 15, no. 3/4 (2001): 543–63.

Zi Teng (A Hong Kong-based NGO), "Research Report on Mainland Chinese Sex Workers: Hong Kong, Macau, and Town B in Pearl River Delta." Hong Kong, 2000.

Index